D0709503

THE THRILL OF
VICTORY

THE THRILL OF
VICTORY

Best Sports
Stories from the
Pages of **MACLEAN'S**

VIKING
CANADA

VIKING CANADA
Penguin Group (Canada), a division of Pearson Penguin Canada Inc.,
    10 Alcorn Avenue, Toronto, Ontario M4V 3B2

Penguin Group (U.K.), 80 Strand, London WC2R 0RL, England
Penguin Group (U.S.), 375 Hudson Street, New York, New York 10014, U.S.A.
Penguin Group (Australia) Inc., 250 Camberwell Road, Camberwell, Victoria 3124, Australia
Penguin Group (Ireland), 25 St. Stephen's Green, Dublin 2, Ireland
Penguin Books India (P) Ltd, 11, Community Centre, Panchsheel Park,
    New Delhi – 110 017, India
Penguin Group (New Zealand), cnr Rosedale and Airborne Roads, Albany, Auckland 1310,
    New Zealand
Penguin Books (South Africa) (Pty) Ltd, 24 Sturdee Avenue, Rosebank 2196, South Africa

Penguin Group, Registered Offices: 80 Strand, London WC2R 0RL, England

First published 2003

1 2 3 4 5 6 7 8 9 10 (FR)

Copyright © Rogers Publishing Ltd., 2003

All rights reserved. Without limiting the rights under copyright reserved above, no part
of this publication may be reproduced, stored in or introduced into a retrieval system,
or transmitted in any form or by any means (electronic, mechanical, photocopying,
recording or otherwise), without the prior written permission of both the copyright
owner and the above publisher of this book.

Manufactured in Canada.

NATIONAL LIBRARY OF CANADA CATALOGUING IN PUBLICATION

The thrill of victory : best sports stories from the pages of Maclean's / Michael Benedict,
editor.

ISBN 0-670-04434-2

1. Sports—Canada—History—20th century. I. Benedict, Michael, 1947–

GV585.T46 2003   796'.0971'0904   C2003-901831-8

Visit the Penguin Group (Canada) website at **www.penguin.ca**

CONTENTS

FOOTBALL

GOLF

IN THE RING

FOREWORD

Roy MacGregor

FOR A YOUNG, FIRST-YEAR JOURNALIST, it was a bit like riding up to heaven with the gods.

I was 24 years of age. I had just landed my first job in journalism—assistant editor of *Office Equipment & Methods*, a business trade magazine where I wrote reviews of staplers and paper clips and dreamed of escape—and every lunch hour found me standing inside the Dundas Street entrance of the old Maclean-Hunter building on Toronto's University Avenue, waiting for the elevator to take me to the third floor and another afternoon of wishing I were on the seventh floor.

The seventh floor was where they put out *Maclean's*. The people who worked there did not wear ties and ill-fitting suits. They had no rules about hair. They seemed to come and go as they pleased. The elevator often smelled of their smoke, sometimes of exotic French cigarettes, once in a while of sweet marijuana. And they had, to my mind, the greatest jobs on earth.

This particular winter day I was waiting for the elevator when the side door of the building opened with a slap of cold air and three men burst in, oblivious to the young man in the bad suit. Two of them, I knew, were senior *Maclean's* editors—

Tom Hedley, who had once worked for *Esquire*, and Don Obe, who wore leather jackets and invariably had a cigarette poking through his massive moustache—and the other, I would later learn, was Winnipeg novelist Jack Ludwig, who limped, wore a flamboyant Western hat and spoke in a loud voice.

For three floors I was privy to the talk of the trade. They had had a working lunch—liquid, obviously—and they were talking hockey. About the '72 Summit Series then just months past. About goaltender Ken Dryden, who had played so well for Team Canada against the Soviets. And about whether it was too much of a stretch to compare hockey fights to the "stare signals" of rhesus monkeys in the wild.

The elevator was notoriously slow, but on this day it rose far too quickly. I wanted more. I wanted to understand the connections. I wanted to know what sort of mind could tie monkey behaviour to professional sport. Two months later, when Ludwig's feature on the intellectual goaltender—"Ken Dryden, Hockey's Lonely Forerunner"—appeared in *Maclean's*, I understood.

February 1973 was the same month that I received a call from Peter C. Newman, the editor of the then-monthly magazine, to see whether I would like to leave the business division—at no increase in salary, of course—and join *Maclean's* as a lowly assistant editor in charge of the "slush pile," the unsolicited manuscripts that came in from all over the country and were always read before being rejected. It would be my job to choose the form letter we would send out; my job, as well, to poke through the pile in search of that rarest of magazine achievements, the unsolicited piece that gains acceptance. I was finally on the sacred seventh floor.

I loved *Maclean's*, and I loved sports, and I adored the way *Maclean's* treated sports. It was as if sport were a large house and, while the other media types were trapped within the walls— beat writers unable to escape the same room as the athletes they covered—the magazine journalists had access to the windows; they could stand just slightly outside and stare in from whatever perspective they chose, coming and going as they pleased. It was when reading a 1973 *Maclean's* article on Alan Eagleson by the legendary Trent Frayne—one of his six in this collection—that I first wondered whether Eagleson was not quite what he had seemed in everything else I had ever read of the man who carried off the 1972 Summit Series.

Not everyone at the magazine was interested in sports. Alan Walker, who spent 16 years at *Maclean's* before retiring as executive editor in 1993—and who, much to our mutual surprise, turned out to be a distant cousin—used to put on surgical gloves before handling any sports copy and would move the offending pieces from in-tray to out-tray with obstetrical forceps. He called every sports profile "Reggie" on the grounds that, in his experience, all athletes went by the same name: Reggie Fleming, Reggie Jackson, Reggie Leach . . . The bizarrely eccentric Walker was also a brilliant editor who dramatically improved all copy, sports included, and was a great loss to us all when he died three years after retirement at age 56.

In a way, I understood the cerebral Walker's attitude toward sports writing, for it has always been an awkward niche in Canadian literature. This has long puzzled me, and it should puzzle the reader who sits down with the superb literature held within these pages; but there can be little doubt that Canadian literature is its own animal, with precious little, if any, time for sportswriters—quite unlike both the American and the British English-language experience. Perhaps this indifference is caused by the simple economics of writing in this thinly populated country. Canadian literature tends to be more academically based for the obvious reason that so few can make a living on their writing alone. This, in turn, has odd repercussions; small sales cause authors to become far more prolific than their

American and British cohorts, often to their own detriment, and short stories have become so ubiquitous—thanks to so many creative writing classes, where the short story fits into the time frame, and so many small magazines—that Canada has become oddly known as the country of the "short story." More accurately, we are the country of the "short-story economic model."

The effect of such academic concentration has been that sports—that bastion of the uneducated, the lower classes, the beer drinkers, the active—tends to be thought rather less of, both as physical activity and as literary activity. Although American writers from Ernest Hemingway to George Plimpton have regarded sport as valid a topic for examination as war, it is impossible to imagine Robertson Davies writing on hockey fights or Alice Munro on the highs and lows of small-town curling.

Maclean's, to its great credit, always fought against such snobbery. Whenever the magazine could, it would assign a Canadian literary type such as Mordecai Richler or Jack Ludwig to the Canadian condition as they might find it in sport. Far more significantly, however, the magazine gave talented journalists the page length and the time to delve far more deeply into sport than the daily press could ever provide. The list of great writers who wrote about hockey and football and lacrosse and baseball and so many other games for *Maclean's* is, in large part, a list of the best journalists of their day: Trent Frayne, Jim Coleman, Harry Bruce, Hal Quinn, all of whom are found in this volume, and dozens of other names right up to today's Marci McDonald, Michael Posner, James Deacon, the sports editor of *Maclean's*, and Ken MacQueen, the magazine's Vancouver bureau chief.

Maclean's executive editor Michael Benedict, a lifelong sports fan, has collected the best of their work here. He has chosen, carefully and well, stories that show the country as it was and is today, stories that demonstrate clearly that race was not the only barrier to scale in sport—and how far women have come since they stood up for their own rights to play.

There is nearly a century here of good reading, nearly a century of Canadian achievement—great writing being, in this humble opinion, as much an achievement as winning the Stanley Cup or the Queen's Plate.

These stories, after all, are about writers at the top of their games, as well.

And for me, reading them is like riding once again up to the seventh floor, where the doors open on the wonders of great magazine writing.

PREFACE

J AMES DEACON, who now presides over matters of sport at Maclean's, is also wise about the history of sports writing. When told that, from its earliest days, the magazine featured sports coverage in its editorial mix, Deacon guessed that, at first, three sports dominated the coverage: boxing, horse racing and baseball. Correctly, as it turned out, he explained that these were the three glamour sports in North America before the Second World War and that only baseball has since maintained its popularity.

Of course, hockey has been atop the heap since the war and has attracted many of Canada's finest writers, including Deacon, to the game—and to the pages of Maclean's. Four of his hockey stories are included in this collection, the same number of hockey stories as selected from the work of the legendary Trent Frayne, who first wrote for Maclean's in 1941 and still occasionally contributes a finely crafted essay. Others in the Maclean's pantheon of hockey writers are Mordecai Richler and Jack Ludwig, proof that the magazine has always brought a wider perspective to its sports pages.

Within months of the first issue of Maclean's in 1905 (until 1911 it was known first as The Business Magazine and then as The Busy Man's Magazine), a story appeared on salmon fishing in Newfoundland and Labrador, four decades before the island colony became part of Canada. Since then, the magazine has taken many shapes and forms over its nearly century-long history—it began as a collection of articles that had originally appeared elsewhere—but sports coverage has remained a constant.

Not all the stories are a source of pride. In October 1936, H. H. Roxborough, a frequent contributor of the time, wrote on the Berlin Olympics solely as a sporting event, oblivious to the Nazi propaganda purposes served by the Games. Roxborough's story matter of factly mentions Hitler's presence at the opening ceremonies and then goes on to recount the achievements and disappointments of the Canadian team, ending with the now familiar lament that our amateur athletes are woefully underfunded.

Fifty years later, another not-so-great moment in *Maclean's* sports history was recorded in the October 3, 1988, cover package featuring Ben Johnson, "The King of Seoul." It was written in the euphoria of Johnson's record-breaking Olympic gold medal in the 100 m, making him the fastest man in the world, and was on the press just hours before he was disqualified after performance-enhancing drugs were found in his urine. Nevertheless, that issue was one of the best sellers of the year.

The 47 articles in this collection provide a survey of Canadian sports history, both highs and low, but mostly highs, including the hockey victories over the Soviets in 1972 and the United States in the 2002 Olympic gold medal game. We meet many world champions, from the Edmonton Grads women's basketball team of the 1920s to the World Series–winning Blue Jays of the early 1990s.

An important constant over the years at *Maclean's* has been providing our readers with stories that they cannot find elsewhere—oftentimes, stories that are quirky and entertaining. In this volume, we have a piece from 1944 about female bowlers threatening a male preserve, another on six-day bicycle races and a thoroughly delightful account of a 1960 world curling championship in Scotland. And, yes, there is a piece about fishing—the joys of capturing small-mouth black bass in 1936. The articles reprinted here appear essentially as they did originally. Some have been shortened in order to fit a greater variety of pieces into the collection.

Maclean's researcher-reporter Michael MacLean did his usual estimable job of finding those who have left few tracks, whether it be the writers who produced the pieces or the athletes themselves. The brief summaries at the end of nearly all the stories are the result of his labours. Once again, Kristine Ryall found the photos to illustrate the pieces. Ryall, the magazine's photo editor, has worked on all seven books from our archives in this series, published annually by Penguin Canada. Sean McCluskey, Maclean's director of production and technology, has also worked on all the volumes, ensuring a smooth transfer from the printed page in a magazine to another in this book.

The other person who has more than assisted on all seven books over the years is Cynthia Good. Earlier this year, Cynthia resigned as publisher of Penguin Canada to pursue what will no doubt be a second successful career. Thanks for the memories, and sincerest best wishes.

OCKEY

Conacher, the Versatile

—September 1, 1932—
Harry Shane

SIXTEEN YEARS AGO a big, blond, unassuming fellow by the name of Lionel Conacher won the Amateur Lightweight Wrestling Championship of Ontario. He is still a big, blond, unassuming fellow, but his return to the arena of wrestling this year was accompanied by a professional contract, nearly 200 pounds of solid muscle and an athletic record that is perhaps unparalleled in the annals of sport.

The intervening years have seen Conacher take a hand in almost every competitive sport that time would permit him to engage in. Possessing all the natural and acquired qualities of

Conacher in one of his many starring roles

the perfect athlete—speed, strength, height, weight, stamina and skill—he has left behind him a trail of remarkable feats in rugby, hockey, lacrosse and baseball.

Examination of the most distinguished sporting records of the past decade reveals the names of Howie Morenz, George Young, Percy Williams and Jack Wright. Each has been brilliant in his respective sphere of hockey, swimming, track and tennis. Each has confined himself to the one sport that has brought him success, fame, and perhaps a good livelihood. Athletes of the two-sport variety are not so plentiful; yet the name of Newsy Lalonde comes to mind as an athlete who has been equally brilliant with the hockey and lacrosse stick. The versatility of Conacher has excited the imagination of sport followers both in Canada and in the United States, and his single-handed efforts and last-minute recoveries in tense struggles have stamped him as one of the most colourful personalities that has ever attracted the public to sporting amphitheatres in this country.

Some of Conacher's earliest training took place in the Jesse Ketchum School Park, Toronto, a stone's throw from his birthplace. How early this training took effect is evidenced by the fact that he was a member of the 95-pound champions of the Toronto City Rugby League when he was but 12 years of age.

From this humble beginning, he wrote a very stirring chapter in the rugged game of touchdowns and rubdowns. In 1918, on the middle wing, he helped the Toronto Central Y Football team win the championship of Ontario, and in 1919 he was with the Capital Intermediates, runners-up to Sarnia in the championship series. The autumn of 1920 found him a member of the Toronto Seniors, and in the semi-finals against the Argos that year he almost defeated the scullers single-handedly by his brilliant open-field play.

Beginning with the rugby season of 1921, when he joined the Argonauts, till the end of his football career, Montreal,

Ottawa and Hamilton were treated to individual performances in open-field play that are conceded to be the most sensational exhibitions of football ever seen in this country. He ripped a hole in opposing lines at will, caught with a sure pair of hands, evaded tacklers with apparent ease, and kicked consistently for 40, 50 and 60 yards. His 185 pounds and six-feet, one-inch were the focal point of spectators in every city of the Big Four and the headline topic of every newspaper reporter in Eastern Canada.

During a game against Ottawa in 1922 he gained 120 yards in three downs, an average of 40 yards a down. Against Montreal one afternoon he gained a total of 227 yards, or an average of more than three and a half yards a minute.

Taking up skating and hockey long after most boys have perfected their game, we first hear of Conacher as a member of the Toronto Canoe Club team, Junior Hockey Champions of Canada in 1920; and during that same winter, 1919–1920, he played defence on the Dominion Bank champion Bankers' hockey team of Canada. His decision to forsake senior hockey in 1922 was engendered by an offer of $5,000 that he received from Leo Dandurand to play for the Montreal Canadiens in the National Hockey League. By virtue of his all-round brilliance in lacrosse, baseball and rugby football during 1922 and his effectiveness in senior hockey the previous winter, Dandurand made what was then a phenomenal offer to bolster gate receipts and attract to the hockey arena Conacher's thousands of admirers—certainly a tribute to a great sporting personality.

Conacher's refusal of this contract, which was based largely on his desire to retain his amateur standing and play football the next autumn, was grossly misinterpreted. The incident started many a tongue to wagging. If an amateur could turn down offers like that, what a fortune there must be in amateur sport, was the implication of their remarks. Smarting under the lash of this bitter and unfair criticism, Conacher stepped into intermediate hockey in Toronto and played real hockey all winter. Without any attendant publicity and with a keen desire to play effectively, he proved that the game is the thing and that he could get along without a trumpet and fife to announce his every movement—certainly a gesture of good sportsmanship.

From the arena of amateur hockey, we turn to Scarboro Beach and Hampden Park, Toronto's lacrosse and baseball grounds. To lacrosse Conacher brought stamina and speed from the gridiron, deft footwork from the ring, wherein he had incidentally become a good boxer, and a powerful physique from constant training. In baseball his great power lay in his hitting, just as his great power in lacrosse was his scoring punch.

No more vividly was his point getting and individual force demonstrated than during the events of a Saturday afternoon in the late summer of 1922. Two championship games were scheduled. Hillcrests were to play Monarchs for the baseball championship of Toronto, and Maitlands were to play Brampton for the championship of the Ontario Amateur Lacrosse League. Conacher started at two o'clock with Hillcrests, at Hampden Park. The game was to run seven innings by agreement, and going into the last half of the seventh the Hillcrests were trailing by two runs. After the bags had been filled, Conacher tripled to decide one title, which would be enough for the average fellow. But Conacher was not average. He slipped into a taxicab and raced to Scarboro Beach, where Brampton was leading his teammates by three to nothing. He jumped into a lacrosse outfit, scored four goals himself and assisted in the scoring of a fifth to settle another title dispute the same afternoon.

On another occasion, in the autumn of 1921, he pulled the iron man stunt quite as dramatically. In the afternoon he helped Argo Seniors defeat Edmonton Eskimos for the

Dominion Rugby Football Championship, and in the evening he starred in Aura Lee's defeat of Granites for the Sportsman's Athletic Association Hockey trophy.

In the autumn of 1923, Conacher left the Queen City to study at Bellefonte Academy, near Pittsburgh, and played his first American football with the team representing that college; and during the winter season he joined the Pittsburgh Yellow Jackets along with Harold Cotton and Duke McCurry, two other Toronto boys. During two winter seasons with the Yellow Jackets, his hockey improved considerably and, although he was a defenceman, he became a leading scorer and sensational leader of plays. The Yellow Jackets were champions of the United States Amateur Hockey Association and defeated the leading Canadian amateur teams.

Conacher's plunge into the ranks of moneyed sport came in the autumn of 1925, when the entire Yellow Jacket team "jumped" into professional hockey as the Pittsburgh Pirates under the guidance of Odie Cleghorn. During the summer of 1926 Conacher was recruited to the ranks of the Maple Leafs, Toronto's representatives in Class A baseball, and added a little dynamite to the great Leaf team which was successful in winning the bunting [championship] in both the International League and the Little World Series. A prominent American sports writer compared Conacher to Frankie Frisch and George Sisler, two of the greatest diamond men of all time.

The next winter season he joined the New York Americans [hockey team] and led them to a playoff berth. He remained with the Star Spangled team till the season of 1930–1931, when he returned to Canada to play for the Montreal Maroons. While hockey has never been Conacher's greatest game, and although he has never been the peer of Shore, Cleghorn and other ice demons, he has demonstrated remarkable stamina and the ability to score in the pinches.

When the Indoor Professional Lacrosse League was formed last spring, he joined the Maroons, and with the stick that he had hung up some years previously went out and scored 107 points against his nearest competitor's 56.

That Conacher won the Light Heavyweight Boxing Championship of Canada in 1920 and was the worthy opponent of Jack Dempsey in an exhibition bout in Toronto in 1921; that he goes around a golf course in the 80s; that he once won a number of events in a track and field competition—all those minor triumphs have been obscured in this maze of events.

Conacher has always been news. During his heyday at rugby, lacrosse and baseball play, when the rumour spread that he had signified his intention of taking up soccer, it became news on every sporting page in Toronto and soccer clubs sought his service although he had never played the game before in his life.

There are few sport followers who would deny him the title of Canada's greatest athlete. Those who have taken the trouble to look up records have called Conacher the greatest athlete in the world, and in this respect his name has been associated with that of Jim Thorpe, the Carlisle Indian.

At 32 years of age, the halcyon days of many great athletes, he is embarking on a comparatively new career where rugged tactics are perhaps of greater importance than skill and speed. While his success as a wrestler may still be a debatable point, there is no question about the loyal support of a public that has learned that his presence in the midst of a sporting fray has always been an assurance of thrills and excitement.

Although hockey may not have been Charlie Conacher's best sport, he went on to play for two Stanley Cup champions before retiring in 1937. He also made the first all-star team in 1934 and is a member of the Hockey Hall of Fame, the Canadian Lacrosse Hall of Fame, the Canadian Football Hall of Fame and the Canadian Sports Hall of Fame.

In 1937, Conacher was elected a Liberal member of the Ontario legislature, where he served until 1949, when he went to Ottawa as a MP. Re-elected in 1953, he died in 1954 at the age of 53 of a heart attack after hitting a triple in a charity softball game.

Hockey's Greatest Scoring Machine

—November 1, 1951—
Trent Frayne

A NY MOMENT NOW Maurice Richard will score the 300th goal of his National Hockey League career and sometime early next spring he will break Nels Stewart's all-time record of 324 goals and thus become the greatest goal scorer in professional hockey history. There is a reasonable likelihood that Richard, who plays for the Montreal Canadiens, will score one or both of these goals while he is lying flat on his back, with at least one non-Canadien hockey player clutching his stick, another hacking at his ankles with a pair of skates and a third plucking thoughtfully at his sweater.

He shoots, he scores!

No hockey player living has been so much put upon as Richard by the recent revolution in hockey's cultural standards—a liberalizing process that encourages the referees to ignore all but the most flagrant violations of the written rules and, in turn, encourages poor or indifferent players to cut good or great players down to size by slamming them bodily into the sides of the rinks, massaging their ribs with fibre-padded elbows, inserting the crooked blades of hockey sticks between their legs or under their armpits and generally impeding what used to be considered their lawful progress.

In consequence, modern hockey has produced many teams that stand out above their rivals but few individual players who stand out above the other individuals. For almost a decade Richard has towered over them all, both as a goal scorer and as a piece of property. His annual earnings from the game are in excess of $20,000, approximately 20 per cent more than any other professional hockey player has earned either before his time or during it. For the right to his services the Canadiens management was once offered—and refused—a lump payment of $135,000, the highest value ever placed on a single player.

Considering the completeness of his triumph over adverse working conditions, Richard's attitude toward his work is remarkably restrained. If he revels in his position as the most esteemed and highly rewarded Canadian athlete of his generation, he gives no sign of it. On the ice his darkly Gallic features seldom depart from their melancholy cast except on the occasion of another Richard goal, when they sometimes dissolve into an expression halfway between a glower and a grin. Off the ice he is monosyllabic and uncommunicative even among the players he considers his closest friends.

But behind this impassive facade lie deep wells of sentiment, of sensitivity and of temperament. On an exhibition tour to the west coast he once cried openly when told he would have to accompany the team to California before returning to his family in Montreal. A much better publicized display of feeling occurred last winter when he brooded all one night over a referee's adverse decision and tried to punch the official in the nose when they met next day in a hotel lobby. And although he is commonly believed to be indifferent to the hostility or sympathy of spectators, his employers attribute his almost chronic inability to play his best hockey in Toronto's Maple Leaf Gardens to the profane and persistent heckling of a rather small and elderly lady fan.

But neither psychoanalysts nor hockey experts have ever been able to explain precisely why Richard—who in action frequently looks uninspired and almost awkward—keeps on scoring so many goals. During the war a number of coaches, notably Frank Boucher of the New York Rangers, insisted it was because of inferior opposition but in the last two years, when competition again had reached a peak, Richard scored 85 goals and Boucher now says that black-haired, sallow-cheeked Richard is the most spectacular hockey player he has ever seen. "That includes," adds Boucher with some reverence, "the greatest I'd ever seen before him, Howie Morenz."

Tommy Ivan, the coach of the Detroit Red Wings, says that because of his unorthodoxy there is no way to play Richard legally that will render him harmless. Even his own mistakes sometimes work out to his benefit, according to Ivan, who finds illustration for his point in last spring's Stanley Cup playoffs when Richard's team scored an upset victory over the league champion Red Wings. In each of the first two games on Detroit ice, Richard scored overtime goals. "In that second game," recalls Ivan painfully, "our Red Kelly got the puck in our end and was endeavouring to clear it ahead to Leo Reise. Richard was caught far out of position and the player he was supposed to be checking was breaking for the other blue line. On our club we try to teach our men never to let that happen. Anyway, as Kelly cleared the puck it hit Richard on the leg, bounced back into our zone past Kelly where Richard scurried in to pick it up and score the winning goal."

By a similar freak during the 1944–1945 season, Richard established a record for goals in a single season. By late February he had counted 43 and needed one more to tie the record of Joe Malone who scored 44 in 22 games for the Canadiens in 1918. The tying goal eluded him for several games until one Saturday night when the Canadiens moved into Toronto for a game with the Maple Leafs. Late in the game Richard was checked heavily as he carried the puck near the Leaf net. He was knocked down and was sliding along on his stomach, the puck out of control, when a Leaf defenceman endeavouring to clear the rolling rubber deflected it into the Toronto goal. There was nothing the official scorer could do but credit the goal to Richard since he was the last Canadien player to touch the puck. That ended Richard's brief slump. The next night in Montreal he broke Malone's record and went on to score five more goals before the season expired for a total of 50, still a record.

Richard has a distant taciturn manner when he is with strangers. Glen Harmon, a teammate, says this has stemmed from Richard's early inability to cope with the English language. Unable to understand what most hockey writers were saying to him, Richard would grunt some incomprehensible reply and turn away.

Richard is a slender-looking 175-pounder, slightly less than six feet tall. He has sleek black hair, black eyes and a small thin-lipped mouth, which gives him a surly expression. Elmer Lach, his roommate on road trips, says it is not unusual for Richard to sleep more than 12 hours a day and perhaps it is the energy derived from sleep, plus the strength of his big hands and wrists, that enables him to play hockey with such nerve and tireless-ness. He is a devout Roman Catholic, although he goes through no religious ceremony before a game. Richard says that before he goes out, "I always think about it."

In the summertime he plays better-than-average golf—in the middle 80s—and every fall he moves to the tennis courts because he feels the game sharpens his eyes and tones his leg muscles. He likes fishing and working around his home in Cartierville, a Montreal suburb. He owns a so-called triplex in which the Richards occupy the basement and rent out the two upstairs floors. He paints the house, looks after the carpentry in an owner-putterer sort of way. And at the table he consumes anything his quiet brunette wife Lucille puts in front of him, calls her a good cook and especially appreciates her spaghetti and medium-well sirloin steak. The Richards' three children are Huguette, 7 1/2, Maurice, 6, and Norman, 18 months. The ace scorer doesn't read much and when he does, it's mostly detective story magazines. He doesn't give the sports pages his time because he says, he's not interested in what the hockey writers have to say.

Richard has tried a couple of business ventures, the first a partnership in a bowling alley, called the Bowlorium. He got out of this two years ago claiming there were too many partners. Now he has money in a skate-manufacturing business and when the Maurice Richard skate is attached to the Bobby Bauer boot (Bauer is a former right wing for the Boston Bruins) the result is a $45 professional set, which Richard wears. Possibly this venture will not be permanent because Richard says he'd like to acquire "a little business—maybe a tavern" when his hockey days are over.

Obviously, any player who scores 292 goals in less than nine full seasons of play (Richard, who is now 30, scored only five in his first season, 1942–1943, because a broken ankle confined his activity to 16 games) will collect his share of fluke goals and it is equally apparent that nobody can average 35 goals a season armed with nothing more destructive than a horseshoe. Frank Selke, general manager of the Canadiens, puts down Richard's success to his explosive quality of play and calls him "just enough of a Frenchman to be an artist." The Rangers' Frank Boucher says he has never seen a player so determined to put the puck in the net. "You can see it in his eyes," broods Boucher.

Curiously, the determined Richard has seldom exploded in Toronto and it has taken many a long year to convince that city's devoted hockey populace—and, with it, the national audience that views the Maple Leafs and their opponents through Foster Hewitt's Saturday night nuances—that Richard is anything more than an obscure No. 9 patrolling right wing for the Canadiens. The year Richard scored 50 goals he collected only four of them in seven games in Toronto and there have been scores of games over the years when he has had not even four shots on the net.

Richard is unable to explain this localized kink. At various times he has blamed the heat in Maple Leaf Gardens, the vastness of the place (there are no posts, no balconies and the seats bank seemingly endlessly up from the ice surface) and the fact that he grows over-anxious and tense in his desire to succeed in a city for which he bears absolutely no devotion. Frank Selke, his boss, says Richard hates Toronto because for him it is typified by a woman as abusive as she is well groomed, who sits in an expensive seat near the visiting teams' bench. "She is one of the most foul-mouthed women I have ever heard," says Selke, "and she saves most of her more vitriolic outbursts for Maurice."

It definitely cannot be said that Toronto has devised a defence for Richard of which other teams are incapable, because in Montreal "the Rocket," as sportswriter Baz O'Meara of the Montreal *Daily Star* labelled Richard, finds the Leaf net quite as accessible as any other. In fact, it was against Toronto that he established a playoff record of five goals in a single game. That was in 1944 when Richard scored 12 goals in nine playoff games, still another record, against the Leafs and the Chicago Black Hawks as the Canadiens won the Stanley Cup.

Richard is at his best at home. When he gets wound up on Montreal ice, with the Forum crowds shrieking wildly each time he gets the puck, he becomes a whirling dashing man possessed. One night he arrived at the dressing room an hour before game time and informed coach Dick Irvin he was pooped.

"Pooped?" enquired silver-haired Irvin, "how do you mean pooped?"

"Moved today," replied Richard, whose English is tinged with Jean-Baptiste. "Carried furniture up and down stairs all afternoon. Feel pooped."

This came about three days after Christmas in 1944 and Richard had bought a new home for his family. The Canadiens were playing Detroit that night, always a rugged opponent at the Forum, and the pooped Richard moved lethargically onto the ice. The first time he got the puck, the crowd started to shout his name and since he'd been set up in the clear by Elmer Lach, his centreman, he didn't have too much difficulty scoring. That set him off. Before the night was out, the fizzled Rocket was sizzling; he scored five goals and got three assists as the Canadiens won 9–1. That's another Richard entry in the record book.

Richard seldom makes headlines off the ice, but his attack on referee Hugh McLean in the lobby of New York's Piccadilly Hotel one Sunday morning last season was one of the season's most wildly debated episodes. He did this 12 hours after a game in Montreal in which he'd swung on Detroit's Leo Reise who had jeered at him for getting a penalty. Richard explains: "A man can take just so much. I was skating close to the Detroit net when Sid Abel grabbed me by the chin, nearly twisted my head off and spun me right around. I drew the referee's attention to this. All I said was: 'You must have seen that,' but he laughed in my face. As I skated away I said: 'This is the damnedest thing yet,' and then McLean rushed up and put me off." As he skated toward the penalty box, Reise snickered at him and Richard swung at the Detroit defenceman and drew an additional misconduct penalty from McLean. The following morning, as the Canadiens arrived in New York from Montreal for a Sunday night game with the Rangers, Richard encountered McLean and linesman Jim Primeau in the hotel lobby. He grabbed McLean by the collar and tried to punch him but was restrained by Primeau, who began throwing punches at Richard.

Out of all this, a week after the incident, the Rocket was fined $500 by NHL president Clarence Campbell, who declined to suspend the player (as he had done in earlier and similar cases involving other players) on the fairly implausible grounds that "the suspension of a great hockey star is not justified if it reflects in the gate receipts," to quote Bob Hesketch of the *Toronto Telegram* who interviewed Campbell after the fine was announced. "We're trying to conduct a business," Campbell continued. "If I suspended Richard, a great drawing card wherever he goes, it would affect the attendance of the league."

There is no denying that Richard is a vital cog in the successful financial operation of the Montreal club. General manager Selke says he "might as well give up half the Forum as contemplate a trade involving Richard" in reply to reports that fabulous sums have been offered for the Rocket.

Two years ago, while the Leafs were having trouble holding fourth place, their president, Conn Smythe, sent instructions to his coach, Hap Day, that he was to present a blank cheque to Selke to be filled in with any amount up to $135,000 in exchange for Richard. Smythe, holidaying in Florida at the time, was "grandstanding," according to Selke, who refused even to consider the proposition. Selke says Richard is the sort of competitor that money cannot buy. Richard's salary has never been made public but Selke claims he is getting "at least $5,000 more than any other hockey player, past or present."

Though Richard is not a big man physically, Wally Stanowski, defenceman for the New York Rangers, says he is the hardest man in the league to stop because of his strength. "I've had him completely covered," Stanowski claims, "and he'll make a pass at the blue line. Somehow he'll still manage to cut in on the net, often carrying me on his back, and get his shot away." Turk Broda, Toronto goalkeeper for 15 seasons, says Richard's shot is the most difficult to stop, not because of its velocity but because of its uncanny accuracy from any angle. "He'll be standing in front of the net, maybe 20 feet out, waiting for a pass out," says Broda. "He'll have his back to the goal and he'll be surrounded by our players. But if the puck comes out he somehow can whirl and swipe at it, backhand or the other way, and drive it dead for a corner. I think half the time he doesn't know where it's going himself, yet invariably it will just skim the post and deflect into the net."

Richard, like other great scorers before him such as Charlie Conacher and Nels Stewart, has frequently been charged with being a one-way hockey player; that is, that he is an artist driving toward the enemy goal but no craftsman defending his own. His boss, Dick Irvin, refutes these charges. "He's not the best backchecker in the world by any means," says Irvin, "but if you've watched many of our games, you'll have noticed that I frequently use him to kill off penalties. When we're playing five men against six, I've found that Richard has the speed and the stamina to hound the opposition as well as any player in the league."

There is no question that he is the league's most abused forward. Players charged with keeping Richard in check employ all sorts of clutching, grabbing and holding tactics in an effort to shackle him. Being of explosive temperament, Richard draws his share of penalties for his retaliatory swipes at his molesters. Frank Boucher says the Rangers have had some success in harnessing the Rocket by sticking tough little forward Tony Leswick on him. Leswick, traded to Detroit for Gaye Stewart last summer, found that by verbally needling Richard he was sufficiently able to infuriate him as to render him comparatively ineffective. But Boucher is quick to point out that the Rangers have never cowed Richard.

The most celebrated of all Richard's ice escapades involved Bill Ezinicki and Vic Lynn, forwards for the Maple Leafs in 1947 and now with Boston. In a torrid playoff in Montreal in which the Canadiens were heavily favoured after winning the first game 6–0, the Leafs put on a heavy checking display in the second game and had a 3–0 lead in the second period when Richard slashed Lynn with his stick, opening a four-stitch cut over the Leaf winger's left eye. Then he swung his stick axe-fashion over referee Bill Chadwick's shoulder and onto Ezinicki's head, causing a seven-inch cut clear across the player's scalp. Richard was given a major penalty of five minutes in the first instance, a match misconduct in the second, and league president Campbell suspended him from the third playoff game and appended a $250 fine.

Strong and durable, the Rocket almost didn't get to the starting gate. Born in Montreal, Aug. 4, 1921, he very nearly didn't become an NHL player at all because he showed signs in his youth of being brittle, meaning that bumps and spills frequently produced fractures. He first attracted attention as a scoring star with the Verdun Juniors in the 1939–1940 season and when, as a 19-year-old right-winger (he shoots left-handed), he joined the Montreal Canadiens of the Quebec Senior Hockey League, it was like an expectant mother booking space in the hospital. In the first game of the season, against the Quebec Aces, he was tripped and sent crashing into the boards. He broke his left ankle. "I play aroun' 20 games the next year," he recalls, "still with the Canadiens seniors, and then I fall against the net. This time the left arm is broke."

He got back in time for the playoffs and scored six goals while his team was being eliminated by Ottawa in a four-game semifinal. The NHL Canadiens signed him on the strength of his playoff performance. Teamed as a rookie with Gordie Drillon and Buddy O'Connor he scored five goals and got six assists in 16 games; then he broke his right ankle and once again was out for the season.

Early the following year, the 1943–1944 season, it looked like the same story. After a couple of games he twisted his shoulder and was lost for two weeks. But then he started to roll. He was placed beside Elmer Lach and Toe Black on what became known as the Punch Line and scored 32 goals in collecting 54 points. The next year he produced 50 goals and became the most colourful player in professional hockey. As Ted Reeve of the *Toronto Telegram* once observed: "If I had to pay to get in, it'd be worth the price of admission to see him."

Maurice Richard became the all-time goal-scoring leader at the beginning of the 1952 season. By the time he retired in 1960, he had scored 544 goals, a record that stood until Gordie Howe broke it in 1963. His 50 goals in 50 games standard stood until Wayne Gretzky took just 39 games to score as many in the 1980–1981 season.

Campbell was finally forced to suspend Richard at the end of the 1955 season, after Richard attacked a linesman on the ice. Richard had to sit out the final two games of the season and the entire play-offs, a decision that provoked a riot in the Montreal Forum and in the city's downtown. As a result of the suspension, Richard lost his lead in the scoring championship and the Canadiens lost the Stanley Cup finals to the Detroit Red Wings.

Richard died in Montreal at 78 of stomach cancer in 2000.

Trent Frayne, one of Canada's legendary sportswriters, wrote his first piece for Maclean's in 1941 and has contributed more than 100 articles since then. He has won numerous awards and written 14 books, including six on hockey. Frayne lives in Toronto with his wife, fellow writer and frequent Maclean's contributor June Callwood.

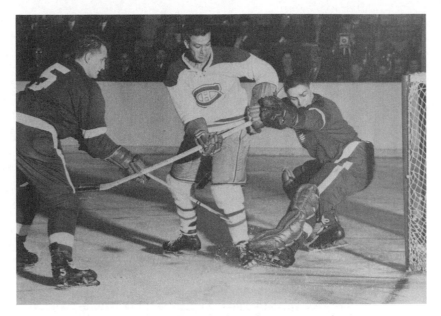

Why Big-League Goalies Crack Up

—*March 19, 1955*—
Trent Frayne

Y OUNG TERRY SAWCHUK was performing acrobatically in
goal for the Detroit Red Wings in a game in the Montreal
Forum one night last spring when Tommy Gorman, an old-time
National Hockey League executive who now heads the Ottawa
Auditorium, got to Montreal for one of his infrequent visits to
an NHL arena. Gorman had not seen Sawchuk in action for
two or three years and his first reaction was one of surprise at
his drawn appearance. After watching the goalkeeper dive and
sprawl to make spectacular stops for two periods, Gorman
turned to a friend.

Sawchuk tying up Bernie Geoffrion

"How old is that boy Sawchuk?" he asked.

"Twenty-four," was the reply.

"Next year," said Gorman, shaking his head, "he'll be 34."

Gorman's remark had a good deal of painful truth to it. The terrible strain on goalkeepers in the modern game ages them quickly and causes an annual turnover that is on the increase. Right now only three goalies—Sawchuk, Toronto's Harry Lumley and Chicago's Al Rollins—have been able to survive in the big league more than *two* seasons. Rollins, who is 28, has shown signs of wear and tear. He was benched in December and again in January to rest his edgy nerves. Sawchuk, too, is battling to hold his job.

In the past five years two goalkeepers, Bill Durnan and Gerry McNeil, both of the Montreal Canadiens, have retired at the peak of their careers because of the pressure of playing major-league hockey, and in the last four years there have been 25 goalies performing at various times for the six teams in the NHL, an incredible average of more than four per club. Through January in this current season alone, the six NHL teams have used 14 different goalkeepers, because of injuries or unsatisfactory performance.

Tension makes misery of goalkeepers' lives. They can't sleep at night. They get ulcers. They throw steaks at their wives. They swing their sticks at rival players. They even become physically ill.

They lose pounds every game because they're under the tension of being unable to move around freely, the tension of physical danger from a rocketing puck and the tension of heavy responsibility. This responsibility increases in the playoffs, when a single mistake by a goaler can cost him and his team-mates $1,500 each in bonus money.

The modern goalkeeper undergoes strains that were unknown to his counterpart of 20 or even 10 years ago. In the Thirties, men like George Hainsworth, Roy Worters, Lorne Chabot, Tiny Thompson and Alex Connell seemingly owned lifetime leases on the goals they guarded. Every one of them had at least a 10-year career, playing schedules of 44, and later 48 games.

In the Forties, the war disrupted the careers of such successors as Turk Broda, Frank Brimsek, Charlie Rayner and Johnny Mowers. More significantly, a series of changes in the rules began whittling away at a goalkeeper's life expectancy. The centre red line, introduced in 1943, permitted attacking teams to shoot the puck into the defensive team's end of the rink from centre ice and set the stage for continuous five-man power plays. The rule caused frenzied pile-ups in front of the nets that were unheard of in the old days.

Worse, from the goalkeeper's point of view, were the rule changes that lengthened the playing schedule. The schedule was gently boosted from 48 to 50 games in 1944–1945, and then it was increased to 60 games two years later. In the 1949–1950 season it went to 70 games. Counting pre-season exhibitions and post-season playoffs, teams often played 80 to 90 games between mid-September when the training season opened and mid-April when the Stanley Cup playoffs ended. They've been doing it every year since 1949 and goalkeepers have been falling like flies. Only Harry Lumley, who entered the NHL as a regular with Detroit in 1944–1945, survives.

One of the first goalers to succumb to the new order of hair-raising traffic jams over long schedules was Frank McCool, an anguished chattel of the Toronto Maple Leafs, who ran up a record three straight shutouts over Detroit in the 1945 Stanley Cup playoffs. The Leafs scored only four goals in the first three games, yet managed to win all of them, largely due to McCool's grim stand in goal. Each victory, however, brought him corresponding misery, for he was nursing an ulcer that the mounting tension aggravated.

The series went the full seven games. The final and deciding game was in Detroit. Halfway through it McCool suddenly called time and skated towards the Toronto bench. White and drawn, he walked past his coach, Clarence (Hap) Day, and silently made his way to the dressing room. He sat down in front of his locker, his elbows on his thighs, and stared at the floor. As Day came into the room McCool reached for a bottle of stomach powder, mixed it in a paper cup, gulped it down and sat silently again.

"How about it, Frank?" Day asked.

McCool didn't answer.

"There's nobody else," said Day. "We've got no sub."

Finally McCool nodded. "I can finish," he said quietly.

They went back into the arena. Halfway through the third period Babe Pratt scored a goal for Toronto and McCool hung on until the end. "Goalkeepers are a race apart, especially in the playoffs," Day says. "For a moment there, when McCool went to the dressing room, I thought that *I* might have to play goal. I can't imagine a worse fate."

McCool's case was extreme but by no means isolated. All goalkeepers undergo a kind of tension that is unique in sports. The very nature of their work prevents them from giving free physical rein to their emotions. Defencemen can rid them-selves of tension by knocking down an opposing forward, and forwards can tear up and down in pursuit of the puck, offset-ting mental pressure with physical impact. But goalies must stick to their nets. "A goalkeeper just stands there, seemingly impassive but actually boiling inside," says Muzz Patrick, coach of the New York Rangers. "Why, they even play a different game. The closest approach in another sport might be the catcher in baseball. But still, he does things that *are* baseball—goes up to hit, chases foul flies and so forth. In hockey, a goaler does nothing that other players do. Except for his sweater, he even dresses completely differently right down to his skates."

Kenny Reardon, a former rambunctious Montreal Canadiens defenceman who is now the team's personnel director, says that before a game players feel like patients quaking at the dentist's. "The strain must be tenfold on a goaler, who can't blow off steam once the game starts," he adds.

In the playoffs, a goaler's single mistake can eliminate his team from the Stanley Cup's cash rewards. Players on a team winning the trophy collect $2,000 each in bonuses; if the team loses in the first round of the playoffs, each man gets only $500. The onus is usually on the goaler whether he and his teammates are going to be $1,500 richer. "For 12 hours before a Stanley Cup game, the modern goalkeeper carries a tension load that is carried by the average person only two or three times in a lifetime," says Lloyd Percival, director of the national research organization Sports College. "Through tests and interviews over the past 10 years, we feel it's the same tension load as that carried by a patient before undergoing an operation, or a man before an important interview for a job that's vital to him."

Coaches, aware of the strain, handle goalies differently from the way they handle other players. King Clancy, the present Toronto coach, never even speaks to Harry Lumley before a game. "I wouldn't dare," he remarked recently. "The slightest thing could throw him off just like that," and the coach snapped his fingers.

Tommy Ivan, now general manager of the Chicago Black Hawks, was excessively careful in conversations with Terry Sawchuk of the Red Wings in the four years he coached the goalie at Detroit. "I used to sit beside him just before we went on the ice," Ivan says. "He'd show the tension he felt by shaking his head unconsciously, a gentle little twitch, over and over. I'd put my hand on his arm, resting it there, and talk quietly about anything but hockey."

Hap Day used to shout at Turk Broda during practice with the Maple Leafs, feeling that the Turk tended to loaf and needed a few rasping phrases to keep him alert, but he left him alone during a game.

Cool has always been the word for goalers who showed skill and unconcern under fire, and it was never applied to any performer more frequently than to the late George Hainsworth, a graceful picture of nonchalance in his years with the Canadiens and the Maple Leafs. But it was merely a front. "Cool!" snorts King Clancy, who played in front of Hainsworth. "He used to die. He'd make a tough stop look easy, and you'd hear the ohs and ahs go up from the crowd. But just by looking at his face you could tell he was dyin'. There'd be little white lines around his mouth, and his eyes'd be this big."

Goalkeepers occasionally have snapped under the tension in public. One night in Montreal in a game between the Canadiens and the old Montreal Maroons, Dave Trottier scored on a long shot, beating Canadiens goaler Wilf Cude with the game's only goal. As he circled the net Trottier laughed in Cude's face and pointed to the puck in the net.

Cude, dejected enough because he'd blown a long shot, took off in wild pursuit of Trottier, swinging his big goaler's stick around his head like a lariat. Cude's heavy equipment kept him from overtaking Trottier before Canadien teammates caught up to him in the Maroon end of the rink and led him back to his cage.

But the most celebrated victims of high tension belong to the modern group—Bill Durnan and Gerry McNeil, both of whom rejected a chance to earn about $15,000 a year from the Canadiens rather than face another season. McNeil even went to training camp last fall before deciding the money wasn't worth the misery.

McNeil, 29, succeeded Durnan in 1950 and was the regular Canadien goaltender for four full seasons. He was sidelined by an injury late last season and replaced by Jacques Plante, who continued to play even after McNeil recovered. But with Plante performing erratically, Detroit won three of the first four games in last spring's Stanley Cup final and Coach Dick Irvin called back McNeil who beat the Red Wings 1–0 and 4–1 to square the series.

In the deciding seventh game Tony Leswick of Detroit fired a long shot in overtime with the score tied 1–1. McNeil set himself to take the puck on his chest protector, but at the last second Doug Harvey, a Canadien defenceman who was standing about six feet in front of McNeil, reached out to catch it. The puck struck his hand, caromed off and squirted into the corner of the net to end the series. "I played that shot over again all summer," McNeil says. "People kept telling me it wasn't my fault, that deflected shots are all part of the game. But I kept thinking that if I'd been standing over just a little, the puck would have hit me instead of the net."

McNeil says that mental replaying of shots that go in the net is an occupational hazard. "After every game, through the season or in the playoffs, I'd toss and turn in bed half the night, playing the game all over again. When I fell off to sleep around three or four in the morning, I'd dream about it."

Bill Durnan had a different kind of problem—the Vezina Trophy. This award, along with a $1,000 cash prize, is given by the NHL to the goalkeeper who allows the least goals over a season. In seven years with the Canadiens, Durnan won the Vezina an unprecedented six times. In each of those six seasons he was voted to the NHL's All-Star team, chosen annually by hockey writers and carrying an award of an additional $1,000 in cash for each player. But after earning the two laurels for the sixth time in 1950, plus playoff money and a salary of $10,000,

Durnan suddenly called a halt to the whole thing. "The Vezina got to be a matter of personal pride with me after I'd won it a couple of times," he says. "But the thing was always hanging over my head. Every time I blew a soft shot I suffered, and then I'd worry about blowing another soft shot and work twice as hard to avoid it."

One night in a game against Toronto, Durnan set himself to stop a long shot by Reggie Hamilton, a defenceman who rarely scored. The puck skimmed along the ice and at the last second it struck a loose chip of ice, changed direction slightly and hopped over Durnan's outstretched foot into the net. Hamilton tried the same type of shot the next opportunity he got, and Durnan recalls that he was as taut as a violin string as he braced himself for the drive. "I was prepared for that puck to hit any piece of ice in the building or for it to change course in any direction," he recalls. "Only trouble was, it didn't hit a damned thing; it went straight through my feet into the net again."

He didn't sleep all night, playing the two shots over and over again. The next day at practice he asked his coach if he'd let a player shoot that kind of long low shot at him after the regular practice session. "I figured a puck might hit a piece of ice like that once in 200 times," Durnan explains, "so I wanted to forget odds like that and concentrate on the 199 shots that *didn't* hit anything. Elmer Lach fired easy ice-skimming shots at me for an hour until I figured I'd prevented the thing from becoming a phobia."

Durnan points out that playing goal involves physical as well as mental strain. "It would be tiring for most people simply to stand all through a game like a goaler does," he says. "In the spring during the playoffs the temperature in those buildings climbs to the 80s. If a game goes into overtime, a goaler might be on his feet under pressure for three hours. I used to lose from five to eight pounds every game. One time, in a playoff, I lost 17."

That game was a Stanley Cup final in 1947 when the Leafs completely outplayed the Canadiens after Buddy O'Connor had put Canadiens ahead in the first minute of play. Toronto finally tied it and in overtime Gus Bodnar scored for the Leafs from a face-off after Durnan had played one of the greatest games in playoff history. Official tabulation showed that he'd stopped 72 shots, against a mere 21 by Broda. A post-game picture in which the defeated Canadiens are congratulating the Stanley Cup–winning Leafs shows Broda and Durnan with their arms around each other, Broda looking harried and Durnan laughing heartily. "I'd just stopped 72 shots," Durnan says, "and the Turk had been having a picnic. But when we met the first thing he said was, 'Jeepers, Bill, I'm getting too old to suffer like this.'"

Broda is considered the most phlegmatic playoff goaler of them all. He is still praised by such men as Durnan, McNeil and his old coach, Day, for his ability to withstand playoff pressure. But Turk says the butterflies used to attack his stomach. Once when he was resting in his darkened room the afternoon of a playoff game, his roommate, Bill Ezinicki, entered with spare goaler Baz Bastien, threw on an overhead light and began playing cribbage. Broda told them a couple of times to beat it but they ignored him. Broda leaped to his feet on the bed, grabbed his pillow, swung it around his head and crashed it against the overhead light fixture. That plunged the room into darkness, broke up the crib game and permitted Broda to continue his rest.

Besides being unable to relieve pent-up emotions by physical movement, a goalkeeper has an added "injury" tension, the unconscious awareness that he can be seriously injured by pucks that travel 100 miles an hour and more. (Gordie Howe, Bernie Geoffrion and Maurice Richard have had their shots officially clocked at 120 miles an hour.) Then there are the deflected shots that quickly change direction and hit a goaler before he can move and screened or hidden shots that zip through a maze of players moving about in front of the goaler, blocking his vision.

There have never been fatal accidents in hockey but fractured cheekbones and noses are commonplace. Charlie Rayner, formerly of the New York Rangers, carried 78 stitches in his face as reminders of flying pucks but he always bore a remarkable attitude towards the danger.

In a game in Chicago some years ago he stopped a shot with his jaw, and four back teeth were broken off. When the swelling went down, the roots of the teeth were dug out. He was still suffering shock from that operation when he skated out the following night for a game in Toronto. A puck whacked his face and he was led, bleeding, to the rink infirmary. As he lay on the operating table waiting for stitches, he shook his head and remarked: "It's a wonder somebody doesn't get badly hurt in this job."

Baz Bastien, a Maple Leaf farmhand at Pittsburgh, had his career ended by a flying puck. In a pre-season practice session at Welland, Ont., in September 1949, a rookie named Don Clark shot a puck Bastien never saw. It struck his right eye squarely and the eye had to be removed. Bastien has stayed in hockey as manager of the Pittsburgh club.

In Montreal one night Bill Durnan's mouth was badly cut in a goal-mouth pile-up and he was led away for stitching. "There was absolutely nothing I feared more than stitches," he recalls. "That needle scared me to death. To top it off there was no Novocaine anaesthetic this night, and the intern kept muttering away about his sutures. 'These damned dull sutures,' he'd say, digging another one into my mouth." Durnan was ready to scream when referee Bill Chadwick walked into the room. "How much longer is this going to take?" he asked.

"Almost finished," said the intern.

"Well, hurry up," grumbled Chadwick, turning to go, "there was a penalty shot on that play and Durnan's gotta get out there."

"The pay was good," Durnan reflects, "but the wear and tear got to be more than I could take. The tension was almost as bad as the stitches."

Tension, says Sports College director Lloyd Percival, is the greatest inhibitor of an athlete's potential. It explains, he says, why a player who fails to hit when the bases are full can deliver when they're empty. Dusty Rhodes, the pinch-hitting star of the 1954 World Series, epitomizes the man who can overcome tension, says Percival, who likes to quote a Rhodes observation. "All these other guys are scared to death," the pinch-hitter kept telling himself as he walked towards the plate, "I'm loosey-goosey, I'm loosey-goosey, I'm loosey-goosey."

Psychologically, modern goalkeepers must cultivate the same attitude, he says, or today's hectic game will continue to cut their careers short and produce tension that will stay with them permanently. "Tension builds up knots in muscles that can be recognized and overcome by compensating muscular exercises," Percival says. "But goalers must work at relaxing just as hard as they work at their trade. By effort and application, they can learn the muscular exercises that will eventually become automatic reflexes the instant tension begins to tighten them up."

Tensed up was indeed the phrase for Wilf Cude, netminder for the Canadiens and Detroit, who long fought nerves and injury and then, suddenly, decided to retire. Like all hockey players, Cude always had an afternoon steak on the day of a game. He liked to pour great quantities of ketchup on it. "One afternoon my wife Beulah had cooked me a nice steak and I'd just started to eat it when she made a casual remark about some unimportant subject," Cude relates. "For no known reason I

picked up my steak and threw it at her. It missed, thank good-
ness, and banged against the wall. The ketchup splattered and
the steak hung there on the wall. Slowly it began to peel, and I
stared at it. Between the time that that steak hit the wall and
then hit the floor I decided I'd been a goalkeeper long enough.
By the time it landed, I'd retired."

*Terry Sawchuk led the Wings to the Stanley Cup in 1955. He
continued to play until he died suddenly in the 1970 off-season of
injuries sustained in a fight with a teammate who was sharing his
New York City–area home. A four-time winner of the Vezina
Trophy, Sawchuk still holds the record for shutouts and games
played, and is second to Patrick Roy for most victories.*

Will Bobby Hull Become
Hockey's Next Superstar?

—*March 26, 1960*—
Trent Frayne

Hull as an 18-year-old rookie

I T WILL COME AS A SHOCK to hockey's millions of fans to
learn that Bobby Hull, a bright young light with the Chicago
Black Hawks for three years and the most sensational performer
in the National Hockey League through most of this season, is
just beginning his career. This, at any rate, is the straight-faced
testimony of numerous qualified observers, including his own
employers.

With a rosy complexion, a jaunty grin, a curling crop of
corn-coloured hair and, heaven help the ladies in the first five

rows, a dimple in his cheek, Hull has gamboled across the league's arenas like a boy skipping school on a warm spring day. By the time he'd turned 21, on Jan. 3, he was the league's leading scorer, and already had scored three goals in one game on three occasions. More important from the team's point of view, Hull and his two young linemates, Bill Hay and Murray Balfour, had brought flight to the wallowing Hawks, lifting them into playoff range after they'd won only one of their first 14 games and were driving their customers into paroxysms of indifference. By February this trio had so excited the jaded legions that 18,396 of them, the largest NHL crowd anywhere in a dozen years, turned out at the Chicago Stadium one Sunday night to watch the Hawks play the Canadiens. The ruckus they raised whenever Hull took the puck was proof that it was this new golden boy they were there to see.

Still, while the fans showed their hoarse delight and some of the sportswriters acclaimed him as the game's new superstar, older scholars talked softly and with reservation. "Bobby Hull is one of the greatest young players who has come along in the last few years," said Jack Adams, the Detroit general manager. "If he doesn't get seriously injured and takes care of himself, he should become one of the finest hockey players of all time."

Once, early in January, after Hull scored his 24th goal, his boss Tommy Ivan, the Chicago general manager, called him into his office in the Stadium. "You're about to start your hockey career, my boy," said the diminutive, dark and handsome Ivan. "From now on the other teams will be giving you special attention. They'll be checking you closer and tougher, much tougher. But if you're the hockey player I think you are you'll rise to it."

Evidence that it's still too soon to know if Hull wears the stamp of a superstar came in an unexpected February thaw when he went nine games without scoring a goal and lost his league scoring leadership. He was the top-heavy choice for the left-wing position on the NHL writers' mid-season all-star team, but in February even his coach, bushy-browed Rudy Pilous, a staunch Hull booster, was showing signs of dismay. "I'm not blaming Bobby for not scoring," Pilous said. "Everyone has a slump in this league. But I do blame him for failing to do a competent defensive job. When he's working at top efficiency we look like a playoff team. But we need his fire and leadership to roll in high gear."

Whatever the future holds for Hull, he already has breathed the spark of individuality into a game whose newcomers over the last decade have borne an assembly-line similarity, as though each had been impressed onto the NHL milieu by the same rubber stamp. By contrast, Hull came straight from a fresh mould. People who never saw a hockey game can be entranced by him, for Hull has a lilt and a swerve unmatched even by Beliveau or Howe, the masters in his trade. He moves with the effortless flair of an icebound Astaire, he can shoot like a cannon and he plays the game hard and fair. On a recent Saturday afternoon in Chicago prior to the CBS nationally televised Hockey Game of the Week, Canadian interviewer Brian McFarlane talked to Hull and to referee Frank Udvari. "Will this fellow give you much trouble this afternoon, Frank?" McFarlane asked the referee, waving his hand toward Hull.

"No, Hull doesn't play the game that way," said Udvari. "He's a fine gentleman."

But he doesn't back away from a disturbance, either. In New York early in January, Lou Fontinato, the rambunctious Ranger defenceman, had trouble with a Hawk player just before the bell ended the first period. Fontinato related afterwards that he became aware as he skated toward the passageway leading to the dressing rooms that a wave of white Chicago sweaters was closing in on him. He turned with his stick raised, anticipating an attack and the stick flashed past the head of Hull who happened to be the closest Hawk. Hull reacted by swishing his stick at Fontinato and a stick-swinging brawl developed between them. Neither was cut or felled in what a wire service report called "the most vicious fight in Madison Square Garden this season," but neither gave ground until other players pulled them apart. Each was assessed a match-misconduct penalty by the referee, Vern Buffey, and fined $100.

Though he rarely has the inclination to fight, Hull has a body built for it, a thick full chest liberally endowed with yellow hair, and the arms of a blacksmith. His 190 pounds are so well distributed on a five-foot, 10-inch frame that, on the ice, he doesn't appear as big or as strong as he actually is. In spite of his youth, sudden success doesn't appear to have affected him. In the dressing room he is a straight-talking young man who gets on easily with his teammates, and in hotel lobbies where fans gather to peer at and talk to athletes, he's as unpretentious as a man twice his age grown accustomed to attention.

In some respects Hull is twice his age. He left home at 14 to begin spending his winters playing hockey, and in the next few years he knew the curious idolatry that's accorded a hockey star in a small town. This is just as real and even more feverish in its own concentrated way than its international counterpart in the NHL's big cities. When Hull was 15 his Woodstock Junior B team won the Ontario championship. In a victory parade through the streets of this western Ontario town, the blond grinning handsome kid who was acclaimed as he sat on top of a fire engine wearing the chief's hat was Bobby Hull.

At 16, he was adored in St. Catharines, a larger community where a sizeable segment of the populace is inclined to regard its adolescent icemen with more veneration than that accorded the mayor, if not the country's prime minister. At 17, in the midst of such comparative adulation, exuberant young Hull was married. He was divorced a year later. When Hull went to the National Hockey League at 18 he had known more public attention than most businessmen receive in a lifetime. By then, all of his teammates were older but not many were wiser in the ways of the world.

Hull's destination was pretty well ordained on the January morning he was born in 1939 in a sand-coloured, two-story stucco house in Point Anne, Ont., a village four miles east of Belleville on the shore of the Bay of Quinte. He was the fifth child and first boy in what ultimately was to be a family of 11— seven girls and four boys. His mother, a comfortably proportioned, serene-looking woman, had the name Robert ready while she carried each of her first four children, who turned out to be Laura, Barbara, Jacqueline and Maxine. His father, a heavy-set shambling man, played junior, intermediate and senior hockey in Belleville and hoped his son would be a hockey player, too. When Bobby was old enough to skate, his dad played hockey with him and his four older sisters on the village's open-air rink or on a cleared area on the Bay of Quinte, a hundred yards from the family's back door.

And being old enough to skate, in Bobby's case, was a mere three years of age. On the Christmas before he turned four, the family bought skates for him and for Jacqueline, who is called Jack, and for Maxine, who is called Mac. The girls then were seven and six. The three of them were sent out to a patch of ice that had formed on the street in front of MacLawrin's General Store. As they left, Mrs. Hull called to them. "Now the first one who comes in," she said, "the skates go back to Santa."

Hull senior swears that Bobby was skating passably well within 15 minutes, and the only way the family could get the three youngsters to return to the house was to go and get them.

In the next eight years the Hulls had six more children, Carolyn, Ronald, Garry, Dennis, Judy and Peggy, the youngest, who is now 12. While he was growing up, it was a rare winter's day that Bobby (who is called Robert by all members of his family) wasn't skating and playing hockey. After heavy snowfalls he'd be the first kid on the bay, skating behind a wide shovel to clear snow. That, he thinks, may account for his heavy chest and arm development; that, and the fact he played all sports energetically and endlessly, and worked on neighbouring farms or at a nearby cement plant in the summertime. He didn't neglect his schooling, even when the Hawks settled him with junior teams in their farm system at Hespeler and then Woodstock and then St. Catharines.

"I didn't get my matriculation," he says, "but now I wish I had it, even though things have gone exceedingly well. I spent three years in high school and got honours for a couple of years. Some day, I'd like to get a degree in business administration, and I think I'd also like to get a farm. I'm not forgetting that a fellow can't expect to play hockey for the rest of his life."

He has helped his brothers with their hockey but he hasn't talked education with them yet. All three are playing Junior B hockey at Belleville and belong to the Black Hawk organization, scouted, as Bobby was, by Chicago's chief scout, Bob Wilson. "I'm not sure what I'd tell those kids if the opportunity came for them to do as I did when I turned pro with the Hawks," Bobby says thoughtfully. "Dennis is a real good student. He's conscientious about his studies. I think I'd be likely to tell him he shouldn't quit school until he has his junior matriculation at least. Garry and Ron aren't all that crazy about school."

Garry (who is called Whitey) is at 17 the blond image of his oldest brother and reportedly is the most exciting hockey prospect.

The family dotes on Bobby and his hockey prominence. When the Hawks are on television, 11 Hulls gather around two or three television sets either at home or at Barbara's (she is

Mrs. Ray Branigan) or at Maxine's (Mrs. Bill Messer). The oldest girl, Laura, watches at Trenton where she lives with her husband Ken Stafford.

Bobby's mother sits rigidly still, with all of the fingers on both hands crossed for luck. Whenever Bobby flashes across the screen she says, barely audibly and to no one in particular, "There's Robert, bless his heart." When the Hawks play in Toronto or Montreal, three or four Hulls drive to the game, usually in Bobby's grey Oldsmobile hardtop, which he leaves in Point Anne during the winter. Sometimes his father can't make it; Bob Hull, now 50, has worked at the Canada Cement plant at Point Anne since 1925. He is mill foreman, working a changing eight-hour shift which, when it's four to midnight, prevents him from taking the trip.

Mrs. Hull says Bobby is always happy when the family turns up to watch his team. Once, when he was with St. Catharines juniors, Mrs. Hull and Maxine drove to Hamilton for a game and arrived late. When Bobby saw them he skated toward the boards during a lull in play, leaned across into the seats and kissed them both. "Robert even stopped to give us a hug once in Montreal, bless his heart," beams Mrs. Hull fondly. She says when he first went away at 14, he was extremely homesick, so in her daily letters to him she rarely mentioned the family and spoke only in generalities. He told her when he got home briefly between games: "Gee, Mom, keep those letters coming with nothing in them."

But Bob Wilson, the chief scout for the Hawks who saw promise in Hull even when the boy was a nipper of 10, has the notion that Hull doesn't play as well in Toronto or Montreal as he does in the rest of the cities. "He must try too hard, or something, to impress the family," says Wilson.

For his part, Coach Rudy Pilous feels Hull "is beginning to learn the game now," after getting 13 goals in his first NHL season, 18 in his second, and better than 30 in his third. By contrast, the great Gordie Howe got seven in his first year, 16 in his second, and didn't top the 30 mark until his fourth season. "Three years are about par for a player to start finding himself in this league," says the bulky, black-browed Chicago coach. "Up to now he's been getting by on his dashing and dancing and youthful exuberance. We've been trying to check that devil-may-care stuff, which causes him to miss a lot of chances, and replace it with the shrewdness of knowing how to move the puck around, when to make his bursts on the net; in short, how to become a leader like Howe and Beliveau. That won't happen until he's curbed the darting and dancing."

Pilous may be right. Still, if that was dancing the young man was doing to startle the customers most of this season, he could have danced all night and they'd still have begged for more.

Bobby Hull led the Hawks in 1961 to their only Stanley Cup since 1938 and stayed with the team—leading the league seven times in goal scoring and three times in total points—until he jumped to the fledgling WHA's Winnipeg Jets in 1972 for $2.5 million. He retired in 1981 and now runs farms and breeding operations across Canada. He lives in North Carolina.

Brother Garry never made it to the NHL, but Dennis did for 13 successful years. Bobby's son Brett, who has won one more Stanley Cup than his father, now plays with Detroit where he holds the team's single season goal-scoring record with 86.

Bad Guys Finish Fourth

—May 4, 1963—
Mordecai Richler

T HIS YEAR the world ice hockey championships were not only held in Stockholm but, for the third time, the Swedes were the incumbent champions and the team to beat. Other serious contenders were the Czechs and the Russians, and the team everyone had come to see humiliated were our own peppery but far from incomparable Trail Smoke Eaters. "No nations can form ties of friendship without there being personal contact between the peoples. In these respects sport builds on principles of long standing," Helge Berglund, president of the Swedish Ice Hockey Association, wrote warmly in

The Smoke Eaters "want to see blood"

the world hockey tournament's 1963 program.

Berglund's bubbly letter of greeting continued, "I do hope the ice hockey players will feel at home here and that you will take advantage of your leisure to study Swedish culture and Swedish life. Welcome to our country."

Welcome?

On the day I arrived in Stockholm a poster on kiosks every-where announced "The Canadians Want to See Blood." (It was advertising a sports magazine.) Only a few days later a headline in the *Toronto Star* read "Ugly Row in Sweden over Our Hockey Team."

I checked into the Hotel Continental, a well-lit teak-ridden place where well on a hundred other reporters, radio and tele-vision men, referees, a hockey priest and a contingent of 27 Russians were staying. I immediately sought out Jim Proudfoot of the *Star*, who had just returned from a cocktail party at the Canadian embassy. "What did the players have to say?" I asked.

"The players weren't invited," he said.

This struck me as incongruous. Rather like having a literary party to which publishers, editors and booksellers—but no writers—were invited.

The next morning things began to sizzle. On Saturday night, according to the most colourful Swedish newspapers, a substi-tute player with the Canadian team, Russ Kowalchuk, tried to smuggle a girl into his room and was knocked senseless by an outraged hotel porter. Kowalchuk, enthusiastically described as a "star" in one Swedish newspaper and "a philandering hoodlum" in another, was not flattered: he denied that there had been a girl involved in the incident and claimed he had been flattened by a sneak punch.

Two things worried me about this essentially commonplace story. While it seemed credible that a hotel porter might be shocked if a hockey player tried to sneak a stuffed rabbit into the elevator, it did seem absurd that he would be shaken to his roots if a man, invited by Helge Berglund to study Swedish life, tried to take a girl to his room. And if the Canadians were such a rough-and-ready lot, if they were determined to crush Swedish bones in Friday night's game, wasn't it deflating that one of their defencemen could be knocked out by a mere porter? More important, mightn't it even hurt the gate?

The Smoke Eaters, as well as the Czech, Russian and American players, were staying at the Malmen—not, to put it mildly, the most fashionable of hotels, a feeling, I might add, obviously shared by the amateur hockey officials associated with the Smoke Eaters, which group wisely put up at the much more elegant Grand Hotel.

When I finally got to the Malmen at noon on Sunday, I found the sidewalk outside all but impassable. Kids clutching autograph books, older boys in black-leather jackets, and comely girls who didn't look like they'd need too much encouragement to come in out of the cold, so to speak, jostled each other by the entrance. An American player stepped out of the hotel and was quickly set upon by a group of autograph-hungry kids.

"Shove off," he said, leading with his elbows, and if the kids (who, incidentally, learn to speak three languages at school) didn't immediately grasp the colloquialism then the player's message, I must say, was implicit in his tone. The kids scattered. The American player, however, stopped a little further down the street for three girls and signed his name for them. I know he *could* sign, too, for unlike the amateurs of other nations, he was neither a reinstated pro, army officer or sports-equipment manufacturer, but a bona fide student. Possibly, he could sign *very well*.

In the lobby of the Malmen, Bobby Kromm—the truculent coach of the Smoke Eaters—was shouting at a Swedish journalist.

Other players, reporters, camp followers, cops, *agents provoca-teurs* and strong-armed hotel staff milled about, seemingly bored. Outside, kids with their noses flattened against the windows tried to attract the attention of the players who slouched in leather chairs. Suddenly the Russian team, off to a game, emerged from the elevators, already in playing uniforms and carrying sticks. A Canadian journalist whispered to me, "Don't they look sinister?" As a matter of fact, if you overlooked the absence of facial stitches, they closely resembled the many Canadians of Ukrainian origin who play in the NHL: but I let it pass.

Bobby Kromm and his assistant manager, Don Freer, were also off to the game, but they agreed to meet me at eight o'clock. When I returned to the Malmen that evening I saw a car parked by the entrance, three girls waiting in the back seat. Kids, also hoping to attract the players' attention, were banging pennies against the lobby windows. The players, sucking on matchsticks, ignored them. Kromm, Freer and I went into the dining room, and while I ordered a cognac I was gratified to see that the reputedly terrifying Smoke Eaters, those behemoths who struck fear into the hearts of both Swedish mothers and Russian defencemen, stuck to coffee and pie.

Kromm, assuming our elderly waiter could understand English, barked his order at him and was somewhat put out— in fact he complained in a voice trained to carry out to centre ice—when the waiter got his order wrong. The waiter began to mutter. "You see," Kromm said, "they just don't like Canadians here."

I nodded sympathetically.

"Why do they serve us pork chops, *cold* pork chops, *for breakfast?*"

"If you don't like it here, why don't you check out and move right into another hotel?" I suggested tentatively.

This wasn't possible, Kromm explained. Their stay at the Malmen was prepaid. It had been arranged by John Ahearne, European president of the International Ice Hockey Federation, who, as it turns out, also runs a travel agency. "If they'd treat us good here," Kromm said, "we'd treat them good."

Freer—an engaging, quiet-spoken man—explained that the Smoke Eaters had nothing against the Swedes, but they felt the press had used them badly.

"They called me a slum," Kromm said. "Am I a slum?"

"No. But what," I asked, "is your big complaint here?"

Bobby Kromm pondered briefly. "We've got nothing to do at night. Why couldn't they give us a ping-pong table?"

Were these men the terror of Stockholm? On the contrary, it seemed to me they would have delighted the heart of any YMCA athletic director. Freer told me proudly that nine of the 21 players on the team had been born and raised in Trail and that 10 worked for the C. M. and S.

"What does that stand for?" I asked.

"I dunno," he said.

It stands for Consolidated Mining and Smelting, and Bobby Kromm is employed as a glass blower by the company. All of them would be compensated for lost pay. Kromm said, "We can't step out of the hotel without feeling like monkeys in a cage. People point you out on the streets and laugh."

"It might help if you didn't wear those blazing red coats everywhere."

"We haven't any other coats."

I asked Kromm why European players didn't go in for body-checking. "They condone it," he said, "that's why."

I must have looked baffled.

"They condone it. Don't you understand?"

I did, once I remembered that when Kromm had been asked by another reporter for his version of the girl-in-the-lobby incident, he had said, "O.K., I'll give you my impersonation of it."

Kromm and Freer were clear about one thing. "We'd never come back here again."

Jackie McLeod, the only player on the team with NHL experience, didn't want to come back again either. I asked him if he had, as reported, been wakened by hostile telephone calls. He had been wakened, he said, but the calls weren't hostile. "Just guys in night clubs wanting us to come out and have a drink with them."

While Canadian and Swedish journalists got excited, very excited, over Kowalchuk's misadventure, the men representing international news agencies found the tournament dull and Stockholm a sub-zero and expensive bore. Late every night the weary reporters, many of whom had sat through three hockey games a day in a cold arena, gathered in the makeshift press club at the Hotel Continental.

"What did Kromm have to say after the game?"

"He said it was tough not to win."

"That guy is getting very quotable. Cassius Clay better look to his laurels."

Genuine melancholy usually set in at 2 a.m.

"If only we could get one of the Russian players to defect."

"You crazy? To work for a lousy smelting factory in Trail? Those guys have it really good, you know."

The lowest paid of all the amateurs were the Americans, who were given $20 spending money for the entire European tour; and the best off, individually, was undoubtedly the Swedish star, Tumba Johansson. Tumba, a $10-a-game amateur, had turned down a Boston Bruin contract offer but not, I feel, because he was intent on keeping his status pure. A national hero, Tumba earns a reputed $40,000 a year through a hockey equipment manufacturer. First night out on the ice not many of the Swedish players wore helmets. "Don't worry," a local reporter said, "they'll be wearing their helmets for Tumba on Wednesday. Wednesday they're on TV."

Stockholm, the largest city in Scandinavia, has been built on a bewildering sequence of islands and is enhanced by the lovely canals that run through it. Swans and brilliantly coloured ducks swim about in partially frozen canals. Steamers can be seen in the middle of town. "We are a most clean and thorough people," a Swede said to me.

A foreign correspondent stationed (or, if you like, exiled to) Stockholm, told me, "Nothing ever happens here. Nothing. The Swedes only react to what happens elsewhere." If our cliché is the long, undefended frontier, then the Swedish one is peace. The Swedes have managed to stand clear of the last two world wars and walking around in gloriously prosperous Stockholm I got the feeling, a nasty feeling—shared, as I recall, by most Danes and Norwegians I ever met—that they have made rather too good a thing of it. Peacemongering for some, it seems, is at least as profitable as warmongering used to be for others. Though the Swedes are compulsively quick to tell you how much they did for escaping Jews and allied airmen, and how they cleverly sold the Germans faulty goods during the last war, the discomforting fact is they didn't care enough about the Nazis to fight them.

Still, it was exhilarating to be a Canadian in Stockholm. Everywhere else I've been to in Europe, I've generally had to explain where and what Canada was, that I was neither an American nor a colonial, and that we even had self-government. But in Sweden there was no need to fumble or apologize. Canadians are known, widely known, and widely disliked. It gave me a charge, this—a real charge—as if I actually came from a country important enough to be feared, like the United States or Russia.

On reflection, however, it seemed likely that the Swedish press had only slandered my countrymen because they grasped the true nature of our kinship. Our countries are, each on its own continent, synonymous with dullness. We have so much in common that it would be impossible not to despise each other.

The affable Helge Berglund, president of the Swedish Ice Hockey Association, claims there are more than 100,000 active players and about 7,000 hockey teams in Sweden. How fitting then, he reflects, that the Johanneshov *isstadion* should be the scene of the world championship competition. "The stadium's fame as the Mecca of ice hockey," he continues in his very own bouncy style, "is once more sustained."

My trouble was I couldn't get into Mecca.

"You say you have just come from London for the *Maclean's*," the official said warily, "but how do I know you are not a . . . chancer?"

With the help of the Canadian embassy I was able to establish that I was an honest reporter. "I could tell you were no chancer," the official said, smiling now, "a man doesn't flow all the way from London just for a free ticket."

"You're very perceptive," I said.

"They think here I am a fool that I do everybody favours— even the Russians. But if I now go to Moscow they do me a favour and if I come to London," he said menacingly, "you are happy to favour me too."

"Call me any time," I said, grabbing my ticket.

Inside the *isstadion*, the Finns were playing the West Germans. A sloppy, lacklustre affair. Very little bodily contact. If a Finn and West German collided they didn't exactly say excuse me: neither did either of them come on like Howie Young. I returned the same night, Monday, to watch the Smoke Eaters play the exhausted, dispirited Americans. Down four goals to begin with, the Canadians easily came back to win 10–4. The game, a dull one, was not altogether uninstructive. I had been placed in the press section and in the seats below me agitated agency men, the unsung reporters of Associated Press, United Press International, Canadian Press and other news organizations, sat with pads on their knees and telephones clapped to their ears. There was a scramble round the American nets and a goal was scored. How, I wondered, are they able to determine, through such a tangle of arms and legs, who actually shoved the puck in for the Smoke Eaters?

"Em, it looked like number 10 to me," one of the agency men ventured.

"No—no—it was number 6."

"Are you sure?"

"Absolutely."

"I'm with Harry," the man from another agency said, "I think it was number 10."

A troubled pause.

"Maybe we ought to wait for the official scorer?"

"Tell you what," somebody said, "as long as we all agree it was number 10—"

"Done."

All at once, the agency men began to talk urgently into their phones.

". . . and the Smoke Eaters add yet another tally. The second counter of the series for . . ."

The next game I saw—Canada vs. Czechoslovakia—was what the sporting writers of my Montreal boyhood used to call the big one, a four-pointer. Whoever lost this one was unlikely to emerge world champion. Sensing the excitement, maybe even hoping for a show of violence, some 15,000 people turned up for the match. Most of them were obliged to stand for the entire game, maybe two hours.

This was an exciting contest, extremely tense, with the lead seesawing back and forth throughout. The Czech amateurs are not only better paid than ours, but also play with infinitely more elegance. Superb stick-handlers, cunning and accurate passers, they skated circles round the Smoke Eaters, overlooking only one thing: in order to score frequently it is necessary to shoot on the nets. While the Czechs seemed loath to part with the puck, the more primitive Canadians couldn't get rid of it quickly enough. Their approach was to wind up and belt the puck in the general direction of the Czech zone, all five players bearing in after it.

The crowd—except for one hoarse and lonely voice that seemed to come from the farthest reaches of Helge Berglund's Mecca—delighted in every Canadian pratfall. From time to time the isolated Canadian supporter called out in a mournful, touching voice, "Come on, Canada."

The Czechs had a built-in cheering section behind their bench. Each time one of their players put stick and puck together a banner was unfurled and at least 100 chunky, broad-shouldered men began to leap up and down and shout something that sounded like, "Umpa-Umpa-Czechoslovakia!"

Whenever a Czech player scored, their bench would empty, everybody spilling out on the ice to embrace, leap into the air and shout joyously. The Canadian team, made of cooler stuff, would confine their scoring celebration to players already out on the ice. With admirable unself-consciousness, I thought, the boys would skate up and down poking each other on the behind with their hockey sticks.

The game, incidentally, ended in a 4–4 tie.

The Canadians want to see blood, the posters said. Hoodlums, one newspaper said. The red jackets go hunting at night, another claimed. George Gross, the *Toronto Telegram*'s outraged reporter, wrote, "Anti-Canadian feeling is so strong here it has become impossible to wear a maple leaf on your lapel without being branded ruffian, hooligan and—since yesterday—sex maniac."

A man—that is to say, a Canadian man—couldn't help but walk taller in such a heady atmosphere, absorbing some of the fabled Smoke Eaters virility by osmosis. You found yourself ordering drinks in a gruffer voice and possibly even growling at girls. In all honesty, however, I must confess that no window shutters were drawn as I walked down the streets. Mothers did not lock up their daughters. I was not called ruffian, hooligan or anything even mildly deprecating, but possibly the trouble was I wore no maple leaf in my lapel.

Anyway, in the end everything worked out fine. On Tuesday morning Russ Kowalchuk's virtue shone with its radiance restored. Earlier, Art Potter, the politically astute president of the Canadian Amateur Hockey Association, had confided to a Canadian reporter, "These are cold-war tactics to demoralize the Canadian team. They always stab us in the back here."

But now even he was satisfied. Witnesses swore there was no girl in lobby. The Malmen hotel apologized. Russ Kowalchuk, after all, was a nice clean-living Canadian boy. In the late watches of the night he did not lust after Swedish girls, but possibly, like Bobby Kromm and Don Freer, yearned for nothing more depraved than a ping-pong table. A McIntosh apple maybe.

Finally, the Smoke Eaters did not behave badly in Stockholm. They were misunderstood. They also finished fourth.

The Smoke Eaters was the last club team to represent Canada at the world championships. It was replaced by an amateur national team until a full professional team was allowed in 1977.

Mordecai Richler, one of Canada's greatest writers, contributed 48 pieces to Maclean's. He died of cancer in 2001 at 69.

The Unreal Derek Is Unreal

—April 1972—
Jack Ludwig

HOCKEY, LIKE ALL PROFESSIONAL SPORTS, depends on its image junkies—advance men, drumbeaters, barkers, sloganeers, con artists, puff writers—to gun the publicity noise machine National Hockey League owners demand, the media supply and fans crave. To be successful, a hockey star should have all the attributes of a well-advertised breakfast cereal. Maybe the greatest publicity winner of all time is a young man of high profile, neatly packaged, instantly identified, Derek Sanderson. He and the image junkies depend on each other. They exploit him and he, by letting himself be exploited, exploits their exploitation.

"A steak and three Pepsis, please"

You know the Sanderson image—Derek the swinger, Derek the class dresser, Derek the sexual satyr, Derek the tough, Derek "the cocksure," "hockey's Joe Namath," the NHL's first "radically hip" nonconformist.

I'm a novelist, not a sportswriter. Fiction leans on the real. I can't write about anybody till I've seen the whites of his or her eyes. As far as I'm concerned, Derek Sanderson had no existence before I met him. I had seen him play hockey, knew all the legends and *then* met him. What I met was a confessedly confused and contradictory shy young man with an extraordinary commitment to his father and mother and sister. Harold Sanderson to Derek is the icon of icons: Derek repeats his dad's words as though every sentiment were newly minted and not easily duplicated in most Canadian Legion halls.

More to the point, the Sanderson who is supposed to be such a nonconformist has the values one finds in many Canadian small towns, and big cities, too, particularly those Ontario communities that generate NHL stars. He refers to French Canadians only half-kiddingly as "Pea Soup," absolutely despises militant athletes, particularly black militants, like Duane Thomas of the Dallas Cowboys. He regards American draft dodgers who have found refuge in Canada as, for the most part, "a bunch of chicken-livered weirdos." In St. Catharines and Niagara Falls, one suspects, such sentiments abound. Between Harold Sanderson's and Derek Sanderson's contemporaries there is little of a generation gap. Derek's about as radically hip as Clarence Campbell, president of the NHL. But then Derek Sanderson never claimed to be radically hip; that's what the publicity machine *said* he was. And that is not the only discrepancy one finds between the image and the real human person Sanderson happens to be.

We met in Toronto a couple of nights after Boston had creamed their rivals for first place in the Eastern Division, the

New York Rangers. In that game Sanderson had scored one goal and played his usual serious penalty-killing, forechecking, unselfish-passing three periods. I see this youngish guy with a rather recalcitrant moustache, his hair is neat and not-quite-shoulder-length: his suit is grey flannel, pinstripe, with a vest yet; he orders a steak done medium-well when any swinger or jet-setter knows steak has to be eaten rarer-than-rare or, to project the proper image, even a little raw! To go with his steak he orders, not champagne, or 20-year-old Scotch, or even a beer! *Three* Pepsis Derek asks for, and the waitress, familiar with his likes, doesn't bat an eye.

In that same restaurant, to compare with Sanderson's "hair" and "moustache," I see three Christs with hair falling down the back, two bearded Che Guevaras, one Fidel Castro, an Allen Ginsberg; I think of a typical college campus with its splendid show of hair, beards, sideburns and moustaches. Among these people Sanderson would not only *sound* but *look* square. The establishment is no enemy of Derek Sanderson's. Its enemies, moreover, are his. The close connection between "money" and having "class" is a staple of the establishment credo to which Sanderson so generously subscribes. After lunch, Sanderson and I walk through the Colonnade on Toronto's Bloor Street. "Hey, you know any good broads in Toronto?" swinger Sanderson asks me. Several pretty girls pass by. Sanderson smiles, bows, makes a sad try at coming up with girl-boy chit-chat. The girls ignore him and move right along. "Everybody thinks I got nothing but women," Sanderson says. "Finding nice broads isn't that easy."

Sanderson has almost had to hide the fact that he, the swinger, has been involved with one woman, Judy Martin, for the past two years. "I'm so close to getting married you wouldn't believe it," he tells me, who believes it. "Not that I don't go in for a one-night stand," Sanderson adds, to relieve my anxiety, "except that apart from sex I don't give those broads nothing."

His loyalty to Judy Martin assumes real class: John Reeves, the *Maclean's* photographer, comes from Toronto looking for fabled Sanderson women to photograph. Sanderson refuses to give out the names of women he has had only casual relations with. He won't do it because it's phony, but, more important, rejects it because of the hurt it might cause Judy Martin and his mother.

By this time I'm not surprised by the signs of feeling and delicacy in Sanderson. In Toronto he tells me how angry he was when his good friend Eddie Shack got traded away from Boston. His eyes glint. "Trades," he says, "kill a man. They hold it over your head all the time. To keep a guy in line." A "radical" would go the next step, of course, and ask how come "they" have so much unchallenged power.

But the Eddie Shack story isn't finished. "You know when I gave up that fighting?" Sanderson tells me. "It's when I'm banging away at somebody in the middle of a game and look up and see—my old buddy, Eddie! Right there and then I realize there's got to be something goddam awful about what I'm doing." To his mother, a cheery Scots lass who hasn't lost her charming Fife lilt, Derek's the essence of reliability—a born penalty killer: "Nobody," she tells me, "has to worry when Derek's around." According to her, Derek tries to hide his sensitivity. "If people ever found out what I'm really like, Mom," he told her, "I'd be finished."

In the Bruin program there's a group picture of the team. Everyone in it—players, managers, trainers—is smiling, except one man, Sanderson. Once he was off in Florida when picture proofs arrived at his home. They had to be judged right away. "You do it, Mom," Derek said over the phone, "but make sure you don't choose one with me smiling." Sanderson works at that particular projection. He backs away from the face-off, skating slowly, almost stiff-legged, then moves in, muttering and growling. The ploy, you see, has worked. Sanderson the scene-stealer has done it again. Bobby Orr may be out on the ice with him, Ken Dryden, the NHL East All-Star goalie, waits at the other end: other All-Stars, Frank Mahovlich, Yvan Cournoyer, J. C. Tremblay, are getting set for the power play, but the guy who to them is no more than a good, not great, player captures all the attention. And attention translates into bucks.

The NHL, rather than being an end in itself, becomes, for those who reach it, the fastest and shortest route to Easy Street. Think of it. All over Canada, and, increasingly, in the U.S. too, thousands upon thousands of kids play hockey with some NHL idol held before them—Gordie Howe, Jean Beliveau and, among the active players, Bobby Orr, Bobby Hull, and at most one or two others. As they move up through tyke, peewee, midget, juvenile, junior and college play, the kids turn into young men in need of a career, a Big Break, a windfall or any old job, even a trade. Of these thousands who wait to be called by the NHL, only 100-odd are chosen, and of these fewer than 30 or so really make it—even in the era of expansion. Of those who make it, only two or three reach the state of being noticed *regularly*. For these the NHL is not only the way up, it's the way out—to a flourishing business setup, a fat stock portfolio, or, in the dream of dreams Sanderson sometimes dreams, to Hollywood, to big-time television, the intersecting avenues of Easy Street.

In the Bruin dressing room after a recent Montreal game I met an old buddy of Sanderson's now tending bar in Montreal. "Can you imagine," he said to me, "I grew up with this guy. And look where he is now!" He meant that, tips included, he could clear $150 a week, maybe $200, and here was his old buddy, Derek, already doing better than $50,000 a year, and inevitably headed for much much more. Without *both* the NHL *and* his image-projecting, Sanderson himself might now, at 25, be earning—if he could find a job in Niagara Falls—$8,000 to $10,000 a year working nine to five, five days a week. With *only* the NHL, Sanderson at this point would be doing well earning $20,000 a year.

The key, obviously, is in that projected image Sanderson helped foster and now, sometimes, hates. If the NHL, and hockey in general, weren't so unbelievably square, Sanderson's image-projecting would not have been so unbelievably easy. The NHL owners are like one of those high-school principals forever suspending kids with long hair or jeans; he himself wears a stiff collar, a knotted tie, a sharkskin suit, his hair cropped—rather imitative of the costume cons wear the day they are sprung from prison.

In Toronto, two kids in hockey sweaters sneak into the area where the Bruins are eating. Orr isn't around, but almost all the other Bruins are: "Hey," a kid says to Phil Esposito, "which one's Derek Sanderson?" Phil shrugs and points, the other players glare, the kid passes almost the entire roster by, gets Sanderson's autograph for himself and his buddy, squeals with delight and leaves. It's almost like that everywhere else. First Orr, then Sanderson—plus Esposito and McKenzie—then the undifferentiated rest. The players glare because though nobody thinks himself as good a player as Bobby Orr, or as good a scorer as Phil Esposito, or as rough a scrapper as Johnny McKenzie or Teddy Green, everyone, almost to a man, thinks of himself as at least Sanderson's hockey equal, if not his superior. Yet there's Sanderson, talking about a dozen pairs of golf slacks he just bought for $35 per. In every city they hit, there's Derek's unsmiling photo. I sit at a table with a couple of players: "I don't want to talk about Derek," a Bruin says quickly. When another player joins the table and is told I'm doing a piece on Sanderson, his immediate response is: "Well, that won't take long, will it?" Even Tom Johnson, Sanderson's coach, can't hide his feelings: "Not another thing about Sanderson?" he says. "Why can't people try something hard for a change?"

Sanderson's comeback is that what he has done is as much a contribution to the NHL and other players as it is to himself: "They don't even know what I did for them," he tells me. "*I* was the first one with long hair in this league, I gave them their first moustache. I was the first guy to mouth the big shots. Nobody else did a thing."

We walk along a Boston sidestreet, pass a sporting goods store. Hanging in the window is a yellow sweatshirt inscribed DEREK IS UNREAL. To go with the printing is a line drawing of Sanderson sans moustache, his hair shorter, his sideburns much more like Elvis's. "That's me two years ago," Sanderson says, "I'm nothing like that anymore." As soon as we leave the store, he mugs a softshoe routine; later, in a costumer's, he puts on a succession of pilgrim hats, Paul Revere triangulars, a Greek helmet, a W. C. Fields busted top hat; he does imitations, clowns around, smiling, having a ball. For an instant all thoughts of The Gimmick are banished, he doesn't have to protect the Unsmiling Image: in front of me is a charming, relaxed, self-mocking, shy Canadian kid, the same one his mother, Caroline, describes, the same one Judy Martin has been telling me about.

Earlier I've been to a Bruin workout at Boston University: Sanderson, the Sunday night before, had scored three goals and had two assists in a nine-to-two slaughter of the Detroit Red Wings. Everybody was cool and kibitzing. After the workout I got into Sanderson's car, and, moving at about two miles an hour, he aimed it at Johnny McKenzie. Without missing a beat, McKenzie vaulted up on the hood, climbed up over the roof, then down off the trunk, as if he'd merely stepped over a hockey stick. Sanderson and the other Bruins watching convulsed with laughter.

Five or six long-haired BU students were watching. To them, undoubtedly, Sanderson looked extremely puckish and neat. But that's the way he came through to me from the very beginning, a rather nice, not unusual boy from a hockey town in southern Ontario, more typical than he thinks, less abrasive than other people think. Derek is real enough. If Trudeau can be contradictory, why can't a hockey player from Niagara Falls? If consistency isn't attained by most philosophers, academics, tycoons, politicos, why should one be surprised when a young man like Derek Sanderson on the very same day blasts draft dodgers and yet signs his autograph "Peace"? If Derek Sanderson is unreal, he's no more unreal than the two-dimensional, four-colour-poster world he thrives in, that needs him more than he needs it.

Derek Sanderson played one more season with the Bruins and then jumped to the WHA's Philadelphia Blazers for $2.6 million, then the richest contract ever signed by any athlete. But he missed Boston and returned to the Bruins, where he became even more famous for his off-ice shenanigans. He became an alcoholic and smoked two packs of cigarettes a day. Nevertheless, he continued in the NHL, off and on, until 1978. By that time he was broke and sleeping on park benches. His road to recovery began when he landed a job as an assistant golf pro in St. Catharines, Ont., for room and board, while pumping gas for spending money. Now Sanderson has turned his life around. He lives in Boston, where he worked successfully for 10 years as an investment specialist for pro athletes. He never married Judy Martin, but he is married now and the father of two.

Jack Ludwig, best known as a short-story writer and novelist, was a contributing editor at Maclean's *in 1973 and 1974 and is the author of* Hockey Night in Moscow.

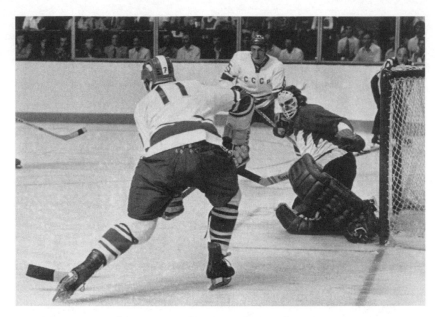

Ken Dryden, Hockey's Lonely Forerunner

—February 1973—
Jack Ludwig

L AST APRIL while I was looking for Ken Dryden up on the
Montreal Forum press-box catwalk, I ran into an NHL
goal judge who told me that if I wanted to find Dryden I should
"look for someone who doesn't look like a hockey player." The
man went further: "He's so *unlike* a hockey player—you'll see.
That isn't all," he added. "He doesn't look like an NHL goalie.
He's six-foot, four-inches. When he stands up we have to crane
around him. Every shot's a screen shot." Just recently, however,
I spoke to Ray Picard, who coached Dryden or managed teams
in Toronto's Humber Valley that Dryden played on from the

Dryden bombarded in the opening game of the Canada-Soviet series time he was seven. "At seven," Picard said, "Kenny looked like an NHL goalie." According to Picard, Dryden had "all the moves and all the poise of a pro" at seven: Picard remembers Dryden as being *small* for his age. Murray Dryden, Ken's father, had built a goal out of two-by-fours for his two sons, Dave (now sharing the Buffalo Sabres' goalie work with Roger Crozier) and Ken: Ken, as Picard recalls, barely rose as high as the crossbar. His brother Dave was six years older and a confirmed goalie. Neighbours remember seeing the Dryden boys taking turns in that net, hour after hour, day after day, summer and winter. Then Ken began to grow and grow and grow.

He's still growing.

When I finally found Ken Dryden I understood what the goal judge had been trying to tell me. Here was this tall young man with slightly shaggy hair not severely sprayed in the best NHL way. Dryden looked more like the Ivy Leaguer he had been at Cornell University for four years, or a law school student on Interview Day. Off the ice he wore horn-rim glasses and looked something like Clark Kent, that un-Canadian Superman. To disqualify himself further from NHL possibilities, Dryden listened intelligently and was shockingly grammatical in speech. When I found him he was answering some sportscaster's question about "your greatest thrill" or "biggest moment"—or maybe it was "biggest thrill" and "greatest moment." Dryden didn't use chummy Dale Carnegie sales techniques such as mentioning the interviewer's first name every third or fourth word: he seemed devoid of athletic nothing talk, or other Method actor tricks such as the modest mumble or the blushing mutter. And yet, of course, nobody could have conformed to the Gee Whiz sports star myth better than this same Dryden.

Up to the time Dryden became Montreal's goalkeeper, there were two ways of guaranteeing a player permanent exclusion from the National Hockey League. One was to play on the Canada team that specialized in losing to Czechs, Russians and other international usurpers of Canada's game; two was to play American *Ivy League* college touch hockey. One could, of course, put in a stint with a Big Ten jock school like the University of Minnesota or a Michigan Tech that Tony Esposito played for. Cornell was another thing. As if being twice-buried weren't enough, Dryden had gone for *three* by attending law school at the University of Manitoba while playing for the national team out of Winnipeg. From Canada's national team he came to the Montreal Voyageurs, the Canadiens' farm team, because he was continuing his education at McGill's Law School. He was the *third* goalie for the Voyageurs, almost exclusively a practice goalie. In training camp in the fall of 1970, Dryden showed up exceptionally well, playing better than any of the other men, Canadiens or Voyageurs. But at the end of camp he was out of The Big Time and off The Big Club. Worse, the first time he started in goal for the Voyageurs, he lost, 5–3. After Christmas that year the Voyageurs played half their home games in Halifax: Dryden decided that, no matter what, he would stay in Montreal and not give up his law studies.

In addition, of course, here was Dryden not only an *anglais* but an *anglais* from Ontario, born in Hamilton, brought up in Toronto, this when the separatist movement was seemingly quite strong. This *anglais*, unlike a confirmed Canadien, had small cussage, and less French. He spoke too softly and didn't carry that big a stick. So what was to worry, eh? And the way the Canadiens treated Dryden when he reported on March 7, 1971, the last call-up date for minor leaguers that season, must have faked goalie Rogatien Vachon out too. The first game Dryden might have played, he didn't even dress for. He sat in the stands like a draft choice, or a third cousin of the Molson family (then owners of the Canadiens). Dryden remembers that night as one of the low points of his life.

But then came a game with Pittsburgh, a trounceable expansion club, and Dryden got his chance. Canadiens, not unexpectedly, won, and Dryden played well. The question remained, though: how would he do against *real* NHL clubs? Dryden could only play six games without being classified as an NHL player for that season. He did. And Montreal won all six. Except for Pittsburgh and one game with Buffalo, all others were against the pre-expansion teams: twice with Dryden Montreal beat the Rangers and once beat Toronto and once Chicago. What had begun as a perfunctory tryout turned into a confirmed takeover.

But Vachon surely had been saved by the bell. The regular season ended. The Canadiens now had to play Stanley Cup hockey. Two or three sports clichés converged, conflicting: one said playoff experience always counted in the playoffs—and gave points to Vachon; another said streaks must end sometimes and are quite often flukes—this was at best a standoff for Dryden; but by far the most compelling sports axiom is that you must always "go with the hot man," which Dryden most certainly was. So there was Dryden when Stanley Cup play began, at least for that game Montreal's number one goalie. The goalkeeper he kept on the bench was daring, acrobatic, talented and young, not some floundering faltering faded flubber. Rogatien Vachon, as any hockey fan with credentials knows, sat out *all* the Stanley Cup games, 20 of them, which ended with the Canadiens winning the Stanley Cup and Dryden winning the Conn Smythe Trophy (and $1,500) as the most valuable player in the series.

What interested me in Ken Dryden, I must confess, was not his hockey credentials or even his ability to stand in as a boys' book hero in a novel I've no desire to write. I was fascinated by what he did the summer of his Stanley Cup success. Instead of using sports, as many Ivy League stars of football and basketball and even hockey do, to set themselves up in business or practice or politics, Dryden worked in a Ralph Nader project dealing with the consequences of pollution.

Spending most of his time in Nader's Washington office but scooting south to Virginia to study firsthand the problem Nader's men were attacking—the effects of pollution on the life and livelihood of commercial fishermen in Virginia—Dryden was as much of a lonely forerunner in the practice of law as he was in his "profession (other)," hockey. When I met him in Montreal on April Fool's Day, 1972, we talked about his summer and about his hopes and plans for Nader work in Canada. As I remember it, we didn't say one word about hockey, though right below us an NHL game was in progress (with Phil Myre in the Canadiens' goal). We talked instead of the backing Nader projects needed in order to support the kind of research Dryden himself had done, hard unglamorous digging to come up with the facts more valuable than opinion.

But it would be foolish to ignore the hockey side of Ken Dryden. It is not at all incidental. It has its existential place in his life. In days to come Dryden will identify himself with what he wins or loses in the practice of the law: hockey is his existential arena at this moment, and, I would think, will continue to be that for some time. And when I say "existential arena" I'm referring to a specific test, one with a beginning, middle and end no less fantastic than Dryden's entry into NHL play. This, of course, was his fabulous downer beginning and over-the-moon end in the Team Canada–USSR series.

This so-called "Match of the Century" featured many players, but nobody's graphed fall and rise so matched the fall and rise of Team Canada as Dryden's did. Dryden had had some experience with the USSR teams before. In December of 1969, playing for the national team, he was given a rough, rough ride by the USSR in Vancouver, losing 9–3. He also gave up four goals to the Czechs in a game the Czechs won 4–0. But anybody hearing of that series would not think, "The USSR and Czechoslovakia must be very good." The common response was "Sure, but that was the Canadian *national* team," which, as everyone knew, was made up of schoolboys, guys too small or too slight or too slow to make the NHL, or a few broken-down ungolden oldies. Few doubted that the NHL All-Stars playing under the rubric of "Team Canada" would beat hell out of the USSR and avenge all previous Canadian losses with a bonus here and there for good measure.

I've already described—in my book on the series—the tumultuous cheering that Dryden got from his people in Montreal as he was introduced the night of the first game on Sept. 2, 1972. There he was, the most popular of the home boys—applauded for the Calder rookie award, applauded for his play as a Canadien, applauded, too, I'm sure because he represents Canada the way most fans would like to see us represented. There he was, gliding around the ice, smiling, chatting with his teammates, doing his warm-up stretches and reaches while skating. And then into the nets for the warm-up, more serious now, the anticipation and the tension starting to build higher and higher.

No Canadian has to be told what happened. Few have to be told what happened to Ken Dryden. Seven times—*seven*—he saw the USSR score against him. Not only that: he knew he had looked bad on a couple of goals and took small consolation that his teammates looked bad on all seven. "Next day was the worst," Dryden told me. In practice, instead of getting most of the work, as befits the "starting goalie," Dryden got the least— less than even the number three goalie got, Eddie Johnston. Nobody said much, Dryden recalled. Everybody was nice— which was chilling. The whole team and its coaches were understandably in a state of shock: each man was probably concentrating on self-rescue.

A goalkeeper, like a quarterback in football or a pitcher in baseball, has no way of not being involved in a game's won-or-lost summing up. Even if a goalie's team scores seven or eight goals there's always the possibility that he'll let in that number, and maybe one or two more. A soccer goalkeeper playing for a superior team might not see the ball cross into his half of the field all game, but a hockey goalie rarely experiences that kind of breather. At any moment anybody is capable of letting go a shot from out far as well as from in close that might well decide a game.

TV instant replay multiplies analysis and assigns error. When a goalie looks bad on a goal now, he looks bad over and over again. Instant replay *might* pick up the forward who missed his check, or the defenceman out of position: what it never fails to pick up is an awkward miss or a faked-out drop to the ice or the nightmarish sight of a puck lurching forward frame by frame to bulge the goal netting with a sudden but slow inevitability. The goalie, more than any other sports figure, is technology's patsy: his one goof may stand recorded in athletic perpetuity as the crucial mismove in a 1–0 game.

Dryden's reaction to a scored goal is interesting. He never says a thing. Other goalies always claim the shot came from inside the crease, or the other team was offside, that the puck didn't go in, etc., etc. Or they glare at a teammate to indicate who really let the goal get by. Dryden has none of these tricks. When we were in Moscow together he told me he hated playing hockey in Sweden because the Swedes were such "actors," always slumping to the ice like Italian soccer players, claiming they were tripped, clipped, gypped.

Dryden at all times, though serious about hockey, has human priorities and personal standards that are more important than winning. He clearly couldn't think he had "won" a game that had been "won" by his tripping someone. Dryden dearly loves to win. In Moscow he told me he hated to have a puck get past him, even in the easiest-going practice. Not from Ken I learned that at least twice, while playing for Cornell, he had left his net with play still in progress to throw himself across a felled injured opposing player. It could be he's a lonely forerunner in this too—a man who is competitive but not combative. In all his hockey-playing years he has never been in a fight.

Which makes Ken's role in NHL hockey something of an anomaly. Commercial prime-time TV hockey, a branch of Show Biz, has encouraged Primitivism at all times, which accentuates Dryden's differences from the mass of hockey players. When he lost that game to the USSR in Montreal, it didn't occur to him that the whole team could and should have been blamed for its part in the debacle. It was *his* inadequacy he thought about. It never occurred to him that he might have tried to behead Valeri Kharlamov or Aleksandr Yakushev. What did worry him was whether he was capable of playing his best hockey against the USSR—and, even more important, if [coach Harry] Sinden would give him that chance. The Sunday after the loss, Dryden told me, "It was almost like you were gone." Departed, that is. Disappeared. Not to be counted in. It took almost 24 hours for him to realize that "things do go on," that he wouldn't be forever fixed in the amber cooked up by lousy statistics.

In the games that followed in Toronto and Winnipeg, Dryden tried to expunge the bad night in Montreal from his memory. That was made mandatory when he got the call to play Game Four in Vancouver. Vancouver, we should recall, was the site of Dryden's 9–3 loss to the USSR three years earlier. Vancouver, as everyone now knows, was the low point in the Team Canada experience. The team was booed, Dryden heard phony applause for easy saves after the USSR scored two quick power play goals. The game ended with the USSR winning 5–3 and, more dismally, leading the series by two games to one with one tied.

In Sweden Tony Esposito played well, Eddie Johnston played exceptionally well. From the moment the team left Canada, Dryden had been preparing himself for the likelihood that he wouldn't play again in the series. After two games he had the terrible average of six—he, a goalie who rarely strayed from the impressive two-goals-a-game average. He began to think, Dryden told me, of the coming season. In Moscow when Tony Esposito got the call for Game Five, that seemed not only fair but deserved. The USSR pouring five goals past Esposito to win 5–4 didn't change Dryden's estimate of his own prospects. Sinden might well have decided to give up on *both* Dryden and Esposito and try, instead, to win with his old Bruin goalie, Johnston.

But Sinden didn't. To Dryden's surprise he named him to start Game Six. Too much has been written about the Team Canada–USSR series for me to repeat how well Dryden played in that 3–2 win. I will say again, however, what he and I spoke about just recently: that the two fast saves he made at the beginning of the game set him up not just for the rest of that one but also for the last game, which followed. One could see the tenseness fall from him. The two days that followed Game Six were the ones he and I spent investigating the Army Sports Club and the Institute of Physical Culture and Sport in Moscow. Ken was totally relaxed now. In practice he was easy and with it. The night before the Big Game he watched the Bolshoi Ballet company do *Anna Karenina* with no tragic analogy to remind him of bad days past.

Game Eight was a team Frank Merriwell performance, complete with Peter Mahovlich's challenge to the cops of the Soviet Union to *come on the ice, I'll take ya all on.* From losing

5–3 at the end of the second period to winning 6–5 with 34 seconds left is the hockey story of the century, of course, and the man who played a fantastic last period in goal was Ken Dryden. Paul Henderson's winning goal lifted all the burdens the series might have loaded on to Dryden's shoulders. The game—and the series—was won, and won well. "You're not going to forget that series for a long time," Dryden told me. "And you couldn't really care if you played that much or not when you got back. It took a while. Then everything fell in place." When that winning goal was scored, Ken's sister Judy was working the cardiac ward at Kingston General Hospital: the doctors kept slapping blood-pressure sleeves on their heart patients, afraid that all the excitement would do them in.

Margaret Dryden, Ken's mother, said she had to keep walking out of the room. She couldn't take it. "Other mothers can take this," she told me. "I can't." In keeping with her role as a kindergarten teacher and innovator, Mrs. Dryden spaced her three children so she could spend time with them growing up. The thought of injury chills her. Dave was once hit in the eye by a puck and had to stay immobile for almost a month while doctors worked to save that eye's sight. His seeing was affected. And so too, I gathered, was Mrs. Dryden as a hockey fan. She tries not to watch her sons in a stadium but prefers— if she has to—to see them on television and be free to walk out of the room when things get tense. She's proud of both her boys because of what they're like, rather than because of what they've accomplished. She told me that Ken didn't relish working for a demolition crew one summer, because he "just doesn't like destruction." The next Cornell summer he got work *building*. A library, she said, which pleased them all. Mrs. Dryden says of hockey: "If the boys are happy in it, I'm happy." What's unsaid is that when the boys *aren't* in hockey she'll be even happier. Dave started teaching school when he was 18;

Judy, as I've already indicated, is a nurse; Ken has just recently passed his law exams. They're lonely forerunners all, these Drydens. Their legends are full of happy endings.

And as for Ken, it's not simply education. It's a commitment to thought and thinking about consequences. Nothing is more difficult, I submit, than being your own man in professional sports. The fans are after you, teammates are after you, opponents, media people. Clichés are shortcuts, terms of surrender, prompt cards, easy ways out. Communication in athletics is most easily done through buffoonery or boozing or cussing or slam-banging. Dryden chooses none of these ways. I should remember, as I vividly do, his rink-length dash to congratulate Paul Henderson who had just scored the winning goal in the Team Canada–USSR series: I'll remember much more pointedly how Dryden smiled as we were pulled into a group pose with the hockey faculty at the Soviet sport institute. He didn't have anything but an open generous attitude to these people who were our hosts. No "star" puffery. No touch-me-not stiffnecked pride. But what stays with me even more is Dryden on the ice with only Red Berenson and Peter Mahovlich after that first game 7–3 loss to the USSR, standing there and waving his stick in salute at the victorious Russians. Frank Merriwell characters are rarely shown losing the big ones. It's the lonely forerunner who does the most serious things well. Dryden is such a one as to build countries on.

Ken Dryden led the Canadiens to a Stanley Cup victory in 1973, winning the Vezina Trophy along the way. He then left the ice for two years to practise law before returning to the Canadiens. He led them to four straight Cups and earned four more Vezinas before retiring in 1979. The author of four best-selling books, Dryden now is president of the Toronto Maple Leafs.

What Makes Alan Eagleson Calm?

—December 1973—
Trent Frayne

T HE EAGLE IS ON THE PHONE. He is talking about his client
Paul Henderson whose two-year contract with the
Toronto Maple Leafs runs out next spring. He is talking to Jim
Gregory, Leaf general manager. "If you want Paul to play for you
next year," says the Eagle, "come up with a five-year package.
We're already holding an offer from the Toronto Toros for
between $800,000 and a million. See you."

The Eagle is dictating letters.

He is writing about his client Bobby Orr to the general
managers of 12 teams in the World Hockey Association. He is

advising them that Orr's five-year million-dollar contract with the Boston Bruins expires in the spring of 1976. He is requesting that they forward to him their offers for Orr's services. The Eagle looks up from his work. "I would suspect Bobby Orr will sign for $2.5 million in the summer of 1976," he says.

The most powerful man in professional hockey leans back in his chair and smiles a long slow smile. "The bidding should be interesting," adds the Eagle.

Until a day in Moscow when I ran into him unexpectedly at an elevator bank during the Canada-Russia hockey series, I'd known Alan Eagleson as a guy of endless energy, always rushing off somewhere waving and grinning and ducking through traffic, one of those people not notably humorous who laughs a lot, a physical-fitness freak, flat bellied, expensively tailored, a nonstop talker delighting in his triumphs, a boy with a toy.

I'd known him since 1967, when he was propelled into prominence as Bobby Orr's lawyer negotiating a landmark contract and then as the organizer of the NHL players' association, another landmark. Not long after he'd become the boss of the hockey players' trade union, he also became president of the Progressive Conservative Association in Ontario, the anti-establishment establishment man, a Bay Street lawyer in a big firm assaulting the Savile Row suits into which the panjandrums of the NHL were stuffed. In those days he looked like Clark Kent, ol' Super Al in his black horn-rims and groomed hair, all lean and athletic. In the last couple of years, like a lot of bushy tails, he'd moved into correctly mod suits, carefully lengthened his hair, switched to wire-rims, and he had become increasingly powerful in hockey's structure, though by September of 1972, at 39, he still had all this bounce, this glee.

I remember meeting him by chance on a Sunday morning in the lobby of the Grand Hotel in Stockholm while Team Canada was there and he said c'mon, he'd show me some marvellous architecture in the courtyard of the Swedish parliament buildings. So we set off across one of the old city's innumerable bridges, and I told him three separate times, for God's sake, what's the hurry, we've got all day, and he laughed and slowed his pace for a few moments but soon he was into his quick relentless gait again. Afterward, we climbed into a sight-seeing launch and cruised the waters of the city with a couple of the players. Forced to sit, he chuckled softly, grinned reflex-ively, and said he had thought it would take him five years to make Bobby Orr a millionaire, but the way things had turned out it had taken a little longer than that, five years and a few months, as I recall.

And so from these few hours on a tranquil Sunday in Stockholm I was entirely unprepared for what transpired some days later when I ran into him at the elevator bank and for the first time saw an Eagleson I'd never known before, the one everybody in Canada was to see on television from the Moscow Ice Palace a few days later. I was waiting to take the down elevator in the Intourist Hotel when the up elevator deposited Eagleson at the sixth floor. This was the day after Canada had blown a 4–1 lead in the third period of the opening game in Moscow to lose 5–4 and go two games down to the Soviets. The Russians had won twice in Canada, lost once and tied once, so now the series stood 3–1–1, and this was the first game I'd seen, because I'd been at the Olympic Games in Munich for the *Toronto Star* while the teams were playing in Canada. Eagleson wanted to know what I'd thought and I told him conversation-ally that I'd never seen a team pass the puck as impressively as the Russians.

"Jesus," he said. "You must be a Communist." He was very intense, his face was pale and drawn, and there was no question he was serious.

"All I said was that the passing knocked me out," I said.

"We lost, you know," he said.

"Yeah, I know we lost."

"We lost, and you're telling me you like their passing."

"That's right."

"Anybody who thinks like you do has to be a bloody Communist."

"What is this?" I said. "I tell you I like their passing and you give me all this ideological gobbledygook. What the hell has . . ."

He interrupted.

"Are you calling what I have to say gobbledygook?" he demanded. "If that's what you're saying, our friendship ends right here."

I was dumbfounded and he was seething and we stood glaring at one another. "Friendship is worth more than that," I said. We were still glaring when the elevator came and I walked into it.

Six days later, in the frenzied emotion of the eighth game, the one that meant everything, practically every human in Canada saw this other Eagleson. Until this single moment, as I've indicated, he had been Ralph Nader in a jockstrap. Six years ago he had stood up to—hell, he'd trampled over—the remote millionaires who'd been manipulating hockey players for generations like cards in a gin game. Late in the summer of 1972 he'd untangled the labyrinths of red tape inherent in Canada vs. Russia, salving egos, puncturing balloons, threatening, cajoling, circumventing, solving and finally bringing off, just this side of single-handedly, the impossible series—the capitalist pros and the Communist amateurs on the same ice floe.

And then in this stupefying moment, his feet had turned to clay right there on the tiny screen in full view of 16 million Canadians (a mere 12 million had watched the first man walk on the moon). When Canada scored the tying goal at 5–5 the red light back of the Russian net did not go on. Eagleson leaped to his feet, screaming, and bounded down an aisle to ice level where he was strong-armed by Russian cops. The milling commotion brought Peter Mahovlich and a wild grim band of stick-waving Canadian players to his rescue and he was escorted by them across the ice to the safety of their bench. Approaching it, face ashen, head bowed, he suddenly shook himself free and turned to the Russian fans across the rink. In a crude gesture, he jerked his arm aloft, once, twice, a digit on his right hand raised. Then he clenched his fist and shook it at the crowd, once, twice, four times, his eyes hot behind the steel-rims, hair tumbling across his forehead, jaw working, a man enraged.

This was surely the moment when he fitted a word the Russians supplied for him. The word was *nekulturny* and, translated loosely, *nekulturny* means yahoo or boor or simply a pain in the ass. John Robertson summed it up in the *Montreal Star*: "I saw us as a bunch of barbarians being led by a man who qualifies as a walking diplomatic disaster." Letters to the editor in papers across the country echoed the sentiment.

But wait.

There is a benefit softball game on July 1, 1967, in the little Ontario town of MacTier up near Georgian Bay. Canada is 100 years old this day and Eagleson, who had been the town's recreation director one summer during his under-graduate days in the 1950s, has been invited back to play in this laugher of a softball game. Also invited are his 19-year-old client, Bobby Orr of nearby Parry Sound, who has just completed his first NHL season, and Bobby's dad Doug, against whom Eagleson had often played ball that summer when he'd been the recreation director. All right. Down 7–6 in the ninth, Bobby Orr is the tying run at third base. Eagleson is batting. As the catcher lazily returns the ball to the pitcher, Orr breaks for the plate. The pitcher whips the ball to the catcher and Orr is clearly dead. But he barrels into the catcher, who drops the ball, and the game is tied. The first baseman, infuriated, rushes Orr and punches him from behind. Outraged, Eagleson drops his bat, tears off his glasses and hammers the first baseman to the ground. Now half a dozen opposing players rush Orr and Eagleson who, standing back to back, flail away as though it's Boston greeting the Rangers. Bobby's sister Pat, a spectator, wants in too, but in her rush down a hill she falls and suffers a shoulder separation. That breaks up the fight, but Orr and Eagleson agree it's been one hell of a fine Centennial Day celebration.

The point of all this is that there is an aspect to Eagleson's makeup that made the arena in massive Moscow no different than the ball park in tiny MacTier, a fact I began to appreciate only after we had stood eyeball to eyeball beside the elevators. Beneath that facade of geniality and garrulousness and energy he is fiercely, even blindly, partisan, and he is competitive to the point of indecency. His wife, Nancy, says that if he beats her five straight sets in tennis, he wants to make it six. He wants to beat every driver on the highway, every amber light on the street. One day last summer when a 16-year-old boy hit Eagleson's eight-year-old daughter, Jill, at a tennis club he told the boy to get his father. The father arrived, angry words ensued and Eagleson knocked the man down. Eagleson was charged with common assault. Then he was advised the charge would be withdrawn if he were to apologize in open court. Long since cooled out, he apologized in open court.

So here we have a partisan, competitive man; anybody who attacks his friend on a ball field, who doesn't turn on the red light when his team scores, who, indeed, admires the Russian passing plays when his team is trailing, has stripped through his facade and bared a nerve. Of course he's a walking diplomatic disaster; whoever charged him with being a diplomat? Of course he was a *nekulturny* in Russia; he went there to win.

Russia is almost a year away by the summer of 1973 and there is a whole new development in professional hockey. Alan Eagleson occupies a cool pedestal where the pressures are negligible. Accordingly, he is the Mr. Smiles-and-Chuckles we knew before Canada-Russia. He sits in the catbird's seat where nobody can threaten him or his friends, the players he represents. The World Hockey Association has come on the scene, challenging the NHL's dominance. A giant auction develops in which Eagleson and lawyers and agents like him deal the most skilful of their clients to the highest bidder. The owners are helpless. They are squeezed in a price war. If they don't meet salary demands of a player whose contract has expired, the player jumps to the other league. When young players graduate from junior ranks their agents offer their services to both leagues. The highest bidder wins. Thus, Eagleson is able to command $250,000 for junior graduate Rick Middleton of the Oshawa Generals on a three-year contract with the New York Rangers. Middleton, 20 years old on Dec. 4, had never been to New York, and when he finally got there this fall he was earning $83,333.33 per year. If the Rangers hadn't come up with the money, Eagleson would have got it, or very close to it, from the Minnesota Fighting Saints of the WHA. The Fighting Saints were very anxious to sign young Middleton.

Eagleson's power is awesome. He and his friend and client Mike Walton decided that Walton had had enough of Boston. The Bruins changed coaches midway through last season. Walton liked the old coach, Tom Johnson. He didn't like the new coach, Bep Guidolin. Mike is what Eagleson describes as "a certifiable psychiatric case." He knows Mike will get understanding from an old friend, Bob Pulford, coach of the Los

Angeles Kings of the NHL. He knows he'll be understood by Harry Neale, coach of the Minnesota Fighting Saints of the WHA. He gets on the phone to Boston where another old friend, Harry Sinden, coach of Team Canada and now a Bruin executive, is advised that Walton is through with Boston now that his two-year contract has expired.

"If you want to keep Mike in the NHL," he says into the phone, "make a deal with Pully in L.A. If you don't, he's gone to the Fighting Saints."

Now he gets on the phone to Pulford in Los Angeles, tilting back in his chair, grinning into the mouthpiece. "Pully, how are you? How's the weather out there? It is? Hell, it's wonderful here. Pully, listen: I've talked to Boston and I've told them Mike's through there. He'll either play for you or he'll play for Minnesota. But you've got to come up with the money. Listen, if he can get 50 goals for Jack Kent Cooke, Jack Kent Cooke's going to come up with a hundred and a half, right? Okay, you and Larry work it out and let me know."

Later, Pulford is back. He and Larry Regan, the general manager, have worked out an offer, a three-year package for Mike Walton—$100,000 for the first year, $115,000 for the second year and $125,000 for the third year. Also, there are incentive bonuses (incentive, yet) starting at 20 goals. For every five goals Walton scores above 20 each season, he receives another $5,000.

Eagleson hangs up and stares into space. "Well, now that I've got him signed at L.A.," he muses, "all I've got to do is get him to L.A."

But he doesn't get him to L.A. Regan and Sinden are unable to work out a deal. Five days later Eagleson and Walton fly to St. Paul for a press conference at which the Minnesota Fighting Saints announce they've signed Mike Walton to a three-year contract for $440,000.

"It's around $440,000," Eagleson says on his return to Toronto. "Actually, it's a basic $405,000 but there are incentives that could bring it to, let's see . . ." He breaks into smiles. ". . . about half a million dollars."

I ask him how he managed to bump a $340,000 base offer from Los Angeles to $405,000 at Minnesota.

"Ah, hell," he grins conspiratorially, "when it became apparent that Boston and L.A. weren't getting together I just sweetened the pot a little at Minnesota. They were glad to get Mike."

Everybody laughed when the Toronto Maple Leafs played hockey last winter. To be charitable, they were lousy. But one of their rare assets was a blond, earnest, solemn young man of 22 named Darryl Glen Sittler out of Kitchener, Ont., six feet, 190 pounds who, after two undistinguished seasons with the Leafs, scored 29 goals last year. Some people these days score that many by Christmas, but don't forget this was Toronto last year.

Just about the time that Sittler's contract was coming up for renewal last spring, Johnny Bassett, tall, slim, moustached, 34, sat in his office at Toronto television station CFTO, where he is a vice-president, and came up with this idea to buy the Ottawa Nationals of the WHA. Using a telephone, he rounded up a dozen friends who, like Bassett, have legal access to money, and, sure enough, in due course they acquired the Nationals, changed the name to the Toronto Toros and set about the business of tearing people away from the ticket wickets at Maple Leaf Gardens. The way to do it, Bassett and friends concluded, was to hit the Maple Leafs where it hurt most: sign Sittler. To salvage at least face out of last year's farce, the Maple Leafs recognized they must go to the moon, if need be, to retain him.

And so the bargaining begins. Well along in it, Eagleson and his wife, Nancy, and Sittler and his wife, Wendy, are dinner guests of Johnny and Sue Bassett in the Bassetts' big and expensive home in a big and expensive neighbourhood in the northern reaches of Toronto where three of Bassett's partners and their wives are assembled, too. It is very congenial. Everybody laughs a lot.

"Well," beams Johnny Bassett, at length, "let's get down to the nitty-gritty, Darryl. What will it take to sign you?"

"Ask the boss," says the shy young Sittler, indicating Eagleson, who has not had to rehearse his speech.

"Five years," he says. "A million dollars."

Nobody drops a drink. "OK," says Bassett.

Levity breaks out. People clink glasses, grin.

"There are a few other things," Eagleson beams.

"Like what?" chuckles Bassett.

"Like legal fees," says Eagleson.

"Yeah," says Bassett. "Legal fees."

"Plus a shopping credit at Eaton's for Darryl and Wendy at a maximum of, oh, let's say $2,000." John C. Eaton, one of the Eatons, is a Bassett partner.

"And a shopping credit for Darryl and Wendy at McDonald's hamburgers." George Cohon, president of McDonald's Restaurants of Canada, is a Bassett partner.

"Al," Bassett chortles, "I'd love to read that in the contract just to see the look on George Cohon's face."

"And a couple of watches for Darryl and Wendy at People's." Irving Gerstein, president of Peoples Credit Jewelers, is a Bassett partner.

"So we've got a deal," says Bassett.

Now the next step seems somewhat vague. Eagleson recalls that he told Bassett he'd have to get in touch with Jim Gregory, Leafs general manager. Bassett recalls that Eagleson picked up the telephone right then and cancelled an appointment with Gregory.

"As far as I'm concerned," Bassett declared several days later when the papers suddenly announced that Darryl Sittler had signed a five-year contract with the Maple Leafs for $750,000, "we had a deal. All that talk about hamburgers and watches and credit at Eaton's was a bunch of nonsense, a lot of hilarity after we'd made a deal. It's my conviction that either Eagleson euchered us or Sittler changed his mind."

Eagleson reconstructs it differently. He says he was entirely in earnest in discussing the fringe benefits. And he says he did call Gregory the next day and told him to get his people together and figure out the best possible deal the Leafs could offer. That deal, he says, was the one for $750,000 for five years.

"I told Darryl to go home and think about the two offers, to talk them over with his wife, and then to let me know," Eagleson recalls. "He told me, finally, that he and Wendy had decided the extra money from the Toros wouldn't mean that much happiness to them, that it'd be cut by taxes anyhow, and that he'd had three happy years with the Leafs and wanted to stay with them. What he told me was this: 'Last year I made $30,000 and I was happy. If I was happy at $30,000, I've got to be happier at five times that.' So what the hell, it was up to him."

Alan Eagleson thinks he will die young. It's not a thought that preys morbidly, only a notion that comes into his mind unexpectedly once or twice a year. "I'll be sitting in a hotel room or maybe setting off on a three- or four-hour plane trip," he says, "and suddenly there it is."

At such times, he writes long and affectionate letters to his parents, his wife and his friend Bobby Orr. A man who has great difficulty expressing affection verbally, he labours to set sentiment to paper. He carries a ton of insurance, keeps his involved financial affairs scrupulously in order. His income reaches $100,000 or more a year, he lives well, though not high, and, through various investments, can see himself reaching millionaire status—if he lives. He is always the loudest man at a party, cocky, animated, childlike in his vanity, often sophomoric though he is not a drinker. Old-line Conservatives deplore these antics, regard him as a clown.

He can't, or won't, discuss the source of his apprehension but apparently because of it he lives day-to-day, reaching for no rainbow, having no specific goal. He wears many hats and all of them fit; he won't look ahead to choose one of them.

For instance, several NHL governors have told him privately they'd like to see him succeed Clarence Campbell one day as NHL president, but he finds the idea too remote from his present position to consider.

Also, one of his law partners, Irwin Pasternak, says he has a brilliant legal mind, that he could become an outstanding criminal lawyer, but Eagleson doesn't think about that anymore.

Also, as executive director of the NHL players' association he wields a very big stick, but although he's talked for two years of resigning, he doesn't know when, or if, that day will come.

Also, one of his close friends, Arthur Harnett, former executive director of the Ontario PCs, says that as PC association president Eagleson is the second most powerful man in the party (second to Premier Bill Davis) and that he could easily become party leader if Davis were to move into the federal field (there's party dissent on this; a man high in the Davis office, requesting what he calls "no attribution," says the association has no real power, that Eagleson likes people to think he has Davis's ear but that he hasn't and that "he couldn't get six votes if he ran for leader"). Eagleson was elected to the provincial legislature 10 years ago at age 30, lost the seat in 1967 and didn't run in 1971. He has been the association's president since 1968 but, again declining to look ahead, he says he rarely thinks in terms of a political future.

One afternoon in his softly lit Toronto office 11 floors above the blaring Bay Street traffic he expands on the subject of his many hats. "I like the variety," he says. "I could give up everything and make $50,000 a year just looking after Bobby's business. But I like what I'm doing now. I take one day at a time, and turn off on weekends with my family—playing tennis or boating, skiing in the winter."

The phone rings—it always rings—and he's off again, grinning and manoeuvring, a man moving up, God knows where.

Alan Eagleson went on to broker the 1976 Canada Cup, the first international tournament involving professional hockey players. Four years later, Bobby Orr dumped Eagleson after the perennial all-star learned he was broke. Still, Eagleson was representing some 350 professionals in 1989 when disgruntled players began a campaign to oust him from the players' association. In 1994, U.S. authorities charged him with 32 theft-related crimes. Four years later, he pleaded guilty to criminal charges on both sides of the border, spending six months in a Toronto jail.

Now disbarred, stripped of his Order of Canada and expelled from the Hockey Hall of Fame, Eagleson lives in Collingwood, Ont., and London, England.

Gordie Howe & Sons Unlimited: Heads Up!

—March 1974—
Jack Ludwig

T HE WINNIPEG JET grinned hugely. He was obviously happy being on the same ice with a hockey "immortal," a live Hall of Famer, Gordie Howe. Not for a moment did it occur to him that Gordie wasn't just as pleased to be on the ice with *him*. Gordie wore his famous number nine, Bobby Hull's famous number, and Bobby was such a nice guy to be on the ice with, boyish, forgiving, patient, masochistic, friendly. Cheerful, full of delight, one of Hull's teammates sailed into the shipping lane between Gordie Howe and the Houston Coliseum boards. He

Gordie with sons Marty (centre) and Mark
before their first game as Houston Aeros

could almost have been tipping an imaginary hat in Gordie's direction.

Gordie's slant shoulders dipped, his stick made a swift, almost imperceptible pitchfork motion, and the Jet turned Catherine wheel, tumbling limbthrashingly in air like someone rebounding off an overly taut trampoline, sprawled finally like a bumpkin making his first contact with a funhouse chute. Gordie didn't break stride or so much as look at the spontaneously acrobatic Jet blurring through Houston Aero space. Jettisoned, the Jet awoke howls of blood in the Houston spectators' throats. Only then did the referee turn.

An NHL referee would have put one and one together immediately—Gordie Howe and a crumpled Jet wreck. The WHA ref had much to learn. Like a London bobby at the scene of an accident, he blew his whistle and a couple of still standing Jets helped their teammate off the ice. Gordie didn't cut a notch in his stick. Neatly, and carefully, he peeled a bit of tape off its blade and courteously handed it to the linesman. In the ensuing face-off no Jet came within 10 feet of old Number Nine. Some learn from experience; others go through life being helped off the ice.

No NFL fan would have been surprised by the Jet's sudden launching and equally sudden landing. He might have observed that Gordie Howe was a little greyer and only slightly heavier than in his last season as a Detroit Red Wing in 1970–1971. He would, of course, have heard about Gordie joining the Houston Aeros with his sons Marty and Mark, ex-Toronto Marlboros of the minor leagues, in the World Hockey Association's second big coup (the first being Bobby Hull's jump to these same Jets from the Chicago Black Hawks). Stories about money abounded—a million for Gordie, half a million each for Marty and Mark, all through the excellent managerial genius of Gordie's wife, Colleen, chief of the now-famous Gordie Howe

Enterprises. Papers and magazines told and retold Gordie's dream—to play on a side with his sons (Mark and Marty, if not with 13-year-old Murray). Money and a dream brought Gordie Howe back after two years of retirement.

Stories soon turned to myth. Take that Jet's unfortunate fall: sportswriters couldn't see a Jet sailing inelegantly through rink air without putting his demise down to Gordie getting even for something the Jet did to Marty or Mark. But nobody who had watched Gordie in the NHL thought of him as someone in need of a goad. Gordie would have flicked Marty or Mark off in the same fashion were either to turn up on an opposing team. The essence of Gordie Howe was and is his disinterested detachment as he goes about his hockey business. Dullards need butt-ends and jabby elbows to awake in them thoughts of revenge: Gordie Howe was, and still is, a purist. From his earliest days as a Red Wing he simply assumed that certain ice areas were his and his alone: behind both goals, say, and in all four corners, and along a four-foot lane running the length and breadth of the rink. Should some aspiring St. George blunder into dragon turf, he would find out instantly that some dragons are never losers.

The next shift Gordie took for Houston was as a penalty killer, and out on the ice was Jet Chris Bordeleau, like Bobby Hull an ex-Black Hawk, one whose rookie season coincided with Gordie Howe's waning years in the NHL. Bordeleau gave Gordie lots of room. Had there been ice on the other side of the boards, doubtless Bordeleau would have chosen to do his playing there. Other Jets—Bobby Hull excepted—treated Gordie as if he were separated from them by a deep pool. Poke checking, they fished a stick tentatively in his direction, hugging the imagined water's edge as if afraid to fall in. It was the old NHL pattern all over again. Shunned and rejected, Gordie picked up loose pucks he either passed off to those Aeros able to shoot straight, or himself let go at the net.

But here a difference was discernible. Gordie's shots don't zip anymore. Sometimes even his flip pass lacks the snap to hit a teammate's stick. Arthritis, which combined with injury made quitting the NHL a wise move, is still with him. Blind myth-makers talk about Gordie as ambidextrous and versatile when they see him poke checking with his right hand, not the hand used by those who shoot right. The explanation for Gordie not using his left hand is quite prosaic: pain, and numbness. Cruising his right-wing lane, Gordie holds his stick "lefty," not to prove himself ambidextrous or versatile, nor to showboat, but to take the pressure off his left wrist. Only when he shoots or tries a hard pass does he assume his natural "righty" position. Yet, so gifted is Gordie Howe, so loaded with moxie, craft and talent, that even with that bad wrist, and a bad shoulder, he looks like Wilt Chamerlain on a basketball court with 10-year-olds. Houston, one must say, is not quite Detroit in Gordie's great days, before NHL expansion; Houston in fact, is more or less a minor league setting for Gordie and his sons. That, I must tell you, is not Gordie Howe's opinion. He's loyal to the WHA and won't let anybody knock it.

One evening, we found an empty dressing room, and Gordie began to talk about why he had come to Houston. Around the other players he indulged in the usual forms of ritual chatter common to North American jock life. He's a fairly easygoing man—though you couldn't prove by the Jet whose fate I've described. He's natural, relaxed, and you never have the feeling, talking with Howe, that he's trying to find the words you want to hear.

But when we were away from the kibitzing and the ceremo-nial jazz, his resentment over his treatment by the Detroit organization broke out of him. Marty knows this about his father, Mark does too, that Gordie, as the greatest scorer in hockey history, who had played all his NHL life with Detroit, naturally assumed that there would be a place for him in the organization, where he could work, make some kind of contribution. The boys know that if Detroit had come through with style and consideration and humanity, Gordie would never have left the Red Wing or the Norris family organization. Houston—no matter how much Gordie wanted to play on the same team as his sons—would never have seen Gordie Howe. Nor, for that matter, Marty and Mark.

"I'd think I was going into some kind of executive training program," Gordie told me, his face angry and disappointed, "and I'd wait for someone to make good on all those promises I'd been hearing. They wouldn't get in touch with me for days. I expected to get into the insurance business—the number of things I thought were going to happen. And—nothing."

Once Detroit made him a vice-president, according to Howe, it was content to let him cool it as sheer window dressing. Slowly it got through to Gordie and Colleen that Gordie's security was not a felt concern of people in and around the Red Wing organization. Slowly they understood that if Gordie— just in his forties and a long, long way from retirement—was going to have an active and financially rewarding life, they would have to do it themselves. Gordon Howe Enterprises, that is, instead of being some form of agribusiness sideline for the Howes, become a serious venture to sustain and support the Howes, their daughter and three sons.

But Gordie Howe had lived for a quarter of a century as a hockey player. It was inconceivable, to him, and to others, that hockey didn't have a place for him somewhere. He didn't want to coach necessarily, but he did want to be closely connected with the team aspect of the game and its organizational side. He wanted to put his hockey to good use. Gordon Howe

Enterprises, then, began to consider alternatives for its biggest assets, Gordie Howe and his two OHA star sons.

The WHA was a natural. Since pulling off the Bobby Hull coup, the league had been trying hard to come up with an encore. Its well-noised capture of Derek Sanderson had ended up as an armful of flypaper. Slowly, then, the obvious came to be. Put together Gordie Howe's Detroit unhappiness with his love of hockey, his need for financial security, his desire to play with his sons, the WHA's feeling that it could sign players of junior age (ostensibly because the Howe boys were Americans), the WHA's need for a dramatic move, solid financial backing in Houston and elsewhere for getting all three Howes at once and there it was—the hockey story of 1973. Not quite on the level of the combined Bobby Hull jump and the Team Canada–USSR series (without Bobby Hull) in 1972, but a big story nevertheless.

But even Houston knew who Gordie Howe was and what a big thing the city had accomplished to get Gordie and his sons playing for the Aeros. On Nov. 28, 1973, with Bobby Hull in town, magazines, newspapers, radio and television, most of which ignored the WHA the rest of the time, swarmed into Houston to see Gordie and Bobby meet head-on. *Sports Illustrated* sent its top hockey writer and one of its best photographers. I went to the Jet dressing room to say hello to Hull, the big man in my hometown of Winnipeg. Bobby recently has been complaining about how difficult it is to keep things going with the Jets. But he himself looked absolutely shining. His head wasn't quite bushy, yet he had clearly had a successful hair transplant job. Thirty-four, he looked in his middle twenties when he grinned—something he was able to do before a Jets game, if not during or after.

Bobby was genuinely glad to see Gordie come out to pose for photographers with him. They shook hands straight, then did a freedom clasp, faked banging into each other and when a photographer insisted on getting down on his back to shoot up at the two of them, they both, quite spontaneously, speared the guy gently in the gut.

During the game, Bobby several times broke into the clear, fast as ever, waiting for a teammate to headman him at the Houston blue line. The puck never came. Four times Bobby beat the man covering him, slipped the puck to a teammate, dodged his check, wide open, waiting. But the Jet he had passed to kept the wanted puck in front of him, dribbling it back and forth as if he were a buyer contemplating a puck purchase. Time after time Bobby did something great, only to have his contribution swallowed up by avid ineptitude all around him. Nobody—not a Hull or a Howe or an Orr—can do it all by himself. Some help, some snap, some rhythm is needed from the other men on the ice. Bobby Hull had taken the tragic leap—out of the NHL and into a hockeyless pit. All game long I kept feeling sorry for him.

But not for Gordie Howe. And not for Mark and Marty, either. Gordie never was a wind-up and roar-the-length-of-the-ice player like Bobby Hull. Gordie didn't go in for Bobby's spectacular slapshooting. His way was not to outskate but to outfox. And dent. Dent recognized the existence of an opponent. A dented opponent was a tutored opponent—nobody likes to be dented day in and day out. Gordie Howe was not only not a rushing madcap Bobby Hull, he wasn't a crease parker like Phil Esposito, either.

Gordie got the puck in roughly two ways: either he pursued it and its hesitant possessor into the corners, or he whacked it free, spun his check, nudged him away, gave him a helping elbow, a hip, a thumb, assorted ends of stick. In the NHL, Gordie's message was instantly retrievable: steer clear. Once the puck came Gordie's way he had lots of plans for it. In 25 years,

Gordie's polished method produced 853 career goals—without one splashy Bobby Hull 50-goal season (in 1952–1953 Gordie did get 49). Gordie at 45 was doing much better in the WHA than Bobby Hull at 34. At midseason, Gordie stood sixth among the WHA scorers. Not Bobby Hull, not Mark, not Marty could be found in the top 10.

In the game with the Jets, Gordie got two assists, the second his feed for a tip-in to tie the game with only seconds left to play and the Houston goalie out of his net. When Gordie shot from the point, no Jet was there to check him; it was all familiar. Though Gordie hadn't made a commitment beyond 1973–1974, one would not be surprised to find him playing in 1974–1975—or even beyond that. Houston, early in 1974, with its three Howes, occupied first place in the division.

The key word (apart from money and security) for Gordie in Houston is fun. Gordie likes to be out on the ice. He likes being out there with Mark and Marty. He enjoys being in the dressing room with them and the rest of the guys before and after the game. He is a cheerful dressing room kibitzer, and all the young Houston players, awed by this superstar of superstars, are amazed at Gordie's style and Gordie's teasing.

After the game, Gordie nudged me.

"Look at Marty," he whispered. "They got him yesterday. Shaved him good."

He broke up looking at Marty, the only player in the dressing room wearing shorts. As a veteran jock, Gordie not only enjoyed but approved the rituals of initiation the Houstons practised. If the guys couldn't play hockey too well, they could play pro.

"They didn't do too rough a job," Gordie said, grinning widely, "but Marty doesn't feel too cool. The guys found out what brand of shaving cream burns the worst."

He looks around.

"Hey, Mark," he yelled to his younger son coming out of the shower, "don't worry about it. There'll be lots more."

Mark had had two easy chances to win the game, but blew them both.

"Look at Mark," Gordie said, "he's real mad at himself. Give him a few more years though."

He stood up on the locker bench.

"Hey, Marty, I never knew you to get your shorts on so fast. You got a date or something?"

Marty grinned good-naturedly. Mark looked sullen. Both boys resemble Gordie. Marty has his upper face. Mark his lower. Marty, though slighter, is built like his father and may fill out to be exactly like him one day. Mark is shorter, squat, thick, but a fast and elegant skater.

"That Mark," Gordie whispered, turning his back so his sons couldn't hear, "we're drawing up contracts and he goes off for a second with the Houston lawyer. What does the guy come up with? A bonus clause saying that if he gets shaved they got to pay him an extra $10,000. He won't sign unless they put it in. So they do! I keep telling him—"slip some guy a couple hundred bucks to do the job, and collect."

Later that night, I saw the Howes' great new house and the huge unfinished swimming pool and patio. Gordie and Colleen and the boys, Colleen's old aunt and uncle from Colorado sat around in the dining room going over the game. The walls were covered with paintings of Gordie, drawings, caricatures. He was having his second time around. Detroit had wasted the talents of an unusually gifted man. Houston didn't seem to be making that mistake.

And yet, as I watched Gordie heave himself aching into his car—refusing to let me call a cab to go back to the hotel—I thought that not hockey alone but all sports fail to do well by the people who make sports thrive. I thought of Willie Mays, crying, speaking into a microphone in Shea Stadium a tortured farewell, a superstar like Gordie Howe, who, injured and hurting like Gordie, couldn't see the strike zone clearly anymore, or get his arm up to throw a ball back to the infield. Immortals with ailing wrists, DiMaggio's bone spurs, Bobby Orr's bad knees, Jacques Plante's fear of flying. Given the fate of most sport stars trying to disengage gingerly, Gordie Howe is a happy ending story. He found something better than beating the kids. He joined them.

Houston may not be much as a hockey team, or the city as a hockey town. But seeing the Howes thrive in Texas made me think that they don't order these matters as well in Toronto, Montreal, New York and, especially, Detroit.

The Howes moved together to the New England (Hartford) Whalers in 1977, and Gordie continued to play until 1980, getting 41 points at age 52. Mark, WHA rookie of the year in 1974, assisted on his father's final goal and played until 1995. He now lives in Philadelphia and works as a Detroit Red Wings scout. Marty retired a decade earlier and is an assistant coach with the Chicago Wolves of the International Hockey League (IHL). Murray, a doctor, never did play pro hockey and now practises radiology in Toledo, Ohio.

For his part, Gordie still holds several NHL records, including most seasons played (26), most games (1,767; including playoffs, 1,924), most 20-or-more goal seasons (22), and most career goals, assists and points by a right-winger. He and Colleen live outside Detroit.

The Gretzky Chase: Mario Lemieux
Is Challenging "The Great One"

—February 20, 1989—
Bruce Wallace

I N THE ROWDY RECENT HISTORY of the National Hockey
League, no player has matched the performance of Wayne
Gretzky. For eight consecutive seasons beginning in 1979, The
Great One dominated professional hockey as few athletes have
ever mastered their sport. His potent scoring ability established
records that may never be beaten. Gretzky's talent and tireless
off-the-ice promotion of his sport made him hockey's foremost
ambassador and its single most identifiable personality.
   Until Mario Lemieux.

Lemieux facing off with Gretzky at the 1986 All-Star Game

With a grace that is surprising for his towering six-foot, four-inch, 210-lb. frame and a flair for scoring spectacular goals, the Pittsburgh Penguins centre is suddenly challenging Gretzky's supremacy as hockey's most talented player and most prolific scorer. With more than 20 games left in the current season, the Penguins star was already 25 points ahead of The Great One in the points race last week. At the same time, Lemieux—along with Gretzky—is assuming a leadership role that is helping to win new fans and transform the image of North American hockey from a violent sideshow to a sport of athletic artistry and skill. A gifted playmaker like Gretzky, the 23-year-old Lemieux seems almost certain this year to lead the once-moribund Penguins into the Stanley Cup playoffs for the first time since 1982. "My goal," Lemieux told *Maclean's*, "is to win three or four Stanley Cups."

Still, the 28-year-old Gretzky clearly remains near the pinnacle of his game and shows no willingness to easily surrender the mantle of greatness. With the torch not yet passed from Gretzky to his younger rival, Canadian hockey may now be in the midst of a new Golden Age. Past hockey eras have boasted their own stars. During the 1960s and 1970s, the sport was dominated at various times by the Chicago Blackhawks Bobby Hull, Bobby Orr of the Boston Bruins and Montreal's Guy Lafleur who, at the age of 37, is currently making an impressive comeback with the New York Rangers. But not since the 1950s, when hockey fans hotly debated whether the Montreal Canadiens Maurice (Rocket) Richard or Gordie Howe of the Detroit Red Wings was the world's greatest player, has the sport had two such supremely talented players in the league at the same time.

The increasing lustre of North American hockey has led to larger salaries for its stars. Gretzky will earn an estimated $23.6 million over the life of his eight-year contract with the Kings.

Lemieux, who first signed with Pittsburgh for about $800,000 over a three-year contract, now earns $1.9 million annually, making him the second-highest-paid NHL player, after Gretzky.

As a hockey star who is not given to flamboyant gestures off the ice, the soft-spoken Lemieux's stardom is a product of his remarkable scoring ability. During the 1987–1988 season, Lemieux scored 70 goals and 98 assists for a total of 168 points. As a result, he seized the league's Hart Trophy as its most valuable player away from Gretzky, who had claimed it for the previous eight years. By last week, with the Penguins in first place in the Patrick Division, Lemieux's point total put him on a course to beat Gretzky's single-season record of 215 points, set during the 1985–1986 season. As well, Lemieux's 50th goal of the season in his team's 46th game made him the only player other than Gretzky—who has done it three times—ever to score 50 goals in fewer than 50 games.

Lemieux's goals are often accomplished with sensational style. He is capable of powerful, accurate shots. Like Gretzky, he has a knack for anticipating plays and making passes to teammates through a maze of sticks and skates. But unlike the 170-lb. Gretzky, Lemieux can use his size and strength to shrug off would-be checkers. Says Montreal Canadiens defenceman Larry Robinson: "When he has the puck, he can shield it with his big body so that no one else can get near it."

Lemieux's talents have made him the toast of Pittsburgh, where he was honoured earlier this month as the city's man of the year. His impact on the city is perhaps best reflected in attendance figures at Pittsburgh's 16,033-seat Civic Arena. In the 1983–1984 season—the year before Lemieux joined the club—the lacklustre Penguins averaged a paltry 6,800 fans and at one stage owner Edward J. DeBartolo considered selling the franchise to a group of investors who planned to move the team to Hamilton. But with Lemieux in the lineup the following year, attendance jumped to an average of 10,000 a game, and this year the average is more than 15,500. "Pittsburgh used to be a football town," said former Steelers linebacker Jack Ham, "but Mario has made it in vogue to be at the hockey games."

Despite his growing status as a celebrity, Lemieux is only beginning to shed his habitual shyness. During his first two seasons as a Penguin, his reserve led some Pittsburgh sports-writers to affectionately nickname him "The Big Goof" for his terse, unexciting responses to questions. Now, with a newly acquired fluency in English, Lemieux is becoming more confi-dent in his assertions about what hockey should be—although, with characteristic modesty, he still acknowledges the greatness of his principal rival. "What Gretzky has to say about hockey is important and should be listened to," Lemieux told *Maclean's*. Adding that on-ice brawling is a destructive feature of the NHL, Lemieux said, "I think that if Gretzky and myself and a few of the other great players in the league get together and demand changes to parts of the game, we could be successful." Lemieux and Gretzky are already changing the style of play. Declared the Canadiens' Robinson: "Wayne and Mario have helped turn the NHL into a scorers' league. The game is faster and it rewards players, like Mario, who have great hockey intu-ition and who can do inventive things with the puck."

Lemieux's stature on the ice has been matched by growing affluence in the star's personal life. He now lives permanently in Pittsburgh, and he is building a house on a double lot in the nearby suburb of Mount Lebanon. Lemieux lives with 22-year-old Nathalie Asselin, a Montreal native who has been his girlfriend for seven years.

Because of his growing celebrity status, he is evidently conscious of the need to serve as a role model for younger fans.

Like Gretzky, he drinks sparingly and quit smoking more than a year ago.

Mario Lemieux has been a closely watched hockey player ever since he emerged as a record-shattering junior star with the Laval Voisins on the northern outskirts of Montreal. The son of retired construction worker Jean-Guy Lemieux and his wife, Pierrette, Lemieux was the youngest of three sons. Growing up in the working-class Montreal district of Ville Emard, Lemieux began playing hockey when he was 3. In his third year with the Laval team, he scored 133 goals in 70 games, making him an eagerly sought player when he became eligible for the NHL draft at 18. Like countless Montreal youngsters before him, Lemieux dreamed of playing for his home-town team. "I think every kid who grows up in Montreal wants to play for the Canadiens, and I was no different," he recalled. "Lafleur was the best player in the world when I was growing up and he was certainly my idol."

But it was the Penguins who finished with the NHL's worst record during the 1983–1984 season and won the privilege of drafting Lemieux. At first, he was wary of playing in Pittsburgh. Although the Penguins' management arranged for him to live with a Pittsburgh family for his first season to help him adapt to the city and improve his English, Lemieux said that he missed his friends and parents. Back in his Montreal childhood home, which is filled with photographs, trophies and plaques honouring Lemieux's hockey accomplishments, Lemieux's parents avidly watched television broadcasts of Penguins games received from a satellite dish that their son had installed on the roof of their house.

Although his 100-point total helped Lemieux win rookie of the year honours during his first NHL season, he also drew scathing criticism from some hockey commentators for what they said was lackadaisical play. "He was a floater," said television analyst and former NHL coach Don Cherry. "He played hard only when the mood hit him." The criticism grew when Lemieux at first refused to join Team Canada for the 1985 world championship tournament in Prague. In the end, Lemieux played with the team, scoring four goals and six assists. Said Warren Young, a friend and former teammate: "He had just lived through an overwhelming year in a strange country where he had not yet mastered English and he was anxious to get home to see his family."

In fact, it was Lemieux's spectacular playing in the 1987 Canada Cup series against the Soviet Union that finally persuaded most critics of Lemieux's star quality. Although team officials expressed concern about his poor physical condition and uninspired play during training sessions, Lemieux excelled in the series, scoring 11 goals in nine games. The most dramatic goal came on a pass from Gretzky in the closing minutes of the final game to beat the Soviets 6–5.

Cherry and other hockey experts point to the series as the turning point in Lemieux's career. "Gretzky showed him that to be the best you can never stop working," declared Cherry. Lemieux said that the series was a watershed in his career. "The Canada Cup came at a time when I was ready for a challenge," he said.

Suddenly more confident on the ice, and comfortable in Pittsburgh, Lemieux roared into the 1987–1988 NHL season. With his 168-point total for the season, he became only the third player in history—the others are Gretzky in seven different years and Boston's Phil Esposito in 1970–1971—to amass more than 150 points in a single season. "There has never been a player of his size, with his raw talent," said Penguins defenceman Paul Coffey, who as an Edmonton Oiler played with Gretzky for seven years. "Wayne is always looking to pass to set up a goal. But Mario is capable of going through three or four players to score himself if he wants."

At the same time, Lemieux's physical strength has contributed to some spectacular goals. In Quebec City last March 27, he skated in on a breakaway and scored, even though the Nordiques' Marc Fortier had jumped onto his back. Said Dave Molinari, a sportswriter for the *Pittsburgh Press:* "What would be great plays for mere mortals are just another play for Mario." Added Pittsburgh forward Rob Brown: "Sometimes, even on the ice, I get caught up watching in awe what Mario can do with the puck."

If the Canada Cup encouraged Lemieux to aim for even greater accomplishments as a player, it also marked a change in his off-ice image. He made a conscious effort to avoid the petulance that sometimes characterized his early career and, instead, tried to emulate Gretzky's model behaviour. Said Thomas Reich, Lemieux's Pittsburgh-based agent: "People expected instant sainthood, but Mario is maturing all the time. He can be as good for hockey's image as Gretzky." The improved image has helped Lemieux expand his portfolio of endorsements. He now endorses Koho hockey equipment, a line of casual sportswear and Toronto-based Effem Foods Ltd.'s Snickers chocolate bars. Earlier this month, Lemieux—wearing jeans and running shoes under hockey equipment—sat in a simulated dressing room in Pittsburgh to film English-speaking parts for a Snickers commercial. Lemieux dutifully took bites from a chocolate bar and spoke his lines before spitting the chocolate out, off-camera.

Now Lemieux's celebrity status—and the local hockey mania sparked by the Penguins' improved play—is making it hard for him to travel around Pittsburgh without being stopped by fans. When Lemieux drops into The Metropol, a fashionable Pittsburgh dance club, he is more likely to slip into a private upstairs lounge than mingle in the crush below. Away from the rink, Lemieux leads a quiet life. He said that he and Asselin plan to get married—eventually. But, he added, "for now, my career comes first."

Besides his remarkable skill as a hockey player, Lemieux is a talented golfer who shoots in the mid-70s. He has even told friends that he might consider trying to join the professional golf tour once his hockey career is over.

For the immediate future, Lemieux's greatest challenge is to help the Penguins to reach the NHL playoffs, a feat that has eluded him through four seasons. Many hockey observers cite the Penguins' failure to even make the playoffs as evidence that Gretzky is a far superior player to Lemieux; in his nine years as an Oiler, Gretzky led his team to four Stanley Cups. But Coffey, who played on three of those teams, remembered that Gretzky, too, was denied recognition as the best in the game until the Oilers finally won a Stanley Cup. Said Coffey: "For years, Wayne had to listen to people claim that he was only an offensive player and that he could not win the big games. That all stopped when we won the Cup. And Mario will hear the same criticism until we win one for Pittsburgh."

Still, Maurice Richard, who is now a public relations official for Molson's Brewery Quebec Ltd. and the Montreal Canadiens, for one, questions whether Lemieux has the intensity to dominate hockey. "Lemieux is a better natural player than I was," said Richard. "But does he have the fire in his eyes the way I did? No." When he was told of Richard's comments, Lemieux responded with an easy smile. "I may be more of a finesse player than Richard was, but that does not mean I lack determination," he said. "If I want to be remembered as one of the best to play the game, I have to be a winner, and that certainly is missing from my game now." To the already converted fans in Pittsburgh, Lemieux's supremacy is unquestioned. With Gretzky's talents still abundantly in evidence while Lemieux comes swiftly up behind him, the hockey world may eventually have to consider which is the greatest player of his era.

Mario Lemieux went on to win his second straight scoring title in 1989, with 85 goals and 199 points. He became only the second player (the other is Wayne Gretzky) to score 70 goals in two seasons. Lemieux won four more scoring championships and led his Penguins to another Stanley Cup in 1992. The following year he was diagnosed with Hodgkin's disease. He returned to the ice that season, scoring a goal and an assist in his first game—which was also his final day of radiation treatment. Lemieux has been plagued by other health problems—a bad back kept him out nearly two seasons—but he returned and won scoring championships in 1996 and 1997. He retired after the 1997 season but made a comeback in 2000, when the team was in a precarious financial state. He married Nathalie Asselin in 1993, and they have four children.

Bruce Wallace, now a European correspondent for Southam News based in London, worked for Maclean's from 1985 to 2000.

The Great One

—April 26, 1999—
James Deacon

Hollywood will no doubt make a movie about Wayne
Gretzky some day, and it will have to include the scene
where he plays his last game in Canada, in Ottawa against the
Senators. It happened like this last week: Gretzky and his New
York Rangers, who had already been eliminated from playoff
contention, were playing the home team to a draw, thus
denying the Senators a chance to boost their own playoff posi-
tion. Yet with 4:45 left in the third period, during one of
Gretzky's shifts, the crowd began to chant "One more year!
One more year!" Then, minutes later during a stoppage in play,

Waving goodbye in Ottawa: Gretzky's final NHL
appearance in Canada, April 15, 1999

the big-screen scoreboard above centre ice replayed highlights from Gretzky's career, and the PA system played Carly Simon's *Nobody Does It Better*. The crowd rose in tribute, and players on both benches stood, too, banging their sticks against the boards and on the ice in the quintessential hockey salute.

When the game finally ended in a 2–2 tie, the Senators lined up, one by one, to shake Gretzky's hand. As for the Corel Centre fans, they stood by their seats long after they would normally have scattered for the parking lots, cheering, whistling, clapping. This from the opposing team's supporters. Most had come to the game wondering if the rumours were true, that The Great One was actually leaving the game he had so profoundly changed. Now, it seemed, they knew, and they were not going to miss their chance to say goodbye. Prodded by his teammates and by the unwavering applause, Gretzky emerged from the dressing room for a curtain call. It was too brief for the crowd, which didn't stop until, a few minutes later, he returned again, without equipment but with his soaked jersey draped over his narrow frame. He stepped out to the bench and waved up into the seats in all directions, but he was too overwrought to bask in the adoration, so he quickly disappeared down the tunnel to the dressing room.

Such is the esteem in which Gretzky is held. For weeks, he had wrestled with whether to finally call it quits, and he had waged the battle mainly by himself. Normally, he would have consulted his father, Walter. But he didn't want even a hint of his plans to leak, and, as one family associate said: "Wally's incapable of telling a lie, so it would have gotten out." Why the secrecy? Modest by superstar standards, Gretzky feared the farewell fuss that would inevitably have occurred at every arena in the league. Nor did he want to distract his teammates when they faced more pressing issues. "I thought about this for a long time," he explained later, "but I kept it extremely quiet because we were in a playoff hunt and I did not want it to disrupt the team."

A team player to the end, Gretzky holds every meaningful NHL goal-scoring record, yet his greatest hockey talent was his knack for setting up other players to score. And in a lengthy list of career accomplishments, one of the more remarkable is that the man who played on a level no one has ever achieved, and who was a leader even when someone else had been designated captain, somehow managed to be "just one of the guys" in the dressing room. So out of respect for the Rangers, Gretzky did not make his retirement official last week until he returned to New York City, when he could be among his teammates in his last hockey home. It was also no surprise that he deflected the lavish praise, crediting everyone from teammates to locker-room attendants for so much of his success. And he had an easy explanation for his unfailingly gracious demeanour during 21 years as a pro: if he had become a role model off the ice as well as on, it was because he was Phyllis and Walter's boy, then and always.

This should be a happy week in the NHL. Sixteen teams, including Ottawa, the Toronto Maple Leafs and Gretzky's former team, the Edmonton Oilers, are beginning the playoffs that lead to the Stanley Cup finals. But his retirement left the hockey world feeling more funereal than joyful. What, after all, was the NHL without The Great One? For two decades, he was the shining constant in a hurly-burly sport that too often bashed itself on the head. He helped lead the transition away from the thuggery of the mid-1970s, when the Philadelphia Flyers ruled by the fist, to a more skilled game that embraces players from around the world. That internationalization is in part why Gretzky insists the sport is thriving and can absorb the loss of its most compelling character. "I've always said no player is bigger than the game," he said, adding: "The game is in great shape."

Maybe so, but try telling that to fans around the NHL, who even in Gretzky's less productive seasons have cherished every sighting. Tell it to the rink rats who secured 99's signature because he was one of sport's all-time great autograph-signers. Tell it to the three new NHL franchises that will begin play over the next three years without their fans being able to see the great Gretzky, except in civvies. Tell it to the NHL marketing department, for whom he is still the only player with transcendent appeal in the United States. Tell it to ABC, the U.S. TV network that just bought the league's broadcast rights for five years and $800 million (U.S.), starting next season. Tell it to the woeful Rangers, embarked on a much-needed rebuilding program but suddenly without their leader.

Then explain it to his family. Gretzky was never just Wayne—Janet, the kids, his dad and his dad's Brantford buddies were all fixtures at every big event, just as they were at Madison Square Garden for the last hurrah on Sunday. "There is going to be a lot of emptiness," Walter told *Maclean's*. "My friends always watch the games with me at our home and, gee whiz, we won't have that anymore. Emptiness." Janet was similarly wistful. She hoped her husband would have a chance to go like Michael Jordan had—with a freshly minted championship. "I didn't want him to leave on a down note," she says, "but he reassured me a thousand times that he was happy with his decision, that this was the right time." Still, she will feel the loss, too. "I'm happy for him, but I'd be lying if I said I won't miss it," she said. "I love to watch him play."

And tell it to the man himself. A significant part of Gretzky's appeal was the childlike joy he took in the game. He loved the company of fellow players, the goofing around in practice and, above all, the competition. The decision to give up hockey had been a long, agonizing process. Hockey had been his life for 35 of his 38 years, and even while he stood in the Madison Square

Garden theatre insisting his last days as a player ought to be fun, he said so with a voice that quavered, with eyes that were red and glistening, and with body language that suggested hockey's loss was no match for the sadness Gretzky would feel when he unlaced his skates one final time. "I am going to miss every single part of the game," he said. "But life goes on."

Gretzky was 10 years old when he got his first tip on how to handle public life. As usual, it came from his dad. "You've got to behave right," Walter told his son back then. "They're going to be watching for every mistake. Remember that. You're a very special person and you're on display."

Why saddle so young a boy with so great a responsibility? The younger Gretzky was a prodigy, hockey's Mozart, whose first symphonies were composed with goals, assists and victories, and whose exploits were being chronicled in national publications. In 1971, Gretzky led his Brantford peewee team to 68 straight victories on the back of his whopping 378 goals (the league's next-best scorer had 40). Despite adding 120 assists that year, Gretzky sparked resentment not only among vanquished opponents but also among some parents of his teammates, who accused the phenom of denying their children a chance to shine. Former Detroit Red Wing goalie Greg Stefan, who played on that peewee team, denies that Gretzky put personal glory ahead of team goals. "Wayne was so competitive," recalls Stefan. "Some of the parents would call him a puck hog, but he would do what it took to win."

Gretzky outgrew hometown hockey and left at 14 to play in Toronto. At 16 he joined the major-junior Greyhounds of Sault Ste. Marie in the Ontario Hockey League, and at 17—a year before his NHL eligibility—he signed with the World Hockey Association's Indianapolis Racers, owned by Vancouver businessman Nelson Skalbania. After eight games, he was traded to the then-WHA Edmonton Oilers. Some veterans were suspicious of the newcomer with the big reputation. "He was just a kid with acne, a scrawny little guy," recalls Al Hamilton, the Oilers captain then. "We wondered what was all the ranting and raving about. We soon realized he had a unique talent, and each time you saw him play you saw something new." His teammates also saw passes coming—like they had never seen them before. "He had an uncanny knack," says Hamilton, "of knowing where the puck was going to go to, and of finding guys—the puck would end up on your stick."

Gretzky's NHL career began the following fall, after the WHA folded and the NHL absorbed the Oilers and three other teams. As a 19-year-old rookie, he tied longtime star Marcel Dionne as the league's top scorer with 51 goals and 86 assists, totals that were mere appetizers. In Edmonton, aided by other talented young players—among them centre Mark Messier, defencemen Paul Coffey and Kevin Lowe, goalie Grant Fuhr and winger Jari Kurri—Gretzky reached unheard-of heights. He scored 92 goals in 1981–1982. Four times he finished with more than 200 points for a season. "He didn't just break records—he blew them out of the water," marvels Dallas Stars winger Brett Hull. "These were records that people had thought were untouchable, and he made a mockery of them."

The team trophies came, too. The Oilers won the Stanley Cup in 1984, 1985, 1987 and 1988, and Gretzky led Canada to two Canada Cup triumphs in the 1980s. He recalls Game 2 of the riveting, three-game series against the Soviets in 1987 as perhaps his greatest-ever game, and he capped Canada's Game 3 triumph by setting up Mario Lemieux's series-winning goal in the dying moments. A magician on the ice, he was no choirboy off it—but he was discreet. "He had his party times," says longtime Oiler broadcaster Ken Brown. "There are legendary stories here in Edmonton, but he knew when to do it and how to do it."

Gretzky was firmly in control of the hockey universe in those last years in Edmonton, and his splashy Edmonton wedding to American actress Janet Jones was the stuff of royalty. What Gretzky didn't know was that the Oilers' owner, Peter Pocklington, was struggling in his other businesses and was getting ready to cash in his most valuable asset. On Aug. 9, 1988, only 25 days after the Gretzky–Jones wedding, Pocklington abruptly shipped his star to the Los Angeles Kings for $15 million (U.S.) in cash.

There were other players involved in the deal to make it look like a trade, but Gretzky wasn't fooled and still refers to being "sold" rather than traded. He felt betrayed and so did Edmontonians, who raged at Pocklington for dispatching their pride and joy—the man who put Edmonton on the international map—down to the States. The deal made Gretzky wary of the business of hockey, and he needed to be. While The Great One made hockey a hit in Hollywood, Kings owner Bruce McNall ran out of money and was later convicted of fraud and sent to jail for four years. Subsequent Kings owners had money problems, too, and Gretzky grew tired of the corporate instability that undercut the quality of the team. In 1996, he asked for a trade and was dealt to St. Louis, where he was briefly teamed with Hull, the Blues' great sniper. When St. Louis opted not to re-sign him that off-season, Gretzky joined the Rangers for what would be his last three seasons.

With age and without much of a supporting cast, Gretzky experienced lean times in New York. Worse, Team Canada failed to win the 1996 World Cup on home ice or the 1998 Olympic title in Nagano, Japan. He was crushed by both defeats, and his apparent misery reflected the feelings of his country. But part of what made Gretzky such a compelling leader was his great perspective. No one took the Nagano loss harder than he did, but he was not about to let it ruin his

Olympic experience. Following the final game, Gretzky returned to the athletes' village and found his teammates, morose and quiet, sprawled in the lounge. Speed skater Catriona LeMay Doan came in about the same time and recalls watching Gretzky adroitly turn the mood around. "Come on, guys," he barked. "It's not so bad that we can't go have a beer." So they all did.

In all the excitement, right there in front of hundreds of TV cameras, reporters and hockey players, Trevor Gretzky, age 6, folded his arms and rested his head on the table in front of him. Understandable, really. The kid was up past midnight the night before, jetting with his mom, his 10-year-old sister Paulina and his brother Ty, 9, up to Ottawa to see his father's final NHL game in Canada before flying straight back to New York. Then he and the family have to sit on a Madison Square Garden stage in front of all these media people so his dad can explain why he decided to retire. The upshot was that dad, who used to go to the rink every day, was going to spend more time at home, with mom and the kids. Trevor contained his excitement well. In fact, he fell asleep, which didn't escape dad's attention. "This guy," said Wayne Gretzky, pointing to his son in the closing moments of his news conference, "he looks really interested, eh?"

How appropriate. While previous speakers hailed Gretzky as the game's greatest player ever and the most important athlete in the history of sports, little Trevor did what Gretzky's family has always done in his otherworldly hockey career—bring him back to Earth. His father, in fact, was the first to denounce the theory that Gretzky could not be replaced. "When Gordie Howe retired, everyone said, 'What is going to happen when

Gordie is gone?'" Walter said last week. "Someone took Gordie's place, and when Wayne goes, there will be others that will step in. It's such a great game."

Others need to be convinced. "It's a big blow to the game," says Dick Irvin, the respected Hockey Night in Canada broad caster. "These people at NHL headquarters are sitting there thinking, 'We're in trouble—who is going to take his place?' There isn't anyone."

Irvin has a point. Gretzky's value to the NHL is far more complex than Howe's was, largely because professional sports are vastly different businesses now than they were even 15 years ago. Gretzky became a marketing vehicle—for sponsors' products, for league visibility and expansion, and for TV ratings. The NHL that he joined in 1979 was poorly managed, had no U.S. network TV contract and had few prospects for growth. Since then, the league has expanded from 21 to 27 teams, and league officials attribute much of that to Gretzky's impact—to the success of the Los Angeles Kings and the subsequent profile it gave the game. Entertainment giants like Disney and Blockbuster suddenly wanted to play, so teams in Anaheim, Calif., and Miami, respectively, were born. Thanks in no small part to Gretzky, the NHL, under new management, could bill itself "The coolest game on earth" without blushing. Speaking of Gretzky's retirement, NHL commissioner Gary Bettman said: "We always knew that we would have to deal with this day. We just hoped it wouldn't be this soon."

Gretzky's remarkable clout has helped sponsors, too. Directed by his longtime agent, Michael Barnett, he saw his off-ice income begin to rival the $8.5 million (U.S.) a year he was getting in Los Angeles. He has helped sell pizzas, camcorders, clothing and, of course, hockey equipment. His first-ever endorsement, in fact, was with Titan hockey sticks, initially for $5,000 a year and all the lumber he could splinter.

When he first started using the sticks, the then-Finnish company was No. 15 in the North American market. When Gretzky took up another brand in 1989, Titan was No. 1 in the world and had built a massive manufacturing plant in Cowansville, Que. "Wayne was responsible for us building that factory in Canada," said Bob Leeder, sales director for Titan. "He made Titan hockey sticks."

What will Gretzky do now? If he knows, he's not saying. "First and foremost, I want to give the time to my family that I haven't been able to give before," he says. No one doubts he will. "You can't underestimate how important his family is to him," says teammate Adam Graves. "He always had his kids at the practice rink, or wherever he was going." But experts who consult with athletes say the first year after retirement is difficult. The sport provided the rhythm in Gretzky's life, his days structured by practices, meals and games, his years reduced to two seasons—hockey and summer. He thrived in that environment, and now he must live by a different beat. "I'm not too concerned about that," he says. "I have a tremendous family, and they will keep me busy."

He is not hurting for cash. A conservative investor, he has socked away millions over his career, enough to consider an ownership position with a team, if he wanted. "I made more money than I ever imagined," he says. Gretzky will someday be open to business proposals that might lead to a second career or a new position in hockey, but not now. "It'll probably be a good year before I decide on anything," he says.

In the end, it was the effort it would take to be Wayne Gretzky that prompted him to retire. Despite an off season, Gretzky remains one of the league's elite players and could certainly play effectively for another couple of seasons. But he is similar to the late, great Joe DiMaggio, who once said that he had to play his best baseball every day because someone might be seeing him for the first time. Over the past few months, Gretzky began to doubt that he could perform at an acceptable level for another 82-game season. And rather than slip below his own remarkable standards, he decided to go.

But he will not disappear. He has already committed to being involved in a summit on the state of Canadian hockey next August, and he will certainly gain immediate induction into the Hockey Hall of Fame. Perhaps those occasions will allow more Canadians a chance to add their voices to the ovation he received in Ottawa, which for now will have to serve as Canada's goodbye. It hardly seems sufficient. In the United States he is a big star, but in Canada he has meant so much more. He was the greatest player in the game Canadians care about most, but he was also Wayne Gretzky from Brantford, a regular guy who happened to earn riches and fame without forsaking family or roots. He was the best playmaker hockey has ever known, but he rarely displayed arrogance or conceit. And going into last Sunday's final game, when he saw the effect of his announcement on his teammates' morale, he did his best to cheer them up. "He wants us to be happy for him," defenceman Brian Leetch said gloomily. "But it's hard for us not to feel sad." Same goes for Canadians.

Wayne Gretzky, a part-owner of the NHL Phoenix Coyotes, was executive director of the Canadian gold-medal-winning hockey team at the 2002 Salt Lake City Olympics.

James Deacon, who has written on sports since joining Maclean's in 1990, is an assistant managing editor at the magazine.

Stand-Up Guy: Brendan Shanahan

—January 14, 2002—
James Deacon

O NLY A MOVIE NUT with a slightly twisted sense of humour—Brendan Shanahan is guilty on both counts—could survive being the star of his own version of *Groundhog Day*. As in the film starring Bill Murray, Shanahan's professional life has a recurring-dream-like quality, but unlike the movie, the recurring part is anything but a comedy. Shanahan's torment, captured on video at the 1998 Winter Games in Nagano, Japan, goes like this: He is playing for Canada against Czech Republic for a berth in the gold-medal men's hockey final. The teams have played to a 1–1 tie through regulation and overtime, and as happens only at the Olympics, the tie has to be broken in a shootout—five penalty shots each. The Czechs score on their first try, then each team fails until Canada has just one final shooter—Shanahan. If he scores, Canada stays alive. He picks up the puck at centre and powers across the blue line towards goaltender Dominik Hasek. Waiting until the last second, he dekes to his right, but the uncanny Hasek stays with him. Shanahan shoots, Hasek saves. The Czechs win, Canada mourns.

How many times has that replay been shown on Canadian TV? Whatever, it's a lot. During a time of intense national insecurity about hockey, that replay has been used to illustrate Canada's lost pre-eminence whenever experts convene to discuss what's wrong with our player-development system. And it was aired even more frequently while the Canadian Hockey Association and Wayne Gretzky were busy choosing the 2002 Olympic team. Only in Canada could the selection of 23 players become the subject of year-long debate and breathless anticipation.

As a result, there are fans and even some reporters who still bombard Shanahan with questions that are phrased in ways that assume, even now, that (a) his life must have been irreparably damaged by his Olympic experience, (b) his Olympic experience irreparably damaged their lives, or (c) all of the above. The inquisitors see his entire career through the prism of that one play: when he suffered through a so-so 1998–1999 season with the Detroit Red Wings, they wondered if he was "still" depressed by what happened in Nagano; when he got off to a blistering start in the current National Hockey League season, they concluded he was "desperate" to make the 2002 Olympic team and "atone" for 1998.

In the flesh, Shanahan doesn't look like a tragic figure. Doesn't look depressed, either. Happy marriage, nice homes, a first-place team and more money than he can spend. Popular, too: he leads all North American vote-getters in balloting for next month's all-star game. Looks like a man in the prime of his life, having fun, doing stuff he loves. He didn't need the Olympic carrot to play well—"I can't remember a single season when, as it was approaching, I felt that I didn't have something to prove," he says. Yet as much as he might like to tell people to get over it, he was simply raised too well, and he knows people believe what they want to believe, facts be damned. Someday, though, he might just lose it—how many times can a guy have his nose rubbed in it and still stay sane?

That question alone makes him the most intriguing player that Canada is sending to the Salt Lake City Olympics next month. But don't count on him cracking. The guy's a glutton for punishment: by playing his way onto the squad, he's certain to face even more questions about 1998. He's definitely used to people trying to mess with his head, too: he has played for, and run afoul of, coaches Mike Keenan and Scotty Bowman, both accomplished mind-game players. And his face is proof he can take the hard going—his scar tissue has scar tissue.

But there's another thing that makes him an interesting pick. Gretzky has deliberately assembled a team with more speed and finesse than the one in 1998, but Shanahan's selection suggests a need for toughness, too. The six-foot, three-inch winger possesses all the modern skills and is one of the NHL's most prolific scorers. But unlike others in the NHL's upper class, the 32-year-old wears his heart on his fists. In that respect, he is akin to great old Red Wings like Ted Lindsay and Gordie Howe, stars who fought their own fights. Altogether, he offers a package that no one else in hockey can match. "That's why he's so difficult to play against—you don't know what you're going to get from him," says Colorado's all-star defenceman Rob Blake. "If he gets even one opportunity, he's going to score.

If you try to run him to throw him off his game, he'll fight you and beat you that way. And if he catches you with your head down, he'll run you over."

The throwback image fits. At a time when self-centred, don't-give-a-damn, go-to-the-highest-bidder athletes dominate the sports pages, Shanahan is thoughtful, passionate and loyal, a guy who loves books and kids and dogs and digging in the garden. But reader beware: in any examination of Brendan Shanahan, there is likely an element of fiction. As a series of pre-Nagano TV commercials showed, he's a natural ham. A voracious reader of historical novels, he's also known for embellishing his CV to reporters who pry into his psyche. As a result, they have reported in good faith that he's spent off-seasons running with the bulls at Pamplona, meditating at a Tibetan monastery and playing a bit part in *Forrest Gump*. He claimed he once stood up in the Wings' dressing room after a tough loss and quoted a passage out of Shakespeare's *A Midsummer Night's Dream*. So how much of what he's saying can we believe? He smiles his crooked smile. "As much as you want," he says.

Sitting in the players' lounge at Detroit's Joe Louis Arena after practice, Shanahan is picking at a salad and pushing ancient history out of the way. For the record: the Nagano shootout hurt like hell at the time. He remembers the aftermath, off by himself, bent at the waist with his head cradled in his hockey-gloved hands as the Czechs celebrated. "I took it very hard, losing at the Olympics," he says. "And maybe I did take it more personally, having been the last guy in the shootout, having the last chance after everybody else missed. And it came down to that one last shot."

That said, the long face didn't last. He eased the pain with the odd pint of Asahi beer even before leaving Nagano and with the assurances of teammates who reminded him that it took all of them to lose that day. Sure, Hasek stoned him, but then Theo Fleury, Ray Bourque, Joe Nieuwendyk and Eric Lindros all were foiled in the shootout before he had his chance. As well, Canada had chances to put the game away in regulation and overtime, but didn't. And even if he had scored, it would only have tied it up; there was no guarantee of victory. Anyway, by the time the NHL playoffs rolled around that spring—he helped Detroit win the Stanley Cup in June—he had done his mourning and moved on. Shanahan remembers a Canadian reporter who arranged an interview during the playoffs and was surprised that the man he found was, well, so normal. "I guess he figured I'd be a chain-smoker or on some kind of antidepressant," Shanahan says. "But that wasn't me at all."

The real Shanahan was revealed in the way he eventually dealt with the situation. He ruminated, weighed things and eventually let emotion give way to reason. After a few weeks, he says, "I had a pretty good perspective, I understood things pretty well." Brett Hull, a teammate in St. Louis in the mid-'90s and now again in Detroit, says he wasn't surprised to see his old pal put the disappointment behind him. "He takes in everything and deals with it very rationally and logically," says Hull. "In some ways, he's always going to be a big kid, which is the great thing about him. But intellectually, he's older than his years, especially in the way he deals with stuff. There'll be situations where I'll be ranting and raving about something, and he'll be calm and say, 'Maybe there's another way of looking at it.'"

That trait comes from his dad, a firefighter and, later, director of fire prevention. Donal, who emigrated from Bantry Bay, Ireland, to Toronto in 1952, died of Alzheimer's disease in 1990, when he was only 58. By that time, Brendan had been away for two years of junior hockey in London, Ont., and three in the NHL with New Jersey. "When everyone saw the forest, he could see the individual tree," Shanahan says. "And when everyone was focused on the little things, he'd step back for the broad picture. He always seemed to be going a different speed from the rest of the crowd. I remember at his funeral listening to one of his co-workers tell a story about how they'd be looking over the scene after a fire, scratching their heads, and Dad'd say, 'Let's take a break.' And sure enough, they'd go for a cup of tea and an hour later, even if they weren't at the site, they'd figure it out."

There are other similarities. Brendan and his wife, Catherine, bought a century-old house near her family's home in Boston several years ago, and during the subsequent restoration, the yards were all torn up. But then the construction debris was finally hauled away and something strange happened. "I had this urge to go and plant things," he says. "I didn't know why—I'd never, ever had the urge before." But he figured it out. "My dad used to get up early in the morning and spend all day in his garden. He had onions, tomatoes, cucumbers, rhubarb and roses in the front yard." The thought makes him laugh. "Growing up, you don't think you're watching, you don't think you're listening, and then one day, you become your parents. It's a cliché, but it's true."

Not in every way, though. He learned to stick up for himself—and have fun doing it—from his three scrap-happy elder brothers, Brian, Danny and Shaun. "My father was the exact opposite," says Brian, a former lacrosse star who now works as a broadcast analyst of National Lacrosse League games in Canada. "We use to drive him crazy with our fighting." Brendan wasn't even the worst of them. He just has a temper. "I'm no angel and there are times when I snap and I wonder, 'Where did that come from?' " His fly-off-the-handle side was worse when he was younger: "In high school, I got into a fight in every sport—basketball, soccer, football and even track and field." Track and field? "It was in the discus pit, with a judge . . ."

At the same time, he's no goon. He just loses it occasionally, and that scares the guys who sign his paycheque, who don't like it when their $6-million-a-season star risks breaking a hand on opponents' heads. But it's not as if Red Wings general manager Ken Holland has any choice. "If they doubled my salary," Shanahan says, "I wouldn't change the way I play."

Shanahan is patrolling the left lane of the freeway in his big black sport-ute, heading from practice in downtown Detroit to a charity event at a car dealership and then to his suburban Birmingham home. The fast lane suits the image of a power forward, although, against the stereotype, Shanahan is surprisingly calm given that he's late for the charity appearance and locked in rush-hour traffic. And an interviewer along for the ride keeps asking personal questions. About his wife, for instance—Catherine, a social worker. "She's very smart—" he begins, but is interrupted by the ring of his cellphone. It's Catherine, ears burning. "How appropriate that you should call just as I'm giving you a compliment," he says, his face twisting into a mischievous grin. "What is it that you do again? Interior decorator? Real estate agent? Teach typing? I forget."

He listens for a while and promises he'll be on time—they have a dinner date with two other couples from their neighbourhood. Then he explains he's in mid-interview and claims his teammates have been talking behind his back. "Igor [Larionov] told this guy that I know way too much about pop culture," he says. "I feel insulted. Should I?" He listens again, and when he hangs up, he turns and says: "My wife says to tell you I have a head full of useless information."

He offers a pained expression, pretending to be cut to the core. "That's just her bitter way of explaining why I always win at *Jeopardy*," he says. But it's true, he's a knowledge sponge and envies the chance his wife had to pursue undergrad and post-grad university degrees. Education was hugely important to his parents—his mother, Rosaleen, refused to let him report to his junior team in London until the Knights agreed to pay his university tuition if he failed to make it as a pro—but because of his hockey commitments, he never finished high school. In retirement, he plans to go to university and study history and literature. "And I don't know if it would necessarily parlay into a job as an English teacher or a history teacher," he says. "Who knows if I'd be any good at it? All I know is I'd be better at it now than when I was 18."

Married three years, Catherine and Brendan are test-driving parenthood. They have three labs and, for fun, they borrow other people's kids and take them to movies. This last revelation comes from Larionov, the Wings' veteran centre and run-ragged father of three. He doesn't always get Shanahan's jokes, but he likes him anyway. "Last week, Shanny and his wife made a date with my two girls," Larionov said while getting changed after practice one day last month. His son Igor, three, was by his side. "They went to *Harry Potter*. Then they went for pizza. And then they went to stores. They spent six hours together, and the girls came home with so many stories. They were so happy."

Shanahan is a natural with kids, a handy coincidence since, early in his pro career, his nickname was "Big" because he looked like Tom Hanks' character in the movie about a boy locked in an adult's body. To Larionov, that rapport with kids says a lot. "Every time he and Catherine come over to my house, he goes down in the basement and plays hockey with this one," he says, tousling little Igor's hair. "Shanny has a big heart, you know, and a very good soul. You can tell that because the kids love him."

We've seen this before. Shanahan is skating in all alone on Dominik Hasek. Will it never end? This time, though, Shanny feints left and, miracle of miracles, the grim-faced goaler goes with the deke, leaving him just slightly out of position when Shanahan deftly shifts back to his right. Hasek desperately throws a leg out, but his momentum is going the wrong way. Shanahan smoothly slides the puck to his forehand and flips a shot up over the pad and into the top right corner of the net.

So what if it's just practice at Joe Louis Arena, another day at the office for members of the Red Wings. Who cares? Any chink in Hasek's armour is welcome news to Canadian fans this close to another Olympics. And Hasek doesn't like giving up goals in his sleep, let alone at practice or, heaven forbid, in a game. He was recently named NHL player of the week after giving up a miserly three goals in four games. And while Shanahan indulged in only a mock celebration after beating his Wings teammate, he doesn't underplay its significance. "You beat Dom, even in practice, and you've done something," he says.

When the Canadian Olympic squad was announced in December, Gretzky at one point gave special mention of Shanahan's hard work and how it helped him win a spot on the team. Shanahan had no choice: he wasn't invited to the mini-camp in Calgary last September until Joe Sakic was injured and a space opened up. But he did well in Calgary, then he went on a scoring tear when the NHL season began. Still, the guys closest to Shanahan insist he's only doing what he usually does. "He's off to a tremendous start, but I don't know the Olympics are any more motivation for him," says Steve Yzerman, Shanahan's roommate on the road. "He always wants to play well."

A lot of factors contributed to his play this year, Shanahan says, including self-doubt. There have been times when he worried he wasn't good enough, or that the game was passing him by. "Fear of losing your abilities, fear of failure—fear's not the only motivation, but it's an ingredient," he says. He was stricken by that fear when he wasn't initially invited to try out for the Olympic team, and in the end, he was less driven by a desire to make the team than by the prospect of not making it.

Even now, even though he knows the downside, Shanahan still dreams the childlike dream of having the chance to score the winning goal. "It's just part of sports—you want to be the guy out there," he says. "When you don't want to be standing up on that stage, that's when you've lost something." He pauses for a second, as if to make sure it's clear he means it. "I don't feel that way," he says. "I want to be the guy." And who knows? He might just be.

A broken thumb restricted Brendan Shanahan's contribution during the Salt Lake City Olympics, but he came home to help the Wings win the Stanley Cup in 2002, scoring two goals, including the game-winner, in the final game.

How Sweet It Is!

—March 11, 2002—
James Deacon

M IKE RICHTER GOT JUST A PIECE of Jarome Iginla's one-time snap shot with four minutes left in the Olympic gold-medal men's hockey game. It was a desperate effort by the American goalie, who was sliding across the crease to his right and had to reach back with his left hand to intercept the Canadian winger's blast. As if in slow motion, the puck tumbled end-over-end off Richter's glove, headed toward the bottom right-hand corner of the gaping net.

Around the packed E Center, there was a collective gasp as fans watched the puck's progress. Its fate was critical: Canada

Mario Lemieux after the gold-medal victory over the U.S.

held a slim 3–2 lead, and with so little time on the clock, the Americans had to keep the score close if they were to have any chance. On the benches, players from both teams stood up to get a better look. In the second deck, the most anxious observers of all—Team Canada managers Wayne Gretzky, Kevin Lowe and Steve Tambellini—leaned out over the balcony in anticipation. And on the ice, Joe Sakic, Iginla's centreman and the person closest to the play, tried to redirect the fluttering puck in mid-air with his stick to make sure it went in. He missed.

Anyone who has followed men's international hockey competition lately knows Canada's ambitions have frequently been thwarted by near-misses and really hot goaltenders. In fact, it was the very same Richter who stoned the Canadians at the 1996 World Cup of Hockey, handing the otherwise out-gunned Americans a major upset. Two years later in Nagano, Dominik Hasek, the Gumby-like goalie for the Czech Republic, was unbeatable in the semifinal shootout and led the Czechs to the gold medal.

But Canada got the bounce this time. The puck dropped inside the post, just before defenceman Tom Poti could get to it and sweep it out of harm's way. On the ice, Iginla, Sakic and Steve Yzerman practically crushed one another in celebration. Canadian fans in the stands, who made up about 30 per cent of the crowd of 10,000, went berserk, waving flags and shouting CA-NA-DA! Gretzky and Co., meanwhile, leaped from their seats, propelled as much by stress relief as joy. The pressure that built over 18 months as the 2002 Olympic team was put together, the frustrations of past but never-forgotten losses and the sleepless nights that preceded Sunday's final were swept away in the exultation of the moment. "Our country desperately needed to win this tournament," an exhausted Gretzky said afterwards.

It was all over but the anthem. And not the tinny rendition that was played over the public-address system during the medal ceremony. With 30 seconds left, red-clad fans rose from their seats all around the arena and belted out their own heart-felt O Canada. By then, Sakic—named the tournament MVP—had made it 5–2, beating Richter on a breakaway. It was spontaneous and sweet and moving, not just for those in the crowd but also for the players. Hearing fans singing the anthem "was just unbelievable," forward Simon Gagne said. "It became tough to focus on the game because it was such a great feeling. It made me so proud to be part of the team that brought the gold medal back after 50 years."

For that alone, the final competition on the 2002 Winter Games schedule deserves to be considered among the defining moments in Canada's collective experience, right there with pivotal elections and Expo 67. The hockey precedent has been set: Game 8 in the 1972 Summit Series against the Soviet Union in Moscow is already there. So too the Montreal Canadiens vs. Red Army confrontation on New Year's Eve in 1975. Ditto Gretzky-to-Lemieux at the 1987 Canada Cup. And a strong case can be made for the women's team's thrilling 3–2 triumph over the United States that gave Canada its first hockey gold here.

According to overnight ratings, the men's final drew an average of 10.25 million viewers on Sunday afternoon, which makes it the most-watched TV program in Canadian history. Viewership peaked at nearly 12.6 million during the closing minutes and post-game celebrations. For fans in the arena, it was once-in-a-lifetime stuff. "What an amazing game—unbelievable," a deliriously happy Seth Boro, 26, of Ottawa, said after the medals had been handed out. "I think this is our generation's '72, without a doubt."

It wasn't just a scoreboard success. The final game was a thing of beauty. It didn't have the last-minute heroics of 1972 and 1987, but it sustained a breathtaking pace from the opening faceoff to the final whistle. Most strikingly to Canadian fans, there was the unshakeable conviction of their team, which had started slowly in the Olympic tournament but had rounded into form at precisely the right time. The big defencemen—Chris Pronger, Rob Blake and Adam Foote especially—had figured out the trick of keeping incoming forwards to the outside on the large ice surface and limiting opposition attacks. And Sakic, Iginla and Gagne had become the most dangerous forward unit at the Games.

On Sunday, even in the pre-game warm-up, the players were deliberate and focused, and once the puck was dropped, their opponents noticed. "You could tell they needed it," said U.S. stalwart Jeremy Roenick. "You could tell in the way they played. Fifty years of emotion was pent up in the way they played. I would have loved to win, but I respect the people who won tremendously. It was an honour to play in today's game."

What a way to conclude an Olympics. Over the final seven days here, Veronica Brenner and Deidra Dionne finished silver-bronze in freestyle aerials. In short-track speed skating, the women's 3,000-m relay team took bronze, while the women's hockey team grabbed their gold. The women's curling rink won bronze and the men followed with silver. Speed skater Clara Hughes produced a gutsy bronze-medal performance in the 5,000 m—a finish that made the former cyclist the first Canadian ever to win medals in both Summer and Winter Games (she earned two bronze medals in 1996). And then, on the eve of the last men's hockey game, three-time Olympian Marc Gagnon and teammate Jonathan Guilmette finished one-two in the 500-m short-track final and then led the men's 5,000-m relay team to yet another gold later that night. Talk about stoked—after a tough start to the Olympics, that great sporting intangible, momentum, had shifted Canada's way.

The women's hockey victory was the most energizing because of its underdog appeal. The two North American teams were the class of the tournament, and the game was played at a ferocious clip. But Canada's women were decided long shots since they had lost eight straight pre-Olympic games to the Americans. And although they cruised easily through earlier games, the Canadians struggled against the Finns in the semi-final before finally getting on track in the third period for a come-from-behind, 7–3 win.

But who can predict an Olympic result? There was plenty of motivation on the Canadian side: they lost the gold medal in 1998 to the Americans, and that memory was still agonizingly fresh for the veterans on the team. So in the championship game here, they set the pace from the start, forechecking the U.S. to a standstill for long stretches. And they achieved that despite an incomprehensibly one-sided effort by the American referee, Stacey Livingston, who at one stage called eight straight penalties against Canada and seemed intent on making sure the home team won. Led by Hayley Wickenheiser and Vicky Sunohara, the Canadian penalty killers did wonders. And even then, the 3–2 final score doesn't quite do justice to the Canadian team's edge in play. There was no doubt that the better team won. "We didn't care about those eight games we lost," captain Cassie Campbell said after the joyous final. "This was the only game that counted."

The men weren't sure bets either, especially in the minds of hockey-obsessed second-guessers who for months debated every single player selection and management appointment. Their criticism turned particularly nasty when the team started so slowly, losing its first game 5–2 to Sweden and only just edging the Germans, 3–2. The players were alarmed, too, especially after the spanking they took in the opener. "After the Sweden game," Sakic said, "there were a lot of doubters. But that game forced us to come together as a team."

As the nail-biter against Germany illustrated, that coming together didn't happen immediately. Gretzky, who isn't used to such widespread criticism, was also feeling the burden of responsibility—his hand-picked group of players appeared to be going in the wrong direction. He admits it was getting to him and that he leaned on old pal Lowe, the Edmonton Oilers general manager, for stability. Yet he summoned a trick learned from his former Oiler coach, Glen Sather, by steering the negative attention away from the players. After Game 3 against the Czechs, a 3–3 tie that was the team's first promising performance, and on the eve of the more important stage of the tournament, Gretzky lashed out uncharacteristically, suggesting, among other odd things, that the whole world wanted Canadian hockey to fail.

It was a thinly veiled "Us vs. the World" call to arms—some U.S. newspapers likened it to Knute Rockne's "Win one for the Gipper." Instantly, Gretzky became the focus of fans' anxiety, and while there's no way of knowing if it helped the players, the gold medal suggests it didn't hurt. "Our team, behind the scenes and everywhere, had taken so much criticism," a tired-looking Gretzky explained after the final. "I felt we weren't comfortable and relaxed. I felt, 'Okay, take some heat off the guys,' and I did. But I didn't sleep for five days."

There was no Paul Henderson here. But the team owed much to its experienced hands. Playing hurt, Mario Lemieux wasn't the imposing figure many had hoped he'd be, but his leading-by-example style, along with that of Yzerman and Sakic, was crucial. After being released by their National Hockey League teams, the players had only one practice day before the Games started. And there were those initial growing pains. "The first couple of games, there wasn't a lot of talk in the dressing room, not a lot of emotion," said centre Joe Nieuwendyk. "Guys were trying to figure out their roles, so it took a while to come together."

It showed, of course, but the veterans stayed calm, Gretzky was unflaggingly confident, at least in public, and eventually 23 players from 15 NHL teams became a unified force. Strong on defence, tough along the boards, dangerous in the offensive zone and, above all, fast. "I wish we could take this team and barnstorm with it—become the Globetrotters," enthused coach Pat Quinn after it was all over.

On the wider international ice surface, it was an exciting, free-wheeling spectacle, the kind that cramped NHL rinks can't accommodate. And these were the greatest players on Earth: Canada, the U.S., Russia, Sweden, Czech Republic and Finland all had dream team-like rosters stocked with NHL stars. "I don't think you'll see any country dominate international hockey again, because everyone's so balanced," said Yzerman. "It's now down to who gets it together. Look at Sweden—they were awesome"—and even then they somehow lost to upstart Belarus. Since the Olympics are supposed to feature the world's best athletes, it makes sense that hockey should showcase its best players, too. "Hopefully, this sends a message to the NHL," said Tom Greenberg, a 26-year-old Torontonian who flew in for the final. "The game belongs here."

As abruptly as they were thrown together, the players dispersed. There will be no men's hockey parade down Ste-Catherine or Yonge or Portage or Granville because the players' employers wanted them back and filling seats in NHL rinks right away. Fair enough—the NHL clubs are the ones paying the big bucks. But for fans, it'll probably take some time to get excited about pro hockey after seeing what the game can be like when the world's best get some room to move. And for the millionaire members of Team Canada, well, it's doubtful they'll ever forget how much fun they had playing for nothing more than national pride.

The Real-Life Dreams of Jarome Iginla

—*October 14, 2002* —
James Deacon

S UMMONING EVERY OUNCE OF NERVE they've got, three small boys approach Jarome Iginla, hoping to speak with hockey's reigning scoring champ now that practice is over. He's discreetly decked out in civvies—black leather jacket, pale blue T-shirt, faded jeans—but they've spotted him anyway, sitting up in Calgary's Pengrowth Saddledome stands. At first they keep a polite distance, since he's already talking to someone else, but it's clear they're leaking courage the longer they wait. So Iginla excuses himself from his conversation to greet the boys with a broad smile and a big right hand, which, one by one, they

Relaxing in the Flames locker room

shake. By then, though, they're too cotton-mouthed to blurt out a "Hi," let alone what they came to say, so the big guy gets things rolling. "How ya doin'? Have a fun summer?" Iginla asks. A couple of nods. "How's school?" he asks. "What grade are you in?" The biggest boy holds up four fingers.

There's more than the usual pressure on Iginla going into the new season, but he's still his usual exuberant self. There's an awkward silence and, finally, one of the boys mumbles the question they came to ask: "Are you playin' tonight?" he wants to know, and all three lean in for the answer. "No," Iginla says, explaining that in pre-season games the coaches want to see the rookies more than the vets. "Sorry about that," he says. Disappointed, the boys turn to go, but Iginla stops them in their tracks. "You guys have anything I can sign?" he asks. They wheel around, happier. "Really?" asks the littlest kid. "Sure," Iginla says, and he proceeds to autograph the scraps of paper they dig out of their pockets. Several thank-yous later, they shuffle off.

Talk about asking for trouble. As soon as he's seen signing things for kids, the professional autograph hounds in the building pounce, thrusting bindered sheets of mint-condition trading cards under Iginla's nose. They don't apologize for interrupting him. They just watch carefully as he signs dozens of cards, calculating, perhaps, what each will soon sell for in card shops and on Web sites. Iginla knew that was the price he'd pay for taking out a pen for the little boys, but he still did it. "It's part of the game," he says.

The sports world is starving for guys like Iginla. The people who buy tickets and jerseys invest a lot of emotion in the migrant millionaires who play for the home teams, and it hurts when their heroes turn out to be zeroes. So fans, kids especially, connect with Iginla. Starting his seventh full National Hockey League season, he still seems to have that pinch-me excitement about playing hockey.

About life in general, in fact. He is resolutely decent, a 25-year-old man whose moral compass is directed by strong but discreet Christian convictions, and who appreciates his great fortune rather than bemoaning the inconveniences of fame. He's putting his mother through university so she can pursue a second career. He contributes both his time and his money to Calgary-area charities. He's the nice guy you'd have liked your daughter to bring home if he weren't already engaged to his junior-high sweetheart. Brad Lukowich, a teammate on Iginla's junior team in Kamloops, B.C., once summarized: "If you took the best player on the ice, the best leader in the locker room, the best community guy with the fans, and put them altogether, that's Jarome."

Iginla's focus was already on making the playoffs. He has enjoyed success at every level, from minor hockey to the Olympic Games. It is fitting then, that his last name means "big tree" in his father's dialect, Yoruba. He needs to be stout because, these days, everyone wants a piece of the muscular right winger who won the NHL scoring title last season—he was the only sniper with 50 or more goals (52). With Joe Sakic and Simon Gagne at the Winter Games in Salt Lake City, he formed Canada's most potent forward line on the men's team that so gloriously won gold. And at season's end, even though the Flames failed to make the playoffs, he was voted the league's most-outstanding player by his peers. He's been inundated with requests from fans, reporters and sponsors (he has deals with EA Sports, Campbell's and General Mills), leaving it to Flames PR director Peter Hanlon to say no: Iginla hasn't learned the word yet.

He is also courted because of his skin colour. His Nigerian-born father, Elvis, is black; his American-born mother, Susan Schuchard, is white. So their son, like Tiger Woods, is a multi-racial star in a predominantly white sport and serves as a role model for visible minorities who might feel shut out of the game. Iginla says race never got in the way of his own hockey opportunities when he was a kid in St. Albert, outside Edmonton, but he knew he stood out. Other kids, and their parents, reminded him of that. "I was aware, and others would say to me, that there weren't many black players in the NHL," he says tactfully. "So it meant a lot to me that Grant Fuhr was playing right there in Edmonton, winning Stanley Cups and being an all-star. It meant a lot to see Tony McKegney and Claude Vilgrain. I followed those guys, so I'm glad if I can be a role model—I know what it meant to me."

And then there is his multi-faceted role with the Flames, who open the new NHL season this week. They haven't qualified for the playoffs since 1996, and Iginla desperately wants to end that dubious streak. Fans, meanwhile, will be expecting him to justify the two-year pact he just signed with the Flames for a whopping US$13 million, a vast sum for a small-market franchise with a tenuous future. Some argue the Flames paid too much, but their financial woes might have been worse had they tried selling tickets without their star attraction. So on top of everything else, he's central to the team's marketing campaign.

Instead of groaning under the load, Iginla's remarkably cool about it. "There's pressure after signing a big deal, pressure to live up to scoring 50 goals, and the way I look at it is this," he explains. "When I was a kid, I saw Wayne Gretzky doing all the interviews, and Mark Messier and Steve Yzerman. They had all these pressures every year, and they still handled it. So that's what I want to do too, you know?"

A lot of people were surprised by Iginla's dominance last season. They shouldn't have been. He decided at age seven he was going to make it to the NHL, after one of his very first games. It soon became clear he was talented, and he succeeded at every level. He won two Memorial Cups for junior-hockey supremacy with the Kamloops Blazers, and the 1996 world junior championship with the national team. Individually, he was named Western Hockey League player of the year in 1995–1996, and was runner-up for NHL rookie of the year the next season.

Iginla wasn't originally chosen to take part in the pre-Olympic camp that Gretzky held in Calgary last year. He was added at the last minute because Gagne was injured, and the chance to play with that elite group had a profound effect. He'd measured up against the game's best. "You could tell it boosted his confidence," his centreman, Craig Conroy, says. "Jarome's got a great shot, and after that camp, he started to use it more."

To the casual observer, Iginla's talent seems more natural than mechanical, and it's true he's a gifted athlete. But a lot of sweat went into his climb into the elite ranks. He has spent hours training with a former decathlete, Rich Hesketh, to add strength and flexibility to his six-foot, one-inch, 200-pound frame. When he reached the NHL, coaches said his skating ought to be better, so he addressed that. "I approach it like a sprinter, trying to get more explosive," Iginla says of the specialized regimen. Last season, the team needed him to score more, so instead of passing in certain situations, he began to shoot. Bingo, more goals.

Iginla says he's just doing whatever it takes to be a better player and to win. But it's an approach that sometimes makes his dad cringe. Elvis hates that his son sometimes has to fight, and he also knows his son isn't blameless—"As mild as he is off the ice," Elvis says, "Jarome can be very physical and passionate on the ice." Iginla is no enforcer, but he knows a fight can sometimes change a team's momentum. Last week against Edmonton, he and Oilers defenceman Eric Brewer mixed it up a bit. No offence was intended, Iginla says—Brewer's a pal from the Olympic team. If anything, Iginla was sending a message to his teammates to play harder in a tight game with a division rival. "That's part of what happens when our two teams get together," was all he'd say about it.

During a practice at training camp, working on power play drills, Iginla cruised into the slot, took a pass from Conroy and fired a rocket that nailed goaltender Roman Turek squarely in the head. The lanky netminder fell like a bag of cement but was slowly returning to his feet by the time everyone gathered to see if he was all right. His helmet was badly dented and askew, but his humour was intact. "Is that the best you've got?" he shouted at Iginla.

If success ever inflates Iginla's head, his teammates will be right there to let out the air. They call him Iggy—how cutting is that? And they rib him for being a dawdler and for arriving late for buses. "That's because he loves to sleep," says defenceman Robyn Regehr. "He'd sleep 'til two in the afternoon every day if he could."

No one in the locker room doubts that Iginla's the real deal. They talk about his shot and his uncanny knack for getting open in the slot. More than that, though, they talk about character. "He doesn't let his emotions get away from him," Conroy says. "He gets a lot of attention from opposing teams, but he keeps his focus and finds ways to get open." Regehr concurs. "I don't see him as a one-hit wonder at all," he says. "His work ethic is phenomenal, and he's driven—he's always striving to be the best."

His motivation has been the same since he was a kid. Some past coaches tried to turn him into a grinder, a 15-goal and 100-penalty-minutes-a-season player. He didn't bite. "Don't get me wrong," he says. "Playing in the NHL is a dream come true and I'd play any role to stay here. But I always dreamed of getting here and being a scorer, an elite player, a star, to be on a winning team, and win Stanley Cups. I know I'm not there yet, but that's still my goal."

Skeptics doubt he'll reach all those goals in Calgary, where the payroll's barely half of what some teams are spending. In fact, some insiders speculate that if the Flames fall out of contention early this season, they might trade Iginla to a wealthier team for inexpensive prospects. But general manager Craig Button says no such plan exists, and his trade last week to acquire forwards Chris Drury and Stephane Yelle from Colorado for defender Derek Morris and forwards Jeff Shantz and Dean McAmmond indicates he's serious about contending. "We're trying to build a successful team," Button says, "and Jarome's a big part of that."

Iginla's anxious to speed that up after watching other teams compete in the playoffs the last six years. "Maybe people'll judge me by goals and points or whatever," he says. "But to me, what really'd be great is being able to make the playoffs and break that cycle of tough times, and share that with the team." He's so focused on that, in fact, that he and his fiancée Kara Kirkland, a physiotherapist, have not set an exact date for their wedding in St. Albert next spring. His hope is he'll be busy playing into June, and she's used to having hockey dictate their schedules. They've been together since they were 13, give or take the odd rough spot.

His full name is Jarome Arthur-Leigh Adekunle Tig Junior Elvis Iginla, and it appears in full on his wrinkled old birth certificate. He was two when his parents divorced, so the only life he remembers is one in which he lived with his mother, who worked long hours outside the home as a massage therapist. His father studied law at the University of Alberta and lived elsewhere, and his maternal grandparents, Richard and Frances Schuchard, looked after him when his mother was at work. It was his grandfather, in fact, who took the boy to his first organized hockey tryout.

Back then, he was exhaustingly energetic. "So my mom got me into everything—bowling, tennis, Little League, you name it," he says. At one point he fancied he might grow into a Bo Jackson–type athlete, playing pro baseball, the game his grandfather taught him, as well as hockey. But then he looked at the calendar. "The seasons don't exactly work out," he says, laughing at himself in retrospect. "And really, I wasn't that good of a ballplayer."

Along with sports, he took everything from piano lessons to public-speaking classes. "My family's very musical," he says. "On my mom's side, my gramma runs a music school in St. Albert, and my mother's back in school studying to be a drama teacher. Anyway, I used to have some battles. They'd put me into music festivals and public-speaking things." He blushes at the memory of a shy boy having to perform in front of an audience. "I kept going up 'til junior high, but after that I gave it up."

By then, he was the star of the St. Albert rep team, and was soon drafted to play for the Blazers. It started badly. "It was tough leaving home at 16 years old and not playing a lot—I was sitting on the bench, playing two shifts a period," he explains. He'd been the star at every level, but now, the dream was in doubt. "I remember talking to my grandpa saying, 'Maybe I should just come home.' But he was like, 'Give it a little longer.' He wasn't saying I couldn't come home, just that I should give it a try. And it did get better."

The story triggers another memory of his family. "I was very fortunate in my situation—I wouldn't change any of it," he says. "Whatever games I had, they'd go and watch, and they were always so positive. I never heard once that I had a bad game from them. I had bad games, obviously, but I had coaches to let me know that." Now, he appreciates the fact they never pushed him. They knew he loved to play, he says, "and they let it be my ambition."

Left to his own devices, he set high standards for himself, not just in hockey but in life. "What really defines Jarome," Elvis

Iginla says, "is his sense of right and wrong. He worries about that a lot, and it spills out into his relationships, his work, everything." That isn't something that concerns some of today's superstars, and Elvis knows that. "I'm happy Jarome's done so well in hockey," his dad adds, "but I am far happier for the person he has become."

FOOTBALL

The Most Feared Football Player in Canada

—November 26, 1955—
Trent Frayne

O N THE EVE OF ANOTHER EPIDEMIC of Canada's favourite disease, an infection called Grey Cup fever, a remark made a year ago by Edmonton's resident football genius, Frank (Pop) Ivy, has virtually been forgotten.

The Edmonton coach had just seen his spindly-legged halfback Jackie Parker pick up a fumble with three minutes to play in the Grey Cup game in Toronto's Varsity Stadium last Nov. 27, and sprint 93 yards for the touchdown that wiped out a lead the Montreal Alouettes had held most of the game. It enabled the 1–4 underdog Eskimos to take a 26–25 lead into the final three minutes. It also filled Ivy with a sort of ecstatic apprehension in what should have been for him the year's high moment. "I was thrilled to be ahead, but for the first time in the game I was scared," said Ivy, probing the paradox on a television program after Edmonton had hung on through the final frantic moments to win the Grey Cup. "I was afraid to death of that Etcheverry."

Sam Etcheverry is an old hand at giving fits to football coaches. Since he joined Montreal Alouettes four seasons ago he has become the most feared and versatile quarterback in the country because no one can ever be sure what he's apt to pull next. In an age of specialization in football the backfielder who can do many jobs well has become an anachronism. But Etcheverry is the exception. He can throw a football with surpassing skill, run deceptively if not with notable speed, punt for good yardage, kick points-after-touchdown, run back opposition kicks and play a fearless tackling game defensively. In addition to all this he is a gambler, and it is this quality that has made him at once anathema to rival coaches and the toast of the volatile Alouette adherents who once booed him.

That was during Etcheverry's first year in Canada in the fall of 1952 when the Alouettes were building their present powerful team. In those days they had a porous line and the opposing linemen made life miserable for the new quarterback. So did the fans whenever he lost yards with the ball. But in the last three seasons, with the Alouettes stronger, he's been winning wild acclaim from the grandstands, as well as from the coaches. "You can't set up a defence for him," says Lew Hayman, who was general manager of the Alouettes when Sam moved to Canada, "because nobody knows what he might pull out of the hat. By nobody, I'm including Sam."

In some respects this is true. Etcheverry recalls one game against Hamilton in 1954 when he called a pass play while the ball rested on his own four-yard line. Halfway through the play he suddenly switched to another. In itself, calling a pass was a daring move in such a position because if the pass were intercepted that close to the Alouette goal line it would almost certainly result in a Hamilton touchdown. The very fact that the play would be unexpected, however, was the element that appealed to Etcheverry. It was designed as a pass to the right end, Red O'Quinn, and as Etcheverry backtracked behind his own goal line to give O'Quinn time to shake loose from the man covering him, he was carefully watching the defensive man shadowing O'Quinn. "Suddenly it dawned on me," he related later, "that the safety man hadn't covered our other end, Hal Patterson, who was a decoy on the play. I took a look and, sure enough, old Hal was wide open. So I pitched it to him."

It was quite a pitch. Patterson took the ball on the 40-yard line and ran the rest of the way for the touchdown. It was, according to Big Four and Western Conference record books, the longest pass-and-run touchdown play ever completed in Canada, 106 yards from the line of scrimmage.

That day, Saturday, Oct. 16, was the most successful in Etcheverry's history in this country. He completed 26 passes in 36 attempts for an all-professional record of 586 yards gained by a passer in a single game. Sparked by Etcheverry's early surprise pass to Patterson, the Alouettes romped to a 46–11 victory.

As a gambling quarterback, he is equally capable of the unexpected when time is running out and the score is close. Just last October in a game against the Toronto Argonauts the Als carried a 30–28 lead into the last three minutes, and the Alouettes had been pushed back to their own 10-yard line. Standard procedure in such circumstances is for the leading team to play it safe and to keep possession of the ball as long as possible, so that the rival team will have neither time nor the possibility of a fumble or an intercepted pass working for it. But Etcheverry, the gambler, didn't figure it that way. Realizing the Argonaut defenders would not be looking for a pass he threw one to his flying wing, Joey Pal, which carried the Alouettes to their own 40-yard line and far from the danger of their own goal line. When the Argonauts finally did get the ball they were deep in their own end and there was not time enough to muster a final threat.

The thought that a pass interception could cost his team the game at so critical a moment had occurred to Etcheverry, "but it was outweighed by my conviction the Argos wouldn't be looking for it," he later explained. "If you start worrying about what *could* go wrong, you'd second-guess yourself right out of a job." And although he's been throwing daring passes from inside his own five-yard line almost since the moment he arrived in Canada, Etcheverry has been discreet enough in calling the play that only once has he been intercepted in that situation in four seasons.

Sam, in fact, has been doing the unpredictable since he arrived in Montreal in 1952 from Denver University, Colorado, an unknown with little more to recommend him than a glossy print in a football record book. The picture was used to illustrate a section that pointed out that Etcheverry had set a running-and-passing record of 1,168 yards gained. The picture, and then the statistic, caught the eye of the Montreal coach Douglas (Peahead) Walker. "I'd never heard of him," Walker confesses, "but there was *something* about that picture. I liked his looks and his trim build and his features."

Walker happened to know the coach at Denver University, Johnny Baker, and he phoned to enquire about the man in the picture. "Baker supplemented what I'd been able to pick up out of that book," Walker relates. "He said Sam was a fine competitor, clean living and not susceptible to injury."

It was a fortuitous phone call. Even in his first year Etcheverry was conceded by press-box occupants to be shoulder pads and helmet above a woeful band of Alouettes who won only two league games all year, and he was named on the Big Four's alternate all-star team. In 1953 he was the unanimous pick for first-team honours, and last year he was named as the most valuable player in the league, and as the outstanding football player in the country in a national poll of broadcasters and newspaper reporters, an annual award worth $1,000.

No one, least of all Etcheverry, would suggest that in a game as combative as football, any player can earn all of these honours single-handed. There are many reasons for any quarterback's success, not the least of which are linemen who are big enough and aggressive enough to keep people off his back while he's winding up to throw, and ends who are deceptive enough and sure-handed enough to get the ball and hold it. He needs adept and/or bruising runners, too, so that he can attack with diversity. Etcheverry has all of these accessories, as have most quarterbacks in Canada whose teams have won more games than they've lost. The one thing that sets Etcheverry apart is that he's unpredictable, a quality that often brings inspiration to his teammates at moments when those with less imaginative quarterbacks might feel they'd picked up enough lumps for one day. "We come from behind in a lot of our games," says Tex Coulter, the mammoth Montreal tackle, "because we don't let down when we get behind. We figure Sam will think of something. You get a kind of zest out of hearing him call a daring play, like a bunch of kids playing follow-the-leader, and you want to help him make it go."

Sometimes, in defying standard procedure, Etcheverry raises goose bumps on his own coach, the squat, white-haired Walker. One of the oldest tenets of quarterbacking, even predating the one about never passing from inside your own 10-yard line, is one that says a passer should "eat the ball"—that is, keep it and be thrown for a loss—if he's trapped by onrushing linemen and can't find a receiver. The principle here is that it's better to lose 10 or 15 yards and retain possession of the ball than throw blindly and risk the interception that would put the opposition in control. In his first year, when the Alouettes had far less material than now and Etcheverry was called upon to do just about everything except massage his own bruises, he often was trapped and thrown for huge losses. In just such circumstances in 1953, when the Alouettes started to become a power in Canadian football, there was a game against the Ottawa Rough Riders in which Sam invented the "submarine."

He was being assailed on all sides by Ottawa players and as he ran for his life, one of his pursuers was so close that Sam couldn't raise his arm to throw. Faced with a big loss as he backpedalled, the quarterback swung his arm behind his back waist-high as he was grabbed about the shoulders, and he flung the ball underhand in a long high arc downfield. Astonished Ottawa defensive backs stared in awe as the ball floated over their heads, and Joey Pal, a Montreal halfback, was galvanized into action almost in time to complete an astounding pass. He made a belated lunge for the ball and it just tipped off his fingers.

However preposterous, the incomplete pass prevented Sam from taking a large loss and it brought yelps of delight from the customers, the antithesis of the groans and abuse that had been heaped on him—and, in fact, that always emanate from grandstands anywhere when the hometown quarterback correctly elects to "eat the ball."

The combination of Etcheverry's inventiveness—he tried his submarine three or four more times in '53 and neither completed it nor had it intercepted—and the growing strength of the Alouettes got the fans off his back that season and he has become the most popular football player in Montreal history. He is rarely called anything but "Sam" and the vast majority of football fans in Montreal know who Sam is in any conversation without the necessity of the surname.

On the field Etcheverry moves with the faintest suggestion of a swagger from the huddle where he calls his plays to the line of scrimmage where the ball is put into play. He seems unruffled and unhurried and confident but these mannerisms are a facade, for beneath them Etcheverry is usually seething with nervous energy. He is seldom able to eat on the day of a game, or, if he does nibble at the scrambled eggs and bacon that are put before the players as they eat together in a hotel dining room, he is unable to keep the food in his stomach. Just before the game starts he becomes physically ill, and occasionally during the course of play he has paused for a moment, stopped down on one knee, and been sick to his stomach. When the team is playing at home in Montreal he refuses to touch any food and the night before a game he tosses fitfully in bed. According to his wife, Nita, he broods silently over a defeat, prowling restlessly around the Etcheverry's two-bedroom apartment in the west end of Montreal, drinking an occasional bottle of beer and mentally replaying parts of the game where the tide turned against the Alouettes.

The Etcheverrys live there from July to December with their sons Steve, who is three, and Mike, 18 months. Mrs. Etcheverry, a quiet pretty girl from Albuquerque, N.M., is expecting a third child. They spend the off-season in Albuquerque where Nita's father, Harold Mulcahy, has a whole-sale sporting goods business for which Sam is a salesman covering New Mexico and Colorado.

Etcheverry is a French Basque whose father, Jean Baptiste Etcheverry, was born and grew up near the village of Urepel in the French Pyrenees, where *his* father was a sheep rancher. Jean

Baptiste emigrated to the United States when he was 18 and joined two older brothers who had found jobs on a sheep ranch near Carlsbad, New Mexico, where Sam was born May 20, 1930. He has two younger sisters and an older brother, Jim, who is a cowboy near El Paso, Texas. Sam probably would have been a cowboy too had he not been adept at football. When the Carlsbad high school, with Etcheverry as quarterback, won the state championship in 1946 when he was 16, he was offered an athletic scholarship at Denver University.

Etcheverry says he had heard of Canadian football before receiving a letter from Walker, from friends at Colorado College in Colorado Springs, near Denver, where numerous Canadian hockey players receive athletic scholarships. It was largely on their reports that he decided to give it a whirl, plus the fact that he was offered $6,000 by the Alouettes. Walker recalls that the first time he saw Etcheverry on the field in Montreal he could tell he had great possibilities. "For one thing, he'd listen; he was no wise guy," says the coach. "When he made mistakes he admitted them; he didn't go around blaming a halfback for not getting a signal. He didn't alibi; he still doesn't."

Many coaches use their quarterbacks as puppets and, in effect, call the signals themselves from the bench. But once a game is under way Walker leaves Etcheverry on his own, which Sam says has built his confidence. Walker confesses "it can be nerve-wracking" when Sam tries an unorthodox play, but adds that he sees no reason to send instructions onto the field, "as long as he keeps us hummin'."

"Football is something like the infantry," says the coach. "One general's trying to figure out in advance what the other general's up to. So it doesn't hurt us any to have an unpredictable boy at the wheel."

✦

With Sam back at the controls this year, the Alouettes picked up just about where they left off last, the best-balanced club in the east, the most colourful to watch and, all fumbles and injuries being equal, the team most likely to be in Vancouver toward the end of this month to face the Western Conference champion in the Grey Cup game. If they are, the largest crowd in Grey Cup history, upwards of 30,000 in Vancouver's Empire Stadium, will get a full measure of entertainment from the country's most versatile quarterback. Part of the entertainment this time will not be located in the newspapers, Sam promises, as it was last year under his signature in the *Toronto Telegram*. On that occasion an indiscreet observation made to the newspaper's Bob Frewin, who ghosted a daily series for him, helped contribute to Edmonton's upset victory.

On the play in which Edmonton's Jackie Parker ran 93 yards with an Alouette fumble to turn the tide in the Eskimos' favour, there was only one man on the field who had a chance to head off Parker after he picked up the loose ball. That man was Etcheverry, who was in position to angle across the field and cut off Parker's course straight down the sidelines. "I didn't know whether to try to outrun him or to slow down and try to fake him," Parker said later. "Then I remembered a story I'd seen in the paper which said he wasn't a very fast runner. I figured the piece had to be authoritative because it was written by a fellow named Sam Etcheverry. So I just put my head down and ran."

Sam Etcheverry led the Als to the Grey Cup final that year and in 1956, but his team lost both times. He finally won a Cup with the Als in 1970, this time as the team's coach. Now retired and living in Montreal, Etcheverry still holds several CFL records.

The West Is Wildest When Regina Cries, "Go, Riders, Go!"

—August 6, 1966—
John Robertson

W HAT STARTED OUT as a perfect August evening for watching football at Regina's Taylor Field unexpectedly turned (unexpectedly, that is, for visiting fans unfamiliar with Regina's weather) into a cloudburst.

Barrie Williams, covering his first Regina game as a football writer of the Hamilton *Spectator*, leaned out the press box window to see how many of the 15,000 unsheltered fans had resisted the urge to flee. None had moved. With the Saskatchewan Roughriders hanging onto the leading end of a

George Reed scoring in Saskatchewan's 1966 Grey Cup victory over Ottawa

5–3 score in the third period, the fans, oblivious to the down-pour, were gargling their team yell, "Go, Riders, Go!"

"Are they crazy?" Williams asked me incredulously.

"Some of them probably are," I assured him on the basis of knowledge gained from covering Regina football. "Some of them are stoned. And the others just don't care as long as the Riders are winning."

In the fourth quarter the Hamilton Tiger-Cats, who had been fruitlessly trying to run holes in a 45-m.p.h. wind, switched ends eagerly to get their backs to the gale. But suddenly the storm reversed direction, as if on cue, until it faced the visitors squarely again. It ultimately reached such velocity that they couldn't have moved the ball, even if the Riders had vacated the field.

The game ended 5–3.

Afterward, we watched the fans make their first move for shelter. They resembled stragglers from a high-society poolside party in which everyone had gone off the deep end. Some of the younger men had removed their shirts. And the chic summer fashions hung limply on the women, like old bird-cage covers. Barrie Williams stowed his dripping portable in its case, shook his head and stomped out into the rain.

I knew he was already conjuring an appropriate lead for his story, or I would have called him back to relate what general manager Herb Capozzi of the British Columbia Lions had said on his last visit to Regina, when someone asked him how he had found Taylor Field: "I looked it up in the yellow pages, under outdoor insane asylums."

It was not that much of an exaggeration. From the standpoint of depth, agility, versatility, belligerent loyalty and raw lung power, the rah-rah raunchies who threaten to split Taylor Field at the seams at every home game are just about the hairiest fans on the continent. They wedge shoulder to shoulder in every available cranny bordering the field, and if the odd foot happens to extend into the playing area—well, that's show business.

Lately, there have been signs that creeping dignity is eroding some of the splendid atavism. That grassy haven between the bleachers and the playing field has been declared out of bounds to the thousands of fans who used to camp there with all the frenzied bias of a lynch mob. On occasion when a play would spill over into the sidelines, these rabid Rider fans had shown an alarming tendency to give only their own players back. So this year, using as an excuse the 3,300-seat extension of the east grandstand, the lawn has been ordered cleared. And somehow, Taylor Field won't seem the same again.

But one thing will never change—the eerie, funereal pall that envelopes the place whenever "the other guys" score a touchdown. It becomes so quiet you can hear the referee's arm-bones click as he reaches skyward to signal the score. However, the general mood is usually a giddy type of insanity, madcap to be sure, but with more warmth than waspishness, because the highly infectious football fever that grips not only Regina, but all of southern Saskatchewan, is born of a glad-to-be-here feeling. The populace knows that a city of 125,000 should not be expected to survive in the ever-escalating economic warfare called professional football. But the Roughriders have survived since 1910. And when the club teetered on the brink of bankruptcy in 1960, with a deficit of $80,000, it was salvaged by a lapel-seizing form of the hard sell that shook the natives with this realistic threat: "Can you imagine living here without pro football?" Apparently few could, because since 1960 the Riders have flourished both competitively and financially. Their bank balance is rumoured to be close to $250,000, but when I asked one official for a more explicit figure, he said, "Look, let's not louse up this 'Poor Little Regina' image. The people might get the idea we don't need them as much now."

It was not an idle assessment, when you consider that the Riders filled Taylor Field to 117 per cent of its seating capacity last year, and only managed to make a profit of $16,000. But statistics hardly explain why the natives of Regina and southern Saskatchewan get so demonstrative about their football.

For instance, could you fathom 3,000 ecstatic Toronto fans jumping into their cars and driving all the way to Toronto's International Airport, well after midnight, just to smother the Argos with huzzahs because they had won a routine league game? Or what would possibly motivate 1,000 people to journey down to the Regina telegraph office to affix their names to a good-luck wire prior to an out-of-town playoff game? That only cost each supporter a dime. But at the other extreme, 900 fans paid $100 apiece to attend the club's booster dinner last year. An average of $75,000 is raised each season in various promotional gimmicks and hat-passing binges that keep Saskatchewan in professional football.

A newcomer to Regina quickly realizes that he really doesn't have much choice but to support the Riders, because his boss— no matter where he works—is probably a member of one of the countless Roughrider executive committees. I once received a phone call at my sports desk at the Regina *Leader-Post*, from a man who had just been transferred into town. "I got a note from my boss this morning saying that I had 30 days to apply for government auto insurance, 45 days to register for medicare, and 60 days to get my Roughrider season tickets."

Season tickets are much, much more than just a status symbol in Regina, because they range from $14 to $42 and are within reach of everybody. In 1963 team executive Jay Brown introduced a novel easy-payment plan whereby a fan could pay for his season tickets at any bank, drug store or place where utility bills are accepted, and he could name his own terms. In many cases, office employees enroll in payroll-deduction plans.

For the absentminded, the club launches a massive tele-phone blitz each spring. Some years ago, so the story goes, a Rider telephone solicitor called a woman to ask why she hadn't renewed her pair of season tickets. "I'm sorry," she said. "But my husband passed away several months ago."

"Gee, that's too bad," said the caller. "But just a minute. We have another woman whose husband died recently. How would you like to double up with her this season?"

"That would be wonderful," she replied. "I haven't missed a game in 11 years, and I was going to stay home rather than go alone."

The unique part of Regina's football fever is that every time the club officials try to ram a certain project down their throats, the fans seem to open wider and beg for more. From Rider president Don MacDonald right down to the grade-school toddlers who pay $4 for kids' season tickets, everyone is sincerely convinced that he or she owns a piece of the action. And this is why their fervour mushrooms into a wacky crescendo every time the gates are opened at Taylor Field.

One night I asked Charlie Underhill, the stadium's ticket custodian, just how many people were in the park. I had esti-mated 18,000, and there were only 14,000 seats. "We'll never know, John baby," he grinned. "The only guy we've turned away is the fire marshal. If he sees this, he'll die."

Up in the press box, a Winnipeg football writer had his own theory on how to count the attendance. Inhaling the rum-flavoured aroma that wafted up from the stands, he said, "All they have to do is count the bottles and multiply by two."

Among Taylor Field's natural hazards is cheering for the visiting team. One Calgary Stampeder fan buttonholed me on the street the morning after a game and lisped through broken teeth that he would never return to Taylor Field. "I was cheering for the Stamps," he said, "and aside from one guy pouring his coffee down my neck, I survived the first half okay. Then I made the mistake of going to the washroom at halftime. I'm in this cubicle minding my own business, when someone next door shouts, 'Yea Roughies.' So I give with a 'Yea Stamps,' and next thing I know, two guys burst in, grab me by the heels and try to drown me. Then they stand me up and punch me in the mouth.

"I stagger outside and collar the nearest cop."

"I guess he fixed them," I said.

"Hell, he took one look at my cowboy hat and ribbons and arrested me for being drunk and disorderly."

Taylor Field partisanship knows no bounds, especially when the B.C. Lions come to town. The Lions are the rich kids of the Western Football Conference, and they never cease to brag—even about their humility. Lions general manager Herb Capozzi usually starts it off by saying that every time he wants to discipline a player he threatens to trade him to Regina.

But there are ways of getting even. The Lions arrived early one evening and went straight to Taylor Field for a practice, only to find the gates locked. No one, it seemed, had the authority to open up for them, or to turn on the lights. Finally, after phoning all over town, the Lions had to settle for practising across the street from the Hotel Saskatchewan, in Victoria Park, an unlighted area adorned by monuments and criss-crossed by sidewalks. Midway through this unhappy workout the coach was seen shaking his fist at a clutch of birds in a nearby elm tree, shouting, "Go ahead—everyone else around here does."

Perhaps the most moving moment in the history of Taylor Field was that frigid November evening in 1963 when the Riders staged their miracle comeback from a 26-point deficit, to oust the Calgary Stampeders from the Western Conference playoffs. They had dropped the opening game of the total-point series 35–9 in Calgary. And two nights later, when it resumed in Regina, only 10,000 shivering supporters turned out to watch what would surely be another rout.

But Bob Shaw, head coach at the time, decided to gamble on a sleeper play the first time the Riders got the ball. Halfback Ray Purdin stayed out of the huddle and "hid" himself right in front of the Calgary bench. But the fans were screaming so loudly the Calgary coaching staff couldn't alert their defensive unit. Rider quarterback Ron Lancaster tossed to Purdin who jogged down the sidelines unmolested. By halftime the deficit had been reduced from 26 points to 10 and suddenly from the press box, all you could see throughout the city were streams of car headlights heading toward the stadium. By the fourth quarter, at least 6,000 latecomers had scrambled through the gates, and when Rider fullback George Reed clawed his way over the goal line for the winning touchdown in the dying minutes, the people were still streaming into the park.

"The fans did it," bubbled Bob Shaw. "Those wacky wonderful fans. Did you hear 'em? We just couldn't let those people down."

In upward of 60 years of trying, the Riders have never managed to win a Grey Cup. "Maybe it would be the worst thing that could happen here," says veteran Rider executive Clair Warner. "What could we give them for an encore?"

At present, it costs the Riders about $700,000 a year to stay in business. Their average attendance of 16,000 per game works out to close to 130,000 people per season, more than the equivalent of Regina's total population. Using population as a yardstick, Toronto and Montreal would have to draw two million fans apiece in one season to equal Regina's fan support.

The Roughriders are community owned, a situation that has not always turned out happily in other Canadian cities. But Reginans work very hard at it. Club executives pay their own way on road trips and even to league meetings. A squad of doctors donate their services, even free surgery.

When I first arrived in Regina in 1963, I soon was made aware that nobody is exempt from pitching in and that few want to be. General manager Ken Preston invited me to the club's dressing room to inspect some renovations. We could hardly squeeze in the door for cinder blocks, mortar bags and wallboard. I was halfway past the supplies when he tapped me on the shoulder and said, "Hey, grab an end—this stuff has to go upstairs." So up we stumbled, groaning as the plywood bit into our fingers. At the top, Preston led me into a shower room, which was done rustically in Early American corroded tin.

"We're retiling all this," he said, beaming. I was about to start rolling up my sleeves when he added, ". . . in a few days."

"What outfit's doing all this work?" I asked.

"The players," he answered, pointing to the freshly mortared partitions and the gleaming new coaches' quarters paneled in imitation oak. "They come up in the afternoons, when they're not working."

"Do you pay them?" I asked. He pointed to a row of empty beer bottles. "So this was what they meant when they called it socialized football?" I said, trying to conceal my astonishment at the ingenuity of the entire operation.

He turned and looked me squarely in the eye. "The hard way," he said, "is better than no way at all."

Led by the "Little General," quarterback Ron Lancaster, and running back George Reed, the Riders won the Cup that year, beating Ottawa 29–14. Taylor Field now holds 27,732 people and the Riders still are a big draw: in 2002, average attendance was 24,226.

John Robertson worked in major newspapers from Regina to Montreal before retiring in 1989. He now lives in Winnipeg Beach, Man.

Football Dynasty on the March

—September 8, 1980—
Hal Quinn

E DMONTON ESKIMO KICKER Dave Cutler sits on the back porch of his farm house 35 km from the city limits and, more important, 40 km from Commonwealth Stadium. Three-and-a-half hours earlier, 42,778 fans had cheered as the scoreboard flashed: "Dave ties pro football field goal record—335." But by the time the crowd quietly filed out of the stadium, the scoreboard read: "Calgary Stampeders 16—Edmonton Eskimos 15." The Grey Cup champions had lost for the first time this season, their second ever at Commonwealth Stadium, and Cutler, the man with the green and gold leg, had *missed* three

Moon receiving a hug from coach Campbell
after winning the 1979 Grey Cup

field goals. Angry, remembering, he stares out toward the lake bordering his farm. Overhead in the moonlight, a flock of geese honks its way south. "Damn, summer's gone."

Later that morning, before heading back to the city and his sales job at rock radio station CHED, the Victoria, B.C., native notices that the leaves on the trees near the lake have begun to turn. Cutler is reminded again of the northern Alberta winter that lies ahead. It adds to the chilling memories of the night before and the "trap" he had allowed himself to fall into.

"Dr. Death" sits in the offices of the Edmonton law firm Lennie, DeBow & Martin, his six-foot, four-inch, 249-lb. frame filling most of the chair and all of his suit. It is the day before the Calgary game, four days before he will be called to the Alberta bar to become David Allan Fennell, lawyer. But this day Fennell is speaking as "Dr. Death," the name he picked up as leader of the Edmonton defensive line—Alberta Crude— that struck fear into the hearts of opposing quarterbacks in the mid-1970s.

"You know," he is saying, "what's amazing to me is that every game we've played this year has been a 'must' game for the other team. Like, Toronto *had* to beat us when we were in Toronto; B.C. *had* to beat us to get into first place; Winnipeg *had* to beat us or their season was over; this week Calgary *has* to beat us; then if Ottawa doesn't beat us it's over for them; then it's back to Calgary on Labour Day; then out to B.C. That's nine *must* games in a row, which creates a lot of pressure. I wish someone would say, 'Well, this is just a normal game. This one's for two points!'"

Disco music blares through the dressing room of the victorious Calgary Stampeders as the players celebrate their one-point victory over the Eskimos. But for the absence of champagne, it is like a Grey Cup championship party. Of course to sip champagne, Canadian football teams have to beat the Eskimos.

Eskimo Head Coach Hugh Campbell is at his desk at the team's offices in the Edmonton Inn early the morning after the loss to Calgary. "Oh, I guess the sun will still shine," he says with a smile. There is an air of calm about the office befitting a command post of a team that has won nine of its past 10 games. "Our local media was talking about our going undefeated and in that sense this loss could really help us. Like, our fans have no idea of what our ability is, they have it vastly inflated. There we were last night playing Calgary, supposed to be our arch-rival, and the fans were watching it like they were watching a play at the theatre." One of the CFL's top receivers when he played for Saskatchewan from 1963 to 1969, Campbell knows the ups and downs of Canadian football well. "The fans are very good here, but they were misled into thinking that we were going to win all our games by a big score."

The Eskimos have been winning the next one for a long time. Between 1950 and 1960, the team was never out of the Western Conference playoffs and appeared in five national championships, winning the Grey Cup three times—in 1954, '55 and '56. The team's fortunes dipped in the '60s as the Saskatchewan Roughriders dominated the West but, after missing the playoffs in 1972, the Eskimos went on to re-establish a football dynasty. They have finished first in the West six of the past seven years, played in the Grey Cup final every year but one since 1973 and won the last two Cups. Thanks to what is probably the league's most sophisticated scouting system—one full-time and 11 part-time U.S. scouts and Frank Morris' reports from 26 Canadian colleges—the Esks are blessed with excellent talent. Their Canadian players are among the best in the league—punter Hank Ilesic, centre Bob Howes, linebackers Tom Towns and Dale Potter and company. Bolstered by such top-class Americans as receivers Waddell Smith, Tom Scott and Brian Kelly, quarterbacks Tom Wilkinson and Warren

Moon, middle linebacker Dan Kepley and running back Jim Germany, the Eskimos have lost only 13 of their last 55 regular season games.

Two days after the loss to Calgary, Cutler was still thinking about the "trap," still angry with himself. As he chatted in his office at CHED, George Blanda's North American pro football record of 335 field goals was uppermost in his mind. Blanda had kicked his last field goal in December 1975, capping a 26-year career in the American and National football leagues. Cutler started this, his 12th year in the CFL, needing 11 field goals to set the new mark. Now after six games, he still needed one more. "I fell into it. I had been thinking about the record so much that it almost became more important than the game. I've never done that before. I've always considered myself to be a team player. Now I just can't wait for the next game. I hope I kick one from the 12-yard line *early* and get this damn thing over with."

The Ottawa Rough Riders came to town five days later. Cutler's chance came early, at 5:56 of the first quarter, not from the 12-yard but from the 48-yard line. He made it. The Esks won 45–20 and Cutler could relax.

Cutler's sense of team is not unique among the Eskimos, nor is it unique to this year's team. Jackie Parker, Hall of Famer, the Shenley awards player of the quarter-century and star of the 1950s Eskimos remembers: "I always felt that other teams then had as much talent as we did, but that we had an edge because we were so close as a team." That closeness, esprit, sense of belonging, is tangible in the violent world of pro football and the precarious lives of professional athletes. It, and a sense of the community in which they live and play, is cultivated by the Eskimos as by no other team in the league.

As the Esks prepared to play Ottawa, shock waves emanated from the locker room of their opponents in their past five Grey

Cup games, the Montreal Alouettes. Quarterback Joe Barnes' wish to be traded was granted on Aug. 22. Then the next day, the Alouettes placed *four* veteran players—kicker Don Sweet (nine years), linemen Gordon Judges (12 years) and Dan Yochum (nine years), defensive back Larry Uteck (7 years)— on waivers. The players said it was a budget move because of the large salaries the team was paying to U.S. college No. 1 draft choice Tom Cousineau and National Football League veteran receiver Fred Biletnikoff. Three days later the new-look Alouettes went out and defeated Toronto Argonauts 43–33.

Eskimo players don't think that sort of trauma could happen to their team. "Here you don't find a lineman blocking for a running back who is making 10 times the salary," says the new lawyer Fennell. "And you'll find that this team will keep a veteran over a rookie or a newcomer because of the contribution made over the years." The Eskimo difference is not lost on recent arrivals, like Canadian running back Neil Lumsden. "When I was traded here from Hamilton in May, you know, [Coach Hugh] Campbell and [executive manager] Norm Kimball talked to me on the phone that night. I was greeted with open arms—'How do you like Edmonton? Can we get your wife a job?'—I was impressed. All organizations are the same; the difference is how they're run. This one happens to run probably as well as any in North America."

The Eskimos are a community-owned, nonprofit business. A nine-man board of directors headed by Don Carlson establishes general policy. "After we've done that it's just a question of getting good people and letting them operate without interference," he says. Getting the people is Kimball's job. With prospective players, too, character is almost as important as ability. "We don't build in problems," Kimball explains. "We don't want any discontented, disinterested people here. We will either sign or trade the player who wants to play out his option—at our leisure, not at his. And in our scheme of things, keeping salaries close is very important."

The harmony "built-in" by management is reflected by the team. Wide receiver John Konihowski, in his seventh year with the Eskimos, is a highly visible figure around Edmonton coaching and conducting track-and-field clinics with his wife, Diane Jones-Konihowski, Canada's premier pentathlete. Lounging in jeans and sneakers before the Calgary game, he talks about the Eskimos. "This organization makes us feel human; we are treated like men. There are no curfews, bed checks, overly long practices. We are expected to act professionally, know our jobs and prepare. It makes the game more enjoyable, and when you're enjoying what you're doing, you give that little extra."

Of course in a sporting world populated by Harold Ballards and George Steinbrenners, harmony and contentment come with winning. As one man riding the crest of the Eskimo success story, Hugh Campbell admits, "I know that one day I'll be fired. My wife keeps asking me when I'll get a *real* job." And few know the vagaries of pro-football life better than Tom "Wilkie" Wilkinson, the 37-year-old quarterback who splits duty with 23-year-old Warren Moon. The beloved Wyoming tumbleweed drifted from the Toronto Rifles of the defunct Continental Football League to the Argonauts, then to the B.C. Lions before coming to rest in Edmonton. According to Cutler, the once-roly-poly, five-foot, 10-inch, 175-lb. Wilkie (who just doesn't *look* like a quarterback) is the key to this team. "Oh, they laugh about his body—I laugh about his body," says the kicker. "But I room with him on the road because I'm a little ego-centred about my own body. Mine is bad compared to anyone else's except his, so I'm the Greek god in our room. Sure he comes off as a clown prince, but he's the guy that leads us by example."

About the records Wilkinson holds, his attitude is the same: "Heck, I've been playing so long I'm bound to pass somebody." When not in uniform on the field or TV screen, Wilkie is a popular figure around the city as an ad salesman for middle-of-the-road radio station CHQT. "You know, in a city of 600,000 rather than, say, two million, you're accepted into the community more."

And win or lose, at home the Eskimos will have their weekly team meeting. "These, of course, are unofficial," Konihowski grins. "We have them in a local pub, and I'll tell you every guy shows up. And on the road they'll gather together."

"That last trip to Winnipeg," says Cutler, "we had 20 of us in the same pub after the game. *Twenty guys*, and the other 12 were back at the hotel, but doing something *together!*" The Eskimos don't operate like other clubs, and with two straight Grey Cups and six wins in their first seven games, they don't play like other clubs either.

After that loss to the Stamps, the Eskimos won five in a row en route to their record-tying third consecutive Grey Cup. They won the next two Cups as well. Warren Moon went to the NFL in 1984 and met with great success until he retired in 2000. David Fennell works for a gold-mining company in B.C. Tom Wilkinson still lives in Edmonton, as does Hugh Campbell, who is now president and CEO of the team.

Hal Quinn, now a national columnist for Scoregolf Magazine *living in North Vancouver, was a writer and editor at* Maclean's *from 1978 to 1993.*

OLF

Out of the Rough:
Sandra Post Is a Big Girl Now

—June 1975—
Marci McDonald

I N THE COFFEE SHOP of a rambling Ramada Inn on Houston's
No. 59 freeway, Sandra Post moved among the tables, chain-
smoking nervously. Other women straggled in around her—big,
square-jawed, rawboned women, freckled and rangy. Not your
ordinary women, it was clear at a glance. Their faces were confi-
dently naked of makeup, skin etched in squint lines and
leathered by an unrelenting sun. Their haircuts were styled with
one eye to the wind, and they walked with a lope from the hip
in long, easy strides. Over the red vinyl booths and morning

coffee, they congregated for the week's $100,000 tournament. They slapped each other on the back in greeting, took playful swipes at passing shoulders, traded loud twangy insults that passed for talk. "Hey Postie!" they called out, the restaurant transformed with instant locker-room fraternity, and Sandra Post hurtled across the room for some reunion heavy with its heartiness. "You know," she says, finally lighting over a paper placemat for breakfast, "it's always good to be back."

It is back after a two-week layoff from the Ladies Professional Golf Association circuit, but for Sandra Post it is even more. It is the comeback of a pro career that had swept off the tee nearly seven years before full of promise and miracle putts when she set off at 19 from Oakville, Ont., a giggling blond bubble gummer who took her hair down from its eternal rollers, dabbed Chanel No. 5 behind her ears and promptly went out to knock off the golfing Goliath, all-time money winner Kathy Whitworth, copping the prestigious LPGA championship in a playoff by a whopping seven strokes. But three years later the girl they'd predicted as the next star of the circuit woke up in hospital one morning on the brink of collapse, a bitter broken marriage on her hands, a listless broken career on the record books, written off at 22, a golf has-been. It is a comeback that has taken two long years etched in hurt and grim determination and served as living testament to the redeeming qualities of that great North American institution, divorce—perhaps the most remarkable comeback in all of women's golfing history. But it has been a journey that Sandra Post has measured out as shrewdly as an alien fairway, savouring every step along the course. "I really believe that I've been given a second chance," she says. "And I wasn't going to blow it this time. I was determined I was gonna make it back or I was gonna die tryin'. I wanted to be a success again and I was willing to sacrifice anything, just anything. I was a desperate little girl."

A trace of that desperation has ebbed now. In December, she wrapped up a 1974 season with $50,000 in winnings, more money than all the Canadian male golfers on the more lucrative men's tour combined. As the '75 circuit rolled into gear, she was already in second place in earnings and was counted enough of a contender again to land a coveted Colgate commercial, which showed her grinning out of a bubblebath in the raw. But the biggest change of all was that Sandra Post had finally won the second tournament of her career, the plum Colgate Far East in Melbourne, Australia, and when she stood up in the wind there to accept her $14,000 cheque before the TV cameras and the clapping, tears had suddenly blistered in her eyes and she hadn't been able to get the words out that would say just what it all meant.

"I just couldn't get it all together. I was so emotional," she said. "I mean, I'd made my money over the last two years. I'd played well. I was layin' them in there. But I wanted to win, I had to win. It was a drive so strong I could taste it. And boy, when I tasted that victory it was sweet. I think I knew then that I'd finally made it again after all these years."

Under the cold fluorescent glare of the coffeeshop, Sandra Post looks little different from the teenager grinning from the sports pages, the first Canadian ever to make the pro tour. The face is a little rounder maybe, the legs a little more solid in her tight patchwork jeans, the tanned cleavage spilling out from her well-unbuttoned shirt a trifle more generous. "I'm the chunky one with the straight hair," she had warned the night before over the phone, self-conscious about the 128 pounds she was carrying on her five-foot, four-inch frame. She doesn't like to talk about her weight and discusses it constantly, obsessively. At the very mention, she orders cold cereal and tea for breakfast. She runs her fingers through the short bleached-blond thatch now left to the vagaries of nature, the constant battle of the curlers abandoned years ago. But at 27, she is still one of the tour's most attractive lures in a solid, spunky, cheerleader sort of way.

The real difference now is that Sandra Post ranks as a veteran. Nothing had pointed it up more than the Orange Blossom Classic a month before in St. Petersburg, Fla.—the same tournament at which she'd once made her pro debut—when a pretty 19-year-old rookie named Amy Alcott with barely a month's experience on the circuit snatched the $5,000 first-prize money from under her nose with a 20-foot putt on the 18th.

Later in the morning when Renee Powell, her former roommate, stops by to congratulate her on that match, Sandra Post will shake her head philosophically. "History repeated itself," she says. "I mean, I beat Whitworth in my rookie year, then Alcott who's a rookie beat me. I knew how she must have felt, though she could probably cope with it better than I did. When I beat Whitworth it was like my 10th tournament. I mean, I didn't believe it. I was just a thrilled little kid. And even though you don't purposely do it, you don't practise as hard after. You get a little lazy. I wouldn't change anything now, but maybe if I'd handled it a little better it might not have taken me another seven years to win again."

Above the practice tee at Westwood Country Club on the concrete shopping centre fringes of Houston, the day hangs limp and dun-coloured, the hint of a Texas thunderstorm thick and threatening in the air. It is an hour later and Sandra Post has pulled a loose white V-neck over her pants, pushed a white cotton porkpie hat low over her eyes and there is a squat, more solid cast to her frame as she lines up in a row beside the others, eyeing the distant yardage markers that loom like white carny shooting-gallery flags out in the field. Since she began her comeback she has not let a day go by without practising.

To watch her now, all sombre concentration, in-turned and grim, you can see the solemn fascination that moulded the short sharp backswing, the quick hard down-drive, the perfect twisting arc as the driver head shocks the ball with a splitting crack and lifts it high and gentle out to the 200-yard mark. Her tour caddy, Chuck, an emaciated looking wisp with a worn face like a tragic mask, stands by handing her clubs with unspoken understanding, but it is not to him that she talks but to the scarlet driver grasped in her scarlet golf glove. "Come on, Big Red," she says. She is lost in the ritual of years of that same motion, hours of standing in one spot knocking them out, a life measured out in buckets of practice balls. In a way it is the only life she has ever known.

A skinny little kid whose fruit farmer father had never quite accustomed himself to the fact that he hadn't had a son, she was dragged off one day on their yearly Florida winter vacation to watch the South Atlantic Ladies Open in Miami with him. "And I was captivated, just captivated," she says. "I went right back home and told them all that I was gonna be a lady golfer." She was five years old.

Not that Cliff Post was a man to take a five-year-old's fantasies lightly. The next year back in Florida she turned up in the LPGA gallery with her own little cut-down club. She took to the rhythm of standing there swinging at the tiny white pocked ball for hours as if she were born to it. She putted as if mesmerized. Years later one of the players she followed, Marilynn Smith, a gentle neatly hair-sprayed lady who is still on the tour today, remembers "this wee little thing, so determined" and the letters penned in a painful childish scribble charting her playing course: at nine, winning her first tournament; shooting in the low 70s by the time she was 13; at 14, in the Ontario Junior scoring a 71.

School, friends, nothing came before golf. "In the summer everybody'd go up north to their cottages or swimming," she says, walking the course now in a practice round. "But I'd hit golf balls all day. My mother'd drop me off at 7 a.m. and I'd come home after dark." Then she would go to the driving range with her father and knock them out again under the eerie neon floodlights' glow. Until the day she turned pro, he was the only coach she'd ever known, a man sometimes regarded as the stage father of the 18-hole set, and there are those who've seen them fighting tooth and club on a fairway over how to play the ball. But he remains probably her closest friend. She still plays with him almost every afternoon when she's home at her Boynton Beach, Fla., condominium and he's down at his winter vacation spot nearby, calls twice a week and after every tournament, and the first thing she did when she won the Colgate Far East was to phone him at 3 a.m. in Florida. Cliff Post was so emotional he couldn't say a word.

"My parents did everything in their power to help me become a lady golfer," she says. "Sure, it set me apart. But that was all right, see, 'cause this was what I was gonna do. I was workin' toward somethin' all the time."

Over the years she never once wavered from the dream. It was a steely determination that earned her the reputation of being cocky early. She was constantly at war with the entrenched Canadian women's golf establishment, always shooting off her mouth. In 1964, just weeks before her 16th birthday, they showed what they thought by leaving her off the Ontario junior team—a slap that, she says, "kinda took the sting outta me. Unless you're a real determined little kid, they'll beat you down." But Sandra Post was a real determined little kid. She talked her father into flying her out to Calgary to compete in the Canadian Junior and promptly walked off with it, beating the entire Ontario elect by eight strokes. She won it the next two years, too. "My biggest sin was they thought I thought I was too good," she says, still resentful. "But I was 15. All I wanted to do was play golf."

Three years later when she turned pro, the veterans marvelled at that same gritty fight. She never once flinched from nerves all through the wearing extra-day playoff with Whitworth; at the end there was no tear of relief in her eye. But afterward sports-writers would make the pilgrimage to the circuit for magazine stories on Sandra Post and come back quietly caustic. "The worst part of my game?" she would crow into their tape recorders. "There really isn't one." She expressed boredom with the circuit, said it was a tough life, no life for a girl, and after all, as she saw it, "I proved to everybody I could do it. I won, not just anything, but a major title; I was rookie of the year; made a lot of money. How many men make $25,000 a year?"

Even today, diplomacy and tact are not among Sandra Post's strong points. At lunch that day I watch her get up in the middle of another player's emotional anecdote about her child-hood, announcing blithely, "Well, I gotta go practise now." But as she says in her brisk adopted Florida twang, "I think I've grown up a lot. When I was waitin' for my [divorce] decree, I got thinkin'. I realized that I could do better than I'd already done. That was just a scratch on the surface. So I came back. What alternative did I have? It's the only thing I know. It's my life. It's in my blood."

The LPGA tour is a tough life. It is a heady, harried wash 'n' wear grind, a tight 100-woman travelling road show where one day's winner may be the next day's loser and there's no time in between for introspection; but it's back into the next plane or rent-a-car for the next motel room on the edge of the next town you never get to see. It is a capsuled unreal existence played out in a searing public spotlight where each flick of the wrist can be seen under the scoreboard's relentless scrutiny, where an unseemly swear word or betrayal of unladylike fury can cost a $50 fine and a girl's only friends are her opponents. It is a life of such fishbowl vulnerability that those on the tour always refer to it as Out Here.

Out Here there is a camaraderie that betrays the loneliness of the long-distance golfer. Out Here, where once she didn't mix much. Sandra Post now visits with a vengeance, running between clumps of girls for quick, bright non-conversations, playing cards late into the night and talking about it like some school-age sorority girl. Now that she has chosen this life, she clings to it tenaciously. Friendships are staked out with a fierceness, cliques formed—and rivalries. Out Here where the prize money has more than doubled to $1.8 million since she started out seven years ago and a player's worth is measured as much in her press clippings as in her pars, there is a wary eye out for the newcomers such as lithe, shapely 20-year-old Laura Baugh whose colour-coordinated miniskirts and vital statistics are paraded all over the sports pages above her scores. The rest of the mainstream may be struggling for a sense of womanhood based on something other than curls and curves, but in ladies golf the lookers are promoted and envied, a lure for the galleries and the take at the tournament gate. "Oh, we're not libbers," says Sandra Post, slightly defensive. "We're not into women's lib at all. I'm not even sure what it's about."

It is late the next night after a lacklustre, sodden pro-am tournament and back in the Ramada Inn coffeeshop around a corner booth, the talk turns to what colour of blond to bleach to, who's pregnant and whose boyfriend is flying in for the weekend, who has managed to mix marriage and golf. Over a slice of lemon pie, Sandra Post suddenly grows uncharacteristically silent. The bounce of earlier that evening, when she'd rocked along the expressway in her rented Chevy with the Top 40 blaring on the car radio, is gone now. It isn't until the following morning, when she lies back on the bed in her motel room waiting out frigid temperatures and the announcement that the tournament would be cancelled, that the story comes spilling out: the disastrous two-year marriage to a good-looking Florida golf pro named John Elliott two years after she turned pro and a month after he got sent home from army service in Vietnam:

her virtual three-year disappearance from golf. She still winces at the memory.

"It was awful," she says. "I was havin' a terrible inner struggle mixin' a married life with golf. When I was out playin', I felt I should be home, and when I was home, I felt I should be out playin'. I got so I didn't hardly play at all. I was shooting bad. I lost my confidence. I'd just completely lost my will for golf."

In the three seasons of her marriage, she played only 39 events for a total of $12,000—less than half of what she'd made in her first year as a pro. She was constantly abandoning the LPGA circuit to fly off to his side. But the fairy tale wedding of two kids who would swing down the fairways of life together was already running into the rough. John Elliott was always better known as Sandra Post's husband and there was no secret he resented it. "A lot of times John would be playing against Sandra's reputation more than against the other golfers," says a friend who played with him. When he failed to qualify for the PGA in the States and came up to join the Canadian summer circuit, he ended up in a series of tantrums with officials, ripping up his scorecard, screaming over rulings, once during the Canadian Open even chalking up a two-week suspension after a verbal set-to. It all blew up one day in Vancouver when she found herself hastily invited to leave his room—and his life. "He just said, 'Out,'" she recalls quietly. "Let's put it this way, he had to get rid of me real fast 'cause *she* was comin' in. See, you can only fight the girlfriends so long. I couldn't believe this was happening to me."

In hysterics she called a 32-year-old wealthy Bostonian law-graduate-turned-entrepreneur named Leigh Kandar who'd known them both. He put her on the next plane for Boston, saw her through the next harrowing six months and the two years since, both as business agent and the current love of her life. "I was such a mess," she says. "I went down to 112 pounds.

I got real sick—oh God, was I sick. I was hemorrhagin' for eight days and they didn't know what it was. I had to go into the hospital. And comin' up out of the anesthetic, there's John beggin' to be taken back."

Leigh Kandar keeps a protective cordon around her now, invests her money, okays all interviews with a rhetorical flourish that would make Richard Nixon's former press secretary Ron Ziegler sound like a master of straightforward English. "I have spoken to Sandra about the matter to which you alluded pertaining to an interview," he had told a reporter over the phone a week earlier. "Sandra would be delighted to serve you in the capacity of interviewee, per se." He doesn't play golf— "doesn't know one end of a golf club from another," she says. But at the time it could hardly have been less of a problem. For six months Sandra Post just lay around her Florida apartment, listless, confused, never picking up a golf club.

"Then one day they called me to come play the Colgate Pro-Am in Miami," she says. "So I drove down, took a look at the prize money and I saw golf was gettin' to be a better place for a woman to make a livin'. I finished 10th and that night I couldn't sleep. I got in the car and drove home at 3 a.m." She drove straight to Leigh Kandar's Florida apartment and when she couldn't get in, she started hammering on the door. "Leigh, Leigh," she hollered. "I just had to tell you this. I'm going back into golf.

"I just felt so good," she says.

She was out practising the very next day. In her first tournament back she made $600—$20,000 by the end of that year. It has been uphill ever since, even if there have been hazards along the way. She spent the first six months back having to watch John Elliott hold hands with Marlene Hagge, the tour's 41-year-old well-preserved bombshell. "Maybe it was part spite," she says. "But it lasted six months and I was playin' every day in front of them, in front of everybody. I did all right Out

There in the day, but boy, you shoulda seen me at night. I was a mess. I don't know how I got through that time." Ironically, she and Marlene Hagge are now inseparable. And Sandra Post looks back on it all as "a good experience. It's made me what I am and I'm glad I went through it. I'm a much happier person now. And all that—it seems like another life."

She lies back on the bed, estimating that she'll stay Out Here another five years but after that, whether the future holds the marriage and kids she once said she wanted more than anything else, more than golf itself . . . she is silent. "I don't know," she says, staring out the window, thoughtful. "My life now is right here. To do the best I can. I'm still very determined to win. And I can't be thinkin' of other things five years from now. I have to take one day at a time."

Suddenly, it seems only natural to ask Sandra Post what changed her mind that life Out Here wasn't the life for a girl. She pauses for a moment and then she smiles. "Maybe it isn't for a girl," she says. "Maybe it's for a woman."

Sandra Post failed to win that year, but she came second in the U.S. Women's Open and finished 10th in earnings with $34,852. She remains the best female golfer in Canadian history, retiring from the main circuit in 1984 with nearly $1 million in career winnings and eight tournament victories. She did not marry Leigh Kandar but did wed former Brian Mulroney cabinet minister and custom golf club maker John McDermid in 1992. They live in Caledon, Ont., and she splits her time between teaching golf and working as a broadcast commentator.

Marci McDonald wrote for Maclean's from 1974 to 1997, working in Paris; Washington, D.C.; and Toronto. She left the magazine to become a senior writer at U.S. News & World Report in Washington, but now lives in Toronto.

The Making of a Master: Mike Weir

—April 9, 2001—
James Deacon

T HE TWIN-ENGINE CESSNA CITATION II had barely lifted off when the wind started tossing it around. Departing from a private field near Jacksonville, Fla., the eight-seat private jet was broadsided by a thumping gust that knocked the plane sideways for an alarming second or two. The turbulence continued as the aircraft climbed high over the Atlantic shore and turned northwest, then subsided a little when the plane reached its cruising altitude above 30,000 feet. But it turned mean again on the descent into Lawrenceville, Ga., the nearest airfield to the BellSouth Classic golf tournament site. The man

Watching his tee shot in San Diego, Feb. 10, 2001

who had chartered the jet was visibly relieved once it touched down. "I don't know about you," said Mike Weir to the only other passenger onboard, "but that did something to my stomach."

Which raises the inevitable question: what the heck is Mike Weir doing flying around in chartered jets? Weirsy, as his pals on the PGA Tour call him, grew up in Brights Grove, Ont., near Sarnia playing hockey in winter and golf on the dry, hardpan fairways of Huron Oaks in summer, and he might happily have opted to pursue a career at the nearby chemical company where his dad worked. Instead, Weir spent a half-dozen years grinding it out on the world's fringe tours and had to play the PGA Tour qualifying tournament just 2 1/2 years ago. Which means it wasn't very long ago that he was playing for hundreds instead of millions.

But aside from last week's stomach-turning flight, there haven't been many bumps on Weir's career path lately. Since earning his PGA Tour card for good in November 1998, he has vaulted into the top ranks of international golf, winning trophies, widespread acclaim and riches beyond anything he imagined even a couple of years ago. That hardly makes him the favourite going into the Masters this week: superstar Tiger Woods, coming off victories in his last two starts, is the man to beat at golf's first "major" in 2001. Still, British oddsmakers tout Weir among the next tier of challengers, and for Canadian golf fans, having one of their own given a reasonable shot at the Augusta National is a rare thrill. The country hasn't had a serious contender for the Masters title and its coveted green jacket since the late George Knudsen finished second in 1969.

Though new to golf's main stage, Weir, 30, has prepared himself well for a star turn. In 1999, he challenged Woods at the gruelling PGA Championship in Chicago, won his first Tour event in Vancouver at the Air Canada Championship, and finished in the top 30 money winners. He improved in 2000, and after winning a spot on the international team at last October's prestigious President's Cup, was the surprise of the event. The internationals lost to the host Americans, but Weir had perhaps the best week of any player on either team, drawing raves from veteran TV announcer Johnny Miller. "He's a star on the rise," Miller said at the time, adding: "He has a good attitude, he's a smart guy and he's played like crazy this week." The craziness continued into early November, when Weir won the season-ending American Express Championship in Sotogrande, Spain.

The victory was worth $1 million (U.S.) to Weir, and boosted his earnings for the season to $2,547,829 (U.S.), sixth-best on Tour. And that doesn't even begin to include endorsement income. A fat wallet allows him the luxury of hiring jets, which gets him home faster to his wife, Bricia, and his daughters, Elle, three, and Lily, nearly one, in Draper, just south of Salt Lake City. "By buying some time on private planes, I get more time with my family," Weir says. "And it makes it a lot easier when my family is travelling with me. You're not dragging kids and suitcases and stuff through airports."

The most valuable professional benefit from last fall's stellar play was the enormous boost to his confidence that Weir got from breaking into the upper echelons of the game. It was one thing to challenge the best, another to actually beat them. At the President's Cup, he went from little-known outsider to key player on a team that included such big names as Ernie Els, Greg Norman and Vijay Singh. At Valderrama, the course in Spain, Weir was sensational in the final two rounds, overcoming an eight-shot deficit to defeat a field that included Woods, Nick Price and other illustrious names. His drives were laser-like in accuracy on the tight, cork tree–lined fairways and he putted brilliantly. Now, he gets a different reaction on Tour.

"You have arrived," he explains, "when the top players know that when they tee it up on Thursday, you're going to be a factor. In my first couple of years on Tour, that wasn't there."

It's difficult for people watching on TV to imagine Weir with the killer instinct necessary to contend, and win, the big events. He appears so mild-mannered, and in interviews he is polite and soft-spoken. It's not an act. "He is the nicest guy," says longtime Canadian Tour executive Dick Grimm. "But inside, he's got the burn in his gut." Grimm was in Augusta to watch Knudsen in 1969 and was commissioner of the Canadian Tour when Weir won the order of merit as top money winner in 1997. And while the swings are different, not the least because Weir is a lefty, there's a similarity in character. "I remember watching George come off the practice tee in '69, and he had his hands wrapped in handkerchiefs," Grimm recalls. "He was hitting balls even when his hands were bleeding. I think Mike is cut from the same cloth, and guys like that don't come along very often."

Last week in Ponte Vedra Beach, Fla., offered a perfect example. Weir stayed behind a day after his final round at the Players Championship to work on the back range at the Tournament Players Club. He had not played well at the TPC, so he hit hundreds of balls, placing a huge mirror behind him so that he could stop and examine his position at different points in his swing. He was there for hours, all alone except for an osprey swooping overhead, looking for lunch in an adjacent lagoon. It looked like a lot of work, but he just shrugs. "I'm lucky," he says. "I like to practise."

He is a great believer in planning. "I set up a game plan for each golf course and stick to it," he says. "When I stick to it, it keeps me in a good rhythm. When I don't, I don't do well." At Augusta, he says, "You have to have patience, know which pins to go for, and you have to be prepared for the unexpected." He will have plenty of on-course support. His parents and older brothers plan to be there, and Bricia will finally get to see him play the Masters: last year, she had just given birth to Lily and didn't attend.

That reminds him of an interviewer's previous question. "You asked what I liked most about my success," he says. "Well, for me, the best thing is that I have been able to do some things for my family." For one thing, he took his dad and brothers to the British Open last year: "We stayed at a house there together, we went out to dinner every night, and it was a fantastic experience. I would never have been able to do that before." Otherwise, he is a cautious consumer. "We have a little bit bigger house with a little bit bigger yard, but that's about it," he says. "I have come from struggling for five or six years on smaller tours, so I'm smart with my money, and I'm not going to go and blow it all."

Weir is aware his image differs from his reality. "It's funny, but when I played hockey, I played a tough role," he says on the flight to Georgia. "I was small, but I loved to hit, loved that aspect of the game." In golf, though, size—he's five-foot, nine-inches, 155 lb.—doesn't matter as much as patience and an even temper, and over the years he has learned to control his emotions on the course. And in the last few years, he's been easing off a little on his intense practice regimen. He used to keep working on his game even when he went home, putting constantly on the carpet. "Once you start having kids, that changes fast," he says. "So now, I leave it at the course."

Besides, practice only takes a guy so far. Golf is a head game, especially when everything is on the line. Former PGA champion Davis Love III once described the pressure of contending in major championships as feeling like, at any minute, he was going to throw up on his shoes. Thanks to a steely resolve, Weir has kept his Foot-Joys dry. "Maybe it's because I grew up trying to keep up with two older brothers, but as a kid, I was trying to beat the scores of the older guys," he says. "And I always felt like I had something to prove for some reason." Now? "I don't feel like I have to prove anything to anybody except myself. I have gotten my game to the point where I can play with the best in the world. Now all I want to do is prove to myself that I can win a major. For me, that's exciting." For a lot of other people, too.

Mike Weir failed to come close to winning the Masters that year or in 2002. But in 2003, Weir won the green jacket in a sudden-death playoff, becoming the first Canadian to win a major tournament.

N THE RING

The Greatest Fighter Who Ever Lived

—February 15, 1955—
Trent Frayne

U PSTAIRS IN A VENERABLE BOARDINGHOUSE in an ancient section of Boston a blind old Negro sits all day rocking backward and forward in a creaking wooden chair. His sightless eyes are masked by a pair of cheap plastic-rimmed spectacles, long since scratched and smudged by age. His greying bullet head is covered by a faded maroon baseball cap and his lean aging body swaddled in a nondescript bathrobe. He is a man with many ailments, few hopes and only one amusement: On Wednesday nights, when the fights come on the little mantel radio, as they do on radios all over the continent, his head cocks and his face lights up as he lives once again in a golden past.

For this is Sam Langford, a living legend from Weymouth, N.S., and perhaps the greatest fighter of his size who ever lived.

Hype Igoe, the most renowned of all boxing writers, made no bones about it in the old New York *Journal*. "Langford is the greatest fighter, pound for pound, who ever lived," he wrote. Just this year, Joe Williams, the respected sports columnist of the New York *World-Telegram*, echoed Igoe's words. "Langford was probably the best the ring ever saw," he wrote in his current TV boxing book. The great Grantland Rice described Langford as "about the best fighting man I've ever watched."

Langford's old manager, Joe Woodman, put it a little more colourfully last month. "At 72,'" he said, meaning 172 pounds, "he'd have eaten Joe Louis."

Langford was a small man—five-feet, six-inches—who took on opponents as much as 10 inches taller and 60 pounds heavier than himself because he couldn't get enough fights with men his own size to keep him busy. He was so good that he could actually name the moment he'd knock out an opponent. One night in 1910 he was fighting a pug named Dewey, who weighed 205 and stood six feet two. The bout was in Cheyenne, Wyo., a section where trains came and went irregularly. His manager was anxious to get back quickly to Los Angeles. When he consulted timetables he discovered that the only train that day left half an hour after the fight was to start.

"Why, I'm surprised you're worrying," Langford said. "That gives us lots of time." Whereupon he knocked out Dewey in one minute and 42 seconds of the first round.

He was so good that he once knocked an opponent smack into the lap of an unfriendly writer. In San Francisco in 1908, when he weighed about 155 pounds, he fought a 210-pound bruiser named Fireman Jim Flynn who was six feet one. In the first round Langford jostled Flynn toward the ropes above the ringside seat of a west-coast sportswriter named H. M. Walker. Walker had written that Flynn ought to stop mixing with "clowns like Langford" if he wanted to prove he was a genuine threat for Jack Johnson's heavyweight crown.

"Mr. Walker," grinned Sam, "here comes your champion." And he knocked Flynn into the writer's lap.

Langford fought in an era when Negroes were in a highly anomalous position as fighters. Jack Johnson, a Negro, was the champion. And largely because of this there was a national wave of sentiment against Johnson in particular and Negroes generally. "Somebody has got to beat him," people said, and managers strove to find a "white hope" who could.

The "white hope" industry was launched in 1908 right after Johnson followed Tommy Burns to Australia and beat him to a pulp in 14 rounds in Sydney to win the world's championship. Johnson thus became the first man to cross the "colour line" established by John L. Sullivan, the first American heavyweight champion of the world, who had refused to meet Peter Jackson, an outstanding Australian Negro. For years the colour line was invoked by each succeeding champion. But Johnson refused to keep what most whites regarded as "his place." As champion he was once compelled to flee to Paris after being charged with violation of the Mann Act—he was accused of transporting a white girl, Lucille Cameron, whom he later married, across a state line for immoral purposes. In Paris he bet lavish sums on race horses, wore a beret and sipped champagne through a straw, habits that swelled the sentiment against his race.

In this turbulent atmosphere, not all white hopes were worthy challengers; rather, many were products of skilful manipulation by their managers and the worked-up fervour of prejudiced fans. White hopes were usually too wary, or their handlers too discreet, to risk their reputations against Negroes of Langford's talents. Woodman told me recently that Sam "almost always" had to "do business" to get a fight with a white man. In other words, white fighters exacted promises that Langford would carry them so far.

To get fights and to keep eating, Langford had a long series of bouts with Harry Wills, Sam McVey and Joe Jeannette, who, with the champion Johnson, were the best prize fighters in the world. During the time Johnson was champion, from 1908 until 1915, the other four tried constantly to track him down, but Johnson avoided them. "On a good night Sam is just liable to beat me or make it close," the champion said when a match with Langford was proposed in Paris in 1914, "and what's the sense of that for the kind of money we'd draw?"

They did meet, once—but that was before Johnson was champion. When Langford weighed 151 pounds in 1906 he fought 15 brutal rounds with Johnson in Boston. Although Johnson, who weighed 186, won the fight, he resolutely refused to meet Langford again. Two years after he became champion, he was cornered by Langford and Joe Woodman in the sports department of the Boston *Globe*, and offered $10,000 if he'd agree to a return bout. He did, but when the two fighters were to meet at 10 o'clock the next morning to sign papers for the fight, Johnson didn't show up. The bout naturally died.

In his fights, Langford invariably got the worst of physical odds. He fought 15 times with the brawling Harry Wills, who outweighed him by almost 50 pounds and was seven inches taller—they were unbelievably violent clashes. Wills, who chased the heavyweight champion Jack Dempsey for a fight in the early Twenties and was bypassed in favour of Gene Tunney, who won the championship in 1926, once knocked Langford down nine times in the first four rounds of a bout in New Orleans in 1916, and then was knocked out by Langford in the

19th round. When Langford was crowding 40 in 1920 he twice knocked out a Negro named George Godfrey, who stood six feet three and weighed 240 pounds.

The phrase, pound for pound, fits naturally into any comparisons with Langford because he was so much smaller than such heavyweight champions as Johnson, Jess Willard, Dempsey and Joe Louis. He had exceptionally long arms, heavy shoulders and a deep thick torso. He started fighting as a youngster in the lightweight division at 132 pounds and when he added weight, almost all of it was in his upper body. He outgrew the lightweight, welterweight (147) and middleweight (160) divisions. Most experts agree his best fighting weight was at 172.

Under his barrel build and with his long strong arms, Langford's short legs gave him a curiously gnomelike appearance. Then, as now, he had a broad flat nose, a cauliflower left ear, thick heavy lips and crisp short curly hair that fitted the broad contours of his head so tightly it looked almost like a skullcap. In the ring, as one San Francisco writer put it, he resembled "a man from the Dark Ages."

Built along the general lines of a gorilla, he would come loping out of his corner, his face impassive, his black skin glinting. He fought in a crouch that made him a difficult target for taller opponents and he usually offset their superior height by working his way inside their defence, pounding solidly to the body and then hooking to the jaw. His judgment of distance was uncanny. One old-time boxing writer in Boston, William A. Hamilton, recently described this talent of Langford's: "He would glide out in a crouch and when his opponent led he'd move just a fraction and let the blow graze his head," Hamilton recalled. "He could hit like a terror with both hands."

Langford was never able to get a fight for a world's championship in any division. Johnson refused to meet him and so did Georges Carpentier when he was the light-heavyweight

champion. When Stanley Ketchell was middleweight champion, his manager, the astute Willus Britt, refused repeated
offers to meet Langford in California, but finally consented to a
no-decision, six-round bout in Philadelphia on April 27, 1910.

Langford had instructions from Woodman to go easy, the
theory being that Ketchell might then consent to a championship bout. Newspaper reports relate that "they gave a pretty
boxing exhibition, with Langford having something of a shade
on points in the first three rounds. After that, Langford
contented himself with blocking Ketchell's punches, without
making any attempt to fight back." Woodman's plan for a
return match faded forever six months later when Ketchell was
shot and killed.

Langford got $300 for fighting Ketchell. Throughout his 21
years in the ring his purses were small. Although one of the greatest ringmen of his time, he never drew more than $10,000 for a
fight and reached that level only once—in London in 1909 when
he knocked out Ian Hague, the English heavyweight champion,
in four rounds. If he wasn't highly paid, Langford was at least
highly regarded in Boston, home of the abolitionists, where a
Negro could rise above the crowd. Sam spent his money on fancy
clothes and feted his friends at the bars. He took a drink himself
and once, before embarking for England, nearly missed the boat
as he said his raucous farewells to well-wishers who danced to
the pier as the gangplank was going up.

In one of his infrequent returns to Canada he was greeted in
Weymouth, N.S., as the hometown boy who made good. In the
province that has the highest proportion of Negroes in Canada
but doesn't always treat them too well, everybody turned out to
greet him and they carried him down the street on their shoulders. At Cape Breton he was acclaimed by miners who came up
from the pits to cheer the Nova Scotian who'd built a world
reputation in the ring.

When Sam was nearing the end of his long career, he made his only appearance in Toronto, where he met Young Peter Jackson on Oct. 18, 1921. The *Toronto Star* story of the fight, in which Langford knocked out Jackson in the second round, appeared under the byline of Lou E. Marsh.

A pickaninny has as much chance in a rassling match with a gorilla as Young Peter Jackson had with Sam Langford . . . They say Langford trained on pork chops. Well! If he did he done gobbled up Mistah Y. P. Jackson in two bites like any other pork chop.

Langford was reportedly in his 40s when he won that fight but as is the case with Jersey Joe Walcott, former heavyweight champion, and Satchel Paige, a venerable baseball pitcher, his age has always been a source of speculation. Some record books note his birth year as 1880 and others make it 1886. He once explained that his father just chopped a notch in a tree when a child was born, and that way kept track of the youngsters if not their birth dates.

On other counts, however, his memory appears excellent, and he can sit by the hour in his dim upstairs room in Boston recounting the past, a smile on his broad flat features, his head tilted back, an occasional slit of the white of his right eye showing briefly through smudged glasses. He is totally blind, but cheerful. His white teeth flash as he throws back his head and laughs, and one gold tooth gleams brightly among them.

He left home around the age of 12 for work in Boston, and after getting in a fight when he was 15 or 16, a mentor encouraged him to get into boxing. "Mike Foley got me some battered old tights and a pair of gloves and in my first fight, there's me and a Scotch fellah. I knock him out and I get a watch that I can hock for $30. I fight a couple more times and then one day

Mike says, 'Sam, do you know a fellah named Joe Woodman?' I say no and Mike says this fellah's a druggist who's interested in fighters and he wants to see me. So I go, and Woodman says, 'You got no business fightin' amateurs. I know where you can get some money.' That's all I wanted to hear. I became a pro and Woodman became my manager."

The record book shows that the year was 1902, when Sam was probably somewhere between 16 and 20. He had four fights, all in Boston, and won them all in six rounds or less. He had 26 fights the next year and lost only one.

On April 26, 1906, Langford met the man he was to pursue for the next 10 years in a fruitless search for the world's heavyweight championship, Jack Johnson. Langford was barely more than a heavy welterweight at 151 pounds and Johnson was a tough established heavyweight, 35 pounds heavier and on his way to the world's championship.

In nearly 50 years since that fight, which Johnson won on a 15-round decision, the story has grown that Langford gave Johnson such a handful that Johnson was afraid to meet him again. But the files of the *Police Gazette*, a sort of boxing bible, relate that "Johnson gave Langford a terrible beating and was awarded the decision."

Sam was so upset by the defeat that in his next bout two weeks later he lost a decision to Young Peter Jackson. The same year in Rochester he knocked out Jackson in five rounds.

In 1908 Langford became a Pacific Coast favourite when he knocked out Jim Barry and Jim Flynn in Los Angeles and San Francisco, respectively. His attack on Flynn was unbelievably ferocious. He broke Flynn's nose in the second round and broke his jaw in the third. When he put him away with a right uppercut, Flynn was unconscious for more than 20 minutes.

Fight promoter Hugh McIntosh then took Sam and the American Negro, Sam McVey, to Australia. Eighteen thousand people saw their first fight in the broiling sun of Sydney on Boxing Day, 1911. McVey won a 20-round decision that was roundly hooted. They were rematched in the same city four months later. Langford won in 20 rounds, and then repeated with another 20-round decision in Sydney on Aug. 3. In Perth on Oct. 10 in a violent brawl, Langford knocked out McVey in 11 rounds, and then, a year to the day after their first meeting in Sydney, Langford knocked him out again, this time in 13 rounds.

The next three years, in the opinion of his manager Woodman and ring historian Nat Fleischer, were the best of Langford's long career. Fighting everywhere from New York to Paris to Denver to Buenos Aires he fought 30 times and lost only two decisions, one to Joe Jeannette and one to Harry Wills.

In the midst of his running battle with Wills, Langford reached the turning point in his career. On June 19, 1917, when he was in his early 30s, he went to Boston for a match with Fred Fulton, a towering 215-pound Kansan. Langford was out of shape—a puffy 181 pounds—and for six rounds he took a dreadful beating that eventually cost him the sight in his left eye. In the sixth he was knocked down for the third time with a left hook to the jaw. Sam climbed to his feet dazed and help-less as Fulton swarmed on him. Fulton drove both hands to Langford's eyes, nose, jaw and stomach and Langford simply rolled along the ropes.

He weathered the round and as he stumbled drunkenly to his corner, his left eye was tightly closed. As the bell sounded for the start of the seventh round, Sam did not rise from his stool. He sat there, tears slowly trickling down his cheeks as he signalled the referee, Matt Hinkel, that he could not continue. He never regained the sight in his left eye. "Sam should have quit fighting then," Woodman, a voluble spry man who still handles fighters, told me recently at Stillman's Gym in New York. "I told him to quit while he still had his senses and one good eye."

"'Are you telling me you're through with me?' Sam said, and I said, 'I'm telling you, you should quit.' But he wouldn't quit. We parted, but he went on fighting for another six years."

Langford had nine more fights with Harry Wills and, incredibly, after being knocked out twice by Wills in Panama in 1918, he won a 15-round decision from him in Tulsa in 1919.

Sam continued to fight until late in 1923, when he was in his 40s. He had three fights in Mexico City, then quit. He stayed in Mexico "six or seven years and then I got sick and tired of it." In San Antonio, Tex., one night he watched a fight card.

"Both my eyes were bad then but I could see a little bit," he recalls. "I knew I could lick the whole bunch put together."

He asked a promoter for a fight. The promoter agreed. The old fighter doesn't remember the name of his opponent but he remembers thinking "they're not teachin' boys to fight these days."

"When we got in there," Sam recalls, "he started swingin' that left hand and I blocked it and he swang again and I blocked it. An' then I knocked him out."

Sam adds that punch line with a grin. He grins a good deal these days, skipping lightly over the hardship he suffered after his last fight, the exhibition in San Antonio around 1929. Ten years ago a New York boxing writer, Al Laney, writing a series about old fighters, went searching for Langford in Harlem. He found him after two weeks "in a dingy hall bedroom on 139th Street down a corridor so dark you had to feel your way." Sam by then was totally blind as well as broke.

Laney's story marked the beginning of a fund that enabled Langford to return to Boston where he lived with his sister until a year ago. Boston writers raised a few thousand dollars in a benefit boxing card. But the funds were just about dissipated when Sam's sister died a year ago.

Then Mrs. Grace Wilkins, a widow who runs a somewhat forlorn rest home in Boston, agreed to look after Sam. Ordinarily, she charges $35 a week to look after old people but there is nothing like that in what remains of Sam's funds. The money, she says, arrives sporadically, an occasional cheque for $49.18 from the New York fund and an infrequent $60 from Boston.

"Mr. Langford uses just about that much in coffee and tobacco and doughnuts," she smiled recently.

Sam is an amiable guest in the dim room on the second floor of the 15-room house at 136 Townsend Street—a big old house from which the paint is peeling and the shutters are hanging at odd angles. But he spends many of his dark hours worrying about money. Mrs. Wilkins, who sometimes buys him pyjamas, underwear and tobacco, says he often expresses deep concern that he is too much of a burden.

"I asked him one time," Mrs. Wilkins says, "I asked him, 'Mr. Langford, what would you like to do now if you could do anything in the world you wanted?' And he replied, 'Missus, I've been everywhere I wanted to go, I've seen everything I wanted to see, and I guess I've eaten just about everything there is to eat. Now I just want to sit here in my room and not cause you any trouble.'"

Sam Langford died on January 12, 1956. Sixteen years later, Weymouth Falls erected a plaque to his memory, calling him "The Boston Terror," the politically correct version of his earlier nickname, "The Boston Tar Baby."

Anatomy of a Championship: How Chuvalo Won by Losing

—May 14, 1966—
John Robertson

M ITCHELL CHUVALO is only six years old and is far too young to be reading the sports pages, or to understand why anyone would call his daddy a punching bag—and an unworthy one at that—before he fought Cassius Clay.

But Mitch was there that night in Maple Leaf Gardens, and he saw those devastating punches welt and disfigure his father's face and make the blood run in twin rivulets from his matted hair. Perhaps it was cruel to expose Mitch to this, but I watched him squirm excitedly in his seat during the last round, and I

Catching his breath in between rounds in the Clay fight

heard him implore the referee to get out of the way, during one clinch, so his dad could sock this guy Clay a good one.

After the final bell, while thousands of grown men stood and applauded the unbelievable, almost-incredible courage of his father, Mitch tugged his mother's hand toward the corner of the ring where the trainers and seconds were ministering to the man he was so proud of, even in defeat.

A friendly hand hoisted him up onto the ring apron, outside the ropes. George saw him and bent his head over the top rope so Mitch could reach up and grip both sides of the towel that encircled his sweaty, bewhiskered face. And there, in front of almost 14,000 people, they embraced, man to man.

Pride gushed from the boy's eyes, and for the first time that night, George Chuvalo gave way to his own emotions and blinked back tears.

Flanked by his manager, Irving Ungerman, and his trainer, Theo McWhorter, the man almost everyone had branded an unfit challenger ducked through the ropes and tottered wearily down the steps, into the beckoning arms of his pretty, redheaded wife, Lynne. His mother, who had refused to even look at the ring for most of the evening, so she wouldn't have to see as well as hear those punches crunch against the face and body of her son, reached past Lynne and caressed the back of George's head with a hand that trembled more with relief than pride.

Referee Jack Silvers and the two judges had unanimously declared Clay (alias Muhammad Ali) the winner, and quite justly so. But to Mitchell, Lynne, Mrs. Chuvalo and thousands of others there that night, there was no loser. Even the men along press row who had been nonbelievers until George had battled and bled for 15 rounds to win them over, flung down their pencils and cheered him at the end.

As I jostled my way to the press interview room through the throng that was still surging toward ringside, other reporters closed ranks in front and behind me and discussed the fight. "The man's not human," one said of Chuvalo. "Clay must have hit him 500 times. He never even flinched." A British voice said, "It was like watching a chap banging on a pub door at closing time. But Chuvalo took it all, and he might just have saved boxing in the process."

This was a crow-eating time for the 360 boxing reporters, most of whom had travelled with mixed feelings to Toronto to cover what many of them considered the biggest championship farce in the lurid history of heavyweight boxing.

Chuvalo had lost three of his last four major fights. His only impressive credential was that although he'd lost 11 of his 47 bouts, he'd never been knocked down. But this said more for his courage and stamina than for his ability.

Clay's image in the United States had deteriorated to the point where he had been forced by public opinion to take his title out of the country to defend it. It was bad enough, all along, to be associated with the Black Muslims, but he had really capped everything with his now-famous crack about his draft status: "I ain't got no quarrel with them Viet Congs."

At the same time, no one questioned Clay's fighting ability. He had knocked out 18 opponents in 22 pro fights and had humiliated two former world champions, Floyd Patterson and Sonny Liston.

So the fight shaped up as a fourth-rate affair, pitting a champion considered too unpopular to fight in his own country against a challenger who had been labelled an unworthy opponent by almost everybody. Sam Leitch of the London *Daily Mirror*, a leading British sports authority, took a cue from his editor and demanded a world boycott of the bout. Leitch's story was headlined: "THE BOSS IS RIGHT . . . I HAVE CANCELED MY TRIP." Typical of United States press reaction was the barb tossed by columnist Arthur Daley of the *New York Times*. He told his readers: "They are charging $100 ringside here for a fight that isn't worth 30 cents." And sports editor Milt Dunnell of the *Toronto Star* had phoned his department all the way from Florida and ordered, "Don't even suggest in any of your advance stories that Chuvalo has a chance, because you and I both know he hasn't."

But on fight night, Chuvalo was to punch holes in their pessimism. After a little-league buildup, he turned in a big-league performance. I saw it from second-row ringside. As I looked up through the ropes, 13,900 fans in the Gardens were shrieking with excitement as Chuvalo plodded out of his corner at the opening bell and took six punishing jabs before he landed a solid left hook to Clay's midsection. But then for round after round he kept doggedly carrying the fight to Clay, who stubbornly refused to back off, throwing faster and often more telling punches at the Canadian champion. It seemed inevitable that Chuvalo would go down. But he absorbed the punishment unflinchingly for the full 15 rounds. His face bled and rose in grotesque lumps, but even in the final moments Chuvalo was punching back. By the time the judges awarded the decision to Clay, Chuvalo had already won something Clay had lost long before, if he'd ever had it: the respect of everyone who saw or heard the fight.

Ironically, it was Clay who came closer than anyone to predicting the exact trend of the fight. He had insisted throughout training camp that Chuvalo would probably take him the full 15 rounds and prove to be his toughest opponent ever. But most sportswriters and fans suspected his motives. Tickets had been going badly at the Gardens, and the once-vast network of closed-circuit television outlets in Canada and the United States had dwindled to a handful. All TV rights were controlled by Main Bout Inc., which is dominated by Black Muslim interests. Was Clay just talking to help sell tickets?

My first clue that he was occurred 11 days before the fight while watching him spar at his Toronto Athletic Club training headquarters, a compact but clean little gym located above a body-and-fender shop on Ossington Avenue. In the third round of a scheduled eight-round session with sparring mate Jimmy Ellis, Clay was knocked to the canvas by an innocuous-looking left hook. He rolled over on his back, blinking up at the popping flash bulbs, and then got up and stomped out of the ring, muttering, "Run, run, run away . . . and live to fight another day."

"I got tired," he told me later, in his dressing room. "I got stunned, and decided to quit." Then after he had accepted my offer of a ride back to his motel, I heard him lean over in the car and ask his manager, Angelo Dundee, "Did it look real? Will it help sell tickets? Did the wire services get a picture of it?"

Clay's entourage—three sparring partners, two bodyguards, a valet, a trainer, a masseur, Dundee and two Muslim cooks—were quartered in a motel near the Toronto lakeshore. The moment we got out of the car, Clay charged ahead into the motel dining room. When I caught up with him, he was sitting at a table, consuming a head of lettuce and a quart pitcher of orange juice. "Listen to this poem," he said, thumping his glass on the table. "I'll say it too quick for you to write it down: 'The politician is not my Shepherd . . . I shall not want . . . He leadeth me down the path to publicity . . . He maketh me fight out of my own country . . . I shall fear no newspapermen . . . My Cadillac gas tank runneth over . . .' " I missed a few lines but he would not repeat them. "Politicians are bad enough. I don't want those preachers against me, too."

Five teenaged boys approached the table, introduced themselves to Clay and asked permission to interview him for their high-school paper. "Sit right on down," he said.

Dundee had already warned me not to ask Clay about his tiff with the draft board—it was too touchy for the champ. So I leaned forward expectantly when one high-school kid asked him bluntly, "Would you consider going to Vietnam to box exhibitions?" Dundee nudged me and whispered, "He won't answer."

But Clay said, "Maybe I would . . . for $10,000 a day. If they're spendin' $160 million a day on the war, they can pay me a little $10,000 . . ."

"Gawd," said Dundee.

"I would join the army only if Elijah Muhammad told me to. He knows everything," Clay went on. He pointed out the window. "See that lake out there? Elijah knows why it don't spill over. He knows how much the earth weighs . . . and the moon, too. You don't learn that stuff in school. I'm an Asiatic black man. That was hundreds of years ago, before some plantation owner gave my family this name 'Clay.' I'm Muhammad Ali now. And I'm nobody's slave."

After several more questions, the students filed toward the door, and Clay called after them, "Don't paint me up as no monster now!"

"See," said Dundee. "He has time for everybody."

Clay pranced down the sidewalk toward his motel room, singing to himself, and shadow-boxing. "I gotta dance . . . [jab, jab] . . . to keep from cryin' . . . [jab, jab] . . . I gotta dance . . . [jab, jab] . . . to keep from cryin'."

The next afternoon, old-time movie comedian Stepin Fetchit, decked out in a leopardskin sports coat, was warming up the crowd at the Toronto A.C. the way a second-rate comic will warm up a TV studio audience. It intrigued me, because I had often read about old Step's role as Clay's personal court jester. If you could believe Step's glossy camp brochure, he was much more than that. He had brought Clay the secret of old Negro heavyweight Jack Johnson's famed "anchor punch." That was the one Clay used to knock out Sonny Liston in Lewiston, Maine. Veteran newspapermen claim it's still a secret.

As Step went through his routine, I moved around the ring beside Sam Saxon, a ranking Muslim and Clay's chief bodyguard. Clay was talking about the fight to a number of newspapermen and Saxon was interrupting to get in another Muslim commercial. "Tell them how we have white Muslims too," said Sam. "Tell them about our pure way of life . . ."

Just then Step's voice blared throughout the hall as he milked the punch line of a stale joke about men on the moon sending messages to earth: "Never mind about the dogs and men in funny suits," he cackled. "Send us up some broads."

Sam Saxon, the puritanical Muslim, winced.

The workout was routine stuff, and after it was over, I again drove Clay back to his motel. On the way, I asked him how often he prayed.

"Five times a day," he said. "And I don't smoke, drink, swear or make love to girls. I divorced my wife and paid her $173,000 alimony because she wouldn't cover up her bare knees." A moment later we stopped at a red light and he nudged me. "Hey," he said. "Pull up just a bit." A pole was obstructing his view of two young women waiting at a bus stop. "I gotta go down to that Yonge Street tonight and get me a look at some of those foxes," he said enthusiastically.

"Sure he likes the foxes," said Dundee. "What the hell. The kid's only human like you and me."

The Lansdowne Athletic Club, where George Chuvalo was training, was not in the best of physical condition, as gymnasiums go. On my first visit, their front doorknob came off in my hand. I gave it to the attendant at the top of the stairs. "Not again," he sighed.

I crossed the bare floor, past a sign that said, "Don't Spit in the Water Pails" and found refuge against a stack of empty soft-drink cases. The sparring was already in progress, and George Chuvalo seemed at his bestial best as he plunged his forehead into the breastbone of his spar-mate Hubert Hilton, delivering a vicious uppercut to the Hilton solar plexus.

"That would smart," a bystander remarked. "But aside from it being a low blow, George is still telegraphing his head butts." A roar erupted as Chuvalo floored Hilton with a chopping left.

Later Hilton talked to reporters. "A knockdown?" he exclaimed. "Heck, I just reached for a rope and it wasn't there. I could belt this stiff out anytime I want."

But a much better boxer was soon to try and fail.

Sitting off in a corner, a husky, round-faced Negro was solemnly watching the workout. He was Drew (Bundini) Brown, Clay's former trainer, who had volunteered to help Chuvalo attempt to dethrone his former pupil. I asked him why. He glowered.

"They run me out of their camp because I wouldn't become a Muslim," he said. "That's why they got rid of Clay's wife Sonji, too. Clay should have been boxing's saviour, but he has become its executioner. Those Muslims turn him on and off like a neon sign. He don't know what he believes in. So I'm here to help Chuvalo, to try to save boxing."

♦

The fight had been over for almost 20 minutes, and in the press room at Maple Leaf Gardens the reporters glanced irritably at their watches. They had deadlines to meet, and they were waiting for Chuvalo and Clay to emerge from their dressing rooms.

Chuvalo and his manager, Irving Ungerman, elbowed their way inside. George's nose was bent and swollen. His eyes were bluish slits, and a patch of skin was missing from his forehead. Many of the same men who had publicly labelled him as unworthy of a title shot, now looked sheepishly at him as he moved to the platform.

"Were you ever in trouble?" someone asked, incredulously.

"He never hurt me," said George, through swollen lips. "I'd like another crack at him. I feel I've earned it."

There were more questions. Yes, he thought Clay was the fastest heavyweight he'd ever fought; but, no, he didn't punch as hard as some others he'd fought. When the questions trailed off, Chuvalo excused himself and began moving slowly out of the room. Some of the same men who had called him unworthy before the fight were applauding him now.

Chuvalo paused at the door, then turned back to face them. For the first time, his battered impassive face was forming a grin. "Listen, you guys, you're all invited back to the Prince George Hotel. The party's on us."

A few minutes later Clay came in, flanked by three Muslim friends. He was wearing evening clothes in midnight blue, and he adjusted his bow tie as he hopped up on the platform. He was unmarked.

"I warned you," he said. "But you wouldn't listen. Chuvalo is the toughest man I've ever fought. Tougher'n Liston, Patterson, Jones and all the rest. His head is the hardest thing I've ever hit." As evidence, he held up his swollen fists.

When the interview was over, his bodyguards cleared the way for him through the throng: "Give him room. Give him a three-foot path . . ."

It was more than Chuvalo had given him all night.

George Chuvalo retired in 1978 as Canadian champion after 97 professional fights — he was never once knocked off his feet. But his boxing glory days became a distant memory in the face of monumental personal tragedies. In 1985, his 20-year-old son, Jesse, committed suicide by shooting himself at the family home. His sons George Lee and Steven became addicted to heroin; in 1987, they were convicted of robbing three pharmacies. In 1993, George Lee, 30, died of a heroin overdose. Four days later, Chuvalo's wife, Lynne, 50, committed suicide at their home by overdosing on sleeping pills. Steven died of a drug overdose in 1996.

Today, daughter Vanessa owns a restaurant, and son Mitchell is a high-school teacher and football and wrestling coach. Chuvalo remarried in 1995, and all live in Toronto, although Chuvalo spends a lot of time on the road, speaking out against drugs.

ON THE TRACK

Johnny Longden Up

—July 15, 1944—
Jim Coleman

I N A BUSINESS THAT ABOUNDS in celebrated screwballs it is notable that two of the world's best jockeys are Canadians. It is notable, too, that these Canadians are among the coolest, most clearheaded and most provident representatives of their craft. These undersized gentlemen are Johnny Longden and George Woolf.

Longden and Woolf grew up together in southern Alberta, a section of the country that has produced many other great riders, but this story is concerned with Longden because he is one of the most fabulously successful figures in the history of the turf.

Bringing home a winner at the Belmont racetrack
in New York City, ca. 1940

In the first place, he has ridden nearly 2,200 winners—a feat excelled only by those two Britons, Gordon Richards and the late Fred Archer. In the second place, the mounts that he rode last year won a total of $573,276, a world's record. In the third place, he has more money than any of the Balkan Countries and the story of his rise would make the average Horatio Alger hero look like an arrant sissy.

Longden was born in Wakefield, England, 34 years ago, but his parents brought him to Canada when he was no taller than a mail-order catalogue. As a matter of fact he isn't much taller now—he stands only four-feet, 10-inches, a fact that annoys him excessively, and he wears lifts in his brogans to fool the public. His wife is of average height and he demands that she wear low-heeled shoes so that they can appear together in public without causing a traffic jam.

Johnny inherited his small stature. His father was more than a shade on the small side. In fact it is recorded that when the Longden family first went to work for a farmer in the Taber district of southern Alberta, Longden père didn't report for supper one night. This caused some astonishment because invariably he was well up among the leaders in the race for the evening victuals. When he failed to appear even in time for the pie course, it was realized something was amiss and a search party was organized. They found him sitting hopefully in the excavation for a potato cellar—a project on which he had been working. He had dug the hole so deep he couldn't climb out.

Being a farm boy, Johnny soon learned about horses, and as a youngster he indulged in some of that whoop-de-doo bareback riding around the smaller country fairs. When he left school to earn a living he went right into the coal mines, where his diminutive stature was a blessing—he was one of the few miners who could stand upright in the underground workings. Incidentally, that hard labour in the mines was responsible for the terrific development of his arms and shoulders, two things that have helped to make him a great rider.

Cardston and Taber are centres of the Mormon sect and, inevitably, Johnny came under the influence of that church. The Mormon "mecca" is Salt Lake City in Utah and in 1925, while still in his teens, he decided to visit the mother temple. He travelled to Salt Lake City by railway, but being a keen enthusiast for the open air, he patronized the side-door Pullmans.

It was purely coincidental that he arrived in Salt Lake City about the time that the racing season opened there. I hesitate to suggest that he shirked his religious obligations but, in some mysterious manner, he managed to get out to the race track every morning. It was there that he met a stalwart steed named Hugo K. Asher. Hugo was an individualist among horses. He could run like a gazelle but he objected strenuously to anyone riding him. Jockeys who attempted to ride Hugo K. Asher were considered to be very poor insurance risks.

There was a deep and abiding affection between Hugo K. Asher and his owner but, in his own peculiar way, Hugo was something of a liability. There was no money in the kitty unless Hugo won races, and Hugo couldn't win races unless he would permit someone to ride him. Things were getting so bad at Salt Lake that Hugo and his owner were sharing the same pail of oats. At this juncture young Longden approached Hugo's owner and pleaded for a chance to ride the equine desperado in a race. The owner looked down at his own ribs, which were protruding through his skin and rattled like a set of castanets when he walked. Hugo's owner decided to take a chance—after all, Longden didn't look as if anyone would miss him if Hugo happened to toss him into a low-hanging cloud bank.

Strong men still shudder when they recall the sight that Longden presented on his first trip to the post. Jim Donovan was the starter at Salt Lake and his chief assistant was a salty character rejoicing in the name of "Wampus" Fuller. Donovan then was—and still is—the official starter on the western Canadian racing circuit and the late-lamented "Wampus" also was a colourfully decorative adjunct to the Canadian racing scene until he departed this life a year ago.

Donovan recalls the scene as if it were yesterday. He was climbing into the starter's stand when "Wampus," white and obviously badly shaken, approached. "Lord love me, Mr. Donovan," said Fuller, "but do you see what I see?"

Donovan took a quick look, wiped his hands across his eyes and vowed that the prohibition beer in Utah was stronger than anyone had imagined. Longden had arrived at the post on Hugo K. Asher. He was wearing the regulation jockeys' silks, but in addition he was wearing a pair of beaded Indian gauntlets, which came up to his elbows. While Donovan looked on, scarcely daring to believe his eyes, Longden calmly dismounted and proceeded to unsaddle good old Hugo—Johnny was going to ride the steed bareback!

Taking a firm grip on himself, Donovan explained to the bewildered Longden that The Jockey Club was a little bit stuffy about horses being ridden bareback on recognized race tracks. Well, to cut it short, Hugo K. Asher finished second. Johnny Longden had ridden his first race and, although it was several years before he rode again, he knew then that he was going to be a jockey.

The story of Longden's return to Canada is a chapter in itself, but, suffice to say, he discovered an Alberta car in the Salt Lake Fair Grounds and sat on the bumper until the two owners appeared. He scrambled into the back seat and stayed there for the entire trip. When his benefactors went into hotels at night Johnny slept on the back seat of the car—he was afraid that they might leave without him. Afterward, when he became a wealthy man, he rewarded his unwilling hosts by financing their business ventures.

It wasn't until 1927 that L. P. Jacques and Fred Johnston, two Calgary horsemen, gave Johnny his chance to be a regular hard-boot. In the meantime he had been clerking in a cigar store. He rode with increasing success on the Western fair circuit and in California, but fees were small and he made a bare living. He and his wife were flatter than soup on a plate on Christmas Eve, 1931, when Johnny showed signs of budding business acumen by wagering $2 on an 80–1 shot in California. He rode Bahamas, which set the pace for the immortal Phar Lap in the 1932 Agua Caliente Handicap, and by the end of the winter racing season he had amassed a bank roll of $2,000.

It was then that he learned a lesson. He stuck his money in a California bank. Two days later President Franklin Roosevelt declared the famous "bank holiday." They say that Johnny was the first man in the line when the bank reopened. He put his money in a shoe box and he slept with the box under his bed. When he arrived back in Calgary that spring he was carrying his money in the box under his arm. He conducted extensive research into the Canadian banking situation and eventually divided his money among five or six Calgary branches. Even now he distrusts American banks and patronizes the Canadian institutions—plenty of them, so that he won't be caught with his cheque book down if one bank collapses.

Johnny rode for many owners but he didn't gain international prominence until 1936 when he hooked up with Alf Tarn, a Winnipeg horseman, and rode Rushaway, the famous "Iron Horse." Longden piloted Rushaway to victories in the Illinois and Louisiana Derbys on successive days. In 1938 Longden became the leading rider in America, winning 236 races.

Since then his services have been in demand by the great stables of the country and he struck his own personal bonanza when he signed up with the establishment of Mrs. John D. Hertz and was introduced to a gangling yearling named Count Fleet. When Johnny is riding Count Fleet, he is riding the gravy-train. Count Fleet is a runnin' hoss, suh—the fastest horse of our day—and it doesn't look as if they'll beat him unless a rival owner shoots him from ambush. Last year he won the Wood Memorial, the Kentucky Derby, the Preakness Stakes, the Withers Stakes and the Belmont Stakes. He won them so easily that Longden's only worry was his income tax returns.

Incidentally, Mrs. Hertz has had singular success with Canadian employees. She has won two Kentucky Derbys, the first in 1928 with Reigh Count, and the other with Count Fleet. Reigh Count was trained by Bert Michel, Calgary, and ridden by Chick Lang, Hamilton. Count Fleet was ridden by Longden and trained by Don Cameron, a native Winnipegger.

Longden is a wealthy man now. His mounts won $573,276 last year and it is probable that he received $50,000 in fees and bonuses from happy owners. In addition he received $1,500 per month from Mrs. Hertz, and from Trainer Jim Fitzsimmons, who had "second call" on his services, he received another $800 monthly—which isn't alfalfa.

In many respects Longden is the antithesis of the average jockey. He isn't eccentric; he isn't colourful. He doesn't eat light globes or razor blades like Paul Keiper, a rider who is held in some awe by his fellows. Unlike Don Meade and Eddie Arcaro, he doesn't get into the newspapers and into jams with the stewards by betting on races. Unlike Conn McCreary he doesn't blow kisses to his admirers when his mount is galloping along in front of the field.

The problem of increasing weight doesn't worry him unduly. He has scaled around 105 pounds for many years and he doesn't show any signs of bulging at the seams. If at times he feels impelled to dine unwisely on lush and fatty viands, he can jump into the steam box and get back to normal within a few hours.

He has a well-proportioned, splendidly muscled torso but his legs are short enough to give the impression that he is walking in a rut. His voice is high and sharp and any tavern waiter who saw Longden from the rear and heard him talk would give him the heave ho, under the impression that a minor was trying to crash the gate.

Two things have contributed to Longden's success as a jockey. In the first place he is an excellent judge of pace. Instinctively he knows the precise moment at which to call on his mount for the supreme effort. He can take a horse into the lead in a race and restrain him slightly so that he will be able to beat off any challenges from his competitors in the closing stages of the race. This, of course, is elementary stuff for regular race trackers but for the benefit of the uninitiated, it is known as "rating" a horse. Longden is equally adept at letting some rival set the pace and then giving his own mount its head for the run through the homestretch. A good judge of pace knows instinctively how close he must keep to the pace setter.

The second thing that has contributed to his success is that Longden keeps his mouth shut—an attribute that endears him to veteran trainers. He follows a trainer's instructions to the final letter. Smart-alecky riders who refuse to heed a trainer's advice have been responsible for getting many a good mount beaten. A *good* jockey can help a horse to win a race; *any kind* of a jockey can make a horse lose a race.

As I said, Longden listens to advice from the men who train the horses. If you doubt the efficacy of this system, I suggest that you examine Longden's record. Longden has a good head and a good body. He keeps his mouth shut, his eyes open, and more than once he has used those supple wrists and steel-sinewed arms to "lift" a tiring horse through that last crucial 16th of a mile to the finish-line.

Among riders his only eccentricity is the fact that he has saved his money. Perhaps he recalls the days when he worked underground in that coal mine near Lethbridge. Longden has joined the ranks of the landed gentry. He owns a ranch in Nevada and he has stocked it with expensive purebred cattle. Mrs. Hertz made him a gift of the good stallion, Count Gallahad, and he is going into the thoroughbred industry, too.

Longden lives simply and he has few extravagances. He doesn't smoke and a whiff of the grape leaves him all in a tizzy. But he does own a fleet of large, superpowered cars, which he drives at reckless speeds. He is so short that he sits upon a raised seat to drive, and even then he peers through the spokes of the steering wheel instead of over it. His only other flamboyant streak is his vast affection for expensive haberdashery. He buys $50 shirts.

Longden, if he wishes, can ride for another eight or 10 years. He can smash every riding record in the book. He can pilot more winners than Richards or Archer. But riding is a perilous business. When you're astride 1,100 pounds of straining, hurtling horseflesh it's something like riding a thunderbolt. A single misstep may mean death. Longden has seen jockeys die and it isn't a pretty sight.

Longden has come a long way from that Alberta coal mine. He has reached the peak of his profession. He is a wealthy man and probably before long he'll retire to his ranch where he can follow his beloved comic strip characters in comfort. Who can blame him? After all, you don't hear of Henry Ford taking rides in a helicopter!

By 1956, Johnny Longden had become thoroughbred racing's winningest rider, a record he held until longtime rival Willie

Shoemaker broke it in 1970. Longden retired in 1966 but continued to visit Taber until the late 1970s. He died at his Banning, Calif., home on Feb. 14, 2003, at the age of 96.

Jim Coleman began his varied newspaper career in 1931 and refused to retire, writing a daily column for the Vancouver Province *until he died at 89 in 2001. His last column appeared on the day of his death.*

Northern Dancer:
A Second Chance at Greatness

—May 1, 1965—
George F. T. Ryall (Audax Minor)

"*I* CANNOT WRITE AN EPITAPH *for Northern Dancer—because his future could very well be more important to Canadian racing than his past." The speaker was George F. T. Ryall, better known as Audax Minor, the almost legendary racetrack sage of The New Yorker magazine. His point was that Northern Dancer was only one (admittedly a very good one, perhaps the best) of many fine Canadian race horses. But as a stallion this horse might give this country what it has not had in the past—and what few countries can boast—a truly superb thoroughbred bloodline stretching into the*

Winning the Kentucky Derby with Bill Hartack in 1964

future and enriching the whole world of racing. "Don't just take my word for this," said Ryall. "Consider that within a few days of the announcement that Northern Dancer was being retired to stud because of a tendon injury, his services, at a fee of $10,000, had been booked up for three years ahead." Here, in the quiet, authoritative style that has made him the most respected of turf writers, Ryall takes a knowing and affectionate look at the past, present and future of Canada's favourite equine invalid.

The story of the ugly duckling is repeated, with variations, year after year in racing. Northern Dancer, however, was never an ugly duckling. There is no vestige of the rise from obscurity motif so dear to tale tellers. He was bred to be a good racehorse, and from the outset he was a good racehorse. Indeed, he is unquestionably the best ever bred in Canada. Apart from the fact that he won the Queen's Plate in a gallop, he met and beat every States-bred three-year-old of any importance in the Flamingo, the Florida Derby, the Blue Grass Stakes, the Kentucky Derby and the Preakness Stakes—something no horse from the Dominion had done before—incidentally earning $490,012. But for bad luck in the Belmont Stakes, in which he finished third, and a mishap while training that ended his racing days in midsummer, he might have been the first horse to win a million in prize money in a single season. Actually, though, he is just beginning his career.

For a decade it has been the custom at Windfields Farm to have a pre-priced sale of all its yearlings every autumn, and for Mr. and Mrs. E. P. Taylor to race those that are not sold. In 1962 the usual number of owners, their trainers and advisers took stock of the lot and bought 15 of the 48 horses offered. Among those left was a short stocky bay colt by Nearctic and Natalma, later to be named Northern Dancer. He had a tag of $25,000 on his halter, the high price of the sale because of his pedigree, but the chances are that he would have had no takers at half that, for he was only 14 hands, two and a half inches high, the average size of a pony. When Northern Dancer was sent to trainer Horatio Luro the following spring along with other Windfields two-year-olds, none of the stablemen wanted to groom him: when a draft of young horses comes to a racing stable there is always competition among the men to take care of the more promising-looking ones for the obvious reason that when a horse wins a race there is always a cash present for the man who rubs him. Which only goes to show that experts can err and racetrackers are human.

This has happened before at Windfields Farm sales. Nobody wanted Victoria Park, who in my opinion was the best Canadian-bred till Northern Dancer came along. Buyers ignored New Providence, who won the 100th running of the Queen's Plate the afternoon the Queen came to Woodbine. Nor would any horseman give $7,500 for Canebora, who was voted Canada's Horse of the Year in 1963, and earned 15 times that amount in his first two seasons of racing. Years ago, in Kentucky, the late John Hertz also used to put price tags on his yearlings. One of the colts left on his hands was the triple-crown winner Count Fleet, to whom some handicappers give a higher speed rating than they do to Man o' War.

With the expectation that in thoroughbred breeding lightning quite often strikes twice in the same place, several buyers showed interest in the full sister of Northern Dancer, who was priced at $100,000—far and away the record for a racehorse in Canada—at Windfields Farm's yearling sale last October. Because he had bought at the sale the year before, and thus under the Windfields system had priority, the bay filly went to Jean-Louis Lévesque, industrialist and president of Blue Bonnets racecourse in Montreal.

It has been said, and never denied, that the late Aga Khan, who was high on the list of winning owners in England for so many years, made his thoroughbred matings with the aid of astrology; but, by and large, the breeding of racehorses is an ordinary procedure. The fun of it and the headaches—the romance, if you like—come through more or less adventitious circumstances. If Natalma had not chipped a bit of bone in one of her knees while training for the Kentucky Oaks the spring of 1960, she might have won the race, but Canada would not have had Northern Dancer. As it was, Natalma was shipped home, and, although it was late in the season, was bred to Nearctic, who at Windfields they think is the best stallion in Canada.

Northern Dancer was foaled shortly after midnight on May 27, 1961, and neither Taylor nor Gil Darlington, the manager of National Stud, who has looked over innumerable newborn thoroughbreds, saw anything notable about him—except that according to the rules of racing, which prescribe that the age of a horse is reckoned as beginning on the first of January in the year in which it is foaled, he was nearly six months old. Later, Joe Thomas, the manager of the racing stable, thought he was an especially good-looking weanling, but as the months passed the Natalma colt, as he was called before he was named, failed to grow and his weight was below average. This was puzzling for he ate heartily and was full of bounce and go as he romped in his paddock.

After the yearling sale, he remained at Windfields, where he was broken to wear a bridle, to be saddled, to carry an exercise boy, and to jog on the training track with colts of his age. Though he responded well to his lessons, as yet he impressed no one. The following March he was assigned to the division of the Windfields horses trained by Horatio Luro because Luro had handled Natalma, and it is recorded in the *Señor's* daybook that on the trip from Windfields to Toronto's Woodbine track, Northern Dancer kicked up a fuss in the van, in the course of which he rapped the coronary band of his left fore foot. (The coronary band is the junction of the horn and the hoof and a very sensitive part.) Months later a quarter crack, of which more anon, appeared on the same foot. And it was in the left foreleg that he suffered a bowed tendon.

The first time I saw Northern Dancer was that autumn at Aqueduct, where he had come after racing at Fort Erie, Woodbine, and Greenwood and winning five of his seven starts, including the prized Coronation Futurity. His objective was the Remsen Stakes, but to accustom him to the track, Luro ran him in the Sir Gaylord Purse, which he won by eight lengths from Bupers, fresh from his victory in The Futurity, New York's Blue Ribband for two-year-olds. As he stood in the winner's circle, he struck me as rather smallish and squarely built, but well-proportioned and possessing great quality—a jaunty fellow with three white feet and a blaze. A week later he led all the way in the Remsen, winning well in hand in the eye-opening time of 1:35 3/5 for the mile. Needless to say, I came away convinced that I had seen the next winner of the Queen's Plate.

It was not generally known till some time later that, when he ran for the Remsen, Northern Dancer had a quarter crack. This is a fissure in the horn composing the wall of the hoof, which may be likened to a split in a fingernail past the quick, and more often than not comes from galloping over hard ground. If not given attention, it can sideline a horse. So, after a veterinarian's consultation it was decided to send for Bill Bane, a California blacksmith noted for his successful treatment of the ailment. One of his prize patients is Su Mac Lad, a well-known trotter. The crack in Northern Dancer's hoof was half an inch long and it could have been a bad one. Bane closed it with Neolite and a special kind of cement, then vulcanized the patch with the heat from an infrared lamp (the operation took all day), and from all accounts the foot has not troubled him since.

Taking one thing with another, Luro says that Northern Dancer was not a hard horse to train. Though he was full of beans, as the *Señor* puts it, he was willing and had a voracious appetite, but horsemen like what they call a good doer. In fact, from the first he was a little glutton. After finishing his ration of oats and hay, he would eat most of the straw bedding in his stall. Luro quickly put a stop to that, substituting a bedding of peat moss, and, to keep him from getting fat, gave him long slow gallops every day. This is the Argentine and English way of training, to which the *Señor* is accustomed, and I could not think of a better one to muscle up a young horse. Northern Dancer's passion was (and still is) lump sugar. Luro says that his shoulders were always black and blue from Northern Dancer grabbing him to get at what he knew should be in his trainer's pockets. (Citation, who also had a sweet tooth, had a different way of attracting attention and sugar. He pawed the sill of his stall door when anyone passed, to the great annoyance of his stable because that sort of thing wore out the toes of his shoes.) Although Northern Dancer played rough, he was never mean. As Luro said once, "He just bites men. He does not bite the girls."

Trainers have a saying that a good horse does everything, or nearly everything, right. Though Northern Dancer was beaten in his first start as a three-year-old, resulting from being bumped and crowded for most of the six furlongs, he won his next, the Flamingo Stakes, easily and followed it up with five more victories in succession. It is generally agreed that the Kentucky Derby was his greatest performance, for the mile and a quarter was run in two minutes flat, breaking the track record set by Decidedly (trained by Luro) in the race two years before. Especially it revealed his ability to quicken his pace intensively and at once when extra speed was needed. (Like kicking in the supercharger of a sports car.) Only top horses can do that. He showed it again in the Queen's Plate. As all who saw that race remember, he was drawn nearest the rails and came out of the starting gate slowly. Passing the stand the first time, he was far behind the leaders and rounding the first turn was completely boxed in. Here he was in a tight spot, for if any of the closely bunched runners in front of him had swerved or stumbled there is no telling what might have happened. Going into the backstretch, Bill Hartack, who was riding him, eased him back till he was last, then steered for the outside and clear sailing. Straightened away, Northern Dancer produced an astonishing burst of speed and, passing the seven other colts as though they were standing, went on to win by seven lengths or so, easing up. In my opinion it was his finest performance.

A fortnight before, he had finished third in the Belmont Stakes to Quadrangle, whom he had beaten in the Flamingo, the Kentucky Derby, and the Preakness, and Roman Brother, whom he had beaten in the Flamingo, the Florida Derby, the Kentucky Derby and the Preakness. There is no intention here of going into a tedious explanation—and there are several—of that defeat. In all of the end-of-the-season polls Northern Dancer was voted the best three-year-old in 1964. I string along with that.

After the Queen's Plate it was his stable's purpose to give Northern Dancer a rest at Belmont Park before readying him for the Travers Stakes at Saratoga in mid-August and another meeting with Quadrangle. But the Classic Stakes, at Arlington Park in Chicago, looked such a soft touch. The distance, one mile, was just the ticket to wind him up for the Travers, and, not at all incidentally, the purse was in the $100,000 bracket. It is customary to give a racer a workout at home before shipping him to a distant track, so Northern Dancer did an easy gallop of seven furlongs over the main course. It was raining and muddy, but nobody saw the colt make a single misstep.

However, as he was being cooled out, Luro noticed a mark or a spot the size of a half dollar on Northern Dancer's left foreleg. The stable vet was called in, examined it, said that it might have been cuffed by a hind foot, and prescribed a mild poultice. Next day the spot had grown larger. Later, it was diagnosed as a bowed tendon.

This is one of the dreaded disabilities that can attack a race-horse—a rupture of the sheath of the tendon that controls the action of the foot, caused by a blow or excessive strain. The injury is marked by a curved protuberance that looks like a bowstring drawn back from the wood of a bow and from which it gets its name. A horse thus afflicted may run again, and many do, but he seldom, if ever, returns to his top form. I daresay that after a long rest, for he was not badly bowed, Northern Dancer could have come back to the races and beaten everything that he was likely to meet at Woodbine and Fort Erie this season, after which he would have been retired to the stud. Still, there would always be the danger in a race that in trying to save his bad leg he would put too much strain on his good one, or that because of the tremendous energy he put into running he might break down completely, and that would be most unfortunate.

It is a popular belief that racing is a rich man's pastime. E. P. Taylor is no dilettante in that fascinating and unpredictable game. The loss of Northern Dancer as a racehorse was great, but the decision to retire him to the stud straightaway was no surprise to me. Though he is a practical man, Taylor has a keen feeling for his horses, knows them as individuals, understands and appreciates their characteristics, their qualities, and their failings when he plans their careers.

Northern Dancer must have at least five crops of foals before any definite conclusion that he is another Bunty Lawless can be reached. His value at the moment—he is insured for $1.5 million—does not lie in the number and class of winners he will get, but the influence he will exert on Canadian racing, for he is something of an idol. He doesn't get as much fan mail as he did last summer, but letters from admirers come daily to Windfields Farm, requesting pictures and asking how he's getting on; high-school students write, saying they want to do themes about him. The afternoon I saw him at National Stud, he looked shaggy in his winter coat, but his whole appearance expressed his individual attributes—courage, stamina, robustness, and that air of quality outstanding horses emanate, which is impossible to describe.

In a loose-box on the other side of the barn was Victoria Park, who, back in 1960 finished second in the Flamingo, the Blue Grass Stakes, and the Preakness; third in the Florida Derby and the Kentucky; and might have won at least one of the spring classics with a little bit of luck. Curiously, also, that July he had a mishap while training for the Hollywood Derby and was retired. Searchers after coincidence might make something of that.

Northern Dancer became a legendary sire, producing 112 stakes winners and 295 offspring that earned $183 million. He died in 1990 at 29.

George Ryall, better known as Audax Minor, wrote for The New Yorker *for 52 years until the age of 91, a year before his death in 1979. Born in Toronto, Minor was educated in England, where he began his journalism career in 1907.*

OFF THE BEATEN TRACK

Is Lacrosse What It Used to Be?

—June 15, 1926—
Fred Jacob

W HENEVER A MAN who plays or admires Canada's national game hears the assertion, "Lacrosse is coming back," he feels intensely irritated. An outsider might think his attitude a trifle illogical, as there is a certain amount of optimism in that statement. But the crumb of optimism is offset by the whole assumption on which the statement is based. It suggests that lacrosse has been put away somewhere for an interval and that it is being revived again, deliberately and hopefully. That is not the fact, as the friends of the game know well. Yet, one of the oldest traditions of lacrosse seems to be

Toronto scores against New York, undated

that it "is coming back." I can remember no time in my experience of the game, which extends back for more than a quarter of a century, when men were not getting to their feet and saying solemnly that they were glad to see how the grand old pastime was coming back. I suppose that the same old speech was being made every year from 1867 onward, and if lacrosse had been the national game before that time, they would have started to make the speech still earlier.

Canada is the only nation with a game of its own that belongs to the soil, that was created by the aborigines, and that was adopted and civilized by the white powers that came into possession of the land by right of sword. Of course, it should be unnecessary to mention that lacrosse played by the Indians was very different from the modern version with which we are familiar. The redmen's conception of sport was not something at which the majority of males looked on. All the able-bodied braves were expected to participate, and the field was proportionately long. To the French pioneers, the implement used by the players suggested the title, lacrosse, which is used today. The rules that were good enough for our copper-skinned fellow citizens have gone, but the habit of tradition remains. I have always had a feeling that some day an ex-player, with a literary turn of mind, will write an interesting book about the pre-white period of lacrosse, ending with the capture of Fort Michilimackinac.

Of course, lacrosse has had its ups and downs. Every season is not entirely like the preceding season, or else a little better. The men in charge of the game have tried experiments, some of which did not turn out as well as they hoped. There have been boom years, followed by slump periods when things were not so prosperous. Occasionally, an interval of success will be followed by the creation of an entirely new set of problems.

It was because senior lacrosse enjoyed too much success about a quarter of a century ago that professional lacrosse came into existence. Now, if ever there was a game that has to remain amateur, it is lacrosse. The essence of professionalism is money-making. It requires the stamina of the performers. Baseball makes an ideal professional game because a man can play it day in and day out for months and be none the worse for wear. In as strenuous a pastime as lacrosse, played when the weather is at its hottest, the average of one game per week is about all you can expect from a team, no matter how perfectly conditioned it may be. In the long run, professional lacrosse could never be made to pay because the gate receipts from weekly games are not sufficient for carrying expenses. After experimenting for about 15 years with professional lacrosse, the magnates concerned laid it upon the shelf and left the field once more to the amateurs.

Look over the lacrosse field as we find it today in Canada. In the Maritime Provinces, the game has never secured a foothold. Quebec was once the great centre of the game, but the teams in recent years have not been what they once were. There has never been better lacrosse played anywhere than can be seen in Ontario at the present time. In Manitoba, they have at no time brought the quality of the game played to the highest state of perfection, probably because most of the teams have been located in and around Winnipeg, so that there has never been sufficient competition. Regarding British Columbia, it is diffi-cult to generalize. The game has not been as extensively organ-ized there as in Ontario, for example, and yet they have always played a sterling brand of lacrosse. Whenever a team has been needed to defend the Mann Cup, a line-up of players has been trotted out by a leading Pacific Coast club, capable of disposing of the best of challengers.

During half a century, lacrosse has gone through a series of improvements, until it is now universally admired by sporting authorities. Still, during all the years of its existence, the younger lacrosse players have been obliged to listen to the old boys singing their never-ending chorus about the days when the game was a greater game than it has become and when the men who played it were giants with the prowess of giants.

Perhaps a few contrasts between tradition and reality will indicate why this harking-back grows so aggravating to those who are closely associated with the game at the present time. The old boys like to talk as though lacrosse ought to be able to push all other summer sports off the Canadian map, if it were played as they used to play it 50 years ago. They say: "Look how our other two national pastimes, hockey and rugby, monopolize their special seasons." They do not stop to think that in the fall and winter, there is not much sporting opposition, but lacrosse is played at a time when more than a dozen strongly organized sports, from the wealthy American baseball to the husky English soccer, are on the green, each with its own followers. Think of the money that is spent to advertise baseball; think of the increased interest taken year after year in golf; look over a sporting page published in 1900 and one published in 1926 and see how many new sorts of champions have been created in the interval. With the increased number of games, the space occupied by each on the horizon during the months of June, July and August is proportionately smaller. Lacrosse is all the more alive because it has to fight for its place in the *Sun*—or in any other newspaper that runs a sporting page.

I have heard the old tradition-mongers maintain that lacrosse was a better game in the days when the rules gave the victory to the team that first scored four goals—in some cases it was three goals. Anyone who is familiar with sport will admit that the assertion does not look at all convincing. That method of declaring a winner could only be better where one team out-classed the other; then the agony would be shortened, and the fans would not sit for 80 minutes to watch the rolling up of a score of 20–2. However, on the other hand, there have been more than a few games in recent years in which one team got away to a flying start and tallied four goals in the first quarter, only to be worn down in the long run and outscored in the end. Among the finest encounters that I have ever witnessed, several games of that type would be included. Of course, you want to find the better team in any game, and the better team is the one that can make the biggest score in a given period, not the one that can score fastest in the first 10 minutes.

On one occasion, a very important and swagger game was being played between the Toronto TK and the Shamrocks of Montreal. It was in the days before the fashionable folk spent their Saturdays at golf clubs or attended weekend parties. The smart people, as well as the sporting fraternity, made their way to the old Toronto lacrosse grounds. For an hour, they were gathering and getting placed in readiness for an exciting afternoon. The teams were known to be very evenly matched and were expected to stage a great struggle. It was to be an occasion. But what happened? The Montrealers got off to a flying start and were victors 10 minutes after the first facing of the ball. Everybody knew that once the Torontos hit their pace, they were strong enough to give the victors a great argument, but it was too late for even the best of teams to settle down after the final whistle had blown. Those lacrosse enthusiasts who arrived a little late that afternoon met the disgusted crowds coming away from the game. Doubtless, there were elderly men in that mob who talked of the good old days of lacrosse, when teams were not so inconsiderate as to win before they had given the public its money's worth.

Another annoying tradition into which one is always running preserves the belief that all the great lacrosse players were pre-war, if not pre-twentieth century. There are still a few old men who talk as though there were no more artistic players after Sir Sam and James L. Hughes ceased performing, in the days when Ross Mackenzie was king of them all. They may grudgingly come down, with a few lean words of praise, as far as the days of Hughie Lambe, of the Torontos, Henry Hoobin, of the Shamrocks, Johnnie Powers, of Ottawa, Dade and Findlayson of Brantford, and the ever-green John White, of Cornwall, but they will not move a step farther. Tradition-mongers of a still younger generation would have us believe that all the best lacrosse players joined the professional ranks in the decade before the Great War and that after they ceased to play, no more were produced. As for Lionel Conacher, he was one of the unique players in lacrosse history. He had not much style, but when he got charging, like a rugby halfback, he was a marvellous man to watch. I have mentioned only a few of the players who have proved their worth over a number of seasons. There are younger stars, too, and if they show consistency in their game, they will not have to take off their hats to anybody in the days to come.

Lacrosse is undergoing a resurgence, with some 200,000 amateur players across the country. The indoor professional National Lacrosse League has a dozen teams, one-third of them Canadian.

Fred Jacob, a playwright, poet, novelist and journalist for a quarter century at the Toronto Mail & Empire, *died of heart failure at 45 in 1928.*

The Gamest Fish

—August 1, 1936—
Ozark Ripley with Dink Carroll

W HENEVER I HEAR A BROTHER angler airing his opinion
(a pretty continuous pastime these days) that the fight-
ingest fish in the world is a muskie, rainbow trout, salmon, or
even a pike, I have to pause and count to 10. If I didn't I'd be
sure to forget he was a brother and start in to shout him down,
or walk out on him in the middle of his silly effusion or maybe
do something still more hostile. For he's all wet when he makes
these claims, wetter than the fish themselves.

The greatest fresh-water fighter, the fish that will give
sportsmen the best fight pound for pound, is none other than

the small-mouth black bass—old bronze-back. There just isn't another fish in all the lakes, rivers and streams of the North American continent in a class with him. Believe me, because I know.

It's part of my business to know most of what there is to know about the fish in Canada's waters and the game in her forests. From early spring until early autumn I'm away on fishing trips. I've taken Atlantic salmon from the rivers of the Maritimes and Eastern Quebec, and bluebacks from British Columbia's waters; worked the lakes and rivers of old Quebec, Ontario and Manitoba for trout, bass, muskie and pike; fished the galloping streams of the Rockies for rainbow and cutthroat trout; and set hooks in every kind of game fish that flourishes in this sportsman's paradise. So I speak from experience when I claim that no other fish in Canadian waters will give you the thrills a three-pound small-mouth will give you from the moment you hook him until he's netted.

Only 10 days ago I took a party on a quest for bronze-backs into the wilderness waters of Ontario's French River district, just north of Georgian Bay. I had fished with them and hunted with them before, so we were old friends.

That first night at camp we discussed fishing ethics. The men on this party were veteran sportsmen who had learned that most of the sport in fishing comes when you have the fish, alive, on the end of your line, and not dead in the bottom of the boat. Though we were after bass, we elected not to use plugs. Sport is sport and there is no sport where the dice are loaded against the fish. A bass has a good chance to lick you if you give him an opportunity to spit the hook or smash your tackle. But if you use a big plug with ganghooks, his chance to escape is minimized, for in the frantic threshing of his fight for freedom he may hook himself several times in the body.

We decided to use flies, maybe Ginger Quills or Brown Hackles, depending upon the weather, and tied on small single hooks. Barbless hooks, too, so that if we didn't want the fish we could release him without injury simply by seizing his lower jaw between thumb and forefinger and disengaging the hook. We would take only as many fish as we could comfortably eat in the party. When I see those pictures of anglers with a great string of fish, I get a feeling of nausea. You learn several things about that man. You know he isn't much of a sportsman, because the first article in the sportsman's code is to leave something for the other fellow; and you know, too, that he's a show-off.

After breakfast next morning we went out in pairs. A little below our camp site I paddled with Bill, my partner, along a stream that meandered through a reedy marsh. The freshness of early morning was on the river, the bush and the hills. The sun was just up, but already it came back warm off the water. The stream finally merged into a small round lake less than a mile long with a shore line of low banks. The eastern part was too shallow and full of rank weeds and bulrushes to promise much bass fishing. We followed the left bank around where the water grew deeper and almost inky black. I prepared to cast and Bill sat back to watch, not in any particular hurry, luxuriating in the prospect of a whole day ahead to fish that lake. I shot my bug against a little rocky bank and in less than half an hour drew out two nice small-mouths after a hard fight. Then I took the paddle and Bill had his turn.

He was in the canoe ahead of me when suddenly, a few minutes later, he had a hard strike. I knew at once that he'd hooked an unusually large small-mouth. There was the slow, sure tension as the hook set and the line tightened, the rod bending like a buggy whip, the reel screaming, and then the flash and frantic leap of a huge bronze-back trying to shake the bug out of its mouth. It fell back into the water with a loud splash and headed for the bottom, boring deep, tugging, tugging with tremendous strength, and darting so fast in so many directions that neither Bill nor I knew its exact whereabouts until it broke the surface again in another of its spectacular vaultings above water. I turned the canoe as quickly as I could and held it close to the bank with the paddle, so as to give Bill plenty of proper fighting room.

Bronze-back was a rapid repeater in jumping, going out of the water with the speed of a rainbow but putting more power in his punches. From the looks of him he might have gone six pounds. For 20 minutes the battle waged, Bill pitting his strength and knowledge against the power, the cunning and the great courage of the fish. That fish put up a fight that would stop your heart. He rushed all over the place, breaking the water in savage three- and four-foot arcs, and once raced right at the canoe and might have succeeded in passing clean underneath if Bill, reeling in like mad, hadn't been able to turn him in time. It was fully 15 minutes before Bill began to master the big bronze-back. He played him carefully, giving line slowly and reeling in rapidly, frustrating the fish's frenzied efforts to get a few loose yards of line by keeping the pressure on. There followed another five minutes fighting, until Bill brought him finally to the side of the canoe with his sides heaving, his strength seeming gone and with nothing left in him, apparently, but a few tired thumps. Bill thought it was all over, too.

"Hand me the net," he called to me.

But somehow as Bill went to take the net from me the fish darted away from the canoe and got a couple of yards of loose line before Bill could jam his thumb securely inside the frame of the reel. It was enough for that bass. He leaped high out of the water once more, and went completely over the landing net that Bill was holding down over the water. The leader caught for an instant right where the handle joined the ring of the net.

In that second, old bronze-back broke the leader and raced away to freedom.

How can you help but admire a fish like that, and where will you find another that will give an equal display of fight? The answer, I think, is nowhere.

That day we must have hooked 50 bass, but we kept only four of them. They were biting everything we cast. Late in the day, when the sun began to die and the shadows lengthened, Bill took an old plug from his tackle box, stripped the hooks off it, and began to cast just for the sheer pleasure of watching the fish strike. He had come a long way and he simply couldn't see too much of them.

But enough about that trip. Let's get back to a discussion of the merits of game fish. The way I'd rate them would be in something like this order: Small-mouth black bass, Atlantic salmon, ouananiche, rainbow trout, speckled brook trout and muskie. The best salmon fishing you'll get anywhere is in the rivers flowing into the Gulf of St. Lawrence down by Gaspé. They'll leap five and six feet in the air, break the surface frequently, spraying water in miniature showers. The ouananiche (landlocked salmon) is an acrobat and has been known to jump as high as 10 feet out of water. Rainbow trout will also give you an aerial display and plenty of excitement. Last year we fished him and his companion, the cutthroat, out at Marvel Lake in the Rockies. A cutthroat will give you a short but intense battle. Muskies are big and, taken with a light line and tackle, provide enough excitement; but taken on hand lines and drowned from the back of a motor boat, as happens to be an all too common practice, there is no sport in it. They're all grand fighting fish, but it's the bronze-back that never knows when he's licked.

Yes, sir, there's just something about a bass that gets most of my admiration. For one thing, he's a good family man; far better, for example, than a trout. In spawning time he watches the nest, protects the fry, and drives away predatory fish. He's no fool, either. If he strikes once and you miss him, you've lost your chance at him because he won't come back. A trout, generally thought to be much cagier, will return several times.

Plenty of people will tell you that a muskie taken with a light line and tackle is the ultimate in fishing excitement. It makes swell reading, too, when the boys write about how the savage muskie got away on them by straightening out the hooks; but all that kind of talk means to me is that they were either poor quality hooks or the angler wasn't playing the fish right. I'll take a three-pound bass in comparison to a 50-pound lunge any day.

Look at it this way. Let's suppose you're a fight fan. Now whom would you prefer to watch—Primo Carnera or, say, Jimmy McLarnin? Carnera, a lumbering giant weighing some 265 pounds, is undoubtedly the harder hitter of the two. But the little man, McLarnin, is far faster, much cleverer, infinitely more resourceful, and no one has ever questioned his great courage. It's McLarnin who gets the nod because you know he'd give you more action in five minutes than Carnera would in five hours. And for exactly the same reasons, I prefer to fish bass to muskie.

There are, of course, factors that affect the fighting qualities of fish, and you want to battle when they're at their best. I've taken my favourite bronze-back when he came in belly up after showing nothing more than a mere flurry of fight. That was in midsummer, with the thermometer crowding 90 and the lake water warm as milk. Even the bass had been slowed up to the point of sluggishness. But get him in the clear, cold-water lakes and rivers of Northern Ontario and Quebec early in the season when he's firm-fleshed and healthy, and he'll give you all the fight you want, more for his weight than any of his finny brethren.

For me, by far the most enjoyable part of fishing is what might be termed the hunting end of it. It's what makes a resourceful fisherman. I find the bush exciting. I like to explore it for myself, make portages, put my judgment to the test by trying new waters. I like to think I can look at a lake or a stream and be reasonably certain about the kind of fish there are in it and just where to find them. I like to use my own judgment, too, in regard to flies. There are so many things to be considered; the weather and the kind of insects you find on the water and so on. And I don't like to take many fish because I learned a long time ago that very little of the sport in fishing lies in capturing the fish. Among other things, I like to give the fish a little edge on me by using small hooks and light lines; then if he beats me I can watch him go without bitterness. Or, better still, if I lick him I can set him free and feel exhilarated by my action.

"You know," a friend once said to me, "catching game fish is a real test of moral fibre. There's no sport on earth as fascinating or exciting where there isn't a referee. There is no referee in fishing except God. It's you and the fish and God. There's no human referee to make you act the part of the sportsman and give a game fighter a fair break."

Morality? Why not? Sentimentality? I don't think so. You're looking for sport when you go fishing, and you won't find it unless you impose certain limitations on yourself. You have to conceive of fishing as a kind of game, and you have to obey the rules even if there is no referee to enforce them. If you break them through ignorance there is no penalty; but if you break them knowingly, the penalty should be in your own feeling of dissatisfaction and disgust with yourself. If you don't feel this dissatisfaction, you may be sure you are no sportsman.

But sportsman or no sportsman, before you lay claim to the fighting championship for muskie or trout or salmon, for anything but the bronze-back, fill your packsack and head for those cold-water lakes and rivers up North. Put your fly over one of those battling beauties, strike just before he does, set the hook, and when you're through with that next wild 10 or 15 minutes, I think you will have changed your mind.

In 2002, Ontario had 1.6 million anglers, with small-mouth black bass second to walleye among them in popularity. The French River had become so popular by the mid-1990s that restrictions had to be imposed on both fish.

Dink Carroll, who popularized "Rocket"' as Maurice Richard's nickname, graduated from law school at McGill University but never practised. Instead, he pursued his love of sports in a journalism career that saw him write columns for the Montreal Gazette for nearly 50 years, from 1941 to 1987. He died in 1991 at 92.

Sallys in Our Alleys

—January 1, 1944—
Larry Gough

A FEW SHORT YEARS AGO when bowling was a game that called for 10 big pins, a 16-pound ball and a hairy-chested man to roll the latter at the former you were about as likely to find a woman bowling as you were to find her playing hockey for the NHL.

But times have changed, and if you don't believe it you either haven't been in a bowling alley in the past few years or else you're living in an all male community. Today the girls are out in force, sliding up to the foul line, rolling the ball with a will and shouting with glee as the pins clatter to the floor. It's generally

Ollie Miller showing her form

accepted that there are now as many women bowling across Canada as there are men, and that means thousands of women according to the men who ought to know—the proprietors of the alleys. Those same gentlemen estimate that approximately one person out of four in the larger towns and cities bowls at least occasionally and that there are a good 800,000 people in Canada who can be classed as dyed-in-the-wool bowling fans.

The female invasion of the game started when tenpins went out of favour and fivepins came in. That was back in the mid-twenties, although the game of fivepins was first introduced to a waiting but not too excited public in 1909 by the brothers Ryan, a pair of Toronto bowlers who thought it was time for a change. History does not record whether or not the Ryan boys designed their game with an eye to the ladies, but whatever their intentions they wound up by producing a sporting delicacy that the fair sex has all but gobbled up whole.

Under the Ryan regime the 16-pound ball gave way to a three-and-a-half-pound replacement, the number of pins was cut in half, the pins themselves were reduced to about half their former dimensions and each one had a rubber band around its middle to make it livelier and to keep the ball from rolling effectively between it and its next-door neighbour. As a result players found, and this appealed particularly to the ladies, that good scores were easier to make and that bowling alleys could be pleasant places to spend an evening playing with pleasant people.

Now the ladies play with men on mixed teams, have leagues of their own and even have a large and growing section of the Canadian Bowling Association all to themselves. What's more, they've mastered the sport to such an extent that the average score of a good lady bowler is only 15 or 20 points lower than the 240 or 245 that a man must consistently score in order to be considered really top flight.

Mabel McDowell, Toronto, president of the ladies' section of the CBA and one of the best of the timber topplers in any league, says that any girl can be a good bowler if she really wants to, even if her hands are doll size and she's never before engaged in any sport more active than a quick kiss on the living room sofa. "There are some natural bowlers," says Mrs. McDowell, "but they're the exception, not the rule. Most girls taking up the sport for the first time will find they're not very good at it but they can and will improve quickly if they bowl regularly."

A right-handed girl, to be in proper balance when she bowls, according to Mrs. McDowell, should step out with her left foot, take a step with her right and then slide a little on the next step with her left foot forward. Her right arm should swing forward with the ball as far as it will go; she shouldn't drop the ball at her feet with a bang and a bounce. If she remembers the steps, the slide and the follow-through she shouldn't have any trouble making a passable score.

"That is, of course," smiles Mrs. McDowell, "if she remembers to hit the head pin every time."

A game of fivepins—by far the most popular variation of the bowling sport in Canada with both men and women—consists of 10 "frames" in each of which not more than three balls are bowled. If all pins are down after the first ball you've scored a "strike." If two balls knock them down it's a "spare." Both strikes and spares give the bowler a chance to count extra points in the next frame, and thus bolster his score. If you bowl strike after strike you wind up with a perfect score of 450 and a lot of envious stares from your friends and acquaintances. If you don't score strike after strike—well, you're just like every other bowler.

In the more than 15 years since the Canadian Bowling Association was founded fewer than a dozen men have bowled perfect games, and no one is on record as having done it twice in league competition. So far none of the ladies has rolled up a perfect score, although several of them have come within a few points of doing so. Scores of 300 or slightly better have become fairly frequent among women as well as men, but a game that approaches 400 is still considered an event in the life of any bowler. Much more common than a near perfect score, in the experience of most bowlers, is a near zero, caused by an off day, an inexplicable loss of coordination or, as some insist, with only the semblance of a smile, the evil eye.

Bowlers who take the game seriously belong to a league of some kind, whether it is a church, club or business group. The cream of the bowlers, both men and women, play in the big-time "city" or "major" leagues. Many teams have a company as sponsor, which pays for the bowling and derives a certain advertising value from whatever prestige the team can win.

It may surprise you to learn that there is such a thing as good or bad bowling weather, but the best bowlers insist this is so. "On a nice, crisp, winter day," says Mrs. McDowell, "the pins fall quickly and sharply. Good scores are easier to get. If it's dull and humid, on the other hand, the pins seem sluggish and won't fall or fly properly at all."

I tried one night, not long ago, to find out at firsthand just what it is that makes women—and for that matter men—like the game of bowling so much. The men I approached seemed to take the attitude that I was trying a new angle to bilk them out of their playing time and steal their alley. Mostly they just looked me up and down and said something like, "We like to hear the racket when the pins fall. Now, on your way, chum."

The ladies, on the other hand, opened up and gave me a few good reasons. Most of them said that bowling appealed because it was a game of good, fast action that didn't demand too much violent exercise. They also liked to think that here was a game in which they could make high scores without taking lessons from a professional. One or two, obviously of a very practical turn of mind, said it was a good way to spend an evening without using up too much of the boy friend's working capital. Another girl, of even a more practical turn, told me in strictest confidence that she had lost 13 pounds since she started to bowl and that she regarded the game as a practical example of the old theory of diminishing returns.

Ollie Miller, a tall, smiling girl who is generally conceded to be in a class by herself among the lady bowlers, has a few tips to offer that might be useful to girls who will be playing the game for the first time this winter.

"The most important thing of all," Mrs. Miller says, "is shoes. Don't bowl in high heels. You can't slide and you can't bowl your best game. Besides, you may turn your ankle and merely succeed in hurting yourself when you should be having fun."

Real bowling shoes, with soft soles and rubber heels, she claims, aren't very expensive and are worth plenty to any girl who expects to spend much time at the game. If you only plan to bowl occasionally and don't want to bother with the real thing, then wear a pair of low-heeled sport shoes.

"Another thing worth some attention," she says, "is your dress. You can't bowl in a tight skirt, but one that's too flaring isn't any good either. A tight one will keep you from bending and sliding properly and a flaring one may get you all tangled up just as you're about to let go of the ball."

Mrs. Miller thinks that the most important factors in becoming a good bowler are an even temperament and the ability to relax and realize that, after all, bowling is only a game. "It should be fun," she says, "not a chore. If you work at it too hard and blow up when you miss or get deadly serious every time you get near a bowling alley, you won't have much fun and you won't do very well at the game. And, what's more, you won't be much fun to play with." She also points out that a bowling alley is no place, these days, to practise that ancient feminine custom of being late.

Aside from the fact that there aren't enough alleys to go around in most communities and the dearth of pin boys, the war hasn't produced many serious problems for bowling fans. The only cause for complaint among the followers of Canada's most indulged-in sport seems to be that somebody else is always using all the alleys. The game, they say, is getting too popular, that's all!

An estimated one million to 1.5 million Canadians now bowl annually, about half of whom are women.

THE BOYS
OF SUMMER

Rusty Staub:
The Making of a Muscular Millionaire

—July 1970—
Harry Bruce

"RUSTEE, RUSTEE," THEY SAID. "Monsieur Staub, Monsieur Staub," and they pushed the ballpoint pens up at his face, and the old baseball programs, the pocket notebooks and the cigarette boxes, and he kept on signing his name, just that, just his name, Rusty Staub, Rusty Staub, Rusty Staub, and he'd pass the pens and the scraps of paper back down to the hands that were like the bills of hungry baby birds, and his mouth was closed over a small comfortable smile, and he'd murmur *bon soir, bon soir, bon soir. Rustee, merci. Merci,*

Le Grand Orange in 1974

merci, merci, Rustee. And they'd go away, feeling good, taking the piece of paper with just his name on it and tucking it away in a special place. You could tell that they were feeling good by watching their eyes and, for anyone who had not seen this ritual of the sports world before, the odd thing about it all was that these guys were not 11- and 12-year-olds; they were not the skinny little "Rusty Staubs" of the sandlots and the back-alley baseball of downtown Montreal. No, these guys were big businessmen, or at least they were as big as they'd been able to make themselves.

They were members of the Richelieu clubs of metropolitan Montreal. The Richelieu is French Canada's most powerful service club, and these men were top beer salesmen, merchants, tailors, stockbrokers, manufacturers, insurance executives and undertakers, and the last organized ball that any of them had ever played was probably a quarter of a century ago, 'way back in the time when they could still get away with shaving only once a day.

But look now, will you just take a look at that Rusty Staub! The Supreme Sports Hero. He hit .302 for the Expos last year and 29 home runs. He's six-foot-two and, this evening anyway, he's down to a good clean 200 pounds. The diet is working. The famous red hair ripples back in neat but gener-ous waves. The hair *fits* his head, and it's laced with gold. The suit is soft green, and it's cut in an edgy, military, Edwardian style that proclaims not only the clean breadth of Staub's shoulders, not only the youth of his waistline, but also a certain knowledge of what's going on, a conviction about where the action is, how to find it, how to exploit it and how to make out. Staub is the tallest, youngest, healthiest and, physically, the most accomplished man in this whole hallful of 300 men and, as if that were not enough, there's something about him that suggests he thinks it's entirely possible that,

one day fairly soon, he will also have more dollars than any of
them. He's the cock of the walk. He's *Le Grand Orange.*

He came to Montreal only about a year and a half ago and
already he's inspired the rhapsodic sort of public adulation that
Jean Beliveau has spent half a lifetime to build for himself.
Indeed, late last summer one of Montreal's French-language
newspapers polled its readers to discover the city's most popular
sports hero, and the winner was not *Le Gros Bill* at all, it was
Le Grand Orange. (Beliveau, a friend and sometimes golfing
partner of Staub, observed mildly that, after all, the hockey
season had not yet started.) Staub's fans insist he's even more
popular than Santa Claus and, as proof, they cite what
happened during the last Grey Cup parade. Eaton's was appre-
hensive about the ways in which assorted political trouble-
makers might react to the company's traditional Christmas
parade, so they called it off and consoled themselves by entering
the old gentleman in the Grey Cup parade. Staub, too, went
along for the ride, and his admirers insist that, all the way
down the long, cheering corridors of Montrealers, Staub got
a louder hand than Santa.

In midwinter, Staub appeared at the Montreal Forum, un-
announced, during a baseball skit performed by the Harlem
Globetrotters' basketball troupe, and there were something
close to 17,000 people there, and they caught sight of that
flaming-red head down among the black basketball players, and
they set up a racket that was louder than anything Staub had
heard since his appearance in an all-star ball game at Houston.
And he'd played for the Houston organization for eight years.
Staub remembers the night at the Forum. "Ah was awed by it,"
he says. "It's hard to get awed by yourself, but Ah was awed by
it. Ah didn't believe it." Until you have heard Rusty Staub say
he was awed by something, really *awed*, you have just not heard
a real Southern accent.

But now, the Richelieu Clubs of Montreal have just given *Le Grand Orange* a fat, brassy plaque. That's the ostensible reason why he's here. To accept that plaque. He is getting the plaque because he took 25 French lessons during the off-season, and it's strange how the press finds these things out, but now everybody knows that *Le Grand Orange* is trying to master the French language and, for Staub, it's all working out as just about the niftiest piece of personal public relations in the modern history of professional sport. This evening, he has thrown away the nice, smooth little speech that the Expos' public relations staff gave him in the afternoon, and he is ad-libbing a few halting sentences in French, and he is getting away with it. He sounds like someone who is trying to say something that is *his*, in French, and his accent is better than that of several thousand WASP politicians in Canada. And, after all, he does come from a closely knit family ("About all we did in the family was goin' to school, eatin' and playin' ball"), and he is a good Catholic, is he not? And did he not grow up only a few blocks from the French quarter in New Orleans?

Now, the House of Seagram—which includes Charles Bronfman, whose millions of dollars helped to bring the Expos to Montreal in the first place—shows the Richelieu Club its bicultural film about the sweet and famous and maybe even lucrative love affair between Montreal and its funny young baseball team and, every time Staub's big, red head goes wagging across the silver screen, all the distinguished members of the Richelieu Club applaud like happy children and, later, one of them stands up and tells *Le Grand Orange* in English that if he really wants to master the French language there's only one thing to do. Get a French girl friend. (One of the Expos' better pitchers, Bill Stoneman of Oak Park, Ill., did just that, and married her, and settled down in Kirkland, Que.) And all of these friendly events give an unusual light of warmth and significance to this strange old rite, whereby a strong young man deigns to hand out his very own signature to adoring boys, to older men, and to other lesser males.

At the back of the room, and some distance from the banquet tables, there's a 36-year-old man sitting on a folding chair and watching Staub with some obvious pride and affection. He smiles, and he smiles and he smiles. He wears horn-rimmed glasses, he is rather bald, and his blue pinstripe suit, with vest, is more conservative than Staub's. The man is a bit chubby but not so chubby as he often says he is. He appears to be very benign and Staub, who knows him as well as he knows any Canadian, has said that he has never seen this man lose his temper. Staub, whose own temperament is anything but mild, said this with respect and amazement. The man is Gerry Patterson, business adviser to Rusty Staub, and to Jean Beliveau, and to Don Drysdale, and to Gordie Howe and, now and then, to Gump Worsley, Bill Stoneman and half a dozen other pro athletes whose names alone may mean money. Patterson is an impossibly sunny combination of business and sales genius, sports fanatic and work addict. ("It's just amazing," he says, "how much work you can get done if you get downtown by 7 a.m.")

Patterson is confident that if Staub plays well for the Expos during the next four years (assuming, of course, that the Expos survive that long), then he, Patterson, will have little trouble turning him, Staub, into a millionaire. At the moment, and for the next couple of years, Staub's straight salary for playing right field for the Expos is a mere $67,000 a year. Patterson, however, has already set up Rusty Staub Inc.—the third member of the board of directors is Marvin Segal, president of Giovanni Inc., and the man responsible for Staub's very snappy clothes—and he has registered the name *Le Grand Orange*. Before too long, you can expect to see *Le Grand Orange* baseball manuals, *Le*

Grand Orange fielders' gloves, *Le Grand Orange* uniforms and, of course, *Le Grand Orange* himself as he tells you all about the super qualities of assorted sports cars, watches, outboard motors, tea, financial institutions and so on, and on and on.

For the moment, however, or for this season anyway, it is part of Patterson's strategy to exploit Staub's remarkably sudden popularity in a cool, solid and respectable way with a few cool, solid and respectable companies. Rusty Staub has a contract with General Mills, which pays him to like Wheaties. He is president of the Bank of Montreal's Young Expo Club. ("Who is 16 or under, eats popcorn, loves baseball and has lots of fun? A Young Expo.") Late this spring, Patterson was also negotiating with American Motors to get for Staub the same sort of auto-endorsement deal that Jean Beliveau enjoys.

Patterson is the president of Sports Administration Inc., vice-president and shareholder of Jean Beliveau Inc., vice-president and shareholder of Rusty Staub Inc., and a director of Gordie Howe Promotions. One of Patterson's hotter schemes is to use the names of Beliveau, Howe and Staub, and perhaps of some Canadian golf ace, to push sports equipment in an entirely new string of outlets across the country. Jean Beliveau Inc. moved into an office in Place Ville Marie as soon as the Canadiens missed the playoffs, and Patterson's ambitions and plots for *Le Gros Bill* are immense, complicated and pretty sure to turn Beliveau into an extremely rich tycoon. And soon.

Headquarters for Rusty Staub Inc. are a desk in Staub's $400-a-month, two-bedroom pad in Westmount Square. (Westmount Square is the sort of place that is invariably described as "posh.") Patterson's plans for Staub relate to what he calls a "dynasty theory" of sports heroes in French Canada. The theory goes like this: when Howie Morenz was a sports idol, Toe Blake was already coming along as the next sports idol; when Toe Blake was the idol, Rocket Richard was already coming along; when the Rocket was the idol, Beliveau was coming along. There was always an overlap but, now, Beliveau is 38, and who is there in the Canadiens' organization to take over that special spot as The Superstar? Savard? Maybe. But maybe nobody. For *Le Grand Orange*, that vacuum could just be the chance of a lifetime. "If he were to win the batting championship," Patterson says, "his opportunities would be just fantastic."

Patterson's firm, Sports Administration Inc., also handles all corporate promotions for the Montreal Baseball Club. Patterson has an office among the Expo front offices, and he's there most days of the week. Since what's good for the Expos is also good for Rusty Staub and, in a sense, what's good for Staub is also good for Patterson, this arrangement suits everyone pretty well except, occasionally, one pretty fagged-out baseball player. One week last winter, Patterson booked Staub into banquets in New York, Toronto, Montreal and London, Ont.; a network television appearance in Toronto; a business meeting with a machinery manufacturer back in Montreal; and appearances with the Expos' promotion caravan in Plattsburgh, N.Y., and Ottawa. Staub was nervous before the television appearance, on CTV's Sports *Hot Seat*.

Staub was one of the seven Expo players who chose to make their off-season home in Montreal. This decision, and the rubber chicken banquet circuit, and the French lessons, and the appearances on French-language television and the generally sweet relations between Patterson-Staub and the press were all part of what Patterson is pleased to call a "quality exposure program"; and, as far back as last January, when Staub had been in Canada only about eight months, Patterson was able to report to him that Sports Administration Inc. had already "established Rusty Staub in the Canadian community with particular emphasis on French Canada." As the night at the Forum proved, and the night at the Richelieu Club, and a lot of other public nights around town, this was an understatement.

There's a temptation to see that benign and smiling man on the sidelines as a fiendishly clever image-maker who turns big bland athletes into robots who need merely flash their dimples (or, in Staub's case, freckles) in order to get people to give them money. Staub himself, however, wrecks this theory. He may talk as though he's just a poor boy from the country who's trying to get ahead but, behind the easy Southern grace, there's a sharp awareness that, for Rusty Staub, Montreal is everything that people used to call The Main Chance. Staub's notorious determination to stay with the Montreal club in the spring of 1969, even though the Houston Astros insisted he return to Texas, made him something of a hero in French Canada even before he'd once swung a genuine, powerized Hillerich and Bradsby Louisville Slugger on behalf of the Expos. "This is the greatest town Ah ever been in," he says, "and mah opportunities are tremendously great here." Staub did not need Gerry Patterson to tell him that, in the United States, the ballplayers who make the real bread *off* the field all live in New York or Los Angeles, and not in Kansas City, or Atlanta, or Houston; and that one way to rake in that New York–style money was to establish himself as *the* baseball hero of the one and only big-league team in all of Canada.

Establishing himself as a baseball hero has not always been easy. There's evidence that, although Staub's batting swing shows the long snapping grace of Ted Williams, he is not exactly the perfect athlete. His first year in the big leagues, with Houston, he hit only .224. True, he was just 19 then but, even a year later, after a painful banishment to a farm team, he hit only .216 for Houston. Three years ago, in the year he hit .333, Philadelphia Manager Gene Mauch said, "The best batting coach Houston ever had is Rusty Staub. That boy made himself into a hitter, and he did one hell of a job." No one had ever heard of the Montreal Expos in those days and it is one of those sweet and rare coincidences of pro baseball that Staub's old admirer, Gene Mauch, is now the Expos manager.

Staub has recurring problems with his ankles, and he is far from the fastest right fielder in baseball. He says he's not so slow as some writers have claimed—"although Ah would not say that Ah am a gazelle at foot"—but that, in any event, he studies his pitchers, and the enemy batters, and thinks about the weather and the conditions of the field, and all this "gives you a knowledge of how to play a guy. You can do more with an intelligent approach than all the speed." Staub's fielding style is distinctly unorthodox. He snags flies with one hand, rather than two, and if the ball's coming low and hard toward his feet he charges it and then, instead of diving for the shoe-string catch, he sits down fast in front of the ball. That way, he argues, even if he misses the catch, the ball cannot scoot past him. His throwing arm is as natural and powerful as his swing, and he likes to point out that, last year, he led National League outfielders in assists, with 16. He also had 10 errors.

Staub reads books about positive thinking, how to think yourself rich, how to make speeches, how to win friends and influence people. If he reads any fiction at all these days, it's stuff by Harold Robbins. He's had to cut down on the less prac-tical reading, however, because hotel rooms are not always too well lighted, buses jounce you around a lot, he found his eyes were stinging, and that scared him a bit. What's a ballplayer with bad vision? He detests air travel too, but what's a ballplayer who won't go up in airplanes? He's not all that crazy either about getting up early in some strange hotel room in a cold country, in the middle of January, and skipping rope, and doing hundreds of sit-ups and, over and over again, swinging a real baseball bat as hard as he possibly can as an imaginary ball rockets up to an imaginary strike zone. But what is a flabby Rusty Staub? What is a Rusty Staub who cannot hit? The answer—despite all the canny efforts of a partner who's as clever as Gerry Patterson—is that a Rusty Staub who can't hit is just another ageing baseball player who will never have a million dollars.

Staub, by comparison with most athletes, really does try harder; and perhaps this is because he *wants* harder; and, surely, with so much future riding on his current performance, he must worry harder, too. He says, "When Ah first came into the big leagues, Ah was desirous of some of the stuff that the established players had, and Ah knew, heck, to attain that Ah had to work mah ass off . . . and Ah did, and this is something Ah worked mah ass off for, to be able to stay in this apartment and pay this rent . . . You worry, sure. You tell yourself you don't worry, you just work. You say what are you worrying about? You're making more money than anyone 26 years old can reasonably expect to make. But some things, like that contract Gerry was talking about a little while ago, it's like when you're hungry, and you could almost taste the food in your mouth. And sure Ah want it, but you just try to go back to the basic thought: *the only thing Ah can do is right now*. It's what's taking place now. It's what you have to apply right now. It's not the last pitch, and it's not the next pitch, but it's *this* pitch. And there's the enchilada."

That was in April and, though the Expos were playing disastrous baseball, Staub was hitting well over .350 and, everywhere he moved in the city, men and soft-eyed young women would recognize him, wave at him, smile at him and wish him well. In a bar, he startled a juicy girl with dark hair by helping her off with her coat. They'd never met. "Actually," he told her, "Ah'm not that nice a gentleman." She smiled right back in his face, and said, "I know, but you're one hell of a baseball player."

If you walk with *Le Grand Orange* almost anywhere in downtown Montreal, the city feels kind and cheerful, the way small towns are supposed to feel, and it is hard to believe that he does not deserve what he can get.

Rusty Staub spent three years with the Expos before being traded in 1972 to the New York Mets. He played for various teams, including briefly for Montreal again in 1979, before retiring in 1985. He lives in New York City where, among other things, he runs a restaurant.

The award-winning Harry Bruce, now a freelance writer living in Moncton, N.B., worked at Maclean's in the early 1960s and has written a dozen books on various subjects.

Baseball Heaven

—November 2, 1992—
Bob Levin

T HERE ARE MOMENTS that swell the heart, race the mind,
stir the soul. They blaze by in all their dizzying techni-
colour glory, bombarding the senses even as the brain is storing
away memories, recording them like a video machine for later
viewing.

Eight days, six baseball games—that is all it was. But it was
so much more. Never mind that the first World Series on
Canadian soil was played on shiny Astroturf, under a steel roof.
Never mind that the paid gladiators who packed SkyDome
with flag-waving Canadians were all Americans, Puerto Ricans

or Dominicans. For one stunning week, a game played with a stitched ball and a wood bat managed to unite Canadians from coast to coast even as the constitutional referendum was dividing them. More than 11 million of them tuned into some contests, and non-Torontonians did not even seem to mind that the centre of their televised attention, puffed up with pride, was hated Hogtown. And in the nation's largest city, the Blue Jays' 4–2 Series triumph over the Atlanta Braves, wrapped up in gut-twisting style down in Dixie, sent a half million people pouring into the streets in a world-class frenzy. "When the final out registered, the city roared," marvelled 44-year-old Toronto police Insp. Gary Grant, watching over the dancing, singing throngs. "I must have high-fived 2,500 people by now—my arm will be on the disabled list tomorrow."

For the Jays themselves, the road to victory was paved with fine pitching, timely hitting and steely nerves. To get there meant overcoming past failures, high expectations and shoddy umpiring, and they seemed to savour every breathless moment of it. Ed Sprague's ninth-inning homer in Game 2 in Atlanta, stopping 50,000 tomahawkers in mid-chop. Devon White's wall-banging catch in Game 3, Jimmy Key's precision pitching in Game 4, Pat Borders's Most Valuable Player performance throughout the Series, and Dave Winfield's 11th-inning double in the classic, cardiac-arresting Game 6 that let the celebrations begin. And no one had more to celebrate than Cito Gaston, the much-criticized Jays skipper who, amid the champagne showers in the winners' clubhouse, stood a vindicated man. "I'm churning inside with joy and happiness for all of us," he said. "I don't hold any grudges."

For all the intensity of the Series, baseball remains a kids' game, and the best-loved players showed an infectious enthusiasm. Take Joe Carter's Game 3 homer, which flew into the left-field press box, off one reporter's hands and into those of

George Grande, a St. Louis Cardinals broadcaster who was doing radio reports on the Series. After the Jays' win that night, Grande, who has known Carter for years, found him in the clubhouse video room, going over his at-bats. Recounted Grande: "I said, 'Boy, that must feel great to hit a World Series home run.' He said, 'Yeah, it's great, it gave us the lead.' I said, 'Too bad you didn't get the ball.' And he said, 'Yeah, but I still have the thrill, I'll always have the memory.' And then I took the ball out and held it up and his eyes got big as saucers and he said, 'No.' And I said 'Yeah.' And he said, 'This is the ball?' And I said, 'Here, it's yours,' and the look on his face was just amazing."

To some Torontonians, the wonderful World Series avenged an earlier Atlanta victory: the right to host the 1996 Summer Olympics, a prize Toronto had also sought. For all their recent rivalry, though, the two cities have much in common. Both are painfully insecure, wary of their portrayals in the U.S. national media. As sick as Canadians are of Americans' image of them as dog-sledding moose-hunters, so Atlantans are tired of their stereotype as tobacco-spittin', hell-raisin' rednecks; locals have even joked that the city's slogan should be: "Atlanta—It's Not Georgia." Just as Toronto wants to be a "world-class city," Atlanta strives to be an "international city."

The main striver of them all, Ted Turner—Braves owner, Cable News Network founder, and Mr. Jane Fonda—has his office in Atlanta's modern Omni complex. It looks out over an atrium filled with fast-food restaurants and, as it happens, the Canadian consulate, where last week Consul General James Elliott draped a Jays banner in the very heart of Braves country. Yet even Canada's man in Atlanta admitted to slightly split loyalties. "I've lived here two years," said the native of London, Ont., "and I know the Braves better than I know the Jays. I've been to the ballpark quite a few times, I've followed them on

TV. So before you know it, the tomahawk chop"—he grabbed his right arm and laughed. "Remember in *Dr. Strangelove*, the rocket scientist kept trying to make a Nazi salute and he had to hold his arm down?"

While baseball is not the traditional sport of choice in either city (Southerners are as fanatic about football as Canadians are about hockey), the Series captivated both places. What is it that makes people pack sports bars, paint their faces funny colours and live or die with every split-fingered fastball and high-arcing fly? "Maybe it's that the fate of baseball teams seems so much like people's own lives," mused one Atlanta fan, 37-year-old Vivian Sandlund. "You struggle and struggle and sometimes things happen that are out of control, and you go through periods of being down and then you have to pick yourself up again." Blue Jays batting coach Larry Hisle opened into a slow smile as he considered the question, posed in mid-Series. "It might be unexplainable," he finally said. "For an entire city to get caught up in whether a team wins or loses is oftentimes mind-boggling to me. In Toronto, I'm quite sure that if we win, the effects will stay with the city for years to come."

The team, the city, the country—all will feel the effects. No one will ever again accuse the Jays of choking. No one will say Canadian fans are too sedate. "No one," said Tom Noble, 35-year-old security supervisor for the Jays, blowing his trumpet in the post-Series street celebrations, "can ever take this away from us."

Joy—sweet, unadulterated joy. It is all too rare.

Bob Levin, who joined the magazine in 1985, is an executive editor at Maclean's.

What a Blast!

—November 1, 1993—
James Deacon

N EITHER PAUL BEESTON NOR PAT GILLICK are in the club-house when the corks are fired. The president and general manager, respectively, of the Toronto Blue Jays let their players celebrate the team's second straight World Series championship in the usual champagne-spraying fashion. Veterans of victory, Gillick and Beeston have no interest in sticky hair and stinging eyes and, instead, savour the triumph in a private box above third base until the storm has passed. By then, thousands of SkyDome faithful have taken their party to the streets. And by then, the clubhouse crush has eased enough that the two

Joe Carter rounding the bases after his 1993 Series-winning homer executives can congratulate the players individually. Gillick, shy and reserved, shakes their hands. Beeston, a man of the players, exchanges jokes and hugs. Though both have been with the club for all of its 17 seasons, neither will accept credit for what has just occurred on the field. "It's the players," Beeston insists. "They are the ones who have to go out there and win the thing."

Despite their denials, the Jays would hardly have become baseball's winningest franchise without Gillick and Beeston. "As long as those two guys have something to do with it, this will always be a winning organization," says Ed Sprague, the team's third baseman. After losing 12 players off the 1992 roster, the Jays' odd couple gave top off-season priority to signing slugging outfielder Joe Carter and free agents Dave Stewart, a pitcher, and Paul Molitor, a Milwaukee Brewers star who longed for a World Series championship. When Toronto beat the Philadelphia Phillies 8–6 to win the Series last Saturday, Stewart was the Jays' starting pitcher, Carter hit the game-winning home run and Molitor won the most valuable player award. Chalk one up for the front office. But, as Beeston and Gillick point out, the old cliché still applies: the game is won between the white lines, where nothing can be taken for granted. Or, in the words of Jays manager Cito Gaston, the man whose calm hand steered the team day to day, "This game will jump up and bite you if you plan too far ahead."

Preparing for the opening game of the Fall Classic on Oct. 16, Toronto gets all dressed up. Blue Jay paraphernalia decorates anything big enough to bear a "Go Jays Go" poster. The underground concourse outside the Jays' clubhouse is festooned with paper banners from grade schools around the country; one child, whose affection for the team outstrips his spelling, writes, "Go Joe Carder." On the eve of the Series, the club throws a gala party at the Ontario Science Centre, where local politicians and celebrities mingle at the buffets with baseball insiders from around the league. The players, as usual, stay away: an autograph-seeker, even in black tie, is still an autograph-seeker. Around town, visiting Phillies fans speak well of their reception—or most do. On game day, two men in red Philly caps, parking in a lot across from SkyDome, are puzzled by the price. "What do you mean, $25?" one demands. "The sign says $5." The proprietor, unapologetic, says simply, "This is the World Series." Toronto the Not-So-Good.

As the two teams gather, media attention focuses on their contrasting images—the buttoned-down, businesslike Blue Jays versus the bad-boy Phils. The embodiment of the latter is bulky, bearded first baseman John Kruk, who tosses off colourful quotes like he swings a bat: unorthodox but effective. Caught smoking by a woman who said an athlete should know better, Kruk provided a credo for his entire team. "Lady," he replied, "I ain't no athlete, I'm a ballplayer." But while hand-drawn banners at SkyDome describe the Phillies as Phat and Philthy, a more accurate description would be Phabulous. The truth is, the Phillies' beards and girth disguise the depth and talent that took them from worst to first in one season and that beat Atlanta for the National League pennant.

On field, the buzz is palpable. Long before his scheduled workout, Philly reliever Mitch Williams, known as "The Wild Thing," paces by his dugout, rhythmically tossing a ball into his glove. Nervous, Mitch? "Nah," he says. "Just getting warmed up." Rickey Henderson, the Jays' late-season conscript, works with batting coach Larry Hisle in an attempt to recover his missing stroke. Henderson's problems at the plate have turned attention to his shaky fielding. Yet he stays in the lineup because, according to Hisle, "his importance in the Series could be immeasurable—he can dominate a game when he's on." Watching nearby, Rich Hacker talks about his role with the

Jays. Hacker, the team's third-base coach, was nearly killed in a horrible car wreck last summer, but he is in uniform, if not in his old job, for the Series. In a sport where superstition reigns, Hacker has been given the task of filling out the lineup card because, when he did so in two playoff games against the Chicago White Sox, the Jays won. "Hey, I'm going for three in a row," he says.

The Phillies plan to beat Toronto with patience and hustle. Their scheme is to avoid swinging at bad balls and force the Jays' starting pitchers, particularly Juan Guzman and Dave Stewart, to throw strikes. Following the blueprint, Lenny Dykstra, the overmuscled Phillies lead-off man, earns a walk off Guzman, steals second and scores on a single by Kruk. Kruk, who moves to second when Dave Hollins gets another walk off Guzman, scores on a single by catcher Darren Daulton. Patience and hustle.

But the best-laid plans are not enough against the Jays this night. The Phillies' Curt Schilling falls into the habit of starting each batter with off-speed pitches, and John Olerud, the Jays' smooth-swinging first baseman, takes note. When he steps to the plate with the teams tied 4–4 in the sixth inning, Olerud wallops a Schilling first-pitch change-up over the right-field fence. The Jays go on to win 8–5. The next day in practice, Schilling seeks out Olerud. "I only throw that pitch maybe four times a year," Schilling says. "That's about as good as it gets." Olerud, ever-quiet, grins sheepishly, as if to say, "Just lucky, I guess."

Some of the Jays' faithful, though, are leaving nothing to luck. That Sunday morning at suburban Etobicoke's Nativity of Our Lord Roman Catholic Church, Father Reg Whelan ends the 11:30 mass by leading his parishioners in a rousing cheer for the Jays, then high-fiving his way down the aisle. Fans at SkyDome that night are having similar thoughts: in the upper deck, a banner dubs the stadium "My Blue Heaven." But Stewart is less than heavenly, and a pitcher struggling for control against the major leagues' most prolific hitting team might as well be bleeding in a pool of piranha. Spectacular fielding plays by Jays second baseman Roberto Alomar keep the score close, but in the third inning, down 2–0, Stewart faces Jim Eisenreich. The Phillies' outfielder suffers from Tourette's Syndrome, a disease that, without proper medication, occasionally renders him unable to control his movements. Released last winter by Kansas City, Eisenreich, like so many Phillies, found a new baseball home in the City of Brotherly Love. "You always think that if you stay healthy and play good fundamental ball, you have a chance to get to the Series," Eisenreich said. "But the longer I was in the game, the more it seemed like that wasn't going to be the case." Against Stewart, Eisenreich makes good on his Series chance, hammering a three-run homer to give Philly a 6–4 win.

Toronto fans, however, are consoled by their first sight of Williams in action. He does finally get the save, but only just. "He's not called the Wild Thing for nothing," Eisenreich says afterwards. In Etobicoke, Father Reg still doesn't think the Phillies have a prayer of taking the Series. "It's going to be the Jays in six," he predicts.

With one victory in hand, Philly Phans go home confident, if somewhat quizzical. "You really notice a difference in Toronto," says Steve Argentina, a Philly season's ticket-holder who saw both Toronto games. "I mean, we were up there two days, wearing our team jackets and cheering for the Phillies, and nobody bothered us. People were asking us if we were having a nice time. That would never happen in Philly." Argentina and brother Perry both sport new beards in unity with their team. In fact, beards are as ubiquitous as red ball caps in Philly. "I started growing this during the stretch drive," says the driver of an airport-hotel shuttle, stroking the still-unfamiliar growth on his face. "I'm not shaving until they win."

The night before Game 3, Phils owner Bill Giles throws a party for visitors and natives that, in the notably penurious owner's view, cost "enough to add another ballplayer to the club." Some partygoers suggest it would have to have been a minor-league ballplayer. In the next morning's Philadelphia *Daily News*, columnist Bill Conlin belittles Toronto and makes disparaging remarks about singer Rita MacNeil's weight. Conlin, it should be noted, weighs 290 lb.

Around town, everyone is aflutter about the Phils. One local TV station devotes all but a few minutes of its 11 p.m. newscast to pre-game stories—including strategies on where to park. World Series mania nearly obscures the fact that pop diva Madonna is playing the Spectrum across the street from Veterans Stadium on the night of the game. It is not difficult to spot the concertgoers, in their leather bustiers, fishnet stockings and riding crops, among the red-clad Phillies fans. Meanwhile, back in Toronto, fans in sports bars and nightclubs have warmed to the Phillies' style. "I mean, how can you hate a guy like John Kruk?" asks 29-year-old musician Jim Casson. "A friend of mine was saying that he likes the Phillies because it gives a guy hope that, with physiques like theirs, anybody can play baseball."

Most of the chatter in Toronto and in Philly, however, is about Gaston's decision to use Molitor at first base in place of Olerud. Olerud is the American League batting champion, but Gaston wants right-handed-hitting Molitor against left-handed pitcher Danny Jackson. Ever-gracious, Olerud takes his extraordinary benching in stride. "It probably makes sense to put Paul out there in his most comfortable position," he says. "There is already a lot of pressure to play well without worrying about playing an unfamiliar position."

Molitor vows that he will do everything he can to make Gaston's decision work—and he proves to be a man of his word. Not long after the tarpaulins are pulled off the field following an hour-long rain delay, Molitor smacks a two-run triple into right-centre field. He tops that in the third inning, slamming a solo home run that nearly hits the 1980 World Series decal hanging beyond the left-field fence. "It looks like Cito made the right decision tonight," Phillies manager Jim Fregosi says later. The major beneficiary is Pat Hentgen, the Jays' 24-year-old starting pitcher who keeps the Phillies off balance and wins a crucial game.

The next day dawns rainy and foggy, obscuring the giant red Phillies cap that a daredevil fan has placed on the head of William Penn, whose statue sits atop the city's beautiful old city hall. From there, Broad Street bisects blue-collar South Philly, home of circular Veterans Stadium. At the ball park, players speculate about the effect of the incessant rain on the thin and uneven artificial turf that is difficult to play on in good conditions. Reporters, meanwhile, scramble to book alternative flights in case of a rain out.

The game starts on time in conditions befitting a horror movie: call it Nightmare on Broad Street. With a thick paste of mist and drizzle swirling over the playing surface, neither team is able to conduct batting practice before the game. So they turn the strange contest itself into batting practice of a sort. In its slow and often brutal progress, the game takes on a savage beauty, with two granite-jawed heavyweights slugging away relentlessly, too proud to go down, too slow to deflect the repeated attacks. Toronto pounds out three runs in the first— take that. Philadelphia responds with a vicious, four-run uppercut in its half of the inning—take THAT. With Toronto starter Todd Stottlemyre's chin already bleeding after a second-inning base-running mishap, Philly strikes again, punching across two more runs in their second at-bat.

On and on it goes. Stottlemyre does not even take the mound in the third inning; the Phils' Tommy Greene does and is pummelled for four more runs. Inning after inning, defence-less defenders scurry across the rain-slick carpet chasing a barrage of base hits. Dykstra, the lifeblood of the Phillies, hits two huge homers and comes within a foot of a third. Relievers come, relievers go. For the Jays, the game seems out of reach when the Phils take a 14–9 lead in the seventh. But in the eighth inning, two remarkable things happen. The Jays hammer the Philly relief corps—including Williams—for six runs, the last two on a seeing-eye triple by centre-fielder Devon White. And the relief combination of Mike Timlin and Duane Ward actually get some batters out. Toronto survives, 15–14.

When it finally ends, Game 4 sets the World Series record for runs in one game, ties the record for hits (32) and blows away the record for the longest nine-inning game (four hours and 14 minutes). And after all the stories about how different the teams are, Game 4 reveals them to be fundamentally similar—powerful hitting clubs that are pitching-weak, particu-larly in middle relief. "That was a war out there," says an incredulous Stewart. "It didn't look like any of the pitchers could get anyone out." But in the Philly clubhouse, there is only remorse over losing a five-run lead. "What can I say, we let it get away," Dykstra says. "You don't have to be a baseball genius to know that we should have won that game."

Still, Philadelphians retain at least a gallows sense of humour. At the Vet the next night, a scraggly-looking man carries a cardboard sign that reads: "Will pitch middle relief for food." But what a difference a day makes. Far from a slugfest, Game 5 offers two dominating pitchers—Guzman and Schilling—a couple of scratched-out Philly runs and some missed scoring opportunities by Toronto. The valiant Schilling is helped by swirling winds that forbid anything less than a cannon shot to qualify for a home run. One smash by Olerud, Dykstra says later, should have reached the upper deck but instead fell benignly into his glove. Facing elimination, the crowd rises anxiously with each close play or noisily to taunt Guzman or boo the umpires. Even between innings, the stadium is abuzz with the antics of the Philly Phanatic, surely sport's best sideline performer. And when Molitor flies to centre, completing Schilling's shutout, the 62,706 at the Vet erupt in a long, ringing cheer that follows the players as they disappear into the clubhouse.

Wrapped in a full-arm ice pack, Schilling meets Fregosi by the interview room beneath the stands. Fregosi gently pats his pitcher's shoulder and says, "Thanks." Robin Roberts, the 67-year-old Phillie Hall of Famer who threw out the game's first pitch, leans in and adds: "That was great, just great."

Not to Toronto fans, 36,302 of whom gathered at SkyDome to watch the game on the Jumbotron. Among the sea of Canadian flags, Jays banners and painted faces, 16-year-old Meaghan Eley is philosophical. "I personally want them to win at home," she says. "And on Saturday night we could party." Nor is the game a total loss in Butlerville, the Newfoundland town that is the ancestral home of Jays back-up outfielder Rob Butler. The 23-year-old Butler, who grew up in Toronto, delivered a pinch-hit single in the eighth inning that left his grandmother, Mildred Butler, "tickled pink." Although the Series sometimes keeps the townspeople awake until two or three in the morning, "I've watched every second of every game," says Rob's uncle, John Butler. "It's unreal—the town's gone right mad."

Toronto is beside itself with excitement at the prospect of a World Series clinching game on Canadian turf. With their team leading three games to two, callers to radio phone-in shows vacillate between confidence and insecurity. That wedge of doubt, however, is seemingly eased when the Jays take their first lick at Terry Mulholland, the Phils' Game 6 starter. The Jays have had trouble hitting left-handers, but Mulholland holds no mystery to the top of the order. Molitor's triple scores one run, and Carter and Alomar drive in another pair before the inning ends. The Phils reply with a single run in the fourth, but Toronto comes back with runs in both the fourth and fifth to go up 5–1.

But the Phillies did not beat Atlanta with mirrors. Unfazed by the deficit much less the rabid SkyDome crowd, the scrappy Phils beat up Stewart and reliever Danny Cox in a seventh inning highlighted by the dynamic Dykstra's fourth homer of the Series. The visitors pull ahead 6–5—and Toronto's doubts are back, only deeper.

The Jays' half of the seventh and eighth innings pass without a run. Reliever Ward holds the Phils at bay, setting the stage for a classic bottom-of-the-ninth confrontation: the top of the Jays' order against the Wild Thing. Williams walks Henderson. He gets White to fly out, but then gives up a solid single to Molitor. Carter, hitless in three at-bats, steps up. On a 2–2 count, Williams throws one low and hard—and Carter, who feasts on low pitches, reaches out and swats a low line drive over the left-field fence.

The crowd reacts slowly—things like this only happen in movies. But the homer is real enough, and the 52,195 fans explode like the SkyDome fireworks. Carter, romping around the bases, is eventually entombed in a pile of bodies, but later says he didn't mind. "Everyone who has ever played baseball has probably dreamed of hitting a home run in the bottom of the ninth to win a World Series," he says long after the final crack of his bat. "I can't tell you what it feels like to actually do it. It's incredible—really incredible." Darnell Coles, a Jays reserve who was preparing to pinch-hit for light-hitting

Alfredo Griffin when Carter's ball left the yard, says simply: "That might be the happiest time in my life that I didn't get to come to bat."

And so it is two in a row. The players and their fans, fighting hangovers, will celebrate the next day with a raucous victory parade. But the achievement of back-to-back championships will take longer to sink in. Certainly, the Jays have plenty of money, but that is not the whole story of their success. "If that's what it took, the New York Mets and California Angels would have won a few," says Tim McCarver, the former catcher who is CBS's baseball analyst on Series broadcasts. The Jays also have an all-star cast of players, but the 1988–1990 Oakland A's had a similarly gifted lineup and won only one title. It all comes back to the organization, one that, by reputation, will do anything for its players—within reason. During the clubhouse celebrations, rookie pitcher Scott Brow tries to douse Beeston with a well-shaken can of beer. The team's president, however, grabs the beer away and hands Brow an empty. Without missing a beat, Beeston says: "I was wondering when someone was going to bring me a beer." With that, he laughs and takes a big swig.

Since their World Series win in 1993, the Jays have never made the playoffs.

EATS OF
ENDURANCE

Six-Day Champ

—June 1, 1932—
H. H. Roxborough

T HE TIME IS NINE O'CLOCK Saturday night. The place may
be the most capacious arena in New York, Chicago,
Philadelphia, Berlin, Paris, Sydney, Vancouver, Montreal,
Toronto or a score of other international centres. The occasion
is the conducting of one of those weird sporting spectacles
familiarly described as a "six-day bike race."

At midnight on the Sunday preceding this particular
Saturday, the firing of a starting gun dispatched about 15 of the
world's most capable wheel-racing teams on a long, torturous
grind. Since that moment the hum of revolving wheels has

Torchy Peden, the "brightest star" in bicycle racing

not ceased. For more than 140 continuous hours these two-men teams have been whirling around the white pine boards of a 10-lap saucer.

During this time some of the competitors have suffered fractured ribs, broken shoulders or severe concussions and are now resting in hospital beds. Others had been painfully abrased or cut and bruised in dangerous crashes. None have escaped the marks of the prolonged mental and physical strain that is associated with so many hours and days of constant effort and excitement.

Nevertheless, the chase for fame and gold has continued. At this moment it is announced that a prominent sportsman has offered $100 to the winner of a special 10-lap sprint.

Quickly, the fastest partners take to the track if they are not already there, and plunge into the initial manoeuvring for position. Heads are down, legs are pumping like well-oiled pistons, the low musical hum expands gradually to a noisy buzz. Up to a speed of 50 miles an hour, almost defying gravitation, chancing spills, taking risks that few other athletes need ever face, the racers streak around the well-worn track, while thousands of spectators stand on seats and wildly shout encouragement.

Soon the terrific sprint ends, and all but one of the wheelers slow up in anticipation of relief. From out of the indifferent pack at this moment there bursts a rider whose speed has not lessened. Before his opponents are aware, he dashes away to a quarter-lap lead.

At full racing speed, there swoops down from the upper portion of the track another rider, wearing the same barber-pole striping as that of the leader. This partner relieves the other man without loss of distance, retains the hard-earned margin, and feverishly proceeds to lengthen it. Once more, the arena becomes charged with sound and fury. Spectators renew their cheers; relief riders jump from bunks and leap to the challenge of the team that is out to grab a lap. Every competitor is on the track. A real "jam" is under way.

Meanwhile, the two would-be lap stealers, the battling heroes of this fast-moving picture, relieve each other every two or three laps, and summon all their riding talent and latent energy to stretch their lead, until, in one frenzied burst of furious pedalling, one of them finally catches the bunch from the rear and thus gains a one-lap lead over the entire field.

To gain this advantage at such an hour requires speed, strength, courage, persistence and judgment in a superlative degree. It may have been the achievement of Reggie McNamara, the Australian "iron man;" or Franco Georgetti, the sensational Italian; or Jean Pijenberg, the newly arrived, spectacular Dutch rider; or Letournier, the youthful French star. But it is even more likely that the leading character in that strategic steal has been "Torchy" Peden, a rugged Canadian lad who has been regularly burning up the bike-racing speedways and has wheeled himself to a position of world prominence in this battling game.

Four years ago the name and reputation of this native son had only provincial significance. Today, this strapping Victoria stalwart, six feet, 2 1/2 inches tall, with a riding weight of 214 pounds, is acclaimed by promoters, fans and contemporaries to be a moneymaker, a crowd pleaser, one of the few riders who can dictate terms, possibly the brightest star in the bicycle-racing firmament. In these times when unemployment is so prevalent, it is cheering to know that in Torchy Peden, Canada has one worker who is now definitely contracted for a solid year of highly remunerative labour.

While this accession to the pedallers' throne has been attained at the youthful age of 24, it was not gained without struggle and determination. Indeed, the athletic career of this "Western russet"—so called because of his red hair—has been so thoroughly drenched with discouragement that his ambitions and hopes might easily have caught cold and died.

During Torchy's first three years of riding, he never won a race. But he persisted until eventually he captured several British Columbia titles. Until he came East in 1928 he had never ridden on a board track, yet he competed against men who were experienced, overcame that formidable handicap, and was chosen to represent Canada at the Ninth Olympiad. At the great Amsterdam games Peden was a starter in the gruelling race of 102 miles but had the misfortune to suffer three delays necessitated by tire troubles and consequently was unplaced.

Such a disappointment might again have written *finis* to the career of a less resolute youth, but this confident athlete, with typical Western spirit, refused to remain discouraged and headed for a racing tour through the bike-racing centres of Europe. This expedition was intended primarily in order to gain experience, but Canada's "Big Bill" quickly picked up the tricks of the game and, whether the tracks were of grass, wood, cinders or concrete, he rode with such success that Europeans realized his talent and prophesied his fame.

Peden returned to Canada with a reputation that he enhanced at the expense of the best amateur racers in the United States; then, having reached the pinnacle of the gold medal and silver trophy fraternity, he decided definitely to pursue the profession of bicycle racing. So, in 1929 this victorious Victorian took out his card in the wheel-pushers' union and began to serve his apprenticeship in the dizziest of sports, the six-day bike races.

This unusual form of human endeavour is not a new pursuit. It has ridden the crest of popularity for more than 40 years. Back in 1891, when the up-to-date man rode a high-wheeled bicycle, the first six-day race was held in Madison Square

Garden in New York City. The first two contests were won by the lofty riders; but in 1893 a rider named Albert Shock rode a "safety" bicycle and his superiority over the elevated pedallists was so pronounced that thenceforth the "underslung" vehicle became the accepted type.

Bicycles have changed only a little since then, but the rules governing six-day races have changed a great deal. Originally the racers rode as individuals for 142 hours. They rested little and plugged along without relief until exhaustion often necessitated retirement. In 1898 the spectacle became so inhuman that legislators insisted that no competitor should ride more than 12 hours a day. Then the promoters, seeking a continuous ride, formed two-man teams, each to race half the time but to alternate as they desired.

Six-day races are not new, but they still have an appeal that can coax more than a quarter of a million dollars for one week of gate receipts. What provides the lure? The unusual setting; the speed and durability of the riders; national fervour; the element of danger; the extravagant publicity. In fact, the things that make a circus great are the features that tend to create a demand for this unique sport.

The six-day panorama is unusually picturesque. Inside the huge arena is a pine track, often sloped to 50 degrees at the ends. Inside this wooden speedway are two-decker bunks, where the riders sing "Home, Sweet Home" for a week less a few hours. The track and bunks are indispensable to six-day racing. So is the dining room, for the appetites of the riders are so tremendous that it has been computed that the average racer consumers four times as much food as an office worker. If that statement seems extravagant just review the menu of one race in New York: 600 pounds of lamb chops, 12 sides of beef, 500 steaks, 400 chickens, 10 boiled hams, 50 pounds of bacon, three barrels of potatoes, four barrels of spinach, four baskets of string beans, 10 dozen cans of asparagus, eight cases of peas, 100 bunches of celery, two bushels of onions, 200 heads of lettuce, 10 quarts of tomatoes, 25 heads of cabbage, 70 pounds of prunes, two barrels of cooking apples for sauce, six boxes of eating apples, 1,000 oranges, 300 grapefruits, 12 dozen lemons, 300 dozen eggs, 700 quarts of milk, 50 pounds of butter, 75 pounds of coffee, 20 pounds of tea, five pounds of cocoa, 50 pounds of rice, 20 pounds of oatmeal, six dozen boxes of corn flakes and 250 pounds of sugar.

Truly, a banquet for gourmands. Is it surprising that the estimated food bill of one Italian rider was $107?

But the life of a six-day racer is not just a season of hard work and feasting. Beneath the excitement and apparent contentment there lurks a grimness that raises its ugly head at least suspected times. In a recent Philadelphia race, Peden and Jules Audy, a 19-year-old French-Canadian, were riding a wonderful race and had become the idols of the fans. From the first night until Thursday afternoon this Canadian pair were "stealing the show" and their popularity was hourly increasing. Then a "jam" started, and suddenly tragedy stalked. Wheels crashed and little Audy suffered a severe head injury. Instantly this confident, courageous lad was reduced to helplessness, and speedily he was transported to the Philadelphia General Hospital.

Such accidents are all too frequent and serious, but the riders seem indifferent to the dangers. I have heard of one racer who crashed in a tangle that wrecked four bicycles and broke the rider's nose. He had it bound with adhesive tape and was back on the track in a few minutes. Half an hour later he locked handlebars with another rider, fell heavily under a pile of wheels, and was dragged out with a damaged skull. Nevertheless he again returned to the track, with new adhesive on his nose, and a football helmet on his injured head. It is not merely chance that prompts promoters to purchase liniments, gauze bandages, and tape in quantities that would stock an average drug store.

Based upon the comparative infrequency of the six-day races, together with the liability to serious injury, it would be assumed that the riders receive large cash rewards. However, when compared with Gene Tunney's million-dollar accumulation or Babe Ruth's $75,000 yearly salary, the remuneration of bicycle racing champions seems quite modest. A newcomer just breaking into the weekly whirl may receive $50 or $75 a day, while a few exceptionally colourful foreign teams have been guaranteed $5,000 a week. I have been told that one outstanding rider was assured that his reward would not be less than $850 a day.

In addition to a guaranteed amount or an arranged percentage of the receipts, the speedier riders garner what they call "spare change" from the cash prizes offered by enthusiastic spectators for special sprints. During the last Madison Square Garden race $700 was distributed to the riders from this source; and, by the way, $335 of that amount, including $100 from one "Gar" Wood, was won by Torchy Peden.

Despite the absence of fabulous financial rewards, applicants for entrance into the grand lodge of working wheelmen are far more numerous than racing opportunities. Six-day promoters are so hard-boiled that little consideration is given to an ambitious youngster unless his merit positively "shouts right out." A friend closely allied with the game has told me that it is easier to crash into New York's so-called 400 than to get an invitation to compete in the classic Madison Square Garden six-day bicycle race.

Once a rider is chosen to compete, he must observe the rules or pay a heavy penalty. There are cynics who assert that the laws are merely false fronts, that behind the scenes lap gains are juggled, certain races are fixed, favoured teams do not cover the mileage credited to them, and unpopular competitors are deliberately fouled. Such charges may be dismissed on the ground that they have never been proved. Regardless of the manner in which they are observed, the rules of the game are clear and fair.

During a race each team wears a number and a distinctive coloured racing shirt. At all times one member of the team must be on the track. No rider is considered replaced until his partner has come up to a position beside him. Stalling is considered unfair. Any rider making an effort to get to the front must be given a fair share of the track. Each rider must provide his own vehicles, with exception of special tires, which are furnished by the management. The team having a clear margin in miles or laps is the winner, but in the event of two or more teams being tied in laps, first place is awarded to the team that has secured the greatest number of points in special sprints held three or four times each day.

Into this unusual profession rode Bill "Torchy" Peden. For months his progress lacked any evidence of being unusual. Opportunities, however, slowly increased. Gradually Torchy's power and endurance became pronounced, until, within the past 15 months, no rider has equalled the outstanding success of the Canadian flyer. During this period Peden competed in 10 six-day races in eight different cities, with seven different partners. In these grinds he was opposed by famous racers from Italy, Holland, Australia, France, Germany, Belgium, Austria and the United States. He never started a race he did not finish. In one of the contests he finished fourth; in one, second; in eight— three at Montreal, the others at Portland, Minneapolis, Vancouver, Milwaukee and the Mecca of all, New York— Peden was a member of the winning team. In eight races he had six different partners.

Not only was Torchy superior in these distance struggles— and, by the way, Peden and his mate rode more than 2,600 miles in one race—but he has also found time to establish a new world's record for one mile behind a pacemaker.

One day last November, Doc Morton measured a 2 1/2-mile course on a paved highway at Fort Snelling, near Minneapolis. Closely pursuing a powerful motor car fitted with steel plate projections, Peden began his race with a three-quarter-mile start, then madly dashed over the certified mile at an accepted average speed of 74 miles an hour. As he completed the mile, the motor car speedometer was registering 81 miles per hour.

Thus this Victoria lad has everything essential to bike-racing success. Youth, weight, height, strength, speed, courage, ambition, confidence, temperament, experience and mentality are combined in the make-up of this genial British Columbia superathlete.

Just how long this native son will continue at the head of the pack is dependent upon desire and freedom from serious injury. But if you ask Torchy who is most likely to continue the dynasty of bike-racing monarchs, he will tell you that Jules Audy, a diminutive, blond-haired, blue-eyed Montreal lad, is the up-and-coming pretender to the throne.

Although six-day races are still run in Europe, interest in North America began to flag in the late 1930s. In total, Peden, who earned up to $60,000 annually, won a record 38 of 148 races. He died in Chicago at 73, in 1980.

H. H. Roxborough, a writer and sports administrator, wrote several books on the Olympics and was a frequent contributor to Maclean's during the 1930s. He died in 1979 at age 88.

The Rise and Fall of Tom Longboat

—February 4, 1956—
Fergus Cronin

A TWO-FOOT WOODEN MARKER over an Indian grave near Brantford, Ont., is the only monument today to a man who once was the best-known athlete in the world. His was a Horatio Alger story in reverse. For him there was no long struggle against odds, no interminable hours of training for a gradual and painful climb to the top. He started very near the top in 1906 and was not long in reaching it. Then, over the years, he worked his way to the bottom. Literally, his was a story of Public Hero to Garbage Collector.

Tom Longboat became undisputed champion long-distance

During the "marathon craze," Tom Longboat ruled the roost

runner of the world in a little more than two years after his name was first heard outside the Six Nations reserve near Brantford, Ont. A cigar was named after him (a high honour 50 years ago) and his popularity reached such heights that police stopped him from taking part in races finishing in Toronto because spectators jammed traffic in the business section. His star was bright but short-lived, and before it faded out, Longboat became the world's most controversial sports figure in the period before the First World War.

He was a naïve, long-limbed youth of 19, five-foot-ten-and-a-half in height and weighing about 140 pounds, when he took time out from his farm work on the reserve to try his luck in the 1906 edition of a race sponsored by the Hamilton *Herald* and known as the Around-the-Bay Race. It was slightly more than 19 miles, beginning and ending at the newspaper office and extending around Hamilton Bay.

It was the year of the discovery of vitamins, the launching of the ill-fated *Lusitania*, the opening of a new mining camp at Cobalt, Ont. A Canadian, Tommy Burns, was heavyweight champion of the world. Sir Wilfrid Laurier was prime minister. It was a prosperous year, and although Canadians worked 10 hours a day for an average annual wage of about $400, they could buy an English-made suit for $10, a fur coat for $21 and a trans-Atlantic trip for $26.

Longboat had developed his running legs chasing cows around the woods and fields of the Brantford reserve. He was a full-blooded Onondaga, one of the six tribes that make up the Iroquois confederacy. At the Caledonia Fair held on the edge of the reserve in the fall of 1905, Tom was an easy winner. Then in 1906 another Indian runner, Bill Davis, began to coach Longboat for the Hamilton *Herald* race. The favourite that year was John D. Marsh, who had set many distance records in England and was now a resident of Winnipeg. There were about

40 contenders. There was plenty of betting on races in those days, and the odds against the gangling Indian boy were 40 to one. It was during this race that Longboat's peculiar style of running was first noted. He had a long slow stride that was deceiving in its speed and seemed to carry him over the ground with the least possible exertion. He held his arms at an awkward angle, and his feet sometimes seemed to kick out sideways.

The Herald reported the next day: "Marsh was the pacemaker in the early part of the race, but right behind him was Longboat, who occasionally shot to the front just to test his speed. They alternated as pacemakers until the Stone Road junction was reached, when Longboat decided that the time had come for him to cut loose. He left Marsh as if he had been standing."

Longboat beat Marsh by a full three minutes, and his time of one hour, 49 minutes and 25 seconds was only 42 seconds behind the record—in spite of the fact that toward the end of the race he had taken a wrong turn and run 75 yards before someone turned him back.

Members of the West End YMCA of Toronto convinced Longboat he should join their ranks and represent them in the Boston Marathon, an annual event since 1897 and the only one of the old running classics still held today. The Boston event was 25 miles in open country, much of it uphill. There were 126 entries, but Longboat was confident. As he climbed aboard the train he told a reporter—with a grin that became his trademark—"No more Tom Longboat. I'm Cyclone Jack now." Before he was through, the public and the newspapers had many pet names for him, probably the favourite of which was "the Bronze Mercury."

April 19, 1907, was a miserable day in Boston. Runners had to buck snow, rain and slush. But Longboat won with ease. He finished in two hours, 24 minutes and 24 seconds, a record that stood for four years and was broken only after the course was made easier. Four days after the race the chairman of Toronto's Civic Reception Committee met Longboat in Niagara Falls. When their train pulled into Toronto's Union Station after dark, thousands of jubilant citizens were waiting for it. A ragged parade formed up behind a car that bore Longboat through cheer-filled streets to the City Hall, with torchbearers marching in front and behind.

Mayor Emerson Coatsworth congratulated the youth on becoming "champion long-distance runner of America" and presented a gold medal to him. But Longboat's greatest day was yet to come—also his worst. It was an era in which the individual champion rather than the team was idolized and, in the fashion of Sullivan and Corbett, the fighters, and Ned Hanlan, the oarsman, Longboat became Public Hero No. 1 to most Canadians and many Americans in a period that came to be known for "the marathon craze."

He was likeable but headstrong. He soon balked at the training rules of the West End Y, claiming, with some truth, that he hadn't done much training before and saw no need for it now. He broke the Y's rules against smoking and drinking and was suspended.

In spite of Longboat's reluctance to train, the prospect of representing Canada in the 1908 Olympic Games in London appealed to him. In 1907, Longboat had won so many races all over the country he was giving away medals and trophies to casual acquaintances. Then some question was raised as to his amateur standing. An indignant Toronto fan, J. H. King, wrote to The Sporting Life, of London, a newspaper called the sporting bible of the day: "It is the method of this [Longboat's] club (the Irish-Canadians) that has caused so much talk . . . What right has any athletic club to have men, practically without means, living in hotels month after month?" He suggested that Longboat fell into the category of "the stall-fed amateur."

Longboat was indeed "stall-fed." All his needs were provided by his club, and when its members realized that the Olympic committee would question the Indian's amateur status if he had no visible means of support, the club set him up as "owner" of a small cigar store on Toronto's King Street. The store was intentionally stocked with a supply of 50-cent cigars so that friends and backers could subsidize Longboat by buying them. The stock was not renewed, however, when it was discovered that Longboat was smoking most of them himself.

In November 1907, the Amateur Athletic Union of the U. S. declared Longboat a professional. The AAU president, J. E. Sullivan, said in New York: "Longboat will never run as an amateur in the United States . . . He has been a professional from the time he began his athletic career. He has always been in the hands of a manager . . . he is taken from town to town by Tom Flanagan with bands and carriages and silk hats . . . He ran all kinds of races at country fairs for money."

The Canadian AAU did not dare professionalize Longboat before the 1908 Olympics—all Canada was confident their Indian brave was the best long-distance runner in the world and Canadian sportsmen would not stand for anyone in their own country interfering with his chance to prove it. Six weeks before the Olympics, held in July, Flanagan took Longboat to Flanagan's birthplace in Ireland's County Limerick, combining a holiday with a training program for Longboat on the country roads around the town of Kilmallock. The runner boasted later that although he did a lot of work under Flanagan's watchful eye, he was able to bribe the dairy maids into spiking his milk with Irish whisky.

The American team used Longboat's expense-free trip as basis for a protest to the Olympic committee that he was ineligible because he was not an amateur. Newspaper columns by the score were written on this issue. The committee decided the evidence was inconclusive and Longboat was not disqualified.

The Olympic Marathon was the longest race Longboat had yet run: 26 miles, 385 yards, the distance run in 490 BC from Marathon to Athens by a Greek soldier with news of victory. And the day of the race was the hottest Londoners had had for many years. The sun was scorching as 55 marathoners from a dozen countries lined up four deep on the east lawn of Windsor Castle. The course lay over winding hilly roads, which watering carts and roller brushes had been working on all morning to keep down the dust. Every cottage on the course was festooned with flags and bunting, and thousands of spectators waited in the sun. Another 70,000, including Queen Alexandra, waited in the stadium at Shepherd's Bush where the race would finish three hours after it started.

At 2:33 p.m. the pistol cracked. Longboat, in a white jersey adorned with a maple leaf and the number 72, leaped to the front like a deer and set a killing pace. He appeared to be in perfect condition and led for a few miles, but the hills and the heat and the pace began to tell on him. At the nine-mile mark, Lord of England was leading and Tom had fallen back to fourth place. At 12 miles, Price of England had taken the lead, followed by Lord, Hefferon of South Africa, Dorando of Italy and Longboat—now in fifth place.

Dorando (his full name was Dorando Pietri) arrived at the stadium first, about two minutes ahead of the American, John J. Hayes. But 50 yards from the finish Dorando collapsed. Track officials helped him to his feet and across the line, thereby unwittingly disqualifying him. The judges then awarded the race to Hayes.

But where was Longboat?

At about the 19-mile mark he had slowed to a walk, then stopped altogether. He proceeded to the stadium in a car and was carried in on a stretcher for medical attention. Later Flanagan said, "It was the heat that beat him. We lost honestly." But Canadians and others could not believe he had failed them and rumours were widespread that Longboat had been doped. Only recently a fan (E. V. E. Harris, of Sacramento, Calif.) wrote in a sports magazine: "I had followed (Longboat) on a bicycle twice while training over the full route and never saw him distressed. You can never convince me that he wasn't 'jobbed' or that possibly $100,000 was not won on his failure."

Back in New York a pair of promoters, Pat Powers and Harry Pollock, proceeded to capitalize on the intense public interest in marathons, sparked by the Olympics. Powers was probably the biggest promoter of his time. He used to book Madison Square Garden 100 nights a year, then find attractions to fill it. Pollock was a sportswriter whom Powers found useful as a press agent. The pair induced Dorando and Hayes to turn professional and run against each other in the Garden over the full marathon distance. The race took place Nov. 23, 1908, and Dorando won by about 60 yards. Then Powers set out to get Longboat, too, to turn pro and race Dorando, but another professional had been vainly trying to take on Longboat since well before the Olympics.

He was Alfred Shrubb, reputed to be a perfect running machine, a cocky little Englishman who held all world-distance records from 1 ½ to 11 miles. He had turned pro in England, and came to America in 1907 in the hope of running a series of races against Longboat. Flanagan, his eye on the Olympics, had refused. And after the Olympics, in spite of a campaign of taunting and ridicule by Shrubb, Flanagan felt that Longboat had to redeem himself if he was to be successful as a professional.

The Indian proceeded to do just that, winning race after race. He led a field of 153 runners to win the Ward Marathon in Toronto for the third year in a row. William Stark, president of the Canadian AAU, said, "I think he has since his return from the Olympics proven himself the greatest long-distance runner of the century."

Sportswriters and the sporting public began to demand a showdown between Longboat and Shrubb, but Powers offered Flanagan a portion of the gate receipts if Longboat would take on Dorando. Flanagan agreed to a race in the Garden on Dec. 15, 1908. It was a sellout. When the pair stood at the starting line, the lanky Indian towered over the stocky Italian. At the pistol a mighty roar went up. Dorando took the lead with short, jaunty steps while Longboat loped along a few yards behind. The Italian led most of the way, but occasionally Longboat would put on a spurt and take the lead amid deafening applause and cheers. In a couple of laps Dorando would again forge ahead. The heat became oppressive and every half mile or so the runners would take a water-soaked sponge from an assistant and wipe the sweat off their faces without slackening the pace.

At 25 miles they were still close together, but Longboat seemed to be weakening. Flanagan then demonstrated his flair for practical psychology: he took Longboat's fiancée, a pretty little Mohawk, to the edge of the track. As Longboat came around again he saw the girl, her hands up and both pride and encouragement in her expression. His sinews seemed to take on new strength and he increased the pace. As the runners vanished around the track there came a roar from the crowd. Dorando, with a bare half mile to go, had suddenly staggered and dropped. Longboat jogged on alone and completed the distance.

It was front-page news on both sides of the Atlantic. In the Toronto *Globe*, the headline, "Tom Longboat Retrieves His

Olympic Defeat," took precedence over news of the ill-health of pleasure-loving King Edward VII, who died 17 months later.

Longboat was now a professional and, at 21, recognized as the best long-distance runner in the world. Little Alfie Shrubb again tried to arrange a series of races and challenged Longboat to three races at 10, 15 and 20 miles. Flanagan refused, explaining that Longboat wanted to be married.

His marriage to Lauretta Maracle, his Mohawk fiancée, took place with Indian ceremony at the Six Nations reserve on Dec. 28, 1908, and a wedding reception for them was held that evening on the stage of Massey Hall in Toronto at the close of a benefit performance for the couple. Hundreds of people filed up a runway to the stage to shake hands with the newlyweds. Five days later Longboat beat Dorando once more in a marathon race at Buffalo.

Longboat's success started a fad for racing among Indians. Several around that time appeared shyly at county fairs and, after a few wins, went on to bigger meets. Fred Simpson, an Ojibway from Hiawatha, Ont., came sixth in the 1908 Olympic marathon, and in the same race Louis Tewanina, from Arizona, came ninth. Since turning professional, Longboat had been giving Flanagan trouble. "He was all right until he started to make money," Flanagan said later. "There were times when he did not feel like running, when he refused to train properly and just generally went prima donna on me."

So Flanagan, who had become manager for Jack Johnson, later to become world's heavyweight boxing champion, sold Longboat's contract to Powers for $2,000. This hurt the runner. He complained to his wife, "He sold me just like a racehorse— to make money."

Then Powers organized the daddy of all marathons—to be held in the open at the New York Polo Grounds, which could hold twice as many spectators as the Garden. The race, held

April 3, 1909, offered $5,000 to the best of six men representing five nations: Longboat, Shrubb, Dorando, Hayes, Matt Maloney (another American) and Henri St. Yves, a dark horse from France, imported by Powers and Pollock and whom no one in America had ever heard of. Another $5,000 would be divided among the losers.

Twenty-five thousand people saw Longboat give up in the 20th mile. Shrubb fell into a walk in the 22nd, St. Yves won and Dorando came second. Longboat, at 21, was on his way down. On May 8, Longboat and Shrubb met again, this time in a 15-mile outdoor race sponsored by the Montreal *Star* on the cinder track of the newly opened Montreal Amateur Athletic Association grounds. The distance was more to Shrubb's liking than a marathon. He won by about 500 yards. Longboat went to Shrubb with his big grin and a handshake and spoke the words that became almost habit between them: "You beat me, but I beat you next time."

Powers sold Longboat's contract to Sol Mintz, of Hamilton, for $700—the price was an indication of Longboat's falling stock—and Mintz immediately arranged for a 20-mile race between the two rivals to be held on the Toronto Island track on June 28. At the gun, Shrubb set out and dragged Longboat for a mile in 4.38, the fastest mile in an American long-distance race since the marathon craze hit the continent. Longboat dropped back after this but at the 14th mile began a sprint that left Shrubb limping. In the 15th mile Shrubb quit and Longboat finished alone.

The Indian was now one up. But the score soon tilted in Shrubb's favour because he would not run the longer distances and was Longboat's superior under 20 miles. He won a 12-mile bout in Toronto and a 16-miler in Winnipeg. The Winnipeg race gave the rubber of five races to Shrubb.

Longboat became his own manager and neglected training. A sports editor wrote: "He may dawdle along beating dubs, but any good man will take his measure now." Tales of his drinking became legendary. In 1911 he was arrested for drunkenness in Toronto and received a suspended sentence.

But Tom Longboat had one more kick in him. On June 8, 1912, he ran a 15-mile race on Toronto Island against Shrubb, A. E. Wood and Billy Queal, holder of the American 10- and 12-mile records. They were billed as "the speediest quartette living." Shrubb, who had sprained his ankle, was forced to quit after leading for 5 miles. Longboat won by about a foot and set a new record of one hour, 18 minutes, 10-2/5 seconds, five seconds better than the previous mark set by Wood. Later it was claimed the Island track was short, but England's *Sporting Chronicle Annual* still shows Longboat's time made that day as the record for the professional 15-mile distance.

When the First World War broke out, Flanagan donned the uniform of a captain. With Col. Dick Greer he formed the 180th Sportsmen's Battalion and Longboat joined as a private. But army discipline did little to change the Indian's unpredictable nature. Once when the 180th was assigned to hold back a crowd and permit the 75th Battalion to entrain from Toronto's Union Station, Longboat was missing when his platoon reformed. Three days later he turned up in Halifax— he had taken a notion to go along with some of his army pals.

Longboat was overseas for the last two years of the war. As a brigade runner he was several times reported dead back home, but he came through unscathed. In February 1917, he turned up in England as Pte. Longboat of the Canadian Pioneers to run in a six-mile race at Woodford Green. In a field of 105 servicemen he came third.

The war ended, but Longboat's troubles had only begun. He found that on one of the occasions he had been reported dead his wife had married another Indian. She had also taken all the furniture from the two-story cement-block house

Longboat had built on the reserve with his early winnings. Longboat recovered his furniture but not his wife, and later he took another squaw, Martha Silversmith, a Cayuga, who bore him four children.

He drifted from job to job—farming in Alberta, working in a steel mill in Buffalo, N.Y., odd jobs anywhere—and in 1922, now 35, he returned penniless to Toronto and a job in a rubber plant. His name flared again briefly when he challenged Paavo Nurmi, the remarkable Finn, but the AAU refused to reinstate Longboat as an amateur. By 1927 he had hit the low point of his career—a job as helper on a Toronto garbage wagon.

What became of the thousands Longboat won in his prime? In his first three years as a professional he earned about $17,000. Recently I asked this question of Tom Flanagan, now 77 and living in Toronto's west end. "The same thing that happened to the money won by Joe Louis and Sugar Ray Robinson and the rest," he said. "Smart fellows show them how to double their money, and the smart fellows wind up with it all."

Longboat blew his money on liquor, fancy clothes and foolish investments in real estate. He had no idea how to handle it. His last race was against Shrubb at the Canadian National Exhibition in 1930. It was a stunt and each man got $300. Shrubb, then 53 and 10 years older than Longboat, jogged a mile and won easily.

Longboat became a mail carrier in Buffalo and in 1946 found he had diabetes. He was treated for a while at Sunnybrook Hospital in Toronto but soon went back to his reserve. "It was too lonely there," he told his wife Martha. On Jan. 9, 1949, he died and was buried on the reservation following a service in the Onondaga tradition.

"He was a better man as an Indian than he was trained as a white man," Flanagan said recently. "I often thought if we could have kept him on the reservation and brought him out just to run, what he could have done would have been even more remarkable."

Canada Post honoured Tom Longboat with a millennium series stamp in 1999. His name lives on in annual 10-km races at the Toronto Islands and at Caledonia, Ont., which are staged by the Six Nations.

Fergus Cronin, who now lives in Peterborough, Ont., worked at the Montreal Star and Toronto Globe and Mail before becoming a freelance writer in the 1950s.

WORLD
CHAMPS

They're World Champions

—January 15, 1929—
Frederick B. Watt

I N 1914, J. PERCY PAGE, principal of the Commercial High
School in Edmonton, began to begrudge the breaking up
of basketball teams turned out under his direction. Mr. Page
was a basketball enthusiast and had formed a habit of producing winning school teams. So the first women's Commercial
Graduates club was formed, comprising outstanding members of
former school lineups. In 1915, they won the Alberta championship on the formation of the provincial league, and they
have won it every year since then.

With monotonous regularity the Grads, as they came to be

The Grads of 1928 with J. Percy Page

known, generally knocked over everything that came their way. Dominion championships for women's basketball were unknown at that time and, as the eastern title was held in London, Ont., in 1922, the first year that the Edmontonians cast their eyes toward a Canadian crown, it appeared that this unsatisfactory state of affairs was to continue indefinitely. The Shamrocks of London could offer no financial guarantee, and a little known aggregation had scant hope of raising funds in a home town that was heavily supporting other sports. But the girls were keen about that Dominion playoff. Finally, with a little outside assistance, they dug down into their own pockets, made the long trip east and won the title.

They've held it ever since.

In 1924 came an even greater ambition. The world's title had been claimed by a United States team, but the Grads, even after whipping these claimants, were not satisfied that they were entitled to the honour with the sport flourishing in Europe and the Strasbourg team claiming the championship on that side of the world. So they went to the now healthy club funds, sailed to Europe, showed the leading exponents of the game— including Strasbourg—how basketball should be played, and came home with the world's championship.

They still hold it, having defended the honour at Paris at the same time that Canada's 1928 Olympic team was covering itself with glory at Amsterdam.

The Grads are known throughout Canada, though they have received nothing like the publicity they deserve. Financed only by themselves and public-spirited citizens of Edmonton, they travelled Europe last summer, from Luxembourg to Italy, and defeated the picked teams of the continent by overwhelming scores. Yet, despite the presence on that side of the water of numerous newspaper correspondents attending the Olympic games, the only word of the Grads' doings came by way of private cables to Edmonton, the import of which was finally relayed to the Dominion at large. No complaint was heard from members of the team, but the fact remains that as remarkable a collection of athletes as ever represented Canada in any sport were allowed to go their way practically ignored by their own country.

Before the make-up of the team is considered, let the statistics tell the story of what this unusual outfit has accomplished.

Since 1914, 308 league, championship and exhibition games have been played against the leading teams of the American and European continents. The Grads have won 301 of them. To accomplish this record they have travelled 54,568 miles—practically twice around the world—since 1922. Naturally this has not been accomplished by five girls alone. Of the team that went to Europe in 1924, not one, not even a substitute player, was on the 1928 lineup. In that lies the wonder of it all and in that lies the greatest tribute to Coach Page—that year after year a team dependent on a single school should be broken up, reorganized and still be able to more than hold its own with anything on this well-known globe. In the present team the old rule of allowing only Edmonton Commercial High School graduates to play was broken for the first time at the urging of citizens who believed that the team should be civic rather than one representing a single institution. Gladys Fry, a University of Alberta graduate, the present centre, is the first girl to fill a regular berth on the team under the new ruling.

For eight months in the year, the Grads practise two nights a week; more when an important series is on the horizon. Apart from that, their recreation is largely physical. For the most part it is pleasure to them to keep up this routine, but when it ceases to amuse them, they continue it just the same.

There are four stages to a Grad. A student on entering Commercial High School is given the opportunity of trying for the junior school team. By the time she has won a place, she has been well sized up by Mr. Page. When she makes the proper weight, she has a chance for the senior lineup. Then, with graduation, or in her last year at school, a place on the Gradettes is hers to win. The Gradettes, younger sisters to the Grads, have the same taking ways in intermediate circles that the world's champions have in the senior group. Finally, if a young lady has basketball "it," there is a black and gold uniform that is known throughout the world waiting for her.

It's the teamwork that does it. Player for player, the Grads have run into many stars who were their match, and sometimes their superiors. They have never yet, however, had their spirit of co-operation equalled. In the United States, where they take their basketball seriously, big commercial institutions, eager to bring their names before the public, finance teams of picked players so generously that in many cases the situation amounts almost to professionalism.

The Grads have played 45 games with the best of these. They lost three—all in a row. It occurred when the Canadians were on tour. They were billed for 10 games in 11 nights, the hours between encounters being almost entirely occupied by travelling. It was at the hands of their ancient foes, the Cleveland Favorite Knits, whom they had defeated originally for the old mythical world's championship, that they met their greatest loss. The American girls took three out of four close tussles from the fagged Canadians and promptly claimed all the honours the Grads held, although the series was billed for only the American title. The Grads debated the controversy a bit, then piped down and waited until the next international series brought the team together again. Cleveland went down under a smothering defeat and the argument came to an abrupt conclusion.

In their 45 games with American teams, the champions have scored 1,514 points against 558, an average of 32 to 11 a game.

In their seven Canadian championship series they have piled up 424 points in the 14 games to 171 against, a point score of 30 to 12. It must be taken into consideration, too, that on only a very few occasions have the Grads given way to rubbing it in to a team that is quite apparently beaten.

It is hardly surprising that a team with such qualifications is being boomed strongly as Canadian representatives at the next Olympic games. Basketball was not included on the 1924 or 1928 Olympic schedules and the Dominion was unable to secure anything but unofficial credit for the girls' brilliant performances. There is a reasonable certainty that the sport will be officially recognized in 1932, however, and the Grads will have an opportunity to obtain the reward they have so long deserved.

One of the greatest objections that has been raised to girls playing basketball under men's rules has been that it is too strenuous a sport for the fair sex and liable to damage their health. Certainly the argument seems to have its points when one sees a miniature rugby match milling beneath the hoop. Mr. Page answers the charge, however, by pointing out that none but the strongest, best-fitted girls are allowed to participate, and once they are members of a team, the compulsory training keeps them in such shape that they can absorb any amount of punishment without permanent harm.

Word of this wonder team has travelled to all parts of the world. Negotiations are under way at the moment for a tour of New Zealand, the authorities from "down under" making every effort to arrange for the bringing of the game's greatest exponents to the Antipodes. Japanese Olympic representatives interviewed Mr. Page to the same purpose in Paris last summer and the scheme is still in the wind.

It is not only the athletic ability of the girls that has won them the esteem of all comers. The moment the final whistle has blown, the players, who a moment before had been giving and taking hard knocks on the unyielding maple floor with the fortitude of rugby players, emerge as thoroughly feminine and entirely likeable young ladies. They are in constant demand at social functions and public gatherings. Best of all, conceit is unknown to them. They are, if anything, too self-effacing.

Two things have been constant in the changing scene of the Grad panorama—the team spirit and Coach Percy Page. Certainly, the man who has directed the destinies of the organization could not have achieved the same heights without some really remarkable players to work with, but it is equally certain that the finest collection of basketball players that could have been assembled would have been halted at a certain point had there been a different skipper at the helm.

The Grads won all 27 games they played in four Olympics between 1924 and 1936, when women's basketball was a demonstration sport. But since it became an official Olympic sport in 1976, the Canadian team has finished no higher than fourth. The Grads disbanded in 1940 after 25 years, a career record of 502–22 (seven out of nine against male teams), and winning the world championship every year between 1923 and 1940.

Coach J. Percy Page went on to serve in the Alberta legislature and was lieutenant-governor of the province from 1959 to 1966. He died in 1973 at 85.

Frederick Watt contributed articles and short stories to Maclean's in the 1920s and 1930s.

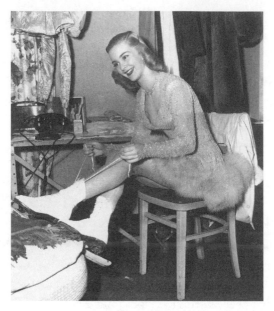

Backstage with Barbara Ann

—February 15, 1949—
Eva-Lis Wuorio

I N THE HALF-LIGHT of a Manhattan dawn last December a
slender girl, her blond hair in pigtails, walked across
Lexington Avenue from a small residential hotel to a small all-
night restaurant for breakfast. It was too early for the hotel coffee
shop to be open. She was carrying a skating costume in a rawhide
overnight bag and a pair of skates in red leather bags, and with
her was a straight-backed, middle-aged woman in a grey English
flannel suit, a tartan bonnet and a long tartan scarf.

Their footsteps echoed on the empty street, for even the
raucous traffic and shrill taxi chorus of New York awaited

Lacing up for her professional debut in New York City

the cockcrow. Barbara Ann Scott and Mrs. Clyde Rutherford Scott were preparing for the professional debut of the world's premier woman skater. The reason for the early rising was the fact that throughout the preceding weeks another show was on the theatre's small ice stage and if Barbara Ann wanted to get any practicing done on the strange ice surface she had to do it before the show troops for the day turned up.

Barbara Ann Scott, Canada's bright young joy and the World, Olympic and North American skating champion recently made her professional debut at New York's Roxy Theatre, the second largest theatre in the world. On the same program was the film *That Wonderful Urge*, starring Tyrone Power and Gene Tierney, and the usual cartoons and newsreels. Also featured with Barbara Ann were the Roxy Skating Bells; Ming and Ling, two Chinese in a Scottish act; and Gautier's Steeplechase, which presented dogs riding ponies with the climax of a monkey riding a dog who was riding a pony. Preceding Barbara Ann's eight-minute "Babes in Toyland" number were the Roxyettes, an ensemble of gals with belts of bells of varying pitch tied about their middles, which they wiggled to a seasonal tune. Barbara Ann had the finale—"Ave Maria" (Schubert) to music by H. Leopold Spitalny's choral ensemble. It was quite a change from the wind-swept Olympic ice fields.

The event made no more ripple on Manhattan's sensation-scarred surface than a fly crossing Fifth Avenue on a summer's day. There wasn't a mention about it in any of the New York papers the next day. In Canada, papers from Halifax to Vancouver were getting, and using, a couple of Canadian Press stories a day on the debut. The Toronto *Globe and Mail* and the Montreal *Standard* sent reporters and photographers to cover the event. The Medicine Hat *Daily News* gave Barbara Ann a whole page as its Christmas-issue feature. And Canadian sports writers chose her, for the third year running, as Canada's outstanding female athlete.

By Dec. 30, a week after her opening, *Variety*, the show-business weekly newspaper, recognized her appearance. It reported that Barbara Ann "gets little chance to show off her more accomplished trick-skating routines due to the confinements of the ice area." But added, "The show is brightly costumed and built in a way that makes her an easy candidate for Hollywood."

Barbara Ann, at 20, a blond, blue-eyed, kind-hearted, well-mannered, healthy young thing, had not wanted this career. Her widowed mother, Mrs. Clyde Rutherford Scott, didn't particularly care either way. But there were many advisers and loquacious friends. They pointed out the obvious fact that Barbara Ann, who had spent her life on perfecting the art of her silver blades, had at this tender age gone as far as she could go as an amateur. There were no more championships for her to win. She'd won them all. She preferred competition to professional skating, always had, but there was no one to compete against any longer.

The advice went something like this. Think of the work, the time, the patience of yourself, your mother, your trainers, that have gone into your life of skating, Barbara Ann. Remember the parties you've missed because you went to bed early. The normal fun at school you haven't had. Why, the advisers said, suppose you had educated your son to be a doctor and he just threw it up when he graduated, how would you feel? Awful waste, there, wouldn't you think?

Perhaps, too, Barbara Ann remembered herself at the age of nine when she gave up going to school to have more time for skating. She'd get up at six and practice all day at the Ottawa Minto Club. Most people would be settling down to their dinners before the small girl would trudge homeward.

There was a time, when she was getting advice about her future, that Barbara Ann used to say, "But you know I'd just like to get married, and learn to cook, and have children." Or, again, "Why couldn't I teach skating to other people, or to children?" It was then pointed out to her that certain obligations always lay heavy on shoulders of those who have risen above their fellows by some gift or ability.

People said, too, "You can make a lot of money."

"I haven't noticed that money makes you particularly happy," she answered.

"But," they said, "the things you could do with it."

That statement was the catapult that landed Barbara Ann Scott on the Roxy stage on a blustery December night, her face more heavily grease-painted than it had ever been before, on her shoulders a marabou cape and, instead of the little skull cap she'd always worn, a marabou-trimmed bonnet on her head.

The first pay cheque from the Roxy for an eight-week engagement, according to Roxy manager Sam Rauch, was about $80,000. This money Barbara Ann did not get. For she'd taken to heart the words about "things you can do with money" and founded the St. Lawrence Foundation to help crippled and underprivileged children. She chose the name in memory of her own happy childhood summers near Brockville, Ont., on Canada's great river.

The foundation is her employer. All her earnings go to it direct. Its officials pay her expenses and a salary. The directors of the foundation are J. S. D. Tory, Toronto lawyer, H. H. Caldwell of Prescott, Ont., Charles F. Lindsey of Ottawa and Robert V. Hicks, Toronto.

In the entertainment world, the foundation and Miss Scott are represented by Musical Corporation of America, which takes 10 per cent of all earnings for its services. It is at the moment considering movie offers from a number of major studios including 20th-Century Fox and Metro-Goldwyn-Mayer; it arranged for the Columbia short "Rhapsody on Ice," which was running at the Astor Theatre concurrently with Barbara Ann's Roxy appearance; and has signed her up for some television shows. Some of the officials seem inclined to favour personal-appearance offers in preference to movies.

When the first professional offers were made her (one of them from Hollywood for $7,500 weekly to Barbara Ann and $3,000 weekly to Mrs. Scott), the Toronto *Globe and Mail* reported Mrs. Scott saying, "Barbara Ann is not considering any contracts. She considers herself a good Canadian but sees no reason why she should work terribly hard and then have to turn most of her earnings over to the government." Under the present arrangement it is possible most of her earnings can go, tax-free, to the St. Lawrence Foundation.

When Barbara Ann turned professional she lost the sunlit world of ice fields, spontaneous adulation, spirited competition. In its stead she stands a chance to make a lot of money. She also got herself a retinue of employees, headed by a Canadian law firm. Her agent is Morris M. Schrier, of M.C.A., who, being an important man in the organization, allots other M.C.A. officials often to look after Barbara Ann. Her publicity agent is George B. Evans (who thought up Sinatra's bobby-sox campaign), who also has people from his office double for him at times. Twentieth-Century Fox representatives also appear on the scene as escorts or advisers.

Long before Barbara Ann's first night a lot of finagling had gone on behind the scenes. George Evans had arranged for the young Canadian girl to be met on her arrival by New York's deputy mayor and given the key to the city. He'd arranged invitations for her to dinners, receptions, and photographing orgies that later blossomed out in papers across the continent. He'd planned radio broadcasts and interviews.

Having a star's dressing room and a weekly salary in five figures doesn't really add up to either glamour or an easy life. Here's a day, typical of those in-training-for-profession times. There'll be many days like this between shows and appearances.

This particular day, Barbara Ann got up just before seven. She wanted a chance to practise on Roxy's ice cube of a rink. She had a glass of orange juice, a piece of brown toast, and a glass of milk for breakfast. She helped a breakfast guest into her coat, held the door open for her mother and, carrying her valise and skates, beamed at the doorman. A cab took her to the theatre, where she tried to glance at her mail while changing into a brief pair of grey shorts and a crisply clean blouse for practicing. Her pianist stuck his head in and announced that he was sleepy but ready.

The mail this morning included a picture from a boy in Willimantic, Conn., a poem from a Midwestern poet, 17 requests for autographed photographs from children to young boys to elderly men, a Christmas card from a real-estate salesman, a request for $3,000 from a Quebec woman, a long letter from a child minding a store in a Nova Scotian village, who wrote, "As soon as mummy comes home and can take over I'm going to go out skating so I thought I'd write you." There was a handkerchief from an invalid farmer, a letter from a boy in boarding school saying thanks for the photograph, it won him a bet from the other guys.

All letters have in common a peculiar familiarity of tone as though the writers were old, close friends of Barbara Ann's. Barbara Ann reads every one of them with obvious interest and pleasure. Every single one is answered.

When she is about ready to go on ice, word comes that a photographer from a Sunday paper is in the theatre. Would she wear something dressy? There have been other sessions for newsreel men when for as long as four hours Barbara Ann has repeated her whirls and airy skimmings until all were satisfied with their shots. This time it is for a colour shot.

Again and again Barbara Ann jumps, spins, leaps, spirals, over the spot the cameraman has marked, to the tune of "Look, honey, just do it again, let's go honey, just once more." She is hot and perspiring but still cheery when it's over. By now the curtain goes down and the early theatregoers fill in for the first show. Behind the thick curtain Barbara Ann prepares for her practicing. The pianist takes his head from his arms and shakes his head drowsily. As the movie blasts out, the girl and the pianist try to concentrate on the routine.

A *Time* writer has turned up and shouts at Mrs. Scott above the noise. "Has she always skated?"

"Always," Mrs. Scott says. "I sometimes wonder why she didn't take up the piano. Easier."

By now the ballet mistress has turned up. She watches Barbara Ann skate and calls out, "You don't make it dramatic enough. Put more PUNCH into it. Lift up your arms for your last bow."

There is hardly time for lunch before an appointment for a broadcast at Radio City. Barbara Ann says wanly she doesn't want any lunch. Mrs. Scott insists on it. It takes 15 minutes with another publicity man on tab for the next step. There is always a representative of M.C.A., 20-Century Fox, or the publicity office with Barbara Ann wherever she goes.

It's a radio program for rebroadcasting for a Sunday-morning breakfast show. Barbara Ann turns, unexpectedly, at the mike, from a quiet shy child into a very self-possessed, amusing raconteuse. The two good-looking veterans of the air are delighted. They say, "Come and visit us. Come for dinner sometime." "Oh, thank you," says Barbara Ann, "I'm so glad to have met you. I've listened to you for such a long time and enjoyed it ever so much."

Now the taxi beats through traffic-jammed streets to Brooks Costumers, on Sixth Avenue. Up a dingy staircase to a well-lit room where designers, seamstresses, hangers-on, costumiers and Canadian newsmen wait. James Stroock, handsome, hook-nosed, grey-haired proprietor of the place, lets it be known that Brooks (trade name for the Stroock enterprise) has "costumed Sonja Henie."

The dress has an immense marabou trim, the bonnet is a vast halo of marabou. Barbara Ann's face looks small and peaked underneath it. Mrs. Scott suggests something a trifle simpler. "We are more accustomed to something simpler," she says.

"This is a different thing," Mr. Stroock says. "It's for the girl's own good. We must glamorize her."

"We were asked to stay the same," Mrs. Scott says. "Don't let them change Barbara Ann, everybody always says to me."

"The Roxy stage is a different thing from a skating competition," Mrs. Stroock points out. "Miss Joan Personette has designed some of the best Roxy effects. B. A. would look like a pygmy in too simple a costume. The public expects an ice queen to look like an ice queen."

There are little huddles of conversation in the room. By the mirrors, between the seamstresses, under the hot bright lights Barbara Ann turns this way and that. "I like quite simple things," she says in a small voice.

"You can't always wear the same things," the designer says crisply.

In the end, for the opening, though the bonnet is not Barbara Ann's own skullcap, it is one third the size of the original.

It's getting on toward late afternoon but there is still an interview with Earl Wilson, the Broadway columnist, at George Evans' office. He is a stodgy little man with a cynical lift to the corner of his mouth. He closes himself up in a room with

Barbara Ann, shutting out Mrs. Scott and George Evans. About an hour later he emerges looking dazed. Says he, "She's the widest-eyed, blue-eyed gal I ever met. And I fear she's real."

George Evans says to Barbara Ann, "Don't forget the Freedom Train Meeting. At eight. Somebody will pick you up."

So Barbara Ann has a couple of hours to herself. The doorman at the hotel greets her warmly. The desk clerk has her mail ready with a smile. The elevator operator hopes she's well.

Up to her room, 16 floors above 50th Street, where the shrill wailing of taxicabs caught in traffic jams rings clearly. Out of one window a glimpse of the East River presents a lighted ship in the early dusk. In her room, Junior, the toy koala bear that, as a mascot, has followed Barbara Ann throughout Europe, stares beady-eyed at his mistress. Pictures of friends are on the dresser. Tidiness rules the room.

"I think I'll just have some corn flakes up here for dinner," Barbara Ann says, "and wash my stockings, and lie down for a bit." Which she does.

The Freedom Train is a United States movement to stress the country's heritage and freedom—among school children by rallies, among adults by a train that carries historical documents from city to city. This is a meeting at a public school. Besides a short program of folk dances the occasion serves to have Barbara Ann Scott present certificates to the best citizen boy and girl. During the presentation the master of ceremonies turns to Barbara Ann and interviews her over the loudspeaker.

Afterward the kids mob Barbara Ann. They stand on chairs and benches and push forward. It takes two big men to get the slight girl to the comparative safety of the platform. And then the day is nearly over. The great city bursts into its nightly jeweled glitter. And its newest star, weary and sniffling a little with a cold, climbs a stool in the drugstore of a small hotel and says, "Could I have a hot lemonade, please?"

"Look, honey," says the counterman, "you need a bun. I'll toast you one."

He looks so delighted at this idea that Barbara Ann nods.

A swarthy, small man on the next stool turns around. "Are you Barbara Ann Scott?" he asked. "I'm from Persia."

While the girl drinks her lemonade and eats her bun, the two strangers in Manhattan talk. It sounds easy and friendly. It ends with the Persian getting off the stool and informing the drug-store generally, "I go to Roxy to see this girl skate. If you smart, you go too."

Last Christmas Day, while the rest of us were carousing about the tree, stuffing ourselves with turkey and visiting friends, young Barbara Ann spent from 11 a.m. to long after midnight at the Roxy, in her dressing room, backstage, on stage, giving five shows.

It's a 10-minute cab trip, across town, from her hotel to the unostentatious stage entrance of the Roxy. At the door the cadaverous but friendly doorman hands her a stack of mail and telegrams. She flips through it quickly to see whether any are from friends. At the end of the ground-floor corridor there is a small elevator that stops just outside her dressing room.

Ernie Adler, the make-up man, comes in while she is still opening her mail and starts to make her up. "Don't make my mouth so large, Ernie, please," Barbara Ann says. "Don't make my eyebrows so dark."

"You have to, for the lights," the stocky man insists in his lisping voice. "You aren't an amateur now."

Backstage, later, he said, "What that girl doesn't know about the theatre could fill a book. I'll have to help her quite a while yet. She hasn't come up the harsh way that teaches you what's what, like the rest of us."

Meanwhile Barbara Ann would be putting on her net stockings, her brilliant-studded, pale-blue, marabou-trimmed

$9,000 costume for the first number, and her skates. Then she would stand backstage in the wings, a slender, shiny figure, her eyes wide, surrounded by the performing ponies, the wise little dogs and other variety artists. She'd go on into the bright lights, and from the vast dark hollow of the theatre would come applause, muted by the wide stage. She concentrates intensely on the moment. But out there in the seats they would see only her flashing, small-girl smile, her easy grace.

Ten times that Christmas Day she changed, laced on shoes, unlaced shoes, tramped up and down between stage and the dressing room. It was a different Christmas from the year before in snow-glistening Davos, amid the Swiss Alps, the world championship in her pocket, and days of sunshine in open air ahead of her. Today she lives in a tinseled make-believe world where she is advised to forget many of those very arts that won her the right to be a star. Now she is told: "Put more oomph into it. This is show business."

And then, as for many nights to follow, as the shows on Broadway began to close and night clubs filled with festive patrons, the young girl and her mother walked home to the hotel, down New York's winter-slushy streets, welcoming the air, and the quiet hours ahead, until tomorrow.

Barbara Ann Scott skated professionally for seven years until 1955, when she married ice-show publicist Tommy King. They lived in Chicago for 43 years, where she trained and showed horses, and served occasionally as a skating judge. In 1988, they retired to Florida.

Eva-Lis Wuorio wrote for Maclean's *for three and a half years. In 1951 the Finnish-born journalist returned to Europe, where she wrote short stories, novels and children's books.*

Canada's World Champions of Curling

—January 7, 1961—
Robert Metcalfe

O NE NIGHT IN MID-MARCH 1959, a Harry Lauder sort of
Scot named Willie Young, Captain of Scotland's champion curling team, sat hunched before a roaring fire in his
farmhouse near Ayr. His florid face was grimly set and his glass
of whisky was untouched. His wife, busy with the supper
dishes, became concerned for her normally cheerful and thirsty
spouse. "Willie," she asked, "What's come over you? You're
awful quiet tonight."

Willie stirred and sighed dejectedly. "Mrs. Young," he slowly
replied, "I just don't know how I'm going to beat those fellows."

Returning home to Regina with the Scotch Cup

"Those fellows" were the Richardsons of Regina, Canada's curling champions and the first to play for the Scotch Cup and the world title in Scotland. Ernie, now 29, his brother Garnet, 27, and their cousin Arnold, 32, were carpenters in Regina; Wesley, 30, another cousin, was an instrument man at a Regina oil refinery. That day they had beaten Willie Young and his middle-aged team rather handily in the first of five games for the curling crown.

"Are they good?" asked Mrs. Young.

"Good?" snorted Willie. "They're too damn good!"

Mrs. Young told the Richardsons of Willie's dilemma shortly before they took him on in the second game. And Willie, who had lost only two of 80 games that season, never did find out how to beat the Richardsons. He lost the next four games as well. Said he, eyeing his aging crew: "Scotland will need younger players if we're to beat those fellows."

But Hughie Neilson, whose 1960 Scottish champions were all in their 30s, wasn't able to beat those fellows either. Like Willie Young, Neilson too lost five games to the Richardsons and watched with chagrin as the upstarts from Canada again won the treasured cup and the curling title.

It was only the second year of the international contest and the cup was on its way back to Regina—bearing only the names of Ernie, Garnet, Arnold and Wesley Richardson. And wasn't curling a Scottish game? There was the rub. But Willie Young and Hughie Neilson had no need to feel alone with the problem of how to beat the Richardsons. The champions of nine Canadian provinces were wondering the same thing.

Just seven years ago the Richardsons, starting to curl for the fun of it, were bungling a game that Ernie as a youth had dismissed as a sport "for old men or muskrats" because it bored him. Today, he and his teammates can't get it out of their system. They mastered the game by spending hundreds of hours at it, almost entirely for the sake of what looks to a non-curler like the somewhat dubious pleasure of playing the game. Their only loot from curling is a jumble of prizes—watches and household goods and gadgets. When they brought the Canadian and world curling championships home to Saskatchewan, they were greeted at the airport by relatives, a few politicians and a victory arch of curling brooms held by women curlers. Only a few hundred Reginans took the time to watch them drive through the city with a mounted RCMP escort.

The hoopla that usually follows sport champions was missing because curling, one of the few truly amateur games we have left, is not a spectator sport. Football fans, some forever mystified by its rules and manoeuvres, will sit for hours in the rain watching grown boys bashing each other about for pay. Curling spectators are usually curlers themselves. Non-curlers can't get excited over men in colour-splashed sweaters and caps with pompons sliding a heavy stone down a strip of ice while teammates dance ahead in an awkward, slithering two-step, polishing the stone's path toward a circular target with furious sweeps of a broom.

Curling is a sports phenomenon in the west, and the Richardsons are only four among thousands of Canadians who have been bitten by the curling bug in the past few years. Prairie youngsters learn to curl with weighted jam tins at community centres; their fathers and mothers curl in Canadian Legion or service-club leagues, or with fellow workers in industry and business. In small towns, the local curling rink is the centre of social life, and farmers, at loose ends after harvest, do little else in winter but curl.

Saskatchewan, home of more curlers per capita than any other province, has some 600 curling clubs, 37,000 men and boys and 10,000 women and girls who curl. The season is no longer limited by freeze-up and thaw; most clubs in Canada have installed or plan to install artificial ice, and the game goes on from early October to the beginning of April.

In eastern Canada, curling has been a common if not a widespread sport for decades. But it wasn't till it had become a craze in the west that the fad started to spread eastward. Now, in many eastern cities, crimp-roofed curling rinks are rising—some of them displaying touches of the most imaginative architecture in Canada. Many of them are going up behind the clubhouses of golf courses, part of the clubs' plans to make year-round athletes of summer golfers and keep the 19th hole open throughout the year.

While its popularity rises in Canada, curling is almost extinct in its native Scotland. The Richardsons found that only rich or leisurely Scots curl today, and the country has fewer than 300 teams—about the total of three good-sized clubs in Canada.

In Saskatchewan, which has produced only one other Dominion champion team, the world champions are touted by some newspapers as "the remarkable Richardsons of Regina." This doesn't go down so well at Stoughton, a south Saskatchewan farming community that only this year got sewers and town status for its 580-odd residents. Most Reginans had never heard of the place until Mrs. Lyle Arthur, correspondent for the Regina *Leader-Post*, objected to Regina's claim on the Richardsons. They didn't belong to Regina, she wrote, but to Stoughton, where they were born. "I couldn't let them get away with that," she said recently.

It was near Stoughton that the Richardsons' paternal grandfather, Samuel Richardson, settled with his wife and five children shortly before the First World War. The curling Richardsons all grew up in and around Stoughton, where townspeople remember Ernie Richardson as a tall, gangling youth who, at 13, took a crack at curling in a high-school bonspiel because a team had to be filled out. He hogged—threw short of the target—all his rocks that day. He preferred to shoot snooker in the local poolroom. A six-foot-four 200-pounder, Ernie has straight black hair and a casual but commanding manner. He has two children, Donald, six, and Judy, four.

His brother Garnet, who throws second on the team, quit school in Regina in Grade 11 against his parents' wishes and, like Ernie, went to work for his father, a housebuilder. At work, the brothers refuse to be separated. Garnet, five foot 11 and 170 pounds, has his brother's dark good looks and is nicknamed Sam after his grandfather. He has a daughter, Brenda Lee, three.

Arnold, the third curling Richardson, quit school after Grade 8 to help his father—Ernie and Garnet's uncle—train and race harness horses, a sport he pursued until 1951. Today, while Ernie, Garnet and their cousin Wes golf (in the low 90s) between curling seasons, Arnold fishes, boats and water-skis on Long Lake near Regina.

Smallest of the four Richardsons (he's five foot eight and weighs 155 pounds), Arnold is also, at 32, the eldest. He's called "the kid" because of his size and youthful appearance. His two boys and two girls are the reason his mother has never seen her son play at the Brier; she's stayed with the children each year so his wife could make the trip.

Of their Scottish trips, the Richardsons are inclined to recall the Scots' "overwhelming hospitality." Says Garnet: "I don't know how a non-drinking team would make out over there."

It was a heartening sight to the Scotch Whisky Association, which sponsors the Scotch Cup games. At first, the whisky barons were skeptical about the Canadians. On the day of the first game, they invited the Richardsons to a directors' banquet, the first outsiders they'd admitted to their hallowed hall. The Richardsons promptly startled their hosts and the waiters by drinking milk. ("There was that game to play," Arnold explains.)

The Macdonald Tobacco people, who give the Brier Tankard, and provide scoreboards for curling sheets, across Canada, haven't fared so well with the Richardsons. None will touch a cigarette, though Arnold and Ernie smoke the odd cigar.

The Richardsons, who like a couple of bottles of beer *after* a game, attended the nightly Brier functions—but they held their thirst in check. At the 1960 Brier in Fort William [now Thunder Bay], Ont., Garnet, holding a full glass at a reception, was stopped by Ken Watson. "You've got five straight wins," said Watson, "But is it any time to start drinking?" Garnet offered Watson a sniff; it was ginger ale. Says Garnet: "I figured the other teams would see us drinking and think 'if the Richardsons are knocking it back we might as well go to it as well.'"

In 1960, the Scots hoped to beat the Canadians with Hughie Neilson, whose expert draw game, they were sure, would solve the Richardsons' knockout style. And in the first game at Ayr, Neilson gave them a run for their money. The second game was played in Edinburgh, and the Richardsons began to aggravate a dour little Scot in the stands. Each time a Richardson rock banged a Neilson rock off the target, he growled: "That's nay curling."

On the fourth end, Neilson had two rocks on the target and one counted; four rocks sat in front of the target with only narrow openings, or ports, between them. Ernie skimmed his first rock through to the edge of the button and the complaining Scot fell silent. When Ernie put his next rock through the narrow port and flush on the button, the Scot roared: "*That* is curling!" Neilson's team didn't recover.

The Richardsons don't worry much about the Brier and Scotch Cup games; their toughest competitors are back home. "When you're clear of Saskatchewan, the tension's off," says Ernie. "Then you can really relax and enjoy yourself."

The Richardsons, who at first curled only 40 games a year, play 150 games a season (including two a week at their home club). They've won 85 per cent of them. "Sometimes," says Ernie, "You'd like a couple of days off. You often have to curl when you don't want to, and play teams you can beat nine times out of 10." But, he figures, "it's a game you can't get perfect at. You get out there with all the confidence in the world—then wonder what happened when you lose."

On the ice, the Richardsons talk very little; they breeze through their games in two and a half hours or less. Eastern teams, they say, talk too much; their games last as long as four hours. Says Garnet: "The game's slow enough without wasting a lot of time talking out there."

Some skips use signals to call for the amount of weight they want on a teammate's throw. The Richardsons tried signals only once. "We got so mixed up we didn't know what was going on," says Arnold. On the road to bonspiels and playoffs, they travel in the same car and always sleep and eat well. Brier tension has bothered them little, on the ice or between games. "You can spot tension in other rinks," says Ernie. "It knocks their calibre of play and a lot of good rinks falter because of it."

Garnet, the rink's morale booster, is full of confidence. In 1959, he brought his daughter a small Scots doll from Scotland, promised her a larger one the next year and made it good. "And next year it'll be an even bigger one," he predicts. His confidence has sometimes irked his brother. After winning their first game at the 1959 Brier, he told Ernie: "We're going to win it all."

Their rise to the top of the curling world hasn't taken the shine off the game for the Richardsons; this season it will take about seven weeks of their time and a few hundred dollars in travelling expenses. It's the time involved that sometimes becomes a sore point with their curling widows. "I suppose you can call us that," says Garnet's wife Kay. "It was getting a bit too much for awhile. But since we've been going to the Briers, it's been worthwhile. Quebec was a wonderful trip." The wives hope to make their first trip to Scotland in 1961.

That depends on Ernie, Garnet, Arnold and Wes. Their fans, they've noticed, are beginning to fall off; Saskatchewan is looking again for an underdog. Many people, though, hope the Richardsons will be the first to win the Canadian championship three years in a row. And if next year's Scottish champions and the champions of the other provinces are expecting to beat the Richardsons, they should know what's going on in Regina.

Although failing to win even the provincial title in 1961, the Richardsons in 1962 became the first rink to win the Brier three times. They also won the world title that year and in 1963. Canada now boasts some 1,300 curling clubs with 300,000 players and another 600,000 curlers who play up to six times a year.

Freelancer Robert Metcalfe wrote for Maclean's between 1958 and 1963.

A Cue for Success

—December 26, 1977—
Michael Posner

O NCE, IN A PREVIOUS INCARNATION, the room had been a dance hall. Couples waltzed and music drifted out of windows and the walls reverberated with the rhythm of the songs. Later, catering to changing tastes, the premises were converted into peep show galleries and later still into something called the Twenty First Century body rub parlour, sad cubicles for the prurient and the peculiar.

Recently there has been a resurrection. The gauzy curtains are gone, replaced by rosewood panelling, and the sound of billiard balls, clicking on 72 square feet of green felt, fills the

Lining up a shot in a quest for a world championship

room with a certain life. Twenty-two stairs above Toronto's
Yonge Street strip, in this room, now known as Cliff Thorburn's
Billiard Club, a pool match is in progress. The principals are
Thorburn himself, a lanky mustachioed young man in blue
jeans, and Bernie Mickelson, a lanky mustachioed young man
in blue jeans. Mickelson is one of the top five amateur snooker
players in the country. Thorburn, a professional, is currently
ranked second in the world. All similarities between the two
men end there.

At Mickelson's request, they are playing pool rather than
snooker because pool is a game that Thorburn occasionally
loses. The same cannot be said of snooker. Only the very rich
or the very dumb play snooker for money with Cliff
Thorburn—even when he gives points.

Thorburn frequently gives points. If he did not give points, he
would have no one to play with, an unenviable position for a
professional. As it is, competition is scarce. Yielding 30 or 40
points, Thorburn can beat 99 per cent of all the snooker players
in Canada. He has been the Canadian champion six times. He
has won two editions of the prestigious Australian TV Masters
championship. He came within an eyelash of winning the 1977
World Snooker Championship at Sheffield, England, last April—
the first Canadian, the first North American, ever to reach the
finals. He is cited in the Guinness Book of World Records for
having recorded 14 perfect games—more than any man in
history—by sinking, alternately, 15 red balls, 15 blacks and all
the other colours, without missing a single shot, for a maximum
of 147 points. (This month, in practice, he shot a 15th.)

In snooker any run of 100 or more points—a "century
break"—is considered an achievement, something to tell the
grandchildren. Thorburn records a century almost as often as
he eats eggs, two or three times a week. Frequently, he scores
them back to back. Once he registered seven in a row.

His knowledge of the game—angles, techniques, probabili-
ties—is awesome. He never forgets a shot and rarely if ever
chooses the wrong ball to shoot. At playing safe or avoiding
being snookered, he is probably without peer. And that he will
win the world championship soon, very soon, seems as certain
as flowers that bloom in the spring.

Bernie Mickelson knows this. That is why he is playing pool.
Pool is not the same as snooker, not at all. For one thing it is
played on a smaller table, which dramatically alters the angles
at which the Vitalite balls rebound from the hard rubber siding.
Thorburn is less familiar with these angles. He is therefore more
prone to error. Since games are won and lost by a fraction of a
millimetre, it is entirely possible that Bernie Mickelson will
win. It is equally possible that Bernie Mickelson will be elected
the King of Siam next week. Not a good bet.

Especially not after Thorburn pots 107 consecutive balls
in the first game. No one in the room has ever seen or heard
of anyone doing that before. It is the approximate equivalent of
sinking 107 consecutive four-foot putts in golf. Thorburn wins
game one handily.

Game Two is tighter. For a time, Mickelson leads. Thorburn
is relaxed, commenting on his play as though he were a sports
announcer. "One of the most exciting performances ever seen
on this table, sports fans," he says, affecting the clipped, nasal
style of broadcasting. "Of course, the table has been here only
three days . . . Now if he sinks this shot, there will be a ticker
tape parade." He misses. Mickelson leads 131–116. The first
player to sink 150 balls wins.

Mickelson misses and Thorburn picks up his $40, made-to-
measure cue, built only a month ago after the previous model
was stolen. He is testing a laminated wood shaft that is said to
vibrate within a smaller field than the ordinary Canadian white
maple wood he uses for snooker. "If you can forget for the whole

game that it's there, then you know you've got a good cue,"
Thorburn says. "Unobtrusive, like." But he prefers the feel of
ordinary wood. The laminate, he says, is "too stiff, too rigid."

One would never know it. He sinks one ball, then another.
He moves around the table like a jaguar stalking prey—an
unhurried, confident lope. His eyes, large and luminous, never
leave the balls.

Thorburn takes less than 15 seconds between shots. He
knows immediately not only which ball he needs to sink, but
how to strike the cue ball so that it spins or caroms or rebounds
to a precise point on the nap, leaving him "position" on the
next object ball and the one after that. As in chess, the possible
execution of B and C depends on the flawless execution of A.
Miss A, leave the cue ball one quarter of an inch beyond where
it should be, and the grand design collapses. Recovery may be
impossible. No sport asks more finesse.

After every shot, Thorburn chalks his cue, then slides the
cube of chalk into his right pant pocket. The motion is quick
and smooth, almost rote, like a coin falling into a slot. Even as
it falls, he is moving again, pacing, thinking. The entire action
seems orchestrated for rhythm, choreographed for flow.

Thorburn's striking motion is equally fluid and efficient.
Bent low from the waist, eyes at table level, he first seeks the
best possible view of "the natural angle" of the balls. When he
shoots, his left leg remains rigid; his right bends at the knee.
The fingers of his left hand splay open on the table, forming—
depending on the shot required—either an open or a closed
"bridge" with his left thumb, a groove for the cue to slide
through. Before he releases, Thorburn brings his chin slowly
down until it barely touches the ebony handle of the cue. Then,
like a hitter in the batter's box, he takes his warm-up strokes,
edging the cue back and forth through the bridge seven or eight
times, carefully adjusting weight and angle, feeling the exact

degree of power needed to sink the object ball and the precise amount of siding needed to put the cue ball in position. Thorburn's cue ball control, his ability to place it just where he wants it to go, where it must go, is utterly uncanny.

Bernie Mickelson sits in stunned silence, watching. Thorburn takes the second game, then the third. He wins $60 for the afternoon.

Clifford Charles Devlin Thorburn got to be one of the world's great snooker players by working very hard at his game. Other men have taken more talent to the table, but few have pursued perfection with more diligence. "I'm only 29, but I'm going on 43," he jokes. "I've seen a lot of life, like. I figure I've played 30,000 hours of snooker. That's since I first picked up a cue, which would be September of the year I turned 15."

Which would have been in Victoria, B.C., where Thorburn, son of a city garbageman, was born, where his parents separated when he was two and where he grew up on the fringe of delinquency, a miserable student but an excellent athlete. He won scoring titles in lacrosse against players who are now professionals. He threw four no-hitters in little league baseball. "But I'm thin, eh? Like, I didn't have enough weight. I could not take a hard jolt. Plus, the coordination in my legs was not too hot. I knew when it was over. The thing with snooker was, I never went more than a month or two without noticing some improvement."

Thorburn had ample opportunity to improve; his academic career ended early. "After my second try at grade nine, my teacher said: 'Cliff. Like, I've passed you, but you really didn't pass, see?' Well, I went to Grade 10 for a couple of weeks and then dropped out. I'll say this though: I was pretty good in math."

Yes. He demonstrated his understanding of geometric principles on the tables of the late Dave Smith's pool emporium in

Victoria almost daily. "There didn't seem much else to do. After I made a few bucks, I figured I was pretty hot, eh? So I went to Vancouver to play Johnny Bear. He hustled me. Sent me home flat broke, tail between my legs. And I started over. But in Victoria, like, there was nobody to measure myself against. I had no idea how good or how bad I was."

So he left. For the next five years, until he was 23, Thorburn thumbed, bused and trained his way across the continent about 15 times. "I think I played in every pool hall in Canada." He'd go to Calgary, take a room in a boardinghouse and stay until he beat the best player in town. Then he'd set out for Regina, then on to Winnipeg, then Sudbury. He watched. He listened. He lost. He won. He played. "It was like going to school."

He played everybody—gamblers, hustlers, sharks, kids, bums—all comers. He played for a dollar and he played (when he had it) for 1,000. He played hot and he played cold. He played from early in the morning to early in the morning and when he wasn't playing the game, he talked it. Talked to men who had seen a lot of snooker. "Now, Cliff," they told him, "you're good. Damn good. But listen, Cliff, listen: Ya gotta go to Toronto to watch George Chenier. Ain't nobody can shoot like George Chenier. You could learn a lot watching him."

Chenier had been the North American champion for 23 consecutive years (1948–1970). What Thorburn learned by watching the master was that his own game needed more work. He went back to Vancouver and started over. By the time he felt ready to play Chenier, the champion was already an old man. "We played at the Golden Mile and I managed to win. I felt terrific at first. Kid from Victoria beats North American champion, eh? The next morning I woke up I felt terrible. Chenier was sick. Dying, like. He couldn't play his game. Beating him was almost meaningless. But I was 21 or 22 and I was oblivious to anything like that."

Chenier said of Thorburn afterward: "I don't know where that boy learned to shoot like that. God knows there was nobody in Victoria to teach him." Other high-ranked snooker players were also impressed. "You could see Cliff had it even then," recalls former Canadian champion Paul Thornely. "Not only the talent, but the desire. The desire to always play his best. If he could run 80 points, hell, he'd run 80 points. He wasn't trying to hide it. He never relaxed on a shot. That's the only way to be world champion."

In fact, Thorburn did hustle occasionally, but only out of absolute necessity. For the most part, he gambled. Once, in Thunder Bay, down to his last $50, he needed to sink a single, simple shot for victory. He missed. He did not hit the cue ball hard enough. "You don't get any better pretending you can't play," he says. "But gambling with your last sawbuck teaches you not to miss."

Broke, Thorburn gambled with money he did not have, double or nothing until he won. "I felt like quitting a thousand times. You're playing badly and you don't understand why. But I was always able, eventually, to figure out why. I have a good mind for the game: quick to make decisions and realistic with myself. I knew when I lined up to shoot I was playing the right shot. And I never thought I was better than I was."

For three months in the summer of 1966, Cliff Thorburn was an apprentice lithographer. For a day and a half in 1970, he picked tobacco in southwestern Ontario. He quit the first job because he did not like being covered with gold dust and he was fired from the second after he failed to turn up one afternoon and was found in the local pool hall. Those are the only jobs he has ever held.

For more than a decade, he earned his living from snooker: tournaments, exhibitions, lessons, gambling. He did not prosper. He travelled by thumb or bus, slept in abandoned cars, and once lived on fruitcake for three days. Everywhere he played, he sported a flashy purple jump suit and white turtle-neck sweater. "I could never understand why I was getting so much action. People looked at me and thought I was a moron."

Success has raised Thorburn's standard of living measurably. He now pays $25 for a haircut. He has traded public transit for a 1976 Ford Granada Ghia. He carries his cue in a handsome, felt-lined leather case that retails for $50. He owns eight $350 three-piece suits from Toronto's celebrity *disegnatore* Lou Myles. He sleeps every night in a comfortable two-bedroom apart-ment, earns $200 a week just for lending his name to two Toronto pool rooms and in Canada alone performs up to 100 shows a year in billiard halls, universities and private clubs. The going rate for an evening of Thorburn's wizardry on cue is $250. He subscribes to *Sports Illustrated,* reads a lot of paperback thrillers (usually during tournaments) and watches his beloved Montreal Canadiens on his colour television every chance he gets.

Still, things might be better than they are. As a sport, snooker is virtually unrecognized in Canada and many people believe that poolrooms are breeding grounds for society's vermin. This accusation is unfair. Vermin may, from time to time, be found in the nation's billiard parlours, but they are bred elsewhere. Besides, some very fine upstanding citizens have (from time to time) passed a pleasant hour or two in the company of a cue. Yet the myths linger and the game suffers.

Oh, to be in England, where snooker is the game of gentle-men. Thorburn's name is practically a household item overseas. People stop him on the street to ask for autographs. When he visits London's swank Sportsmen's Club, his name goes up on the celebrity board. Two former world champions, Joe and Fred Davis, have even been awarded OBEs for—in effect—their cue ball control.

There is also more money abroad. In Australia another former world champion, Eddie Charlton, recently signed a $1.4 million contract with a billiard firm. Most British pros gross $60,000 to $70,000 annually. Cliff Thorburn's Canadian income last year was about $25,000.

Part of the problem is Snooker Canada, an organizing body that is itself disorganized. Torn by warring factions, it spends too much time accusing people of not doing enough for the game. Thorburn himself, acknowledged as the best thing that's happened to snooker in more than a decade, has even been an occasional target of abuse. "I did a two-month tour of Western Canada and just broke even and some high-ranking vice-president, some guy with his diamonds and his Cadillacs, gets up at a meeting and says to me: 'What have you ever done for the game?' I just walked out. I don't have to listen to that."

Tournament prize money is another problem. Existing on the outermost margin of professional sport, snooker has never attracted support from big-buck sponsors. Thorburn collected $1,750 for his last Canadian championship; comparable British and Australian events yield $8,000. "So the organizer says to me: 'Sure, you want a $5,000 first prize, Cliff. You always win.' Well, what am I supposed to do? Wait until there's somebody better than me?

"I'm taking a big gamble even playing in the thing. Any guy could come up hot and beat me. It's happened before. And like suddenly, Johnny Fireman from Rearend, Man., is the Canadian snooker champion and Cliff Thorburn is nowhere. Sure I could make $60,000 a year if I went to England, but I can't do the game much good over here if I'm there. So I think it's important that I make a good living. Like, sometimes it's depressing."

A year ago, Cliff Thorburn nurtured three ambitions in life: to quit smoking, to win the world championship of snooker and to brighten the game's image in Canada. Two months ago he gave up smoking. "It was something I'd accepted that I had to do." In partnership with Terry Haddock, president of Snooker Canada, Thorburn runs two of the nicest poolrooms in the country. More than that, he is himself the game's best diplomat, as polished, mature, likeable and unassuming a champion as one will find.

There remains the world championship, for which he has already started training. "What I've learned lately is that everything comes in good time. I was very impatient before. I wanted to be at the top before I was ready to be there. Now, I'm ready. Somebody is going to have to play awfully well to beat me. I want to play beautifully and be as hard as rock. I want to look good and play the right shot. But more than anything, I want to win." Nobody who bets should bet against him.

In 1980, Cliff Thorburn became the first world champion from outside the British Isles. Now semi-retired with a record 14 Canadian snooker titles, he lives in Markham, Ont., with his wife and two sons.

Michael Posner, now an arts reporter at the Globe and Mail, *was a writer and editor at* Maclean's *in the mid-1970s and from 1980 to 1988.*

Life in the Fast Track

—*February 16, 1981*—
Matthew Fisher

S ʟᴇᴠᴇ ᴘᴏᴅʙᴏʀꜱᴋɪ, the best downhill racer in the world, looked out at the downhill course at Schladming, Austria. The 23-year-old Torontonian had won the race there last year and was favoured to win again, a victory that would make him the first non-European to ever capture the World Cup men's downhill crown. But what Podborski saw was rain.

After two days of heavy snowfall had softened the icy course, the rain came in torrents. Saturday morning found about 40,000 Austrians and tourists huddled in the downpour as organizers of the second-last World Cup downhill race of the

"Glamour boy" Podborski in Austria, 1981

season debated postponement. Finally the jury decided to hold off until the next day, Sunday. "We'll just have to go back to the hotel and reorganize," said John Ritchie, the Canadian team coach.

Though Sunday dawned bright, the rain had made the course unsafe. "It's too bad," said Austrian television commentator Heinz Proeller. "Podborski would have won for sure."

The cancellation left Podborski tied in points with Austria's Harti Weirather, but technically ahead because of his three victories to Weirather's two. As the World Cup race committee debated whether to restage the race in conjunction with the downhill finale in early March in Aspen, Colo.; move it to Lake Louise, Alta., Laax, Switzerland, or Anchorage, Alaska, Podborski and the national team flew home to wait.

"This week has probably been the most tension-filled of Steve's life, but he doesn't show it," says team masseur and confidant Terry Spence, who also acts as a coach at each race start, passing on last-second tidbits received by walkie-talkie from coaches on the course. "Steve just listens to the coaches until he is ready to go," Spence says, "and then, wham, you just know he's going to step on the loud pedal."

At first sight it looks a little ridiculous—a grown man wearing skintight yellow pyjamas, standing at the top of a bitterly cold mountain on two 223-cm-long pieces of plastic. But when Podborski explodes into action, he suddenly becomes much more, hurtling down steep pitches—ones that even the best pleasure skiers only dare sideslip—at speeds of up to 140 km per hour. Steering around hairpin turns onto fall-away sidehill traverses, Podborski sometimes has to lean in at a 45-degree angle to maintain his balance. If he crashes, only one-sixteenth of an inch of woven plastic is between him and the ice, a tree or a rock. The only part of the body that is protected is his head, encased in a hard black plastic sheath, with little more foam rubber inside than you would find in a hockey player's helmet.

Podborski is one of the glamour boys of alpine skiing, one of the fearless breed apart, the downhill racers. To speak with them can be a chilling experience. "The only thing I want to do when I'm going fast is go faster," says Podborski. "You don't think; there is no thought process required in ski racing. You react like an animal. At the finish you can turn on to the real world again and start talking again. During a race you see only the things that are the absolute necessities to maintain life. You only see what you're doing as you move, just like in a car. It's like being scared silly except that it's a controlled thing. After having had a few big wipeouts, I think I can handle any pain that comes along, so there is not much to fear."

Ken Read, who was in the hunt for the World Cup title right up to the final race last season, remarked two years ago that Podborski might one day be the best of the Canadians. While his teammates seemed to have reached a plateau in the late 1970s, Podborski continued to improve by hundredths of a second every season. His ski career began at the age of 2 1/2 when his mother took him to a now-defunct golf course in the Toronto suburb of Don Mills. Steve skied down what little hill there was, cradled between his mother's legs.

In 1974, after success in club and divisional races in Canada, the national team invited Podborski to a ski camp in South America where, as he puts it, "Others decided that I should be a downhill racer."

In 1979 at Morzine, France, Podborski came second but won his first race when Read was disqualified for wearing an illegal suit. Last winter Podborski won at Schladming, only to have the result annulled because fog and rain, similar to last weekend's, made it impossible for later racers (with no chance to win) to navigate the course. Podborski also recorded the best first intermediate times at Val d'Isère, Pra Loup and Kitzbühel before crashing. The Austrian journalists took to calling it *Der Pechvogel der Kanadier* (the incredible bad luck of the Canadian). But he finished the year with promise, a bronze medal at the Olympics and a fourth at a World Cup race in Lake Louise, Alta.

This winter he is the only racer to have finished in the top 15 in all of the eight downhills of the 10 that make up the World Cup. In fact, he's only once been worse than third. "The difference between now and seven or eight years ago is incredible," says the Canadian team's greybeard, 27-year-old Dave Murray. "I always thought Steve had the best natural ability of any racer on the World Cup."

Hans Huber, a journalist for the Vienna daily *Die Presse*, does not feel the oft-used nickname "Crazy Canuck" describes Podborski's racing style. "This term was often used at the beginning of the Canadian era in downhill racing," Huber says. "He's a fine skier, who skis his own line, but he won't take high risks. He's got a very smooth style."

This season's successes have surprised even Podborski, who had been planning to use the year to build up to the world championships in 1982. Last May, while free skiing at Hintertux, Austria, Podborski tore an anterior cruciate ligament in his right knee, the same knee that had been ripped apart in a crash at Kitzbühel in 1976. After the last accident Podborski was operated on in Toronto by Dr. John Kostuik. "This was a serious operation," says Dr. Bernie Lalonde of Ottawa, who oversees the team's medical program. "It was repaired and reconstructed using a band of tissue from the outside of the leg. Many people do not recover to a sufficient level to compete. Steve is the exception and he's very fortunate. He doesn't have a normal knee by your standards or mine, but it is probably as recovered as it will ever be." As another Ottawa doctor, Andy Pipe, who was with the team in December, says, "His competing speaks more of his mind than it does of his knee."

On hard snow, or on days when he pushes himself in training, Podborski's knee swells up. After last month's victory on the rough Hahnenkamm Streif at Kitzbühel, the problem was particularly noticeable. The swelling stops him from doing any running in his dry-land program or joining any of the spontaneous soccer matches that the Europeans are forever organizing.

After reintroducing his knee to World Cup competition with two-thirds and a 10th, Podborski won at St. Moritz just before Christmas, won again at Garmisch and then won ski racing's Super Bowl, Kitzbühel.

When the defending downhill champion, Peter Mueller of Switzerland, fell at Wengen a week later, only three men remained to deprive the English-speaking world its first downhill champion: long shots Toni Buergler (who won at Wengen) and Austria's Peter Wirnsberger, and the more consistent Harti Weirather. To win the title, all Podborski had to do was win one of the last three downhills. Weirather kept his chances alive by winning at St. Anton, Austria.

Podborski's successes have thrust him into an international spotlight. With each victory came new requests for interviews with the shy, smiling Canadian. "If I did what everyone wants me to do, I would never win," he confided in Wengen as he rushed from entertaining a troupe of Swiss schoolgirls who had waited patiently for him for hours in the Hôtel Métropole lobby, to a video room for a CBS interview. But perhaps his most ardent pursuers are a pair of schoolgirls. Tina, from Austria, writes to him everywhere and telephones almost as frequently. Before he crashed at Garmisch, she had hounded Read. Neither racer has ever met her. Then there's an enigmatic Swiss blond who follows Podborski from race to race, camping out for hours in hotel lobbies to catch a glimpse of her hero.

At customs checkpoints, the guards often request one of Podborski's postcards—supplied by his ski manufacturer—before waving him through. At ski resorts, his progress to the front of a lift line causes comments in any number of languages. "There he is. That's him. Steve! Steve!" Podborski and, before him, Read, match Swedish slalom champion Ingemar Stenmark for appeal with the skiing public. Journalist Huber explains, "It's because he is such a sympathetic guy. He's always signing autographs. Mueller might be the most popular in Switzerland, Stenmark in Sweden, and Weirather in Austria, but for all the European countries it might well be Podborski. He is as big as Franz Klammer."

With his fulsome grin, almost oriental eyes and his diamond earring (a legacy from a Toronto romance last year) Podborski appears like a bejewelled gypsy as he holds court in the finish area. While coach John Ritchie of Grand Forks, B.C., screens telephone calls and keeps the more persistent fans away from his star, Podborski tries to rest and read between races. A speed reader with a passion for science fiction, Podborski admits, his reading time has been drastically reduced in the past few weeks. "Some people have been quite obnoxious about getting to talk with me. I have to try to keep everything in perspective. I'm a ski racer and nothing should prevent me from preparing for my job, but there is no doubt I am in an unusual situation. I don't expect a hockey player is phoned by a Canadian reporter he doesn't know, expecting an interview at 10 at night, before a big game." Watching the parade of journalists and fans with detached amusement, teammate Murray says, "I'm sure Steve realizes he has gone beyond skiing for the pure joy of it. He has certain obligations now. I don't think it is affecting him adversely."

Sweden's Stenmark continues to win almost all the slalom and giant slalom races and everyone admires his superb technique, but only a handful of people, many of them Scandinavian tourists holidaying in the Alps, come to watch *him* race. However, when a downhill race is scheduled, Alpine Europe comes to a halt, in much the way Canada does for a hockey match with the Soviet Union. And nowhere is downhill racing bigger than in Austria, the country that has dominated the sport for years. Heads roll at the various ski companies and on the national team when good results aren't produced. It is surprising that Podborski, and before him Read, Dave Irwin and Dave Murray, can challenge Austria and other European nations when all the sport's races, money and technical resources are not to be found in Canada. The Canadian Ski Association spends about $1 million a year on its race program (men and women)—less than half that available to the national teams from Italy, France, West Germany, Switzerland and the United States. The money available to the Austrians is impossible to calculate, so vast are their provincial programs.

A little more than half of the Canadian team's money is provided by the federal government through Sport Canada. Of the rest, about half comes from donations from Canadian companies. European ski manufacturers contribute several hundred thousand dollars through the national association's ski pool. As well as supplying money, they also provide the equip-ment.

The manufacturers' return on their investment is evident every time Podborski wins a race. Within seconds of crossing the finish line his skis are off, turned horizontally, and placed across the front of his body so the television cameras can't miss the trade name. Later Podborski does a round of television interviews in his official team cap. His goggles, bindings, poles and gloves—and their obvious brands—may also find their way into a camera shot. For his efforts on the hill and in the finish area, Podborski receives considerable financial rewards. While estimates of Stenmark's yearly income go as high as $3 million, Podborski and Read earn much less. But they are still among the sport's top earners. If Podborski wins the downhill crown this season, he will probably become the highest paid Canadian athlete in history, earning even more than Marcel Dionne's $650,000 a year.

Podborski has his eye on the world championships in Schladming in 1982 and has committed himself and his tender right knee to at least one more season of World Cup racing. For now, the pressure of winning, and pleasing the public and journalists in a sport where victory is almost always measured in hundredths of seconds, and where the difference between handling a difficult turn perfectly and torpedoing into a fence is measured in centimetres, seems to have no effect on Podborski's personality. Coach Ritchie calls it accepting victory and superstardom, "in the Canadian tradition."

Adds Dr. Lalonde: "I first met Steve when he joined the team seven years ago. The striking thing, the very nice thing about it, is that the only thing that has changed is that he has matured a bit. His attitude, his liveliness, his joie de vivre, that hasn't changed. He's the same old great guy who first arrived on the ski team."

Steve Podborski had to wait until the following year to become the first Canadian to win the season's downhill title. Now living in Whistler, B.C., he is a member of the Vancouver-Whistler 2010 Olympic bid committee.

Matthew Fisher is the Moscow-based European bureau chief for the National Post. He has reported from more than 140 countries since launching his career as a freelance radio reporter in 1970. He travelled with Podborski and the Crazy Canucks for eight years and wrote about his experiences in White Circus, co-authored with skiier Ken Read.

Eyes on the Prize

—June 16, 1997—
Bruce Wallace

I N THE SELECT FRATERNITY of race-car drivers—men who squeeze behind the wheel of the "tub" and turn a skeleton of thin carbon fibre into a howling, fuel-slurping, rubber-sizzling bullet—talk among the brethren sometimes turns to fear. "Of course we talk about it," says Jacques Villeneuve, the 26-year-old Quebec driver who leads the pack as the road show known as the Formula One World Championship arrives in Montreal for its June 15 race. "Fear is not a taboo subject with drivers, and neither is death, though not everyone talks about that. But I believe you have to laugh about everything in life," says the

---

In the driver's seat in Argentina, 1997

quietly confident young man who right now just may be Canada's most famous international athlete. "And I have never yet felt fear in racing."

"Well, I've felt it," says Jackie Stewart, the best driver in the world during his day in the late-1960s and '70s. "I think we all feel fear, if we're honest." Stewart is back in Formula One now, this time as a team owner. On this late May morning, he has returned to the rolling countryside of Fife in southern Scotland to unveil a statue to local hero Jim Clark, a former world champion driver and Stewart's friend and rival, killed in a crash while racing in 1968. Stewart recalls eyeballing death himself during one rainy race in Rome, when he overtook another driver to get out from behind his spray. "I pulled out to pass," says Stewart, turning his hands as if showing how he drives the family van, "and poof, there's an ambulance on the track going 50, 60 miles an hour—and I'm going 160. Don't tell me I didn't get a fright! You don't have lingering fear. It's more a major moment of 'Oh shit.'"

Formula One may bill itself as the thinking man's motor sport, but the risk of death still provides it with its essential drama. Without risk, drivers would just be projectiles stamped with corporate logos. With it, they are hi-tech gladiators. "It's a callous statement, but I've heard it said at the highest levels of the sport that Ayrton Senna's death was good for F1 commercially," says Matt Bishop, editor of Britain's monthly *F1 Racing* magazine, referring to the Brazilian world champion who was killed in 1994. "Racing fans need heroes. And they need to know that even the best can die." It is telling that three years after his death, Senna's cult following outstrips that of any living driver. Senna, agrees Stewart, has become "bigger than life, bigger than reality. And sometimes," he says sadly, "you have to die for that to happen."

Jacques Villeneuve knows all about competing against the legends of the quick and the dead. His runaway victory in

Barcelona on May 25 was his seventh Grand Prix win in less than two full seasons—one more career victory than his late father, Gilles, accumulated over five years in Formula One. Gilles Villeneuve was an acrobat behind the wheel who lived to drive and seemed to toss away the calibrations of risk. He was thrown from his somersaulting, blood-red Ferrari and killed while qualifying for the 1982 Belgian Grand Prix, thereby entering Formula One's pantheon of deities. Comparisons are inevitable, especially when Jacques returns to race on the Gilles Villeneuve Circuit in Montreal. It comes with the genes. "That's the negative side about racing in Montreal, but it's been like that since I started, so I don't really care any more," said Villeneuve this month after final tests of his Williams-Renault car in England. "I understand why people ask those questions, but I've never felt I was racing because of my father."

But many people still wish for the son to reincarnate the father's bravado. Even uncle Jacques Villeneuve, Gilles' brother, has complained that his nephew lacks aggressiveness, misses his father's pure passion for having to be the quickest driver on the track, and wins only because the Williams car is the best in the business. "Yeah, yeah, I know what he says," replies the son with a wince. He is sitting in the paddock at quayside in Monaco on the weekend of the principality's famous race. "No, I don't live and breathe the sport," he responds after a pause. "I live and breathe the competition and the edge. I never grew up saying: 'Ah, I want to be an F1 driver.' I grew up saying: 'I need that edge, that speed.' It could come from anywhere, from any sport."

Villeneuve was a talented skier but has acknowledged he lacked the discipline to train hard enough to become a pro— and was always destined to drive. He was born in St-Jean-sur-Richelieu just outside Montreal, but his father moved to France's Cote d'Azur when Jacques was seven. Along with his mother, Joann, and younger sister, Melanie, the Villeneuves travelled Europe's racing circuit in a motor home plastered with Montreal Canadiens stickers before moving to Monaco in 1981. After his father's death, Jacques was sent to a Swiss boarding school, though he returned to Quebec each summer. But Monaco remains home. Canadian businesswoman Lynn Beauregard remembers being a passenger in a car with a teenage Villeneuve driving, bombing up Monaco's narrow, steep streets after a Canada Day party. "I thought he was out of his mind," she recalls with a laugh. "He got offended when I put my seat-belt on."

It seems strange, taunting trouble this way. One wonders: how can the slightly built young man, with unkempt hair and slouching posture that makes him look like he would be more at home playing computer chess, rattle down straight-aways in the sport that killed his father? How can he worry his mother like this? "I never heard that phrase in my family," he says, surprised at the question. "And I feel lucky that I never did. My family allowed me to risk getting hurt—if I was stupid enough. So I learned how not to." Because more than anything, says Jacques Villeneuve in his poised, clipped manner as he casually munches a peach, "you do not want to get hurt."

Defying death certainly sells tickets. Formula One is now a multibillion-dollar business, attracting bigger worldwide television audiences than any sporting event other than the Olympics and soccer's World Cup—and those are staged just once every four years. Formula One runs 16 Grand Prix races every year, between March and October. Its Big Top is Europe, where the sport began and where fans see themselves as motor sport's sophisticates compared with what they snobbishly regard as the beer-guzzling gearheads who patronize North American car racing.

But beyond soccer, it is perhaps the only sport with a truly global reach. Formula One is established in Latin and North America. And it now seems set to explode into Asia, where advertising laws and social customs conveniently welcome the tobacco companies, which use speeding cars as sexy promotional vehicles for their brands. Financial rewards for drivers have risen in step. Villeneuve's estimated annual income is about $10 million—high, but not as great as German driver Michael Schumacher, who earns more than $30 million in keeping with his reputation as the circuit's most skilled driver.

As Formula One grows richer from its fat TV contracts, however, many longtime fans lament the increasing professionalism that wraps its stars in a cocoon of media and sponsors. The days when rich dilettantes would show up to race their latest motor toy are gone. Formula One has become a hi-tech showcase, where teams hire aerospace engineers for design improvements and guard their trade secrets the way NASA hid rocket blueprints from the Soviets. Even the suspiciously blond groupies, once a Grand Prix staple, have been chased away from the paddocks in the necessary clampdown on security.

Yet there is more that is checkered in Formula One's prospects than the finish line flags. Critics complain the circuit lacks the charismatic personalities and the stirring rivalries on which every sport relies for drama. The races have become too predictable, with too little passing. While everyone accepts that a great driver can shave tenths of a second off a lap time, too often an average driver can ride the best car to victory (the complainers point to Briton Damon Hill, last year's world champion driving for Williams-Renault, who has yet to finish a race this year behind the wheel of the new Arrows cars). In short, many races have become circuses without suspense.

In the past, the European press has sniffed at Villeneuve's sloppy dress sense—baggy pants and untucked shirts—and complained about his less-than-exuberant persona. "Photographers really dread a Villeneuve win," says F1 Racing's Bishop. "Schumacher sprays champagne around forever, but Villeneuve is two quick spurts and he's off the podium." And some criticize the Canadian for spending too much non-driving time away from the paddock, dabbling at computer games when he should be working with the engineers on his car. "I've never been into cars mechanically," he says unapologetically. "I understand how the car works. But I couldn't build an engine. And I couldn't fix one."

The Monaco Grand Prix is Formula One's Wimbledon. They have been running races through the principality's twisting downtown streets, crammed between the seafront and the mountain, since 1929. "You can't really race here," says Villeneuve of his home course. "There's no room to overtake." But swish crowds still come for the weekend's social spectacle. Elegant bars overlooking the Mediterranean resound with foreign accents and the clink of champagne glasses. Race-day breakfast in the deluxe Hotel de Paris costs $200. And crowds converge on hotel parking lots to peer at Europe's finest sports cars: brightly coloured Ferraris and Lamborghinis with front ends lower to the ground than a vacuum cleaner. When the driver of a four-door rental car has the temerity to toot his horn to get through the gawkers, a British voice yells out: "Relax buddy. You're driving a Fiesta."

The atmosphere at Monaco has changed along with F1. Fatal accidents ended the days when spectators could line the sidewalks behind simple guardrails (Monaco's most famous car crash—Princess Grace's fatal plunge off a cliff—occurred just outside the principality's borders). "You used to be so close that tiny pieces of hot rubber from the tires would hit you as they went by," recalls 65-year-old Rosie Balbo with an endearing, crinkly smile. Balbo ran the Chatham Bar from 1949 until it closed last year. The bar was better-known as Rosie's and was one of the places where drivers used to gather to relax. "Drivers used to mix more, they were friends then," says Rosie. "Mechanics from one team would help other guys out if somebody needed a tool. Now, it's all professional secrets and money, money, money. The soul is gone, and that's a pity."

In a tent set up in the harbourside paddock to block out any snoopy competitors, the Williams engineers fine-tune Villeneuve's car. The gleaming beast sits on an elevated stand, seemingly more a patient in an operating theatre than a machine in a garage. Laptop computers crunch data. No oil streaks the blue shorts and T-shirts of the Williams engineers. The car snorts to life when they fire up the engine, and every press of the accelerator emits raging screams as if wounded animals were being gored.

Villeneuve still complains that the Williams team sometimes pays more heed to the data than the driver. "The guys on the team are sometimes too computer-oriented," he said in Monaco, where his longstanding girlfriend, Sandrine Gros d'Aillon, a film production assistant, had flown in from Montreal to watch him race. "I love computers and technology, but don't want to mix them with everything. Too much is taken away from the human side, from the feel."

A steady rain was falling two days later when the drivers lined up to start the race. Most drivers chose to run on treaded tires, giving them added traction on the wet pavement. But the Williams team relied on a weather forecast predicting the rain would stop. They stayed with "slicks," the bald tires that add speed on dry surfaces by putting more rubber on the road. When the green light flashed, Villeneuve slipped and spun as if he were on ice, falling quickly to the back of the pack. He never finished the race, retiring midway through after sliding into a guardrail.

Imagine, a Canadian getting caught with the wrong tires on his car.

Until Villeneuve, Canada had a limited history in Formula One. George Eaton raced for a while but is better known for piloting the now-troubled department store chain. In the mid-1970s, Walter Wolf operated a team that won the 1977 Monaco Grand Prix with Jody Schecter at the wheel. In Canada, Wolf is best remembered as the shadowy figure who helped fund Brian Mulroney's conquest of the Tory party in the early 1980s. He still travels the world on business (his Wolf brand cigarettes are big in Bosnia), but he has long left the Formula One world. "Walter didn't like working with sponsors," Rod Campbell, who was on the Wolf team, recalls with a laugh. "He thought their logos ruined the look of his cars."

Villeneuve is the latest athlete in a line from the Crazy Canuck downhillers to Canada's ferocious hockey players who challenge the myth that Canadians are a cautious, colourless people. "We're a crazy population—six months a year under snow and 40 below makes you stronger," says Villeneuve, acknowledging that he grew up in a "crazier family" than most. "When you grow up in the countryside," he said, recalling those Quebec summers, "it's easy to find an old motorbike and fix it up and just go nuts."

Skier Steve Podborski understands the rush Villeneuve gets from speed. Podborski met Gilles Villeneuve on a French ski hill in 1981, and the two became friends. He remembers 10-year-old Jacques whipping him in a video game of Space Invaders. "I was quite sure the drivers were crazy, and they thought we were nuts to be hanging it out in a skintight suit and a brain bucket," says Podborski, who now lives in Whistler, B.C., and still races the senior downhill circuit. "They're the best," Podborski continues. "Going that fast is normal to them. They have," he says, "the magic that lets them pull it off."

But, of course, sometimes the magic deserts them. It abandoned Gilles Villeneuve that day in Zolder. And it was not around for two-time world champion Jim Clark at Hockenheim, Germany, in 1968. "That day in Hockenheim has taken one of Scotland's greatest sons," Jackie Stewart told the hushed townspeople of tiny Kilmany who gathered to unveil the statue to Clark. The statue's pose was taken from his mother's favourite photograph, showing Clark, hands shoved in his uniform pockets, striding through the pit lane. Afterwards, Stewart and his wife, Helen, lingered so people could take their picture standing beside the image of their long-gone friend. "We used to have so much fun, the three of us," said Helen Stewart, poignantly touching the statue on the shoulder as cameras snapped and children pushed forward looking for autographs. Clark was 32 when he died. "Oh, I wish I could just walk with him again," she said.

After the debacle at Monaco, Villeneuve stormed back with a crushing victory in Barcelona to retake the lead in the drivers' championship from Schumacher. He won despite driving on tires that were blistering from the hot track, careful to push the car fast enough to stay first, but not to speeds that would have shredded the tires.

Everyone agreed that he won by driving smart. He showed no desire to become another dead legend.

Jacques Villeneuve went on to win seven races that year and the overall championship, his best year to date.

THE OLYMPICS

How Percy Williams Swept the Olympics

—November 24, 1956—
Ray Gardner

O N JULY 30, 1928, in Amsterdam, Percy Williams, a
runner who a few weeks before had won the sprints at the
Vancouver high schools' sports day, startled the world by
winning the 100-m event at the Olympic Games. Two days
later, Williams, just turned 20 and so light of build he was
described as delicate, won the 200-m sprint to become the
sensation of the ninth modern Olympiad. They called him
the World's Fastest Human.

Never before or since has any but a United States runner won
both Olympic sprints, the classic events of the Games. But only

Williams being held aloft after his gold medal wins in Amsterdam

Percy Williams sprinted out of obscurity to do it. It was a triumph that stands today as Canada's brightest moment in Olympic Games history—perhaps in all the annals of Canadian sport.

Forty thousand spectators in Amsterdam's new Olympic Stadium went wild as the lithe Canadian breasted the tape in the 200-m to become a double champion. The Canadian athletes were almost hysterical with excitement. The British, South Africans, and Australians were in an uproar. To them it was a triumph of Empire.

In Canada the victory inspired a national rejoicing that wasn't to subside until weeks later when Williams crossed the country in triumph, lionized in Quebec, Montreal, Hamilton, Toronto, Winnipeg, Calgary and finally Vancouver. No other Canadian has ever taken the country by storm as did Percy Williams in those September days of 1928. His youth, his modesty and his achievement touched the national pride. The picture of Percy standing at ease and wearing his white track suit, the Maple Leaf emblem and "Canada" across his chest, became familiar to every Canadian who even glanced at a newspaper.

They shut down the schools and 30,000 children were part of the great crowd that welcomed "Vancouver's Lindbergh"—as all the newspapers called him. The crowd "hailed him like a Caesar," the Vancouver *Daily Province* noted. The city gave him a sporty blue Graham-Paige coupe. Money (eventually $14,500) poured into a trust fund to provide for his education. Kids munched Our Percy chocolate bars, the product of a swift-moving Edmonton candy merchant.

Only Percy Williams himself was able to take his victory calmly. He sat on his cot in Amsterdam's third-rate Holland Hotel and recorded in the pocket diary he had kept for his mother his own impressions of victory and the first rewards of fame:

August 1—Well, it's done. Won the 200 M. Not so bad. Telegrams galore. The girls' team sent flowers to me. Hot dog!

Williams' times were not record-breaking; they were even considered slow: 10.8 seconds for the 100-m and 21.8 seconds for the 200-m. The Olympic records then were 10.6 and 21.6. But this was of no real account for Williams' strategy always was to beat the man, not the clock. Trained to a razor's edge, Williams weighed only 126 pounds, the lightest runner ever to win an Olympic sprint. After his victory in the 100, they said he'd never last out the grueling preliminary heats of the 200. Yet in four days Williams ran eight races, winning six and placing second in two.

His rout of the favourites was so stunning a blow that General Douglas MacArthur, then president of the United States Olympic Committee, felt it necessary to make a public explanation. Only once before had the United States failed to win at least one of the two sprints. "The Canadian, Percy Williams," said MacArthur, "is the greatest sprinter the world has ever seen and he will be even greater before his career is ended."

He did run faster races—in 1930 he set a new world's record of 10.3 seconds for the 100-m—but he never won greater glory than in those four days at Amsterdam. The first Canadian to reach Williams as he flung himself across the finish line in the 200-m was Bobby Kerr, of Hamilton, who himself had won the event at the 1908 Olympics. "Won't Granger be pleased," Williams gasped. A few hours later he told the droves of reporters who sought him out, "Whatever I've done has been through my coach, Bob Granger."

It was not a routine tribute to a helper. Williams meant it literally. Even today, more than a quarter of a century later, Williams says emphatically: "Granger was everything. *Everything*."

A florid man with flaming red hair and a freckled face, Granger was 33 when he first saw Percy Williams run in the spring of 1926. Percy then 18, was to Granger "a puny 110-pound kid." Some time that same year he decided the boy would win the 1928 Olympics. It was a decision, not a dream.

Dr. Harry Warren, now professor of geology at the University of British Columbia, knows the Granger-Williams story as well as anyone. Trained by Granger, Warren was Canada's reserve sprinter at Amsterdam and was one of three athletes who shared a small hotel room with Percy. The heavily favoured United States team lived aboard the chartered luxury liner *President Roosevelt.*

"Granger was unique," says Dr. Warren. "And so, in his way, was Percy. Percy's victory was a blending of these two amazing personalities. Granger *knew* that Percy would win the Olympics. He told me so in 1926. He was absolutely sure of it. Percy didn't love running—Granger drove him to it. Percy was a delicate boy and Granger wouldn't let him out of his sight for a minute if he could help it."

Oblivious to all else in life, Granger studied every technique of coaching and conditioning athletes, especially sprinters. He had a library of books on the subject, but he went beyond what the books taught to evolve his own theories. At Amsterdam the Swedish trainers were astounded by his knowledge of muscle therapy. Stewart says, "He was a genius in his own field." No detail escaped him. In his day sprinters didn't use starting blocks as they do today, but dug their own starting holes with a trowel. Granger experimented endlessly until he discovered the ideal specification—depth and angle—for starting holes.

In 1926 Granger was coaching rugby and track at Vancouver's King George High School. One of his protégés was Wally Scott, the city sprint champion. The students at King Edward High School had promoted a match race between their star, Percy Williams, and Scott. Granger was amazed to see Percy run his own champion to a dead heat. Granger later commented that he had never seen worse style in a boy who could run like Williams did. "I think he violated every known principle of the running game," said the coach. "He ran with his arms glued to his sides. It actually made me tired to watch him."

From the summer of 1926 till the eve of the Olympics Granger slaved over Williams to perfect his starting and running form. Day after day, in spring and summer, Granger got a group of boys together and had them demonstrate starts and arm motion. Mostly, Percy just watched—and learned. Granger called this "visualization." It was a way of conserving the boy's energy. At home, Percy practised by the hour before a mirror. He did setting-up exercises to strengthen stomach and chest muscles. His hands were developed to give him an extra spring off the mark.

At 15, Percy had been stricken by rheumatic fever and, the doctors said, left with a damaged heart. He was even warned to avoid excitement. In any case, he was extremely light and far from robust. His Amsterdam weight was 126 pounds, compared with Americans Charlie Paddock's 175 pounds and Bob McAllister's 170.

While heavier runners might work themselves into condition, Granger took infinite pains to bring Williams slowly up to racing pitch. He spoke of the boy's "precious energy." On a cold day, he would rub Percy before a race with cocoa butter and dress him in as many as three track suits and four sweaters to prevent loss of body heat ("precious energy"). He concocted an amazing variety of rubdown lotions. One was a mixture of olive oil, wintergreen and liniment. He gave him Finnish massages and Swedish massages.

To Granger, psychology was as vital as muscular therapy in his campaign to make Williams an Olympic champion.

And so he set out to make the boy as confident of victory as he himself was. He called him the Vancouver Gazelle, after the world's fastest beast, and continually showed him how his times were beginning to compare with those of the world's fastest men.

Once—in August 1927—he arranged an exhibition race in which he announced Williams would attempt to break the famed Paddock's world record of 17.8 seconds for 175 yards. It was a smart piece of promotion intended to draw a crowd and so raise money for a trip to an eastern track meet, but Granger also had something else in mind. Actually, no record was officially recognized for 175 yards. Paddock, a clever showman as well as a fast sprinter, often ran freak distances simply to be able to claim a new record. Granger deliberately picked this ersatz record because he knew it would be easier to beat than any of Paddock's authentic marks. Breaking a world's record, no matter how artificial it might be, would bolster Percy's confidence. As Granger had foreseen, Percy had beat Paddock's time—by a whole second. And, in appreciation, the crowd donated $160.

Granger succeeded in making track enthusiasts of the boy's family and had them dreaming of Olympic victories. Percy, an only child, lived with his mother, Mrs. Charlotte Williams, who worked as a theatre cashier, and her parents. Williams has always been extremely devoted to his mother and even during the Olympics wrote her every other day.

In the spring and summer of 1927 and the spring of 1928, Granger kept Williams running—and winning—in every local meet. He ran what were, for a schoolboy, some remarkable times: 9.9 seconds for the 100 yards, 22 seconds for the 220. In June 1928, he took his first stride toward Amsterdam by winning the British Columbia Olympic trials. He tied the Olympic record of 10.6 seconds for the 100-m, running against a breeze and on a grass track that dipped up and down like a roller coaster.

Percy Williams became the unexpected star of the national trials in Hamilton. Against a field of topnotch Canadian sprinters, most of them trained in American colleges, he won the 100-m in 10.6 seconds, again equalling the Olympic record, and the 200-m 22 seconds.

June 30—Well, the day of miracles is not passed. I can't quite understand yet but they say winning the 100 metres puts me on the boat for Amsterdam.

But it didn't put Granger on the boat. In response to urgent appeals from Granger, Percy's mother canvassed all over Vancouver trying to raise money for the coach's ocean passage. The Canadian Olympic team sailed from Montreal on July 11 aboard the liner *Albertic*. The *Albertic* left without Granger, but the next day money arrived and he sailed on the CPR freighter, the SS *Minnedosa*.

Granger had counted on nine days at sea to perfect Percy's starts. Eventually he reached Amsterdam and, in Percy's room at the Holland Hotel, he drilled the youth in his starting. A mattress was placed against one wall, as a buffer, and Percy would take off from across the room. The management, not sharing Granger's obsession, objected. But nevertheless it was there in the Holland Hotel, so Granger said, that the World's Fastest Human learned how to get off the mark in a hurry.

On Sunday, July 29, Percy Williams began his dash to glory. Eighty-seven sprinters were entered in the 100-m. The overwhelming favourite was Frank Wykoff, an 18-year-old Californian schoolboy who four times had tied the Olympic record and had beaten Paddock in a race billed as "the spring of the century." Should Wykoff fail, there was Bob McAllister, the

Flying Bowery Cop, and Claude Bracey, pride of Rice University. These three were specializing in the 100-m while other U.S. runners were saved for the 200-m.

Percy Williams won his first heat easily, in 11 seconds, but was forced to run his fastest race of the Games, 10.6 seconds, to win his second heat and enter the semifinals. His diary entry showed extreme modesty:

July 29—My ideals of the Olympic Games are all shot. I always imagined it was a game of heroes. Well, I'm in the semifinals myself so it can't be so hot.

At 2 p.m. on Monday, July 30, Bob Granger suffered a moment of supreme anguish when, for a split second, Williams was caught on his haunches at the start of the 100-m semifinal. He recovered brilliantly to finish four inches behind McAllister who had to equal the Olympic record to win. Second place qualified Williams for the final.

There were now two hours to kill before the final. Granger took Williams to the dressing room and gave him a book to read. As race time neared, Percy warmed up, and then Granger rubbed him down with the last precious piece of the cocoa butter he had brought from Canada.

"Keep calm, it's only another Sunday school race," he told the boy.

When they lined up for the final, the young Canadian was dwarfed by the brawny McAllister and Jack London, a 200-pound British Negro. Frank Wykoff, George Lammers, of Germany, and Wilfred Legg, of South Africa, completed the field.

There were two false starts—first Legg broke, then Wykoff. Each time the crowd surged to its feet, then subsided again. The third start was perfect. Williams shot away with the gun, the rest on his heels. With 30 metres to go, Williams was still in front. Then London made a valiant effort to catch him, but missed by a yard.

July 30—Well, well, well. So I'm supposed to be the World's 100 M Champion. (Crushed apples.) No more fun in running now.

Now began two days of grueling running in the 200-m. The favourite was the flaxen-haired California Comet, Charles Borah, who had won the United States trials in 21.6 seconds, equalling Olympic record. To break him up, the United States had the veteran Paddock and Jackson V. Scholz, who had won the 200 in the 1924 Games in the record time of 21.6. Germany had a strong contender in Helmut Koernig, an almost flawless runner.

Williams wasn't conceded a chance against these fresh, more experienced and, on the record, faster runners. His best time, 22 seconds, was two-fifths of a second off their pace. The secret of Williams' success—as Paddock, after Granger, was the first to perceive—was an ability to switch styles while running. Williams would take off with a driving start and keep driving until he had reached his maximum speed. Then he would shift into an easy, flowing style, a sort of overdrive. Near the finish, as his speed diminished, he would drive again, hitting the tape at top speed. "It was," Williams explains today, "like pedalling a bike downhill. There was no use trying to go faster, it would break my stride to try."

On Tuesday, July 31, Williams romped through his first heat and was resting in his dressing room when Harry Warren burst in with the news that, by luck of the draw, Borah, Koernig and Williams, with three others, were drawn to run in the next heat. "I can still remember my horror," says Warren. "It meant that one of these three great runners was to be eliminated even before the semifinals. Only the first two would qualify."

Granger gave Williams his instructions. "Don't try to win," he said. "Run to heat whoever is running second, Borah or Koernig." Then, to make the boy perspire without exertion, he smothered him under a pile of a dozen coats and blankets.

Koernig, the pride of Germany, flashed out in front from the start of the race, with Borah on his trail. At the halfway mark Williams was running third, four yards behind Borah. It was then that Williams, already travelling at top speed, tried to drive himself faster too soon. Momentarily he faltered, almost breaking his stride, and dropped farther behind. With 60 metres to go it appeared impossible for him to catch Borah. Now he shifted gears again—and this time moved smoothly into his drive, flashing past Borah in the last two yards. Driven by Borah and Williams, Koernig had equalled the Olympic mark of 21.6 in winning.

Granger, who had watched every race in agony, was now beside himself. He spent the night in the corridor outside Williams' room. At intervals he slipped notes under the door to Williams' roommate, Harry Warren. Percy had a habit of pulling the covers over his face as he slept—Warren was to pull them down. "He must have oxygen!" Granger wrote. In another note he asked "Is he breathing easily?"

The afternoon of Wednesday, Aug. 1, Williams won his semifinal race easily, with Paddock fourth. Now only one race stood between Percy Williams and a double Olympic championship. When they lined up for the final, Williams faced Koernig and Jacob Schuller of Germany, John Fitzpatrick, a Canadian from Hamilton, Jackson Scholz, of the United States, the 1924 champion and Walter Rangeley, of Great Britain.

Even before Amsterdam, Granger knew almost all there was to know about all the internationally known sprinters. Now, at Amsterdam, he had studied them in the flesh until, as Williams remarks today, "He even knew who their grandfathers were."

"Koernig is your man to beat," he told Williams. "He is a front runner—an inspirational runner—and if you come out of the curve even with him, or just ahead of him, you will kill his inspiration and win."

This strategy, and Williams' ability to carry it out, was to beat Koernig, who could actually run the distance faster than Percy could. As they came out of the curve, Koernig and Williams were in the field, running neck and neck. They ran that way until the last 50 metres. The crowd came to its feet as the Canadian ran on even terms with the great German. Thousands of Koernig's countrymen urged him on. Then Williams shifted gears, out of his flowing stride and into a blinding driving finish. For an instant the amazed Koernig seemed to hesitate. The skinny kid from Canada flashed by him and won by a yard over Rangeley, the Briton, who had come up fast to place second. Koernig finished third, in a dead heat with Scholz.

The crowd broke loose in the wildest demonstration that ever followed an Olympic victory. Granger, who had mentally run every stride with Williams, was limp. In his excitement, he had clenched his hands on a barbed-wire barrier and they were drenched in blood.

At the Holland Hotel, the cables arrived in a deluge—from Prime Minister Mackenzie King, from almost every Canadian provincial premier and most mayors. There were offers for Williams to run in New York, Berlin, Stockholm, Britain and Australia. Reporters surrounded him. "It doesn't feel any different being Olympic champion," he told them. "My lucky coin in the race was a good start." Then he had a supper of salad and mineral water and went to bed.

When Peerless Percy—as the papers called him—came home in September, he was met by his mother in Quebec and together they travelled across the land in triumph, their arrival in each city the headline news of the day. In Quebec, Mayor Oscar Auger gave Percy a gold watch and said, "We want to prove that we are Canadians." Montreal's Mayor Camillien Houde told him, "You're a great kid, Percy. I say to you, stay Canadian." Hamilton gave him a golden key to the city. In Toronto thousands cheered Percy and his mother at the CNE. At Winnipeg the CPR station was packed with people, and it was Percy Williams Day at the Polo Park racetrack. At Calgary he had only a 15-minute stop but hundreds came to the depot to get just a glimpse of the champion.

In Vancouver, the streets for blocks around the CPR station were a solid mass of people that morning of September 14, when Percy and his mother finally reached home. Granger had travelled on ahead and was there to meet them. The moment Percy stepped off the train, the sun broke through dark rain clouds. A schoolboy band struck up *See the Conquering Hero Comes*.

Two thousand schoolchildren marched ahead of the big touring car that carried Percy, Bob Granger, Mayor Louis Taylor and Premier S. F. Tolmie past cheering crowds to Stanley Park. There 20,000 gathered to see Percy presented with a car and Granger with a purse of $500 in gold.

For the next three years, Canada watched and marvelled as the World's Fastest Human kept on running and winning. A few scoffers, mostly U.S. sportswriters, said he had been favoured by the soft, slow track built on Amsterdam's marshlands. In February of 1929 he invaded the hard, fast, indoor tracks of the United States and took New York, Boston, Philadelphia, Newark and Detroit by storm as he reeled off a series of truly phenomenal victories over outstanding runners, most of whom specialized in indoor running. In Detroit he beat Eddie Tolan, the famous Midnight Express, in a 40-yard dash— and thereby began one of running's most intense rivalries.

Twenty thousand people jammed Vancouver's Hastings Park on July 13, 1929, to see Williams win over Tolan by two inches in the 100 yards. A year later, in the same setting, 10,000 spectators groaned as he ran third to Tolan in the 100-m. On August 9, 1930, in Toronto, Williams ran his fastest race, setting a new world's record of 10.3 seconds for the 100.

Now a classic duel between Williams and Tolan was anticipated for the 1932 Olympic Games, to be held in Los Angeles. But Percy had run his last really great race. The beginning of the end came on August 23, 1930, in the 100-yard final of the first British Empire Games, at Hamilton. The day was cold and, after they had taken off their warm training suits, the finalists were kept standing in their flimsy track suits for almost 10 minutes. It was the very situation Granger had always feared. Williams was flying almost certainly to a new world's record when, with 35 yards to go, he pulled a muscle in his left thigh. In agony, he kept running, staggering out of his lane at the tape. He won in the remarkable time of 9.9 seconds—and then crumpled to the track. His leg was never right again.

The end came—as fame had come—at the Olympic Games. He went to Los Angeles without Granger (they had quarrelled over a petty matter) and certain he had only two good races left in him. He ran third in two 100-m heats and then, in the semifinal, ran fourth and out, to Eddie Tolan. Tolan went on to become a double champion.

The late Lou Marsh, of the *Toronto Star*, wrote from Los Angeles, "Williams went down fighting gallantly, but the legs were gone."

After that Williams stepped deliberately out of the limelight and devoted himself to business and to golf.

Since then, little has been heard of Granger. Williams has lost touch with him and so have Granger's own brothers and sisters. He did bob up at the 1954 Empire Games in

Vancouver—to tell the press they'd never see the likes of Percy Williams again—and then dropped from sight once more. For a while, after Amsterdam, Granger sold insurance, including a big annuity to boxer Jimmy McLarnin, but then moved on from job to job, taking them as they came. His family believes he may be working in a logging camp somewhere on Vancouver Island but are not sure. He never married.

Today, at 48, Percy Williams is a successful insurance agent with a passionate interest in golf, virtually none in track and field, and with so faded a memory of 1928 he could scarcely live in the past if he wanted to. He still looks younger than his years, as he did at Amsterdam.

A bachelor, he shares an apartment in Vancouver's west end with his mother, who still thrills to the memory of the day her son became the World's Fastest Human. Now and then Percy's day of glory is recalled—the last time when Vancouver began to build a stadium for the 1954 Empire Games and there was a campaign to have it named after him. Percy did turn the first sod but the name decided on was Empire Stadium. He didn't attend the Games but watched the Miracle Mile on television at his golf club.

Looking back over the years, Percy tries to remember how he reacted to sudden fame. "I was just like any kid of 20," he says. "I was simply bewildered by it all. I didn't like the running. Oh, I was so glad to get out of it all."

Percy Williams lived a life of relative obscurity with his mother in Vancouver and never married. He committed suicide in 1982 at 74.

Ray Gardner was a staff writer for Maclean's from 1959 to 1961 and then worked at the Toronto Star until his retirement in 1985. He died at the age of 77 in 1997.

What Happened at Berlin

—October 1, 1936—
H. H. Roxborough

O N AN AUGUST SATURDAY AFTERNOON I sat high up in the Reich Sports Field Stadium in Berlin, directly above the box of Adolf Hitler, and watched one of the most unusual dramas in history.

The actors had been preparing for four years and nearly every one was a national champion. The participants came from 50 countries and their number approached 5,000. The audience was estimated to be at least 100,000, and the stage for this unusual panorama cost at least $1.5 million.

Despite the multiplicity of heads and dollars, the show lasted only two hours and its run was just one performance. But what a spectacle was packed into those 120 minutes! Trumpeters on towers played the Olympic fanfare, Hitler entered the stadium, a 200-piece orchestra played "The March of Allegiance," the flags of all participating nations were simultaneously raised on half a hundred staffs, and the Olympic bell rang out its notes of welcome. The sportsmen of the world, dressed in colourful costumes, from the pale blue of India through the scarlet of Canada to the green of Australia, marched into the midst of the cheering mob, saluted the loges of honour, paraded the track and covered the infield. Following the proclamation of the German leader, the Olympic flag was hoisted, salutes were fired by the artillery squad, 30,000 pigeons soared, the trumpeters again played, a choir of 2,000 voices sang the Olympic hymn, the last torch relay runner ran down the track and lighted the Olympic fire, the winner of the 1896 Marathon handed an Athenian olive branch to Hitler, the Olympic oath of an amateur was taken, Handel's "Halleluiah Chorus" was magnificently sung in that cathedral that had only sky for roof, the athletes marched to the exits, Hitler left the stadium and the games of the 11th Olympiad were dedicated.

Fifteen days later, the stream of traffic no longer flowed to the Reich Sports Field, the stands were bare, the flagstaffs became just wooden sticks, the Olympic flame had been extinguished, even the entrances were barred, to prevent the casually curious from quietly strolling through the deserted amphitheatre. In little more than two weeks, the thrill, the glamour, the life had departed; only stone, steel, earth and clay remained.

Was it all worthwhile? Was four years of planning and constructing just a reckless dissipation of energy? Could the monetary expenditure have been more wisely used? Are Olympic Games a monument to an impractical ideal?

What does an Olympiad cost? Nobody accurately knows, but even if it be $5 million, it still is not a waste of money. Why not? Well, the money is not destroyed; it is distributed among the stonemasons, carpenters, labourers, cooks, printers, flag-makers, tailors and all those workers whose livelihood depends upon transportation of people and goods.

The structures, too, are not worthless. Germany intends using its stadium as a national centre for public gatherings, and the Army has already taken over Olympic Village for the training of officers. Moreover, let the financial critics remember that the Los Angeles games were profitable, that Berlin is satisfied with its balance sheet, and that Tokyo, London and Rome were each very willing to become hosts for the 1940 Olympiad.

During the Berlin Olympiad, there were at least 500 events. In the boxing and wrestling matches, there were, as is usual, differences of opinion and a booing of decisions; in a football game between two South American republics, there were evidences of ill-will. But, despite the high stakes and the hundreds of opportunities, outside the incidents mentioned the events were more peacefully conducted than those in a corner lot near our own Main Street.

In eight days of field and track competition, there was only one occasion when a protest might have been lodged. In the 1,600-m relay race, an American unwisely cut in and retarded the progress of a Canadian. But the Dominion officials called it "racing luck," withheld complaint, and kept the stadium events free from even a single protest.

But it is not enough for us to say that Olympic Games do not cause war. It is much more important to claim that the same competitions do promote international good will. One morning, on the Olympic Village track, United States coaches were instructing half a dozen of their own sprinters. The athletes of other nations stood around, watching and listening.

Then, as one American would retire, an athlete from another country would get down on his knees, dig himself a couple of holes and join the starting line. Finally, the lineup included two Americans, an Italian, a Colombian, a Japanese and an Australian; all facing the six lanes, listening to the advice of a United States coach and waiting the commands to "get on the mark" and "get set" as they came in the German tongue from a Deutschland starter.

Another morning, the Bermuda team entered the Village and, as customary, were escorted to their house by band and procession. In front of the house was a flagpole, and as the flag was being raised, the German Army Band played "God Save the King." Immediately, in the field facing the Bermudian home, scores of athletes ceased jumping, stopped running, dropped javelins and shots, rolled away the basketballs and, without any volition but their own, respectfully stood at attention and honoured the national hymn and flag of the little Bermudian delegation.

The friendly chatter of a dozen nationalities in an *Olympische Dorf* bus, the exchange of team badges, the unexpected salute of 300 French men and women to Hitler, the respect of all the larger teams as they separately paraded and laid a wreath on the tomb of Germany's Unknown Soldier were just a few of the many evidences that Olympic Games, at comparatively little cost, do promote peace on earth. If there is Olympic discord, the causes can be traced to national cussedness, for the truth is that every team gets along much better with its international neighbours than it does in its own household.

But apart from the virtues of Olympic Games, didn't the Berlin competitions demonstrate that Canadians are athletically decadent? Were we not chagrined by our mediocre performances?

Strangely, every competing nation asks such questions, and the critics of every country agree that "if we can't do better, we should stay away from Japan in 1940." For instance, the British had won the 800-m race since 1920 and were really disappointed when they failed to finish in even the first three places; the United States did not win a race above 800 metres; Germany, which led the other nations in total points, did not win a first place in any one of the 17 events which finished on the track; the Finns were beaten in their greatly coveted javelin throw; the Jap swimmers failed to show their Los Angeles superiority. Where 50 nations compete, every country has some cause for grief, and the pessimists could have an inning at any national wailing wall.

Canadians, too, could have a real good "lament," for all too often our hopes were dashed. But the closer one came to the contests, the sweeter were the results. Just turn the searchlight on some of the performances. "Howie" McPhee, Vancouver sprinter, in his 100-m semi-final, defeated the champions of Great Britain and Hungary, in time good enough to win seven of the modern Olympiads. Lee Orr, another British Columbia lad, equalled the Olympic record in his 200-m heat, and when only 12 of the original 56 starters remained in that event, three of that last dozen were Canadians. In the final, such countries as Italy, Germany, France and Britain did not have a starter—but Canada did.

The Dominion did even better in the 400-m flat race. Forty-eight athletes were entered in this one event, and when only six remained for the last race, two of that six—Bill Fritz and Johnny Loaring—were from Canada. Loaring, in the 400-m hurdle race, contributed a fine performance. Prior to the Berlin Games this sturdy University of Western Ontario lad had run only one 400-m hurdle race in his entire athletic career, that being the Canadian championship that qualified him for the

Olympic quest. In his semi-final race at Berlin, he finished ahead of the timber-toppers from Germany, Brazil, Belgium, Philippines and Hungary, and knocked nearly two seconds from his Canadian time.

While Loaring's performance was sufficient to remind Europeans that Canadians were not dependent on former reputations, other native sons and daughters were going places in fast times. Phil Edwards, for example, after 21 others had been eliminated, finished third in the 800-m race. A couple of days later, in his fifth important event in four days, in a race that many considered the greatest of all time and that bettered the famous Paavo Nurmi's time by nearly three seconds, Edwards broke the Olympic record for 1,500-m by nearly a second, yet finished only fifth.

In the men's 110-m hurdle race, only four countries were left in the final, and Larry O'Connor, Toronto University athlete, finished sixth in a time that would have won six Olympiad titles.

In the girls' 80-m hurdle race, Betty Taylor, a young Hamilton miss, twice equalled the Olympic record. In the final, the finish was so close that only the camera's eye could do the placing and Betty Taylor earned third place.

In the relay events, only three nations qualified for all the finals and Canada was one of the three. Never did Canada have a better balanced team, or a group capable of such speeds. But track and field results do not tell the complete story, for we had many other causes for rejoicing.

Frank Amyot, powerful Ottawa canoeist, proved to be the world's best singles paddler; his teammates added a second and a third, and were responsible for three stadium flag raisings. In the wrestling ring, Joe Schleimer, Toronto, narrowly missed a first place.

One of our most notable successes in Berlin was contributed by the basketball team from Windsor and a sprinkling of

Vancouver lads. Basketball is now a universal pastime, and 23 nations answered the Berlin call. Canadians won the first four rounds by substantial scores. In the final game, played on a rain-soaked field against a team of American All-Stars none of whom was less than six feet, five inches high, they were defeated.

If "crêpe-hangers" can take any satisfaction from such a record, let them have it. It was the freely expressed opinion of Olympic Villagers that Canadians are still in the upper circle of successful athletes. But they can do better. Give the athletes sounder financing, more competition and better organization, and they will not be surpassed in their specialties by any other country.

Olympic titles cannot be bought. No, but money can coach, develop and equip the athletes. The Finland government gave $20,000 to its team, and Finland is just around the corner from Germany. The Australian Commonwealth contributed a pound for every personally contributed pound; the Japanese government bestowed yens equalling $125,000. Yet not a single civic or provincial government gave a nickel to Canada's Olympic Fund, and the Dominion Government gave only $10,000 to cover both winter and summer games.

By the way, every Olympic official paid his own expenses; indeed most of them not only paid their own way but also contributed to the general fund. All other costs, save that $10,000, were paid personally by the competitors or raised by friends.

How does this financial stringency retard a team? Here is one way: There were not sufficient funds to permit Canadian boxers to hold trials a month earlier, return home, then report at sailing time in sound physical condition. Instead, the championships were concluded on a Wednesday night; all Thursday the boxers had to "wangle" dollars from friends;

Friday morning the boat sailed. All the way to Germany the fighters were nursing injuries; when they arrived in Berlin every one of the seven had to report at the hospital for ailments varying from swollen knuckles to a fractured jaw. Every injury would have healed in a month's time; but the athletes had to make the team, raise the money and catch the boat in less than three days.

Because of money stringency, the competitors, just a week prior to the opening ceremony, were compelled to sit in day coaches through an 18-hour journey from Paris to Berlin—and some never fully recovered.

Contrast such scenes with the opportunities given by Japan. A little Jap middle-distance star spent two months in Finland, training with the Finns. To my knowledge, no other team travelled at such little national expense to accomplish so much as did the Canadians.

More competitions would also improve the performances. Canadians have the faculty of doing their best when the competition is keenest. Select the best, send them to the United States championships, and the testing fire will bring out the gold. Orr, Fritz, Loaring, Edwards, O'Connor, Conway and Betty Taylor never equalled in Canada the times they recorded in Berlin; while Johnny Courtright, who had never thrown a javelin more than 197 feet, won first place in the British Empire–United States meet with a toss exceeding 217 feet.

The Olympics of modern times are not intended to be social engagements; they are stern contests. From observation and conversations, I hold to the opinion that the presence of competitive girls, either while travelling or in the Games themselves, does not add to strength, skill or endurance, nor does it contribute to the discipline and harmony so essential if the best athletic results are to be obtained. It is still possible for Women's Olympics to be held at some other time and place.

Heroes of the XXI Olympiad

—August 1976—
Michael Posner

T HE AMERICANS LANDED on Mars and an earthquake
flattened Tangshan. There were riots in South Africa,
murders in Northern Ireland, carnage in Lebanon. Pitcher
Randy Jones won his 18th game and Jerry Pate captured the
Canadian Open. Sony Inc. reported that second quarter profits
were up 100 per cent. The franc dropped against the dollar and
the price of gold dipped to a three-year low. It rained, at last, in
Europe.

All of this the world briefly noted and then ignored. For 16
days last month, the attention of millions was riveted else-

Comaneci, the 14-year-old "princess of the balance beam"

where, on the city of Montreal and the Games of the XXI Olympiad. Nothing rivalled it. For several hours every day North Americans sat enthralled before their television sets, suddenly learned in the finer points of Greco-Roman wrestling. Even *Sesame Street* was pre-empted. The world's leading newspapers ran Olympics stories on page one. No fewer than seven magazines displayed the pubescent form of gymnast Nadia Comaneci—the first woman to score a perfect mark in the Olympics—on their covers. In Montreal, scalpers exchanged $30 seats for $200 in hard cash. Spectators lined up for hours to secure standing room tickets or a brief glimpse of the Olympic Village. Telly Savalas, Mick Jagger and Queen Elizabeth came to call. In the streets of a city in which even the women who hawk Jehovah's Witnesses literature are chic, there was singing until 3 a.m.

It was an occasion. Conceived in fantasy and reared amid controversy, the Montreal games—to the surprise of everyone—were executed with near-flawless precision. Predictably, there were complaints about security, but the indefatigable presence of Canadian army officers clearly had its intended effect. The closest approximation to an incident was the crashing of the closing ceremonies by a lone streaker. In the end, even Roger Taillibert's Stade Olympique, an edifice of classic proportions, was ready (if not finished). And though the debt for this fortnight's festival was estimated at $1.5 billion and still climbing, Montrealers seemed to accept it with Gallic indifference. Spent or misspent, the money had already changed hands; one might as well enjoy it.

Every Olympiad engenders its own set of heroes, new demigods of sport. To the scrolls that bear the now legendary names of Kuts and Zatopek and Nurmi, the Montreal games will add Lasse Viren, the inscrutable Finnish game warden, and the first man to win both the 5,000- and 10,000-m races in consecutive Olympics; Nadia Comaneci, the sullen 14-year-old princess of the balance beam, a child in everything but grace; Vasili Alexeyev, the strongest man in the world; Alberto Juantorena, a six-foot, two-inch Cuban revolutionary with the speed of Secretariat and the strength of Man O' War—it is not for nothing that his teammates call him El Caballo; Irena Szewinska, a 30-year-old Polish housewife and mother, competing in her fourth Olympics and winning the 400-m (her seventh medal) in world record time; Bruce Jenner, the essence of the American Way and quite simply the finest all-round athlete in the world; and Kornelia Ender, owner of four gold medals, the fastest swimmer of her generation.

♦

There once was a time when North Americans knew little and cared less about the sport of gymnastics. That was before Olga Korbut. In league with ABC, the network of the Olympics, Korbut's acrobatic flourishes in Munich created an instant audience of millions. Its high risks, intense pressures and demanding skills were perfectly suited to the television medium.

Four years ago, the Russians—Korbut, Ludmila Tourischeva, Nelli Kim—were the best in the world. But in Montreal they were all eclipsed by a four-foot, six-inch, sad-eyed elf named Nadia Comaneci, who in the opinion of the judges and the crowd, could do no wrong. Seemingly oblivious to the frantic whirr of movie cameras and motor drives, the crackle of flash bulbs or the fierce stress of Olympic competition, Comaneci moved through her daring routines with unflappable cool— never missing so much as a toe point. On the balance beam— a four-inch width of padded spruce, four feet above the floor, she flipped effortlessly into somersaults, handstands and splits.

On the uneven bars, she whipped her elastic body through breathtaking manoeuvres: handstands and full twists at high speed. Against this unerring daughter of a Romanian garage mechanic, Korbut, Tourischeva and the others scarcely had a chance. Seven times during the competition, perhaps swayed by the volatile crowds in the Montreal Forum, the judges accorded Comaneci the sport's highest honour—a mark of 10. But her victory dance seemed as programmed as her routines: a wave of the arms and a frozen smile that vanished the moment the television cameras turned away.

Comaneci was equally at ease with the horde of international journalists clamouring for her secret.

"How did Nadia feel about receiving perfect scores?"

"It is nothing special. I have done it before."

"Is Nadia afraid of anything?"

"Only when I fight with my brother."

Individuals aside, the single most impressive achievement of the Montreal games was the performance of the German Democratic Republic. In all, GDR won 90 medals, including 40 golds—more than the United States or Japan or Great Britain. But the tally does not begin to suggest the East Germans' depth. In most competitions, GDR athletes scored as many fourth, fifth and sixth place finishes as they did firsts, seconds and thirds. By 1980, presumably, the second rank will have developed into champions, and a new breed of juniors will have taken their place. They will be graduates of the most awesomely efficient sports system in the world, launched a mere 15 years ago.

There is no magic in the GDR program. From kindergarten through university, athletic abilities are screened and tested. Those who show special talent are enrolled in special sports schools, studying in the morning, training in the afternoon. Equipment, facilities, coaching—everything is provided by the state. The package is complete. Its motivation may be blatantly political and the system of selection, by Western standards, undemocratic—but after Montreal no one would dare pretend that it does not work. That a nation of 17 million people can produce 90 Olympic medallists is a staggering achievement.

The GDR juggernaut was best witnessed in the Olympic swimming pool, a handsome, 10-lane affair conducive—it had been forecast—to fast times. And so it was: East German women set eight world records en route to winning 11 of 13 events. For most finals, the only issue in doubt was who would win second and third. First place almost invariably went to a strapping East German fraulein, usually named Kornelia (Konny) Ender, a 17-year-old swimming machine blessed with size 36 shoulders and a pair of biceps most men would be proud to claim. "She has a good stroke, she's as tough as nails and she's about as attractive as the East Germans get," said American backstroke specialist John Naber—a compliment Ender might justifiably ignore. "She swims like a man," noted Mark Spitz, ABC-TV's colour commentator. "I don't mean that pejoratively either. The male stroke is just more efficient. So is hers."

North Americans saw ample evidence of Ender's efficiency. At one evening session, she won two gold medals within 27 minutes (in the 100-metre butterfly and the 200-metre freestyle), an achievement roughly comparable to running and winning a 400-metre and a 1,500-metre race in the same day; it isn't done. Far from wearying at the end, she turned into her last 50 metres head to head with arch-rival Shirley Babashoff of the United States, then simply geared into overdrive to win by a full length and one-half. "No one's going to beat Ender," said Canadian coach Deryk Snelling. "She's ahead of her time. Eventually, the rest of us may catch up, but for the moment she's unquestionably the best in the world."

In the continued assault of American expectations and traditions, there was but one notable exception: Bruce Jenner,

a six-foot, two-inch, 215-pound specimen of athletic perfection. Packaged and sold as only prime time television can sell,
Jenner is to track and field what Nadia Comaneci is to
gymnastics. He can do everything. During two exhausting
days, he outran, outjumped and outhurled the world's best
athletes, to set a world record (8,618 points) in the decathlon
and win a gold medal. The Americans badly needed Jenner's
victory. He restored their faith in the system. He defended the
flag. East Germany might win nine of 14 medals in women's
events, but there were no Bruce Jenners in the German
Democratic Republic—no one with his clean-cut good looks,
his total talents, his assurance before a microphone.

Traditionally, the decathlon's 10 events leave competitors
physically and emotionally drained. But barely 30 minutes after
he had run the last event—1,500 metres in the enviable time
of 4.12 minutes—Jenner looked like a man who had just slept
eight hours as he launched into a detailed 20-minute analysis of
the competition. The adrenalin was still flowing. He was an
athlete at the absolute apogee of his form. "Well, I did the third
lap in 68 seconds and felt the best I've ever felt. And the more
I picked up the pace, the better I felt. I couldn't believe it. I
knew I was close to 8,600 points and I wanted to score 8,600 in
the last meet of my life. So I couldn't let down. When I crossed
the line and saw my time, it was the happiest moment of my
life. I wasn't even tired. I've enjoyed the climb to the top. I've
set goals and met every one of them. I hate to say our system
wins, but I grew up in a country that let me do whatever I
wanted to do." The Americans had found a hero.

It was not an Olympics the Soviet Union will fondly remember. The Russian soccer squad, boasting the finest players
(amateur or professional) in the game, finished a disappointing
third. After a critical 2–1 loss to East Germany, a senior Soviet
football official noted: "Well, we'll have to get rid of these guys.

They obviously lack a proper sense of obligation to their
country." By those standards, a number of other Soviet athletes
may likewise have their performances reviewed. Sprinter Valery
Borzov, a double gold medallist at Munich, finished third in the
100 metres and then failed to turn up for his qualifying heat in
the 200 metres, sparking unfounded rumours of his defection.
(Another Russian athlete, 17-year-old diver Sergei Nemtsanov,
did defect, reportedly with the aid of his American girl friend.)
The men's basketball squad, gold medallists in 1972, were humiliated by Yugoslavia and forced to settle for bronze. The men's
volleyball team finished second to Poland, then consoled themselves with a four-hour shopping spree on suedes, leathers and
blue jeans. Heavyweight boxer Viktor Ivanov, touted as a distinct
threat to Cuba's Teofilo Stevenson, didn't make it past the tournament's second round. But the most crushing Soviet embarrass-
ment was occasioned by 45-year-old fencer Boris Oneschenko,
who carried his quest for Olympic victory beyond good taste: he
cheated, rigging the handle of his épée with sophisticated electronic circuitry, enabling him to record a "hit" on his opponent
even when he hadn't. Had he been more discreet he might never
have been caught. Instead, he began registering "hits" even when
he had not come close to his opponent. Finally a hit was challenged, the weapon seized and inspected and Oneschenko flown
home in disgrace, though not before he was overheard screaming
at his coach, "You made me do this."

Typically, the Soviets kept close watch over all their
athletes—winners and losers alike. For the first 10 days, they
were allowed outside the residential block only to eat and to
train. Visits to the international sector, with its discotheques,
cinemas, boutiques and videotape replay rooms for every sport
were forbidden.

And what of Canada—the first host nation in Olympic
history that failed to win a single gold medal? On paper, the

country's 11-medal total (eight alone in the swimming pool) is not exactly imposing. But the Canadian effort was actually a vast improvement over the team's performance in Munich. In the silver medals of high-jumper Greg Joy, canoeist John Wood and equestrian Michel Vaillancourt; in the performance of the sprint relay teams, in the stubborn determination of Jack Donohue's basketball squad (which finished fourth), there are grounds for optimism.

Every Olympiad carries its own asterisk. In 1968 at Mexico City, the army opened fire on protesting students, killing eight. In 1972 at Munich, the violence moved indoors: 11 Israelis dead from the guns of Arab terrorists. In 1976, a 29-nation walkout, the largest boycott in Olympic history. Politics has never been far removed from international sport, but seldom have their diverging interests been so ensnarled. First, to the dismay of an American press corps grimly determined to misunderstand the issue, Ottawa told the International Olympic Committee that Taiwan, otherwise known as the Republic of China, could not pretend to represent the interests of mainland China to 22 million Canadians who knew better. The Taiwanese could fly their flag and play their anthem, but they could hardly be allowed to imperil Sino-Canadian relations by calling themselves the Republic of China. Unwilling to accept this compromise, the Taiwanese withdrew—perhaps permanently—an exit that now facilitates the long-awaited admission of the People's Republic of China to the IOC fraternity. But even while Taiwan's athletes were packing their bags and heading for home, thousands of Olympics visitors were buying souvenirs stamped MADE IN TAIWAN.

Far more serious was the black African walkout (28 nations in all), ostensibly in protest of a tour of South Africa by a New Zealand rugby team. "Sports ties with the racist regime of South Africa constitute implicit support for apartheid," declared one

African official. "This must not go unnoticed. If New Zealand stays, we leave." The African position conveniently ignored the fact that rugby is not an Olympic sport, that many other nations (including Canada) maintain sports ties with South Africa and that their own black athletes—including such exciting runners as Filbert Bayi and Miruts Yifter—suffered most from the boycott, denied a chance to test their talent against the world after years of training. The Africans earned some headlines but not much more. Only a handful of competitions missed their presence.

The long-term effects of the African power play are difficult to read. In any event, it is just one of myriad problems the IOC must soon grapple with. If politics does not savage the games, the costs of staging them may, and the IOC must soon decide whether lofty Olympic ideals are worth a billion dollars and the threat of terrorism, whether all 21 Olympic sports are worth keeping; whether a permanent site in Greece (or elsewhere) ought not to be established. In the months to come, in the cozy salons of Geneva and Lausanne, the IOC will do its work. The heroes of the XXI Olympiad have done theirs and taken their rightful place in history.

Kornelia Ender was a product of an East German sports system that, it was later revealed, relied heavily on performance-enhancing drugs, although Ender says she never knowingly took any. She quit competitive swimming after the Montreal Olympics and now is a physiotherapist living in Germany.

Nadia Comaneci won two more gold medals in 1980 and defected to the United States in 1989. She married U.S. gymnast Bart Conner. They live in Norman, Okla., where they own a gymnastics school.

Stars in the Spotlight

—March 7, 1988—
Jane O'Hara

F ROM THE BEGINNING, it was supposed to be a two-star
event. East German Katarina Witt and America Debi
Thomas would fight it out for the Olympic gold medal: two
Carmens, two contenders. But suddenly, near the end of the
night, the script was torn up and Canada found itself with a
freshly minted heroine. Elizabeth Manley, 22, of Ottawa, skated
onto the ice dressed in shocking pink—and that was just the
start of the electricity. Turning in the performance of her career,
Manley skated off with the silver medal after winning the long
program, worth 50 per cent of the final mark. She finished a

Manley after her surprise win in the long free-skating program barely perceptible four-tenths of a point behind Witt, who skated flawlessly to win her second Olympic gold. But, clearly, Thomas crumbled under the Olympic strain, settling for the bronze. Said an elated Manley, who had started the evening in third place: "I never really felt the pressure. It's been the Debi and Katarina story here." During her triumphant performance, Manley was buoyed by the cheers of a highly partisan crowd. "It sounded like the world was caving in," said the tiny skater. "There was so much love in the crowd I could have stayed out there all night." In fact, the crowd was so loud that at times Manley could barely hear her own music. But the pert and perky five-foot, 105-lb. skater triple-jumped her way through an energetic program. Known for her jumping skills, the three-time Canadian champion has often been plagued by nerves in her six-year international career. But during her daunting four-minute program, Manley, who was recovering from the flu, looked as composed and confident as she had all week.

In the year leading up to the Olympics, Manley had increased her training to eight hours a day from two, under the eye of her coach, Peter Dunfield. She lost seven pounds, mostly from around her hips, and gained some newfound confidence after consulting with sports psychologist Peter Jensen of Toronto. "I believed I could be on the podium," said Manley. "This was a dream." In fact, Manley had the dream two weeks ago. While training in Ontario in order to avoid the overheated Olympic atmosphere, she dreamt that her mother, Joan, ran down the Saddledome steps to congratulate her. It was a good omen for the highly superstitious skater, who travels to every competition with one of her 30 teddy bears. On Saturday morning, just hours before her triumph, Manley received yet another handmade bear from her doting mother, the emotional bedrock in her life. Manley thanked her, then headed to the dressing room to change as her mother yelled after her, "I love you."

The women's competition boiled down to the dramatic long program last Saturday night, but the pot started bubbling well before that. After Thursday night's short performance, in which Witt placed first, Thomas second and Manley third, Thomas and her coach, Alex McGowan, complained bitterly that the judges had favoured Witt's European elegance to Thomas's Yankee pizzazz. Said McGowan, who held his nose when Thomas's marks came up on the scoreboard: "I'm concerned that, no matter what Debi does, the die has been cast."

In the short performance, Witt appeared cautious and nervous. Standing at the boards before the performance, she held hands with her coach, Jutta Muller. Looking like a member of the Rockette's chorus line in an outfit of rhinestones and blue plumes, Witt jumped, spun and tapdanced to a medley of Broadway tunes. She charmed, but failed to enchant, the 19,000 spectators in the Saddledome. But the judges rewarded her clean performance with high marks.

Minutes later when Thomas stepped on the ice in a black, sequin-studded body stocking, the crowd roared. As she started her program, Witt, skate laces untied, stood at rink-side and watched icily. Skating to the percussive, funky beat of *Something in My House,* Thomas jived her way into the hearts of the crowd, flawlessly completing the seven required elements. At the end, she received a standing ovation and mediocre marks from the judges. Thomas was clearly disappointed when she appeared at a news conference after the event. When a reporter asked whether she thought Witt had tried to upset her by watching her skate, Thomas replied: "I don't think I would have stood there. She was right beside my coach."

Witt, 22, a three-time world champion and gold medallist at the 1984 Olympics in Sarajevo, entered the Games with her heady credentials intact. The 20-year-old Thomas, who defeated Witt at the world championships in 1986, was the underdog. But because both women chose to skate their long programs to Bizet's *Carmen*, there was an opportunity for direct comparison. "The battle between them has been going on for years," said Peggy Fleming, the 1968 U.S. Olympic gold medallist in figure skating. "The comparisons became very stark."

There was also mounting tension between the two women. According to insiders, the demure Witt does not like the flamboyant Thomas. When told that Thomas was studying German in order to speak to Witt in her native tongue, Witt replied, "Doesn't she know I speak English?" Meanwhile, Thomas, who once described herself as invincible, took a shot at Witt last Friday. Asked to sum up her opponent in one word, she said: "How about silver? She sure as hell isn't going to get the gold." At times last week, Thomas reflected the strain by displaying the volatility of a prima donna. She openly argued with her coach, made funny faces at her boyfriend, Brian Vanden Hogan, and sulked whenever she fell.

There were no histrionics during Witt's practice sessions. When she took to the ice, she became the ultimate skating machine—with her coach, Muller, firmly at the controls. Said Fleming: "Mrs. Muller is responsible for every detail of that performance." The East German beauty has been turning heads since her arrival in Calgary. At the athletes' Olympic Village, 40 messages awaited her, including one from the Canadian bobsleigh team inviting her to the village disco. Canadian figure skater Kurt Browning was also smitten by Witt. After skating his long program on Feb. 20, Browning sat in the stands to watch the remainder of the competition. In the seat next to him was Witt. Browning said simply, "God put me there."

Not everybody was as smitten. Last week Witt was lambasted by Dunfield, who claimed that her suggestive outfits would affect the nine judges—seven of whom are men. "We're here to skate in a dress and not a G-string," he added. "It's a circus." Thomas entered the debate, saying, "Her costumes belong in an X-rated movie, rather than a world-class skating competition." It was not the first time that Dunfield has created a stir, hoping to raise Manley's profile. After Thomas beat Manley in Skate Canada last November, Dunfield declared that Thomas skated at a lethargic pace of "10 miles per hour." Last week, in silent rebuttal, Thomas wore a sweatshirt with a 10 m.p.h. speed limit sign emblazoned on the front. On the back, the script read: "Trying for 60 m.p.h."

But when it came to the final test, Manley's speed and spunk were clearly superior. For Manley, capturing the silver medal, Canada's second of the Games, was a dream come true. For Canadians, it was an Olympian moment to treasure for years to come.

Elizabeth Manley was "Canada's Sweetheart" after her surprising Calgary performance. She then turned professional with the Ice Capades and skated professionally for several years. She now lives and coaches in Florida.

Debi Thomas also turned pro for a while, but is now an ortho-pedic surgeon in Los Angeles.

Katarina Witt has parlayed her gold medals into a professional skating and multimillion-dollar show business career. She lives in Berlin.

Maclean's contributing editor Jane O'Hara worked at the magazine as a senior writer from 1978 to 1988 and as an award-winning investigative reporter from 1998 to 2001.

The King of Seoul

—October 3, 1988—
Hal Quinn and Chris Wood

I N THE BRILLIANT SUNSHINE of a warm Saturday afternoon
in Seoul, Ben Johnson did what no man has ever done
before, and few, beyond Johnson, thought humanly possible. In
a few unforgettable seconds, Johnson redefined man's ability to
propel himself by the sheer power of body and will. Last week,
on sport's grandest stage, the Summer Olympics, in sport's most
elemental event, the 100-m sprint, the 26-year-old Canadian
toyed with the seven fastest men the rest of the human race had
to offer and became the King of Seoul. The contest won, the
gold medal secure, Johnson glanced over his left shoulder at his

---

The magazine was printed hours before Johnson was stripped of gold closest rival, American Carl Lewis, raised his right arm in a victory salute and glided over the finish line. Looking up from Lane 3, Lewis saw the clock and, like the 70,000 spectators in Olympic Stadium, he stared in disbelief. The clock read 9.79 seconds. The man who in Rome in August 1987 became the first man ever to run 100 m in 9.83 seconds, had suddenly broken the 9.8-second barrier. Just as quickly, Ben Johnson had entered another realm.

The voyage to the gold medal—and a new world record—in the dash began amidst the hype of a worldwide television audience and the anticipation of athletes and spectators at the stadium. As the eight fastest men in the world limbered up, along the runway on the stadium's east side, Hristo Markov of Bulgaria and Igor Lapchine of the Soviet Union were competing for the triple-jump gold. At two pits at the south end, male high jumpers, hoping to qualify for the following day's finals, stretched between loping challenges to the bar. Finally, a hush descended over the crowd as the public address announcer requested "quiet at the start, please" of the men's 100-m final. As Lewis settled into the block in Lane 3 and Johnson spread his massive arms to the width of Lane 6 to take his signature position, the calm was but faint forewarning of the fury to follow.

When the starting gun sounded, Johnson—in brilliant red shorts and singlet top—erupted from the block. In Rome, his start was timed at 0.129 second off the block. In Seoul, it was 0.123 second. In the next few moments—the stadium infield quiet, the circling pigeons ignored—the audience, like a north-south wave, rose to its feet involuntarily, perhaps hoping to see more, yet knowing it would not understand.

Johnson reached the 50-m mark in 5.52 seconds, 0.13 second ahead of his longtime rival Lewis. The observers in the stadium knew that Lewis, even when he lost to Johnson in

Rome, was the faster man over the final 50 m of the dash. But not last Saturday. Johnson turned on what his coach, Charles Francis, calls the "second acceleration." As the metres blurred by, Johnson at 60 m was 0.16 second ahead of Lewis. At the 80-m mark he was 0.17 second in front. From the gun, the race was never in doubt—just as Johnson had predicted weeks earlier when he said, "When the gun go, the race be over." As the roar from the stadium swelled with each step, Johnson—like a true Olympian—raised his right arm triumphantly.

There was nothing in the months leading up to the XXIVth Summer Olympics to guarantee that the afternoon of Sept. 24 in South Korea—the evening of Sept. 23 in North America—would become a milestone in the history of Canadian sport. After setting the world record in Rome, Johnson suffered a debilitating hamstring injury at a meet in Tokyo on May 13. Next came an embarrassing public feud over his rehabilitation with his personal coach, Francis. Then, in August, after winning the Canadian trials with a time of 9.90, Johnson confronted Lewis—the flamboyant 27-year-old winner of the 1984 Olympic gold to Johnson's bronze—in Zurich. Accelerating through the final 50 m, Lewis won easily. Johnson went on to race in Cologne, West Germany, and finished a distant third in an undistinguished field.

Having completed barely a half-dozen 100-m finals since his record run in Rome, Johnson arrived in Seoul from his training base in the outskirts of Tokyo. Said Francis: "He has been running his best times ever over 200 m, and his starts for the 100 are great." Training in Seoul last week, Johnson also recorded his best personal time over the 80-m distance and, later in the weight room, bench-pressed 396 lb., the most the 175-pounder had ever done. Then Johnson rested up for his races.

In the first qualifying heat on Sept. 23 in Seoul, Lewis and Johnson easily advanced. But in the second round, Johnson stopped hearts back home. Only the top two finishers in each of the six heats—and four other sprinters with the best overall times—would go to the semifinals. While Lewis dominated his heat in 9.99 seconds, Johnson eased up in his and finished third in a time of 10.17. In the end, that was enough to advance to the semis—but that became clear only after all the heat times had been computed. Later, Johnson's agent, Larry Heidebrecht, conceded that Johnson did not know the rules governing the Round 2 races for reaching the semifinals. Just 90 minutes before the final, Johnson and Lewis ran in separate semifinals— and both finished first. Then, moments before Johnson entered the stadium later that day for the gold-medal final, he turned to Francis and said, "I'm ready."

Before the race began, Lewis sought out Johnson and shook his hand. Attempting to gain a final advantage in the eight-man field, Johnson settled last into the block, trying to minimize the time he would have to lock his powerful frame into a ready position. When the gun sounded, he powered into the lead. Lewis said later that he did not see his rival running three lanes away until the race was almost over. But television replays clearly revealed that Lewis snuck three peeks at Johnson, the first at the midpoint—and his look indicated that Lewis knew the race was over.

As Johnson crossed the finish line, the cheers thundered across the Olympic Stadium and the winner jogged victoriously to the foot of the Olympic torch, holding a Canadian flag. In the stands, an elated Gloria Johnson of Toronto said of her son's triumph, "I closed my eyes and said a little prayer." In Falmouth, Jamaica, where television service was still out because of hurricane Gilbert, Ben Johnson Sr., 63, a telephone company supervisor, listened to the race outside his home on a portable radio. Later, leaning on a fence post overlooking Market Street, he said: "They love my boy. Joy for me." Nearby, his brother Harold, 74, likened Ben Johnson's rise to a bi-national house-raising. "We supplied the rocks, and Canada, the bricks," he said. "Canada deserves the medal."

Almost overlooked on the track in Seoul were the strong performances of the rest of the field. For the first time in Olympic history, four runners broke the 10-second mark: Lewis with a time of 9.92; Linford Christie of Britain, the bronze-medal winner with a time of 9.97; and fourth-place finisher Calvin Smith of the United States with a time of 9.99. As well, Canada's Desai Williams, Johnson's Mazda Optimist Club teammate in Toronto, finished seventh with an impressive personal best of 10.11.

Lewis, meanwhile, stood alone at the end of the 100-m track looking stunned. Johnson furled the flag, dropped it along the rail and climbed the stairs of the stadium for a live interview during CBC-TV's national news—during which he took a congratulatory call from Prime Minister Brian Mulroney in Ottawa. Finally, Johnson emerged, resplendent in white, for the medal ceremony—his right pant leg clinging inside a sock.

A double row of 18 trumpeters—their instruments bannered in gold and their hats plumed in white—heralded the beginning of the medal awards. Johnson, at five feet, 10 inches tall the smallest man of the three, stepped up on the centre podium and watched calmly as the Canadian flag rose. And during the playing of the national anthem, among all those savouring the moment it was Ben Johnson who, perhaps alone, had never doubted that it would arrive. "I have been waiting for this moment for the last 12 years," he told reporters afterward. "In the last Olympic Games in 1984, I finished third. I said, my time will come."

Later, Johnson spoke at a news conference, whose start was postponed for more than 90 minutes while the world's fastest human tried to produce a urine sample for drug-testing. Said

Johnson: "I knew Carl Lewis and Calvin Smith were the major guys. They both beat me early in the season in Zurich," he said. "I didn't get upset. I went home to work on my endurance and my starts. Those meets were part of my training." As for Lewis's daunting qualifying times, they were no more than milestones to be passed on the road to the record. "Carl Lewis was trying to impress me with his 9.99 and his 9.97. I just concentrated on the race." But Johnson obviously remembered the times.

Johnson's grace on the track was matched by Lewis away from the lanes. The Olympic gold medallist of 1984 had run the fastest 100 m of his life and the fastest of any American in history. He was the first to congratulate Johnson after the race. Later, Lewis faced more than 1,000 reporters in a temporary news conference theatre set up especially for the event at the Olympic Stadium. He said: "I ran the best I could. I am happy with the way I performed. So no matter what place I came in, I am happy with my race."

The gold medal—Canada's first at the Games and the first in track since Percy Williams won in the 100- and 200-m sprints in 1928—was one of few bright spots in an otherwise uninspiring opening week of the Games for the Canadian team. As the Olympians retired at the midpoint of the Games to their village of highrise apartments—five kilometres away, but 45 minutes by taxi from the heart of Seoul—they could look back on hour-long waits for lunch at the athletes' cafeteria, friendships formed in the "International Zone" and medals won and lost by millimetres and microseconds. Of the more than 9,600 young people, for the sake of whose excellence the Olympic Games are dedicated, a precious few could aspire to some day match the accomplishments of Ben Johnson. As for the spectators and members of a worldwide television audience, they could only applaud Johnson's proud new claim: "I could have broken 9.75 seconds.

I'm saving that for next year." On a shining Saturday in Seoul, Johnson had made them all believers.

Ben Johnson lost his gold medal 62 hours after crossing the finish line, following tests that confirmed he had used banned anabolic steroids to enhance his performance. It was too late for Maclean's that week, which had a victorious Johnson on its cover. Both Johnson and his coach, Charlie Francis, denied the runner used steroids until testifying before a subsequent Royal Commission into drug use in sports. Johnson, who lives in the Toronto area, is a coach and personal trainer.

Indelible Memories

—December 2, 1991—
Brian Orser

I T SEEMS INCREDIBLE that nearly four years have gone by since the Olympic Winter Games in Calgary and that in less than three short months, our national teams will be battling for Olympic gold in Albertville, France. Just the thought of the tough competition that our athletes will soon face stirs my own deeply competitive instincts, sending a rush of adrenaline surging through my body. Looking ahead to the Games also brings back a flood of vivid memories from Calgary. I will never forget how my heart pounded when the huge crowd of 60,000 people in McMahon Stadium jumped to their feet and cheered wildly as I carried the Canadian flag into the opening ceremonies.

Nor can I erase the memory of how that warm reception quickly gave way to the mounting pressure to vanquish my archrival, Brian Boitano of the United States, and win the gold medal for all of Canada. In my mind's eye, I can still clearly see the tiny mistake in the triple jump that cost me the gold, but on the final day of the Games, my feeling of disappointment gave way to a sense of melancholy as the Olympic flame flickered and went out—a tumultuous week in my life was over.

It was not supposed to end the way it did. I was the world champion and had won the silver medal at the 1984 Games in Sarajevo, Yugoslavia. The whole country was eagerly anticipating a gold-medal performance in Calgary. When my name was finally called and I skated out onto the ice, the Olympic Saddledome seemed to be crackling with energy. Suddenly, there I was—Brian Orser, from small-town Ontario, completely alone in the middle of the rink in front of 20,000 people. I was saying to myself over and over, "This is it, this is the Olympics."

Then, the first strains of *The Bolt*, Dmitri Shostakovich's epic composition celebrating the Russian Revolution, started, and for the next four minutes I was lost in a world of my own. I poured every ounce of concentration and energy I could muster into my routine, and when I landed my final triple jump, the Saddledome was vibrating with thunderous applause. Like the partisan throng, I felt that I had skated one of the best routines in my life and that the gold medal was mine. All that remained was for me to climb the podium and accept it. For the next couple of minutes, with the medal all but in my grasp, I was filled with a feeling of overwhelming joy. I finally knew what it felt like to win the gold.

Then came the crushing, gut-twisting letdown. I knew that Boitano had also skated exceptionally well, and then I got the signal that still burns in my memory today. The head official slowly raised two fingers in the air. It seemed impossible, but suddenly I was second, and my illusion of Olympic gold vanished into the cold Calgary night. With the whole country, if not the entire sporting world, watching me on television, I had to come back down to earth without showing my deep disappointment.

As I look back, I am still amazed that I could have soared so high and fallen so low in just a flicker of time. But as the months went by, I took solace in the fact that just to compete in the Olympic Games is a rare and wonderful experience. After all, only a handful of the world's top athletes ever get an opportunity to compete in the Games. And only a very few of them leave the Games with a medal.

And even though I was the reigning world champion at the time, I never thought for one second that winning the Olympic gold was going to be easy. In fact, my preparations for the Games actually began when I met with my coach and manager, Doug Leigh, in June, 1987, a full nine months before our Canadian team's entrance into McMahon Stadium. In our meeting, we set a daunting goal: to win nothing less than the gold medal in Calgary.

Almost immediately, we set monthly, weekly and daily training goals, but to take the gold in Calgary, we knew that I would have to peak at the highest level of physical and mental training, almost on the very eve of the competition. To peak precisely at that point, however, required complete harmony among Coach Leigh, my choreographer, Uschi Keszler, and myself.

That is not easy to accomplish in an Olympic year. Demands from the media and the prestige of the Games not only increase the pressure on the athletes, but also create hundreds of distractions. The television networks, newspapers and magazines all wanted time for interviews, and I felt that as national and world champion, I had to accommodate everyone. But finally, Leigh intervened and literally locked the door of the Orillia, Ont., arena, where we were training, behind us.

Despite the iron control that Leigh exerted over our training regimen, the pressure to win the gold in Calgary continued to mount. If someone even hinted that I might fall short of my goal, it would trigger a rush of negative thoughts. As a result, the actions and responsibilities of the people surrounding me were as critical as my own performance. Every time my coach was asked, "How is Brian doing?" his reply was always, "We are right on track." In the end, the intimacy that we created on that small ice rink in Orillia between my coach, choreographer and family was quite beautiful.

But winning takes more than harmony and positive thinking. It also requires brute determination. And during the early summer of 1987, I stuck doggedly to the set plan. I started each day at 5 a.m. with a high-energy breakfast of organic food, including granola, oats, raisins, nuts, freshly squeezed orange juice and coffee. Then, I left for the Orillia arena for six hours of intense, uninterrupted training. In 1988, figure skating still contained a compulsory figures requirement, and I would spend the first two or three hours working on my highly demanding figures routine, tracing intricate patterns into the ice with my skates.

After three hours of work, I would eat another high-energy meal. That one usually consisted of what we called "power balls," home-made from protein powder, oats, almonds, peanut butter, nuts and brewer's yeast. Following that, I practised my actual Olympic routine for about three hours. I had my own apartment in Orillia, and when I arrived home I would usually prepare a hearty meal of chicken or fish, along with fresh organically grown vegetables. But despite the heavy workload, my training was not over. In the evening, I would either head to the Orillia YMCA or back to the rink for an hour of weight training and running. Finally, at about 9 p.m., I would wind down by watching a movie video—and prepare to do it all over the next day.

By sticking with a tightly controlled training program, I was able to take some of the pressure off myself because I could carefully measure my progress. But for many other figure skaters, a more relaxed approach seems to work better. Canadian and three-time world champion Kurt Browning of Caroline, Alta., for one, takes a completely different approach. In situations where I would try to ease the pressure through a methodical training program, Browning actually tries to add to the pressure he is under—to improve his performance. If the competition is unimportant and the pressure is not there, he does not train well. In fact, the normal pattern for Browning is to skate below his capabilities just before world championships. Then, when everyone is starting to worry that he is not ready for the big event, Browning arrives and skates like the great champion that he is.

Browning's main rival for Olympic gold, Victor Petrenko of the Soviet Union, on the other hand, follows a training pattern similar to my own. Browning and Petrenko will also have to battle Christopher Bowman of the United States, who is now living in Toronto and training with former Canadian champion Toller Cranston. The stress of the upcoming Olympics may be getting even to Bowman, who is known for his casual approach to training: earlier this month, he showed up at the rink with his black hair bleached blond.

As they train, those great skaters will become increasingly aware that the Olympics are tantalizingly close at hand. For them, just to persevere through the three months deserves a gold medal. They are about to live through one of the most high-powered and intense periods of their lives. I was fortunate enough to experience both the thrill of top international competition and the spirit of the Games in Sarajevo and Calgary. And with the Olympics well behind me now, the most important advice that I could give to our athletes would be simply to enjoy and cherish every moment of the Albertville Games—because when the Olympic flame finally dims and goes out, their memories will linger, but their lives will never be the same.

An eight-time Canadian champion, two-time Olympic silver medallist and 1987's World Champion, Brian Orser is one of the finest figure skaters Canada has ever produced. He lives in Ottawa and works as director and choreographer, touring professional shows such as Skate the Nation and Holiday Festival on Ice.

Banyoles Bonanza:
Canada Shines on the Rowing Lake

—August 10, 1992—
Chris Wood

MARNIE MCBEAN WAS TALKING about Silken Laumann.
"She is one of the main components that makes our
team so strong," said the Canadian rower. "She's been an inspiration and a motivator." But McBean and her pairs partner,
Kathleen Heddle, are a formidable force in their own right.
And for all the attention paid to Laumann—the 1991 world
singles champion making a dramatic recovery from a near-
crippling leg injury—it was Canada's other women rowers who
led the remarkable medal haul at Lake Banyoles last weekend.

Laumann courageously winning bronze after her leg injury

Early Saturday, the women's four crew powered down the 2,000-m course to grab the first gold, and Heddle and McBean followed with a decisive victory a half hour later. Then, on Sunday, Laumann completed her improbable comeback with a stirring last-minute surge to beat back an American challenge and take the bronze. "I thought, I'm not coming in fourth," she said later. By then, the Canadians had copped two more medals: golds in the women's and men's eights. "It was nice," said Laumann, "to see the Canadian flag being put up for the fourth time in the regatta."

The triumphant weekend firmly entrenched Canada as a world power in rowing—a gruelling sport that combines brute strength with physical and mental endurance. Actually, Canadians have excelled at the sport before: rowing produced the country's first world champions just days after Confederation when four men from Saint John, N.B.—a light-house keeper and three fishermen—stroked to victory in homemade boats at the 1867 Paris Exhibition. And Ned Hanlan, a flamboyant oarsman from Toronto, captured the world sculling title on the Thames in England in 1880—just one of his more than 300 rowing victories. Other Canadians went on to win 19 Olympic medals, culminating in six trips to the podium at the Eastern Bloc–boycotted Los Angeles Games in 1984, where Laumann and her sister, Danielle, grabbed bronze in the double scull event.

Heavily favoured to win gold in Barcelona, Laumann suffered a devastating injury in May when a German pairs boat accidentally rammed her shell at a regatta in Germany—driving wood splinters into her flesh and breaking her right ankle. But she persevered and, one month and five operations later, crawled into her shell at Elk Lake to begin the struggle back. It seemed amazing that she was racing at all, let alone finishing third in the Olympic final won by Romanian

Elisabeta Lipa—and wishing she had finished higher. "I prefer gold," Laumann said, but added: "I don't think you can ever predict what would have been, and I wouldn't want to take that away from the winner."

It was after the success of Laumann and her teammates at the 1984 Olympics that Toronto's Marnie McBean was introduced to rowing. The makers of Coffee Crisp chocolate bars featured the sport in a TV commercial the next spring, just as McBean, then 17, was looking for something new to absorb her fierce competitive energies. "I had gone through high school being really aggressive at every sport," she recalls, "but I was never talented at any of them. I would always foul at basketball or get myself bruised up in soccer." In frustration, she phoned the Argonaut Rowing Club, whose Lake Ontario boat shed she often passed on her bicycle, and signed up for a learn-to-row course. "I just loved it right from the beginning," she says.

Five months later, Kathleen Heddle, then 19, was crowding into the gymnasium at the University of British Columbia in Vancouver to register for her third-year studies in psychology when she felt a tap on her shoulder. It was the UBC rowing coach scouting the milling bodies for rowing potential. He persuaded Heddle to try the sport. "Right away," she remembers, "I was good at it."

Formally, the two women compete as a "coxless pair"—their slender 28-foot plastic rowing shell does not have a helmsman in the stern guiding their direction. Neither does the women's four. The rowers' success, the coaches say, resulted from supreme intensity and dedication. But, inevitably, there have been tensions along the way. Until now, the media focus on Laumann has overshadowed—and at times irritated—other rowers. And even McBean and Heddle acknowledge that their close teamwork occasionally produces friction. "Sometimes there's tension," Heddle says. "We are very different people."

In fact, the blond Vancouverite is temperamentally the opposite of her dark-haired crew mate. While Heddle, according to women's coach Al Morrow, conceals deep reserves of personal strength behind a shy demeanour, McBean is engagingly assertive and outspoken. "Kathleen is Vancouver," says Morrow. "She's West Coast laid back and Marnie is hustle-bustle Toronto. The beauty of it is that as a pair, they offer each other those strengths." And in the two years that they have rowed together, they have plainly forged close bonds. "There's a lot of faith between the two of us," says McBean.

There needs to be. Rowing a featherweight craft demands something close to shared intuition. "She sets the pace," notes McBean. "She has to believe that I'm following her exactly." At the same time, she says, "if I want the rate [of strokes] to go up, I can't just start going faster. I have to ask her, 'Let's take it up a bit.' If either one of us does anything apart from each other, it will screw us up."

But off the water, says McBean, "we give each other personal time to get away—especially when it's getting intense like this." Since resuming full-time training in January after an autumn break, neither rower has had much freedom for other pursuits. McBean spends much of her limited spare time reading—American author John Irving is a favourite. Heddle, meanwhile, has found a boyfriend among the small circle of Canadian rowers: for the past several months she has been going out with Don Telfer, a 31-year-old Calgarian whose four-man crew was eliminated in the Olympic semifinals. A demanding schedule left all the rowers little time for sightseeing, despite having been in Europe since May for a series of pre-Olympic regattas. "I don't really feel like we're in Europe," says Heddle. "We might as well be in Indianapolis."

Canada's rowers put other pursuits aside, in most cases since 1990, to concentrate on the Games. Says Morrow, with evident pride in their dedication: "It is basically full-time, without pay." Not entirely: team members receive stipends from Sport Canada.

Still, rowing offers few of the avenues to wealth that such high-profile Olympic sports as track and field do—let alone such spectacles as professional baseball or basketball. Heddle and McBean acknowledge that after the Games, they may have to look for more lucrative pursuits. McBean plans to return to her interrupted studies in physical education at the University of Western Ontario in London, where she will also work as a rowing coach. Heddle, meanwhile, in true laid-back West Coast fashion, has no firm plans. But she is buying a boat: a $5,000 single scull.

Silken Laumann rested her injury for a year and then resumed competition, winning a silver at the 1996 Atlanta Olympics. She retired in 1999, lives in Victoria and does motivational speaking.

Kathleen Heddle retired after the 1996 Olympics with nine Olympic and world championship medals. She lives in Vancouver where she is a sports administration consultant.

Marnie McBean won a gold medal with Heddle at Atlanta and retired in 2000 with 12 Olympic and world championship medals. She lives in Toronto and is active in charity efforts and motivational speaking.

Chris Wood, an award-winning Vancouver-based freelance writer and author, worked for Maclean's *from 1985 to 2001.*

High-Speed Dream Team

—February 23, 1998—
James Deacon

TOMOMI OKAZAKI HAD JUST FINISHED posting the fastest time of the day at the M-Wave in Nagano, but as she passed by stands full of adoring fans, she held her finger to her lips, asking for quiet. Trying to direct the crowd's attention to the featured race of the day, Okazaki pointed back towards the start line, where Canada's Catriona LeMay Doan and Susan Auch were getting set for the last pairing of the two-day sprint final. The audience responded and, for a second, there was quiet inside the cavernous M-Wave, all eyes on the two women in red and black awaiting the gun. They didn't disappoint.

LeMay Doan flashes her million-watt smile after winning gold at Nagano

Pitted against one another because they were the top skaters in the previous day's heats, LeMay Doan and Auch blasted through the first 100 m on their way to the fastest 500-m pairing ever clocked in Olympic women's competition. LeMay Doan crossed first, beating Auch by a mere three-tenths of a second. "What a great race," a breathless but thrilled LeMay Doan said afterward. "Susan really pushed me."

For the Canadians who were lucky enough to be there, the colours of Valentine's Day will from here on be gold and silver. LeMay Doan and Auch came into the race saddled with huge expectations—they finished the World Cup season ranked first and second, respectively, in the 500 m. "I felt really nervous," said Auch, who also captured silver at the Lillehammer Games in 1994. "But I had done well under pressure before, and that gave me confidence." Auch jumped into an early lead and forced LeMay Doan into overdrive. "I had to tell myself that I was the strongest skater out there," LeMay Doan said, "and trust that I could make up the ground on the back stretch."

What a week at the races, and what a show of strength from what has suddenly become the dominant team on the Canadian Winter Olympics roster. In five days, the long-track speed-skating team grabbed one gold, two silver and a bronze, and there were prospects for more this week. LeMay Doan holds the world record in the women's 1,000 m and was entered in the 1,500. Among the short-track skaters, sprinters Isabelle Charest and Marc Gagnon are contenders in four events. Watching the men's 500 at the M-Wave, 1994 double-silver medallist Nathalie Lambert was already looking ahead to this week's short-track competition. "Isabelle and Marc are both skating really well," says Lambert, who was sidelined last fall with a broken ankle. "I think we could get three medals in short-track."

Jeremy Wotherspoon and Kevin Overland started it all by capturing silver and bronze in a thrilling 500-m men's long-track competition, won by local hero Hiroyasu Shimizu. Two more Canadians, Sylvain Bouchard and Patrick Bouchard (no relation), finished right behind Overland, giving Canada four of the top five spots. But in the 1,000 m on Sunday, Wotherspoon, a tall, slender 21-year-old from Red Deer, Alta., who holds the world record in the event, had a disappointing skate and the Canadians finished out of the medals.

Despite the grim overcast and cold drizzle in Nagano, it was all sweetness and light inside the spectacular M-Wave. There were the usual nationalist rivalries among the more than 10,000 who ringed the oval—the stands at a speed-skating competition are nothing if not tribal. The Dutch in their neon-orange outfits, the Japanese in blue-and-white, Germans, Poles and clumps of red-and-white Canucks waved flags, blew horns, sang songs and cheered their racers. But everyone applauded good performances, no matter the skater's nationality, and LeMay Doan crossed the finish line to a thunderous ovation that followed her around the oval as she flashed her million-watt smile. More personally, she was congratulated while coasting down the backstretch by her husband, Bart, a rodeo bull rider who drives the Zamboni at the Calgary Oval.

LeMay Doan and Auch are each other's toughest rivals, but it is a friendly rivalry. They credit sprint coach Derrick Auch—Susan's brother—with promoting a team ethic that has eased whatever tensions have arisen. A lawyer who put off joining a Calgary firm so he could continue coaching the sprinters through Nagano, Derrick, 30, has an easygoing manner, and even in the minutes before the gold-medal race, he had the skaters loose and laughing. He says it helps both skaters to be able to train regularly with their fastest competition. And before taking their stances at the starting line, the two skaters wished each other luck. "I was genuinely happy to see her win," Auch said, "to see her arms raised when she crossed the line."

That suits the culture of the sport. There is apparent camaraderie and respect among competitors, whatever their country. At the post-medal ceremony after the men's 500, Overland praised the diminutive Shimizu who had won out over him and Wotherspoon. "He has the best technique of any of the sprinters," Overland said, adding, "I am proud to be on the podium with these guys."

The revolutionary clap skate, with its hinged toe, has enabled all competitors to go faster. But it is Calgary's Olympic Oval, a legacy of the 1988 Games, that is the biggest reason for the Canadians' remarkable rise. It is the fastest ice in the world, which helps skaters learn to cope with higher speeds. And it is open 10 months a year, far more than most European tracks. (The Viking Ship arena built for the Lillehammer Games is open only 60 days a year because of the high cost of maintaining the ice.) At Nagano's Holland House, a bar-restaurant near the M-Wave that provides a little home cooking for rabid Dutch fans, Egon Boesten says his 15-year-old son, Jan, is on the Dutch junior team and wants to attend school in Calgary so he can train at the Olympic Oval. "Everyone wants to go to Canada," Boesten says.

Watching the medal bonanza last week, Gaetan Boucher wondered what might have been. He was Canada's hero at the Sarajevo Games in 1984, winning two golds and a bronze. But at the time there was no indoor oval—he had to train in Europe. And there were no major purses until the twilight of his career. Top competitors now can earn $100,000 annually from endorsements and international victories. "For skating, that's a lot of money," says Boucher, who works for Bauer, the skate manufacturer. "When the World Cup was first started [in the mid-1980s], I won a race in Switzerland and received 50 francs."

The skaters don't expect their Nagano success to spur construction of ovals in every neighbourhood, but they hope their medals have some impact. "It'd be nice to see lots of little kids signing up at clubs next year," Susan Auch said. LeMay Doan wasn't thinking about next year—she had more immediate concerns. "Now I can relax a bit," she said, threading her way through a gauntlet of reporters. "Then it'll be time to get ready for the next race."

Catriona LeMay Doan won gold again in the 500 m at Salt Lake City and holds the world record for that distance.

Susan Auch competed in her fifth Games at Salt Lake but failed to win a medal. Still a member of the national team, she lives in Calgary.

Jeremy Wotherspoon has dominated in the 500 m and 1,000 m since 1998, winning 12 world titles.

The Girl Games

—*October 9, 2000*—
James Deacon

ANNE MONTMINY AND EMILIE HEYMANS didn't have much time to train for the synchronized 10-m diving event. It was not a top priority for competitors who were medal contenders in the individual tower event at the Summer Games. But since they both live in the Montreal area, they got together for an occasional hour and made plans to resume training once the individual event was finished. It took a while to get their rhythm right, and after that it was simply a matter of standing up on the tower and going on the count of three. According to their head coach, the 25-year-old Montminy—as

Heymans (left) and Montminy diving for silver in Sydney

the veteran—counted it down to Heymans, 18. But after towelling off with a silver medal to their credit, the pair revealed that their coach was wrong. "Emilie only hears out of her left ear," Montminy confided. "So she ran the show."

It made sense that, for the Canadian team in Sydney, a thrown-together arrangement made out of last-minute necessity delivered such a sterling reward. Montminy, having already won bronze in the individual tower, became Canada's first double medallist in Sydney in an event that was making its Olympic debut. In fact, Canada did splendidly in new events: Simon Whitfield won gold in the triathlon, Karen Cockburn and Mathieu Turgeon captured bronze in the women's and men's trampoline, respectively, and Winnipeg's Dominique Bosshart, coming from behind in her final match, grabbed bronze in tae kwon do.

It was also fitting that, with a third-place finish in synchronized swimming—and champion kayaker Caroline Brunet scheduled to race after press time—so many of Canada's medals came from women. After all, these were the so-called Girl Games—or, as one Australian newspaper cheekily put it, The Games of the Dames. Right from the start, when opening ceremonies organizers chose to honour the centennial of female athletes competing in the Olympics, the focus has been on women. Throughout the Games, they bore the weightiest pressure and reaped the brightest worldwide spotlight for their efforts. And there were more of them: just under 40 per cent of the 11,084 athletes in Sydney were women. By 2004, Olympic officials predict, the number of women will finally reach half the athlete population, a huge increase over the 20 per cent who attended the Montreal Games in 1976.

Canada has already done its part to tip the balance. For the second straight Games, its team had more female athletes than male. "We have been leaders in making sporting opportunities available to women," said Sue Hyland, who headed Canada's team operations in Sydney. "We have a pretty progressive country, and women have done well by it." They have done well, period. In the pool, the eight-woman synchronized swim team dazzled fans to win bronze-medal marks with a performance that evoked images of other sports at the Summer Games—from hurdlers and high jumpers to archers and cyclists. In synchro's most competitive Olympic final ever, the Canadians had by far the most athletic performance of the eight in the last group. "The sport has really come a long, long way even since 1996," explained synchro-swimmer Jacinthe Taillon of St-Eustache, Que. "A lot of countries that weren't on the map four years ago are really strong now. And it will be better in another four years."

It wasn't a bad week for Canadian men. There was wrestler Daniel Igali, fighting his way into the gold-medal match on the weekend. Tennis stars Daniel Nestor and Sebastien Lareau won gold in men's doubles. And veteran canoeist Steve Giles paddled to a bronze in the 1,000-m sprint final with a blistering kick at the end. "The finish was awesome," said an exhausted Giles.

Undeniably, some women's sports drew attention as much for their sex appeal as for the level of competition. Canada's highly ranked women's water polo team sank early in its Olympic debut, but the sport was hugely popular—it's fast, tough and easy for viewers to follow—and there is always the prospect of a torn bathing suit to bring out the gawkers. In fact, the biggest controversy about the Girl Games was over the role sex played in the selling of their sports. Some top performers got nearly as much ink for their makeup, their painted nails and their skintight outfits, and a few posed nude for pre-Games photos. But if some critics questioned deliberate attempts at attention-getting, others were more philosophical. "There's no one way for women to think—there are many voices, many faces," said Bryna Kopelow, chair of the Canadian Association for the Advancement of Women and Sport. "Women do things in different ways and we have to honour and respect this."

Gains in popularity and endorsement opportunities may not be enough to keep some Canadian veterans in competition. Brunet, who has kept a punishing training schedule for years, is plain worn out. Three-time world champion rower Emma Robinson is heading for medical school. And Montminy has been called to the bar and is weighing an offer to article with a Montreal firm. But Montminy says work is the last thing on her mind, and she is considering studying for a master's degree at the University of California at Berkeley. "I don't even know if I want to be a lawyer," she told Maclean's. "I just want to spend a year being a student, because I haven't been able to do that properly. And I want to do some partying, hang out, go somewhere where it's warm for a while."

Still, retirement from sports is hard to do, even for Montminy. There was that moment in the 10-m final when, with a couple of solid dives, she could have overtaken the American and two Chinese, and grabbed the title of Olympic champion. "It was right there," Montminy said, holding two fingers millimetres apart. That has left her with a competitive itch that can only be scratched in Athens in 2004. "Those were two dives I can do better in my sleep," she groaned. "Come back? Sure, definitely, that's still in my mind. Very much."

For Canadian athletes, perhaps the best result in Sydney is the pressure that a disappointing performance has brought to the debate over sport funding. There is a school of thought that federal cutbacks to an already stretched sports budget have stripped sport federations of their ability to field competitive teams and athletes. Another positive result here is that the success of Canada's female athletes is already attracting girls to sports. In Calgary, 12-year-old Ashley Andersen says she has always played soccer, basketball and volleyball at school. But now she has a new ambition. "Seeing Anne dive," she says of Montminy, "makes me feel like I want to do that, too." In today's sports world, she'll have a pretty good chance to fulfil that dream.

Emilie Heymans still competes and won three championships at the 2003 Canadian Nationals.

Anne Montminy has retired and in 2002 married Daniel Goldman, who had interviewed her for NBC during the Olympics. She is a lawyer, and they are living in San Francisco.

Ashley Andersen never did pursue diving, but she is on her school's rugby team.

Thanks for the Memories

—March 11, 2002—
Ken MacQueen

I T'S THE LAST SATURDAY of the 19th Winter Games—the
night before the Big Game—and Canadians have comman-
deered the student union building at the University of Utah.
It's Canada's night to howl.

The timing is superb and the casting inspired. Labatt has
spent large to sponsor this bash for the Canadian Olympic
Association, for athletes, staff, media and hangers-on. Real beer
is flowing in a Mormon town, and real Canadian rock is being
pumped out by the Tragically Hip. Songs like *Fifty-Mission Cap*
and *Fireworks*, which weave hockey into the cultural and

Jamie Sale and David Pelletier at the Salt Lake City closing ceremonies emotional landscape, hit home tonight as never before.

If there's a goal that everyone remembers, it was back in ol' '72. We all squeezed the stick and we all pulled the trigger. If the allusion to 1972, and Paul Henderson's series-winning goal against the Soviet team, is lost on many athletes gyrating on the dance floor, it's because they weren't born 30 years ago. They are looking to these Games, to contests already won and to the Canada–U.S. hockey final looming tomorrow afternoon—to create a new shared memory, a new national touchstone.

And why not? After two roller-coaster weeks that saw too many medal contenders fall short, Canada is sprinting to a record finish. Canada's speed skaters have just delivered a four-medal day—two golds and a silver in short track, and a gutsy bronze by long-track skater Clara Hughes in the 5,000 m. Disappointments are set aside. All things are possible.

The ubiquitous figure-skating team of Jamie Sale and David Pelletier have just been voted, by their fellow athletes, as the Canadian flag-bearers for Sunday's closing ceremonies. Pelletier graciously tells the crowd that the honour could have easily gone to tonight's short-track hero, Marc Gagnon, a wily veteran of three Olympics. The Chicoutimi native, who'd won an earlier bronze in the 1,500 m, added two golds tonight in the 500 m and in the 5,000-m relay, with teammates Jonathan Guilmette, Francois-Louis Tremblay, Mathieu Turcotte and Eric Bedard. Guilmette also took silver in the 500 m. That—and the upcoming gold in men's hockey—would lift Canada to 17 medals, two above its previous record of 15, to the great relief of Canadian Olympic officials. With five medals over three Games, Gagnon also surpassed legendary skater Gaetan Boucher as the country's most decorated Winter Olympian.

As the Hip take to the stage they're joined by Canada's gold-medal women's hockey team, whose underdog victory Thursday over the U.S. is viewed by many of Canada's 157 athletes as an emotional turning point of the Games. The women's team has been everywhere since their win, hitting the bars and cheerleading fellow athletes.

It seems half of Salt Lake City is in love. A cab driver rhapsodizes about having a team member hang her medal around his neck. "She called me the gold-medal driver of Salt Lake City," he says, sounding like a teenager after his first date. "God, she was beautiful." Men's coach Pat Quinn wept after the women's win, and his team members drew heavily on the victory.

"They've got rhythm," howls the Hip's lead singer Gord Downie as the women, some a bit reluctantly, leave the stage after grinding out the band's opening song. Rhythm and, finally for this Canadian contingent, a sense of momentum.

It was early days in the Games, and long-track skater Clara Hughes of Winnipeg, beloved by the Canadian male sportswriting fraternity for her unaffected decency, has just completed a top-10 performance in the 3,000 m. She is lavishing praise on teammate Cindy Klassen, who just beat her to win bronze and Canada's first medal of the Games. "She's the most humble athlete I've ever met and a really nice person," she says of Klassen. "She's just a Prairie girl at heart." The description could as easily be applied to 29-year-old Hughes.

She's waving her hands as she talks. On her left, she's written in pen in bold capitals, "EKWA." The word was given her by a friend in La Ronge, Sask. It's Cree for "now." Her friend had advised: "'Now, Clara, be in the moment,'" she says. "It really gave me the perspective I wanted for today and for this whole Olympic Games."

The questions turn to the 5,000-m race Hughes will skate on the last Saturday of the Games. "I know for me, the longer the better," she says. "I've got 5,000-m legs right now." Hughes is among that rare class of athlete who excels in both winter and summer sports. As a distance cyclist, she won two bronze medals at the 1996 Summer Games. "Cycling," she says, "is what brought me here." As for the upcoming race, she offers only a secret smile: "I'm not telling anyone what my goals are. My coach knows, my husband and that's it. I'll let you know after."

And she does. On race day, clocking 5,000 m in 6:53:53, she glides to a bench, collapses and curls up. If she's in the moment, that moment is pain. But it yields to a dawning triumph. She delivered on a dream she was too self-conscious to say aloud. She's on the podium—with a bronze, and an even rarer accomplishment. She's the first Canadian, and the fourth Olympian ever, to win medals in both Summer and Winter Olympic Games. "I can't believe this," she says, back to her usual candour now that her dream is out of the bag. "I'm so happy I actually feel like I'm going to throw up."

What worked about these Games is most everything, though it was often hard to realize from the headlines and newscasts. The Olympic figure-skating judging scandal ate the first week and made international stars of Sale and Pelletier. Then, in the Games' closing hours, there arrived, with depressing inevitability, the latest doping scandal. Three cross-country skiers, all multiple-medallists, tested positive for darbepoetin, a red-cell boosting agent intended to heighten endurance. Two skiers, Russian Larissa Lazutina and Spain's Johann Muhlegg, were stripped of their final gold medals, and a third, Russian Olga Danilova, was expelled from the Games. Under existing rules, none lost medals earned in races previous to the positive tests. As a result, Canadian cross-country skier Beckie Scott—an outspoken critic of Olympic testing standards—won bronze in an electrifying photo finish in the five-km free pursuit, behind Danilova and Lazutina, two accused cheats. They keep the gold and silver respectively, while Scott keeps bronze and the knowledge she raced clean. "They may technically be Olympic champions," International Olympic Committee President Jacques Rogge said of the disqualified skiers, "morally it's a very different issue."

And yet, these Games succeeded on many levels. Some US$300 million bought the safest event money could buy, which is to say that about the only things that blew up were a few unattended box lunches detonated by security staff in Park City. Financially, the Games are expected to break even, despite a staggering price tag of nearly US$2 billion. Organizationally, they were such a triumph that Salt Lake Organizing Committee President Mitt Romney, a moneyed merchant banker from Boston, is now considering a political career, possibly a Republican run for governor of Massachusetts.

The closest the clean-living Mormon came to trouble was a run-in with a zealous security officer who, because of a credentials mix-up, backed up 75 buses, causing some 2,300 people to miss the start of a ski event. In a scandal that could happen only in Utah, Romney angrily confronted the officer and was accused in the local media of using a word that rhymes with truck. Not so, said Romney, who claimed he hadn't used that word since high school. "I used the H-word," he told the Mormon-owned *Desert News*. "It takes a lot of frustration to get me to say the H-word." Many trees died as the local press thoroughly canvassed the issue, proving, if nothing else, that the Olympics didn't corrupt Utah's standards of piety and propriety.

❦

Americans revelled in the storybook ending of Sale and Pelletier's story, their eventual winning of Olympic gold. Among their own heroes, they also sought out those who'd overcome adversity or suffered loss. It was as though, in their choice of champions, they expressed a national resolve to recover, to restore and to move on after the shattering events of Sept. 11.

Thus, the gold-medal bobsled run of Vonetta Flowers and Jill Bakken is a lesson in loyalty. Flowers stays with her partner, Bakken, defies the odds and wins. Favoured sled pilot Jean Racine dumps her former best friend as brakeman and finishes a humiliating fifth. Jim Shea's gold in skeleton is a lesson in family. He tucks a picture in his helmet of his late grandfather Jack Shea, a two-time gold medallist in speed skating killed recently by a drunk driver. Young Shea speeds to victory, the third-generation Olympian in his family, his father cheering him on.

Snowboarder Chris Klug's medal is a lesson in perseverance. Two years after a liver transplant, he wins bronze in parallel giant slalom—the day after National Donor Day. The gold-medal skate of Sarah Hughes, all of 16, is a lesson in hope. Stuck in fourth, she seemingly can't vault over a formidable field to win the women's figure-skating title—except she does.

In all, not bad role models for anyone.

Near the close of every Winter Games there is an ice show of the best dancers and figure skaters. As often happens, it seemed to get lost last week in the final frantic scramble for medals, in the excitement of the hockey finals and in the high dudgeon of international affairs.

It was an exhibition. There were no judges, and it seemed a great weight was lifted from the skaters, for it had long since been decided who among them would be honoured with medals. So, they had fun. Canadians Shae-Lynn Bourne and Victor Kraatz danced to *Mack the Knife*. It was a crowd-pleaser and a bittersweet farewell in what was likely their final Olympic appearance. A fall nights earlier had cost them all hope of a bronze. Tonight, when it really didn't matter, they were loose and assured and near-flawless, such is the cruelty of sport.

Sale and Pelletier skated, and the crowd went nuts. Afterwards, bouquets rained down, amid a standing ovation. It was nice, but not as nice as this: the sight later that night of them skating with their co-gold medallists, the Russian pair of Elena Berezhnaya and Anton Sikharulidze—all four linked at one point in a perfect, ice-sweeping, death spiral. Who knows, after all the intrigue, if their smiles were genuine. But for a few magic minutes, the crowd wanted to believe it was so—that despite all the noise, sport can still make us better.

The hockey game ends as it had to, in the perfect world of the Canadian imagination. It seemed a continuation of the party the night before and the start of all the parties that would follow. They'd sung O Canada at the beer bash the previous night to coax back the Tragically Hip for an encore. And they sang O Canada in the stands in the final seconds of the match, when the last best gold of the Winter Games was such a lock that high in his box, team executive director Wayne Gretzky had finally cracked a grin and pumped his fists and hugged his wife Janet.

He'd delivered a win as he'd promised. His team had overcome the doubters and the critics back home, and the crushing need of a country for a new golden moment. *Isn't it amazing what you can accomplish*, the Hip sang, *When you don't let the nation get in your way.*

And that's the way it is at these Olympics, with so much pride on the line. You win because of your people, and in spite of them, too.

Ken MacQueen, who has covered three Winter Olympics, has been Vancouver bureau chief for Maclean's *since 2000.*

PHOTO CREDITS